Praise for *Game of Queens*

'Gristwood handles multiple narrative strands with tremendous finesse ... Densely packed with fascinating material, this immensely ambitious undertaking succeeds triumphantly.'

Literary Review

'A magnificent exploration of a most remarkable group ... Gristwood gives us impeccable research, incisive attention to detail and exquisite writing as she investigates these truly fascinating women and their lives of courage, tribulation and determination. Absolutely unputdownable.'

Kate Williams, author of *The Storms of War*

'Gristwood interweaves the drama of monarchy with its more domestic moments.'

Telegraph

'The complete portrait that emerges reveals a complexity of interactions and relationships among these exceptional, now legendary women, their families, and their nations that greatly contributed to the political, intellectual, and cultural achievements as well as the climate of the Renaissance era. A fascinating work of world and women's history.'

Booklist

'Sarah Gristwood's study of the brilliant, beleaguered and often bloody difficult women who kept Europe going in the sixteenth century is compelling, clear-eyed, beautifully rendered and never-more-timely.'

Jessie Childs

'A fast-paced chronological narrative bursting with intrigue.'

Publishers Weekly

'Gristwood brings them all to life with her usual mix of character study and pacy narrative.'

History Revealed

THE TUDORS IN LOVE

The Courtly Code Behind
the Last Medieval Dynasty

SARAH GRISTWOOD

ONEWORLD

A Oneworld Book

First published in Great Britain, the Republic of Ireland, Europe
and Australia by Oneworld Publications in 2021

ISBN 978-1-78607-894-0
eISBN 978-1-78607-895-7

Typeset by Hewer Text UK Ltd, Edinburgh
Printed and bound in Great Britain by Clays Ltd, Elcograf S.p.A.

Oneworld Publications
10 Bloomsbury Street
London WC1B 3SR
England

Stay up to date with the latest books,
special offers, and exclusive content from
Oneworld with our newsletter

Sign up on our website
oneworld-publications.com

MIX
Paper from
responsible sources
FSC
www.fsc.org   FSC® C018072

For my niece, Freya West

Contents

Prologue

The tiltyard, York House, 2 March 1522

THE SHROVE TUESDAY festivities had a theme to them, and that theme was the heart. Palpitating, vulnerable, many times wounded, the symbol was everywhere.

The Earl of Devonshire and Lord Roos jousted in white velvet embroidered with a heart divided in two by a chain. Written on the borders was the motto 'My heart in between joy and pain'. Anthony Kingston and Anthony Knyvet wore crimson satin with a heart confined in blue lace, and written in gold 'My heart is bound'. Nicholas Darrel's black satin was covered in hearts overthrown or rent asunder, and his motto, in letters of silver, read 'My heart is broken'. But of course, there was only one heart that really mattered, and that was the heart of King Henry VIII.

The courser the king rode on was decked in cloth of silver, records the chronicler Edward Hall, embroidered with letters of gold. His device was 'a heart of a man wounded', and his motto declared '*Elle mon coeur a navera*' – she hath wounded my heart. It was the old passion of uplifting pain, the lover elevated by his adoration of a lady who held him at bay, which had gripped the imaginations of aristocratic Europe for centuries. No wonder a later age dubbed it 'courtly' love. No wonder, too, that the Tudors – that grasping, groping, reading dynasty – seized upon it so ardently.

The dynasty's founder, Henry VII, used Arthurian legend and the tropes of chivalry to sanction Tudor entry into the royal club; Henry VIII saw courtly love as validation for his eventful marital history. And in the end Henry VIII's daughter Elizabeth would convert its imagery to give a language to her controversial female monarchy.

The ritual of the joust, with its carefully choreographed charade of warfare, embodied all the pageantry of the Tudor court. In a world where a king's 'magnificence' was an important function of the monarchical role, parade and even pretence were key. Drama was all. At a feast, the very food might aim as much at provoking wonder as hunger – a cooked peacock 'in its feathers' paraded around the hall, or a mythical 'cockatrice' (the front half of a capon sewn to the back half of a pig). For their entertainment, visitors might expect to be surprised by some elaborate fantasy, and delighted to pay tribute with suspension of disbelief.

On Shrove Tuesday, after the joust, the king's chief minister Cardinal Wolsey gave a supper for Henry, his courtiers and the attentive ambassadors. York Place (later the Palace of Whitehall), Wolsey's great London house, was a byword for luxury and extravagance. Observers noted he had so many eye-wateringly expensive tapestries that he was able to have his walls rehung every week. Tales from the Bible depicted there were as colourful (in every sense) as those from classical mythology; the scenes from daily life – hunting and harvesting, lovemaking and lute-playing – were reimagined into timeless scenes of story. (The great tapestry known as 'The Triumph of Chastity over Love', based on Petrarch's work, would wind up in the king's collection, ironically.)

At table, vegetable 'sallats' and cheeses followed a bewildering array of meats. After all, the cheerless, meatless, season of Lent was about to follow, however expertly king and cardinal's cooks might dress the eels and salt cod, the sea and freshwater fishes. Next, Wolsey's guests were led to a great chamber, decked by branches laden with costly wax tapers.

At the end of the room stood a castle built of wood and painted green – the kind of lavish conceit, designed to last just for the night, at which the Tudor court excelled. Long lists in the royal accounts detail expenditure on these brief dramatic spectacles: on tinsel and costume, timber and carpentry. Just a couple of years later, the court would wonder for weeks over the military management of another such pretend castle, delighted to decide that it 'could not be won by sport, but by earnest'. A latter-day equivalent might be the set for a stage production, or a movie.[*] But this was half a century before the British Isles' first playhouse was built in London; and though the Church might excel in both ceremony and popular pageantry, to enact the secular religion of chivalry there was no better stage than this one – no better place to be than the court.

The castle was made up of three towers each hung with a banner – a banner of three hearts rent asunder; of a lady gripping a man's heart; of a lady turning a man's heart. The castle was a staple of such pageant-'disguises', suggesting either a danger from which ladies had to be rescued, or the lady's heart itself. A fortress defended by ladies throwing roses had featured in that medieval bestseller of courtly love, the *Roman de la Rose*. These three towers were occupied by eight women dressed in white satin, with their names picked out in gold. Beauty and Honour, Mercy and Bounty, Constance and Perseverance, Kindness and Pity – the qualities of the perfect courtly lady. If these pageants were the indoor equivalent of the tourney – as much an arena for competition and display – then the difference was that here, women might take centre stage.

Underneath the castle, as if in parody, were eight other 'ladies' (boy choristers of the Chapel Royal, decked out in 'Indian' dress) with names like Disdain and Jealousy, Scorn and Unkindness. They stood poised to defend the 'Château Vert', for now entered masquers: disguised lords in gold caps and blue cloaks, with names that bore tribute to the chivalric virtues. Nobleness, Youth, Loyalty, Gentleness. Their spokesman, Ardent Desire, was dressed 'all in crimson satin with burning flames of gold'. The knights begged the ladies to come down, but Scorn and Disdain said they would resist, and Ardent Desire gave the order to attack.

As real cannons boomed from outside the building, the knights pelted the castle with dates and oranges. The ladies fought back with

---

[*] Many years ago, when I was working as a film journalist, I visited the set of *Braveheart*, the movie. It was a night shoot, and the ruins of an Irish castle were standing in for the English subject of a brutal siege. What I remember most vividly is that only by tapping them could one tell the fake walls, created out of fibreglass by the production crew, from the ancient stone reality.

rosewater and comfits (though the fake ladies, Scorn and her company, went as far as to use 'bows and balls'); but 'at last the place was won'. As Scorn and Disdain fled, the lords took 'the ladies of honour' prisoner by the hand and led them down from the castle towers, and they 'danced together very pleasantly'. The elaborate steps of a court dance reflected the elaborate moves of the game of love, as did the moves of a game of chance or skill. The successful courtier, male or female, had to display their skill at all, and at 'luf talk' – love talking, the courtly language – too.

But who, at this elaborate festivity, was the 'she' who pierced Henry's heart with the darts of love? It should have been Henry's queen, Catherine of Aragon, under whose colours he had so often jousted. This joust was, after all, staged to honour ambassadors from her Imperial family. But Catherine was ageing now, facing the end of her thirties, and her childbearing years, with a doughty fortitude marred only by the bitter knowledge she had never presented Henry with a living son.

The 'she' could have been Mary Boleyn, whose pliant charms would make her the king's mistress. But only hindsight notes the presence here – making her first recorded appearance at the English court – of another 'she' who would go down in history. A dark-haired figure; not beautiful, but polished to the hard glitter of a gemstone by a youth spent at the continental courts. An accomplished performer and markswoman whose arrows would indeed strike right to Henry's heart, but who would in the end be herself the one destroyed by the courtly fantasy.

At the end of the evening came the banquet: a final course to the conspicuously recherché consumption. Custards and candied fruits, gilded gingerbread and flavoured spirits of wine. First, however, the masquers all divested themselves of their disguises. To no one's surprise (however well they might feign astonishment) King Henry had himself been leader of the lords. Beauty was in fact his sister Mary Tudor. Kindness, all too aptly, was Mary Boleyn. Constancy was Jane Parker, soon to marry Mary's brother George Boleyn, and Perseverance was her sister, that newcomer to court, that expert court performer . . . Her name was Anne Boleyn.

Introduction

THIS IS A book about the Tudors in love – a family whose deadly dramas belie the fact they were besotted with the idea of loving. A dynasty reflecting the late afterglow of the Middle Ages just as surely as they were foreshadowing a modern world, where marriage for love (like a sugar-rich diet, a money-based economy and, eventually, a constitutional monarchy) would come to be the norm.

But it is also a book about the history of 'courtly love': that elusive but overwhelmingly pervasive ideal that dominated the life of the European mind for centuries. As such, it may answer some of the most compelling questions about the Tudor dynasty. Why did Henry VIII marry six times? Why did Anne Boleyn have to die? How could Elizabeth I's courtiers – Leicester, Hatton, Ralegh and the rest – hail her as a goddess come to earth?

To look at the Tudor saga through the lens of courtly love explains as nothing else has done some of the conundrums about our most intriguing dynasty. To understand the roots of that fantasy, it is necessary to go even further back in time from the Tudor age: to go back more than another three hundred years. But restoring the context of the past – past even to the Tudors themselves – casts a new light on events that otherwise seem strange or inexplicable, viewed solely from today's perspective.

The rules of courtly love made possible the long courtship of Anne Boleyn by Henry VIII and, in the end, perhaps, brought about Anne's downfall. A crush on Anne Boleyn is something of an occupational hazard for students of Tudor history. Writing this book, I found myself circling her figure like a wary hunter, afraid the very intensity of my interest would cause my quarry to start up and shy away. But in all the morass of creeds and theories about Anne, the one true heresy, for believers, may be to say that her extraordinary tale is best seen as one chapter in a very long story.

That same courtly creed would – refreshed and reimagined – play a vital part in framing the sovereignty of Anne's daughter Elizabeth. This would be, perhaps, its last great gasp. But to look at the Tudors from this perspective doesn't only give us a new angle on the best-known stories. It gives fresh importance to, for example, Henry's niece Margaret Douglas, and the so-called Devonshire Manuscript: the collection of poems through which she and her friends communicated. It casts a fresh light on Henry's sister Mary; on his later marriages – perhaps even on his daughter's husband, Philip of Spain. It gives (corrupted and attenuated though the game had become by then) some understanding of that most puzzling – and hitherto underexplored – relationship of Elizabeth's last years: her relationship with the Earl of Essex.

Remember the kaleidoscopes that sparked wonder, when we were children? How you shook one, held it up to your eye, and the tiny coloured particles magically reformed into a perfect pattern. Courtly love seems likewise to give a key, a code, to the relationships that shape the sixteenth century. I completed this book against the background of a global pandemic, and personal bereavement. But I was sustained by the sense that never, in twenty years of writing about the Tudors, have I had so strongly the sense of a story that 'wanted' to be told.

Courtly love began as a literary fantasy – a stylish and stylised game subversive enough to capture the imaginations of the intellectuals, and sweeping enough to be seized upon by many who only dimly grasped its subtleties. Its central image was of the knightly lover bound to serve; without reward if necessary, since his mistress was often already married to someone else, and a lady of higher rank than he.

The fantasy was at odds with all reality, at a time when the law left women wholly subservient to men, and aristocratic marriage was a matter of parental arrangement and property, dynastic advancement and political necessity. But despite – or just possibly because of – that, its hold on the hearts and minds of Europe's elite never lost its potency.

Courtly love was never going to stay within the literary box. As we in our own age of fake news know all too well, there is nothing more powerful than a good story.

The dream of courtly love was born out of a real human need: a dissatisfaction with the harsh constraints that Church and state alike sought to impose on affection and sensuality. If the rules said that marriage was a matter of pragmatism and politics – if sexual desire could be tolerated only in the cause of producing babies – why not conceive different laws, in an alternative, more acceptable, reality? This all-powerful imaginary edifice had already survived for more than three hundred years when it came to form the expectations of the Tudor family. And, perhaps it would outlive them.

To offer 'love' in the title of a book invites dismissal. It could easily sound like a soft-centred chocolate of an option, mustily perfumed as a violet cream. But the topic of courtly love is, on the contrary, profoundly contentious. In 1936, in his classic *The Allegory of Love*, C.S. Lewis (a great medievalist, as well as author of the *Narnia* chronicles) described it as a centuries-long force compared to which 'the Renaissance was a mere ripple on the surface of literature'. Yet its very existence (other than as a purely literary game) is questioned by many modern historians. In 1968 (and an epoch that prided itself on shaking off the veils from matters of sexuality), D.W. Robertson complained that the whole concept lacked intellectual respectability; that some of his colleagues were 'teaching medieval texts to the tune of "Hearts and Flowers" '. Many others would have agreed – though in fact the saga of courtly love is also one of obsession, extreme violence and emotional cruelty.[*]

Few today would suggest – as was playfully pictured by writers of the twelfth century, and painstakingly described by scholars of many centuries since – that Eleanor of Aquitaine and her contemporaries presided over actual 'courts of love'; discussing such knotty points as whether love, a matter of the heart's free choice, could even exist within the humdrum constraints of matrimony. But to dismiss the emotional

---

[*] There is, such doubters say, no evidence for its existence beyond the page. I hope to prove that the evidence is there – they were just looking for it in the wrong century.

power of a concept behind the artistic life of four centuries is to deny ourselves access to a whole range of experience. (To say nothing of courtly love's role in nourishing and colouring the broader vision of romantic love still dominant today.) To disenfranchise ourselves this way seems a particularly odd choice at the moment when – due partly but not wholly to Covid-19 – the world seems to be shrinking or opening up according to our own conception of it, independent of the busy clatter of outside reality.

The emotional creed that governed the Tudors is as worth studying as the laws they passed or the battles they fought. Though maybe the fact that emotion has traditionally been regarded as a female sphere – that courtly love is in theory at least a culture which privileges the feminine – explains some of the scepticism around it. Other approaches to Tudor or medieval history – the military, the diplomatic, the legal or constitutional – tend inevitably to foreground the experience of men, who fought the wars and passed the laws.

The biographical approach *does* often foreground the stories of the few prominent women whose lives were sufficiently well recorded. But it is often circumscribed by lack of information as to the subject's inner life, leaving her as two-dimensional as an illustration in a manuscript.

(Some years ago, when writing *Blood Sisters: The Women Behind the Wars of the Roses*, I was painfully struck by the fact that while we know Cecily Neville – mother to Edward IV and Richard III – had to see one of her sons, Clarence, executed on the orders of another, and a third suspected of murdering her grandsons, the 'Princes in the Tower', we have no evidence as to what she thought or felt about it, whose side she was on. Perhaps one reason for our perennial fascination with the Tudors is that the range of available sources turns suddenly from famine to feast, leaving us far less prey to such frustrating uncertainty.)

Instead of querying the validity of the concept of courtly love, we might do better to think in terms of its utility. Utility, firstly, to a Tudor dynasty taking advantage of old stories to give credibility to a new regime. Though with hindsight we may see them as ushering in the modern era, the Tudors' own urgent desire was to paint themselves as legitimate heirs to a long and noble tradition of medieval monarchy. Whatever far-reaching innovations marked the reigns of Henry or Elizabeth, the past, not the future, was their preferred currency. The courtly creed had utility, too, for the women scrabbling for a place in the adventurous sixteenth century, and falling gratefully upon a code that seemed to give them autonomy – even mastery.

Today, study of the courtly creed has utility, also, for those anxious to find windows into the medieval mind. It allows us the rare chance to stand alongside the Tudors on terms of equality; relishing the same works of historical fiction. They were consumers of the courtly fantasy just as we are. We do not have any illustration of the Siege of the Château Vert in 1522; but we do have the kind of image that inspired it.

The three hundred-odd brilliantly illumined vellum leaves of the *Luttrell Psalter*, commissioned by a Lincolnshire gentleman in the first half of the 1300s, saw a team of anonymous illustrators let loose on idealised scenes of daily life; on reflections of Sir Geoffrey Luttrell's career and chivalry; and on the strange, half-human animal figures with which the Middle Ages expressed the nightmare side of its tenets. But they also showed a Siege of the Castle of Love: an image with its roots in the turrets and baileys of the Virgin Mary's unassailable chastity. While knights in gilded armour busily attempt to scale the walls of a tower, the ladies ensconced within it energetically (if somewhat ineffectually) defend themselves by throwing flowers. The knights, one feels, probably could take this castle. As for whether they *should* . . . That was a question which went to the heart of the courtly message; albeit that it seemed to have been resolved in male favour by the sixteenth century.

The Siege of the Castle of Love is an image designed less to reflect reality than to invite fantasy. There is another image, a century later, which serves the latter function for me. A panel of the so-called Werl Triptych, painted in Cologne in the 1430s and now in the Prado in Madrid, shows – we think – St Barbara reading. (To find medieval images of female saints reading is surprisingly, and encouragingly, easy.) Engrossed in her book, luxuriously but comfortably dressed, she sits on puffy cushions with an iris in a vase beside her and a glowing fire behind. Outside the open window of her room, in the distance, a tower is being built – the place of her imprisonment; and indeed it is this which identifies the image as St Barbara, whose pagan father enclosed her in a vain attempt to keep her away from the pernicious influences both of suitors and of Christianity.

We can assume the book she holds up to her face is a work of Christian theology – nonetheless, both the book and the open window give the sense of an imagination let free. Too easy an identification with the modern world is of course a historian's trap, and one that ignores profound differences in attitude and assumption over the centuries. Even so, it is hard here not to think of ourselves – of any bookish, imaginative teenager today.

From a triptych in the Prado – and a tower in the fifteenth century – to a provincial Odeon cinema in the 1970s may seem something of a reach. But this is also a book about the long afterlife of the ghost called courtly love; and this particular bookish teenager first encountered it in an atmosphere of shabby carpets and cartons of Kia-Ora, at a Saturday matinee of *Camelot*, the movie.

First released in 1967, but reappearing year after year, it was my first 'proper' movie. I wanted to be Vanessa Redgrave's Guinevere, in her sparkling white furs and metal-encrusted gauntlets, adored by two men in Lerner and Loewe's slightly mocking fantasy. I was, crucially, too young to be wholly aware of that mockery. But I wanted those gloves. Medieval meets Space Age, you might say.

I went on, of course, to watch *Anne of the Thousand Days*, with Geneviève Bujold in the title role making triumph out of tragedy. But mine was the generation that also saw the television advert of a man going to absurd lengths to fulfil his demanding beloved's wishes. The tag line read: 'And all because the lady loves Milk Tray.' From the Tudor court to Camelot is not such a long reach – it is one, indeed, the Tudors themselves made in their day. From the chivalric code to over-sweet confectionery may seem a longer one. But that's a ghost for you. That's how it operates. Close the door, bar the windows, but the ghost of courtly love simply will not go away.

For better or worse, the idea – the ideal – still survives, for all that it has been normalised to the point of unrecognisability by story, film and music (both classical *and* popular: from manuscript to Meat Loaf, you might say). The pervasive influence of the romantic obsession called courtly love still governs us today. Implicit within its long history is the great question: can the magic last? Last within marriage, or its modern-day equivalent, specifically. But its literature tackles, explicitly, other big conundrums. Is love supposed to hurt? Do I have to love someone just because he loves me?

The ghost of courtly love is the guiding force behind some of our most dangerous romantic tenets, as well as some of our most basic traditional courtesies. It was there on the decks of the *Titanic*, when the ladies took first place in the lifeboats; it is there whenever a man holds open a door for a woman today. There on the tarmac in *Casablanca*, when Humphrey Bogart hands Ingrid Bergman back to her husband and turns away, ennobled by her love as surely as any knight in story. There when W.B. Yeats lauded the Irish revolutionary Maud Gonne – 'half lion, half child', another Helen of Troy, with 'beauty like a tightened bow' – who turned from him to another man:

Why should I blame her that she filled my days
With misery, or that she would of late
Have taught to ignorant men most violent ways

Perhaps – to drop from the sublime to the merely royal, if not ridiculous – it was even there when Prince Harry told British courtiers: 'What Meghan wants, Meghan gets' . . .

That may be one reason we're so fascinated by the Tudors – that this still-familiar game could there be seen played out to its last, fatal, extremity. But understanding the courtly code also helps us (as women, particularly) understand a good many of our own most fundamental assumptions. The romantic fallacy that still holds us in thrall seemed to offer women power, in an era when in fact they had none. But it concealed at its heart a deadly trap.

While the man had the power of action and of choice, the woman had to be both passive and perfect. Though courtly love managed not to divide women into 'Madonnas or whores', it *did* cast them as either the goal, the prize, the deity, or else the already-gained, the available. The disposable, basically. Anne Boleyn would not be the last to find she had morphed from one to the other in the course of her and her partner's romantic history. At a moment when we are questioning many of our preconceptions about the relations between the sexes, this is one we need to debate, and urgently. A system of romance that seemed to be validating a woman's right to her own physical integrity would in the end wind up normalising a 'token' resistance – eventually to be overcome – as part of the courtship game. The lady's elaborately performative denial becomes merely a move on the board.

Though I could not have known it then, as moviemakers set about working their magic on Guinevere and Anne Boleyn, Germaine Greer was preparing *The Female Eunuch*. The feminists of the mid-/late twentieth century seem to have found it worthwhile contemplating the subject of courtly love in all its complexity. In a chapter entitled 'The Middle-Class Myth of Love and Marriage' Greer points out that 'there was a far different concept of love which prevailed not so long ago, a concept not only separate from pre-nuptial courtship, but quite inimical to marriage'.

Born into the 1960s with which Greer's feminism is so strongly identified, I belong to the generation who grew up in the knowledge that our mothers had fought for the right to say 'yes'. To be, indeed, the ones who did the asking. What we lacked was the right to say 'no': an issue with which the #MeToo movement is grappling only today. The credo that crept down the centuries from courtly love *seemed* to promise to give us back that power, albeit that there could be a heavy price to pay.

Though the lady may be cast as the all-important object of the courtly quest, she can be curiously undeveloped as a character in her own right. And anything that positions the woman as chiefly the *object* of sexual desire, the 'sex object', fosters a climate in which sexual violence can take place.*

In the Tudor century, Baldassare Castiglione's *Book of the Courtier* described how a woman must: 'keep a certain mean very hard [strike

---

* I can't but think of the old story of the World War II airmen, and the American who said: 'In the States we put our women on a pedestal.' 'Good idea,' said the British flyer. 'You can see their legs better that way.' Courtly love is all about looking; from Dante glimpsing Beatrice to Snow White in her glass coffin or Sleeping Beauty in her tower, waiting to be spied by the Prince who has broken through the allegorical barrier of thorns.

a very difficult balance] and . . . come just to certain limits, but not to pass them'. Every date-rape case proves just how hard that mean still is today. Any wonder that this powerfully mixed onslaught of messages could lead impressionable girls astray?

A friend of the young Diana Spencer reported that, in the 1970s, she had him drive her round and round Buckingham Palace. It might be rather fun to marry Prince Charles, she said, 'like Anne Boleyn or Guinevere'. Of course, Lady Diana's education was famously limited – but surely she knew how those two wound up? The one headless, the other juggling death at the stake with incarceration in a nunnery. Maybe she did know, but still saw them as figures whose mythic influence gave them a kind of potency. Who might show a directionless, but not unambitious, young girl a way . . . Maybe, since we are of the same generation, she just watched the same movies.

Curiously, Guinevere, just as much as Anne Boleyn, is a leading figure in my story. Two women who refused to stay in their box, you might say.

Deal, Kent, January 2021

PART I
Origins

Cortezia, cortoisie: the virtues of the lover as a code of
procedure to be followed

What so she wills, so will I
When she will sit, I kneel by

John Gower, *Confessio Amantis*, c.1389

Chrétien, the Countess and the Chaplain

12th century

OVER THE CENTURIES, the Once and Future Queen has appeared in many guises. But the dominant image of Arthur's Queen Guinevere, the one that has come down to us, was created by Chrétien de Troyes, at the court of the County of Champagne, in the latter half of the twelfth century.

When Lancelot saw the queen leaning upon the window ledge behind the thick iron bars, he greeted her softly. She returned his greeting promptly, since she had great desire for him, as he did for her. They did not waste their time speaking of base or tiresome matters. They drew near to one another, and held each other's hands.

She was dressed – described Chrétien in his *Lancelot* – in a spotless white shift and 'a short mantle of scarlet and marmot fur': the equivalent, perhaps, of those covetable gauntlets in *Camelot*! Lancelot boasts that if the queen allows him to enter her room, he will not be prevented by the iron bars. Though the iron slices through the flesh of his fingers, he feels no pain, and forces the mighty bars from their sockets.

The Queen stretched out her arms towards him, embraced him, clasped him to her breast, and drew him into the bed beside her, showing him all the love she could . . . Her love-play seemed so gentle and good to him, both her kisses and caresses, that in truth the two of them felt a joy and wonder the equal of which has never been heard or known. But I shall let it remain a secret for ever, since it should not be written of: the most delightful and choicest pleasure is that which is hinted at, but never told.

The strangeness of this strikes like a slap in the face. A married woman about to commit adultery – and with her husband's best friend – who is yet presented as the very image of beauty and sensitivity? So too, of course, does the absurdity; for Lancelot's love for Guinevere – courtly love – assumed a degree of infatuation that now looks remarkably like folly.

Earlier in the tale, Lancelot finds a comb by the roadside with a few of her golden hairs caught in it and begins: 'to adore the hairs; a hundred thousand times he touched them to his eyes, his mouth, his forehead and his cheeks'. He would not exchange them, Chrétien wrote, for a cartload of precious stones. Watching Guinevere through a window, as she passes out of sight, he tries to climb out and shatter his body on the ground below. For her love he submits himself to shame by clambering into the cart usually used to transport a common criminal (an alternative title for Lancelot is 'The Knight of the Cart'). Guinevere blames him that he hesitated for an instant before doing so. He crawls bleeding to rescue her over a bridge made of a sword blade and, hardest of all, he bows to an order from the queen that, to please her, he should do not his best but his worst in a tournament.[*]

The Church saw women as daughters of sinful Eve: 'the devil's doorway', in Tertullian's words; the most dangerous of all savage beasts, according to St John Chrysostom. Yet Chrétien's Lancelot genuflects as he leaves Guinevere's bedchamber, as if at a religious shrine. It sounds extraordinary for its own Church-driven, male-dominated medieval society and still gives pause in the modern one – for in fact, of course, the story of Lancelot and Queen Guinevere *has* been told countless times over the years and is still being retold today.[†]

Across more than eight hundred years the puzzles of courtly love have never ceased to fascinate. Neither its element of absurdity (for it

---

[*] Today one might urge him to get a grip, yet that last trope was plausibly repeated in *A Knight's Tale* of 2001, a Hollywood movie starring Heath Ledger.
[†] See Appendix: The Many Faces of Guinevere.

can indeed sound as though the tongue crept into the cheek early), nor yet its central dichotomy of passion versus principle – or, rather, of where the highest principle or duty truly lies. Yet at a time when in the real world women held the legal status of chattels – when the married lady who took a lover could face the most deadly penalties – a whole international aristocratic society bowed its head and snuffed the heady scent of this most bizarre of fantasies.

But what *was* courtly love? – or *fin'amor*, or *cortoisie*, or *amour courtois*; for the name 'courtly love' came into widespread use only in the nineteenth century. A social ritual, a collective fantasy; a game, as witness the analogy often drawn by contemporaries between the chess game and the cult of love. It started as a literary convention, on the lips of the troubadours who flourished in southern France from the late eleventh century, writing in their native *langue d'oc*. Rock star rebels of their day, we know the names of some 450 of these lyric poets (including some twenty female troubadours, or *trobairitz*) who often moved in aristocratic society and dared comment freely on society's rules and religion's theories.

Soon northern France knew the *trouvères*, writing in their *langue d'oïl*; before long the same essential ideas could be seen in Italy and in the German *Minnesang*. Chrétien de Troyes's work would be translated not only into German but into Middle Dutch, Old Welsh and Norse. The popular *chansons de geste* – epic songs of heroic deeds, geared towards a masculine audience – took on the more refined hues of the *chansons d'amour*; and the *romans* (romances) which followed blended armed adventure, adoration of ladies, aspiration towards a moral goal, and often elements of the supernatural too.

Courtly love grew out of the conditions of the age in which it was born. (What is interesting here is that some of those conditions would once again find echoes in the Tudor century.) The service a lover owed his lady was modelled on the feudal contract that laid down what a villein owed his lord, or a knight his king. C.S. Lewis pointed out that, etymologically, '*midons*', a lover's address to his courtly lady, meant not 'my lady' but 'my lord'. Bernart de Ventadorn, the troubadour who followed Eleanor of Aquitaine to England, promises in one poem to serve his lady 'as I would a good lord'.

But feudalism itself was changing – declining, some scholars say – in a world that saw a more centralised government, an increasingly money-based economy and, importantly, the promotion of new men into the ranks of the nobility. Such men had a vested interest in a creed that believed nobility was founded in behaviour rather than birth. And such a phenomenon, of course, would fuel the Tudor age.

This was a moment when, in the words of the medievalist D.D.R. Owen, Western civilisation was 'feeling the need for a reassessment'. There was a shifting, in broad terms, from the general to the individual; a progressive focus on personal feelings, personal conduct – towards what Stephen Greenblatt, writing of the Renaissance era, would call a new 'self-fashioning'. The so-called twelfth-century Renaissance prefigured Europe's 'rebirth' several centuries later, not least in a new awareness, growing over the coming centuries, of the texts of Classical Antiquity.

The 'twelfth-century Renaissance' saw the building of the great Gothic cathedrals, and also the growth of writing in the vernacular, which gave a new market of women readers who would not know Latin. The great game of courtly love was part of a general sweetening of life in a time when people lived better, read more, travelled more. In this age Church and emerging nation states sought to steer the unfettered operations of a mounted warrior class into either the Holy Land Crusades (which paralleled the quests of Camelot) or the safer and more regulated competition of the tournament. Easy to see what useful propaganda the stories of King Arthur and his Round Table could be.

But the compensatory fantasy of courtly love also grew out of a social structure in aristocratic society that was marked by a huge imbalance between the sexes.* In the medieval castle, where even the domestic work was mostly done by males, men could outnumber women by as many as ten to one. In the twelfth century the phenomenon was accentuated by the armies that went to the Holy Land, leaving a lady to rule in her lord's stead. This imbalance continued to be seen in the royal court, and would later be particularly noteworthy

---

* The same imbalance may lie behind the simultaneous rejection of and reverence for women (white, virtuous women) in that unexpectedly courtly form, the traditional Western.

under Elizabeth I who, despite her own gender, preferred her courtiers to be unaccompanied.

At odds with everything decreed on sex and marriage, both by the Church and by feudal society, courtly love was a gesture against what has been called 'the harsh authoritarian world of masculine kingship'. Kingship both actual and domestic, perhaps. It may be no coincidence that the dream of courtly love was born just as the institution of marriage, juxtaposed with the cult of celibacy, took an ever-stronger hold on society. It was only in the late eleventh century that marriage first became a holy sacrament, to be celebrated only by a priest; that celibacy was required of all clergy. The result was increasingly to disempower women. The most important arrangement of their lives, their marriage, had fallen into the control of a Church which saw them as agents of a sinful sexuality; and they found themselves ever more alienated from learning and scholarship now centred in the new, all-male, universities.

To the Church, Eve was the weak, the sinful, aspect of Adam; yet the lady of courtly literature was exalted as arbiter, adjudicator – ruler, even, and moral superior. Perhaps the blanket rejection of all sexuality displayed by the Church from the twelfth century itself bred a reaction. The thirteenth-century friar Vincent de Beauvais would write that 'a man who loves his wife too eagerly is an adulterer': yes, of course adultery was an evil, but so too were the joys of the marriage bed. Small wonder if fallible humans, warned that *all* pleasure in sex was wrong, decided in that case that one sin was little worse than another.

Courtly love has also been seen as worldly counterpart to the cult of the Virgin Mary – has been called 'a religion of profane love'. (Roger Boase called troubadours the 'harbingers of the Reformation'.) The twelfth and thirteenth centuries saw a mounting ardour for the Mother of God; an ardour itself couched by male writers in personalised, almost erotic terms. St Bernard of Clairvaux, reforming founder of the Cistercian order, advocated a purer faith in which Mary was to be man's intercessor with God, and the knights of St Bernard were called the 'knights of Mary'.

Another theory holds that courtly love 'grew out of the Cathar or Albigensian heresy'. The Cathars were flourishing in the south of France just when courtly love was born; they were beginning increasingly to suffer persecution when courtly love reached its apogee. Cathars and troubadours both set themselves against the papacy, seeking a return to the 'simplicity and purity' of the apostolic Church. The Cathars (says Boase) 'recommended sexual continence and, in an ideal world, would reject marriage, which legitimised it'. Courtly love, 'being chaste and adulterous', perfectly fitted their bill.

Some Cathar beliefs – denying the supremacy of the Pope, the use of prayers for the dead and the existence of Purgatory – echo those of Reformation Protestantism. The Cathar movement owed much to the great ladies who supported it: great ladies would likewise be instrumental in the early sixteenth-century movement for Church reform.

Courtly love has even been envisaged as an actual survival of the pagan cult of Cybele/Maia, and of a pre-Christian matriarchal tradition in northern Europe in which women were revered for their divine powers, though the evidence is scanty. And it has been seen as evolving out of the folk traditions and ritual dances of Europe, especially those associated with the rites of spring. The troubadour songs for May Day traditionally mocked marriage. The association with spring still informs our picture of love and – at the risk of sounding like a stuck record! – certainly did, as we shall see, at the time of the Tudor dynasty.

But the single most widely accepted theory of courtly love has it imported into the south of France from Moorish Spain, strongly influenced by the culture, poetry and philosophy of the Arabs who for so long ruled much of the peninsula. Discernible links can be seen in music, instruments, rhyme and poetic forms – even in that use of the masculine form for the lady; the stress on 'the pathological nature of love', the elevation of the lady and the poet's submission and the need for secrecy. Even the very verb *trobar* – to compose poetry, hence 'troubadour' – may come from the Arabic *tarab*, music or song. The immensely influential Persian thinker Ibn Sina (known in the West as Avicenna) had declared in the eleventh century that if a man 'loves a pleasing form with an intellectual consideration' – as opposed to 'an animal desire' – 'then this is to be considered an approximation to nobility and an increase in goodness'; while *The Ring of the Dove* by his contemporary Ibn Hazm displays not only the belief that love ennobles the lover but the same unreasonable demands from the lady that Guinevere would make of Lancelot.

There were myriad points of contact between Moors and Christians, paving the way for exchange of ideas through word of mouth – royal intermarriages, even. In 980 the King of Navarre offered his daughter in marriage to al-Mansur and she 'subsequently became a fervent convert to Islam'; Richard 'the Lionheart' attempted to marry his sister to Saladin's brother. (Richard I also wrote some eloquent poetry of his own; but in Aquitaine, he stood accused of carrying off his subjects' wives and daughters 'by force and making them his concubines' – afterwards handing them on to his men. There was a dark side to chivalry.)

There were Moorish musicians in every princely retinue, and two Christian royals celebrated their marriage in the palace of an Arab prince. Of course, over the coming centuries, Moors and Christians often found themselves in conflict; culminating in the late fifteenth century when Ferdinand and Isabella drove the Moors from Spain. But Catherine of Aragon, Ferdinand and Isabella's daughter, grew up among the fountain-rich gardens, redolent of Moorish poetry, they left behind: the gardens of the Alhambra.

The different theories do not necessarily contradict each other. It took a concatenation of different circumstances to spawn this extraordinary social movement. Courtly love was born out of contradictions and anomalies.* Oddly enough, that very flexibility within the framing of courtly love may allow it still to be relevant today.

Their exaltation in the literature of courtly love led to no actual, direct improvement in women's lot; legally, economically or physically. The men who listened complacently to these stories seem to have felt no impulse to translate their moral into an inconvenient actuality. Unless, unless . . .

Unless the stories led to an awareness of possibilities; if not in the knight's mind, then at least in the lady's.

*   *   *

---

* Many such anomalies are inherent in the attitudes of the Church itself. Diarmaid MacCulloch points out that the Church which proclaimed the supremacy of celibacy also set up and licensed brothels – on the theory, voiced by Thomas Aquinas, that 'even the most splendid palace must have a sewer system to survive'. MacCulloch describes how supposedly celibate monks were responsible for a flood of homoerotic poetry. 'The Church had always said that homosexuality was one of the greatest sins. Now the clergy were openly glorying in sin.'

As courtly love reached outwards, different strands would be woven into the tapestry; but one of the broadest strands would remain that of the Arthurian stories – not only those of Camelot but of Tristan and Iseult.

The story of King Arthur as such was already long familiar before Chrétien de Troyes's version, albeit that he added romance into the mix. Legends of King Arthur may date back to a fifth- or sixth-century Celtic war leader, defending Britain against Saxon invaders. But they had been given huge credibility for the medieval age by the Welsh cleric Geoffrey of Monmouth and his *Historia Regum Britanniae* (History of the Kings of Britain). Written probably in the 1130s, Geoffrey's work reads to us very clearly as a work of fiction. But at the time it was received as the first authoritative and historically veracious version of the Arthurian story.

Geoffrey's work was a bestseller. It survives today in some two hundred medieval manuscripts, when most texts have come down to us in just two or three surviving manuscripts, and even the *Canterbury Tales* centuries later in only eighty-four. Geoffrey makes little play with Arthur's queen, Guinevere – albeit that her adultery, and her infertility, play a part in the downfall of his kingdom. But in fact she too had featured in the earliest stories: often a sorceress, a wonder worker; a figure of anger and potency. A roll call of Arthur's great queens features in the medieval manuscripts of the Welsh Triads – 'Gwenhwyvar daughter of Guryt Guent, Gwenhwyvar daughter of Uthyr son of Greidiaul, and Guenhuyvar daughter of Ocvran the Giant'. But it is only with Chrétien de Troyes that Guinevere becomes just the romantic heroine any medieval lady might long to be. And it is only with Chrétien that her lover Lancelot (like Camelot itself) enters the story.

From the first tales Guinevere was abducted time and time again: by Melwas, the otherworldly ruler of 'the summer country'; by Arthur's nephew Mordred – with or without her consent. (The earliest stories of Guinevere's adultery partner her with Mordred, not Lancelot. It is Mordred who, in one notably gruesome legend, ends shut up in a cell with the corpse of Guinevere, until forced to dine off her decaying body.) When she consents to her abduction or seduction she is condemned for it, a traitorous wife and danger to the kingdom. In Chrétien's story, too, Guinevere is abducted, to be rescued by her husband's greatest knight. But since theirs was a game played by the new rules of courtly love, she and Lancelot are not deemed guilty for *their* ensuing adultery, but honoured for their ardour.

It was, of course, very often left unclear whether the passion of courtly lovers did end in actual, physical adultery. The noble early troubadour Jaufre Rudel was noted for developing the concept of *amor de lonh*, love from afar – but he could also write: 'Me, I prefer loving and trembling for the one / Who does not refuse her reward.' The literature of courtly love presented slightly different faces in different territories, from the 'how to' manuals of France to the later spiritual elevation of Italy. But there could be contradictions even within the same story.

Time and again the Arthurian tales see a lady in jeopardy coming to a knight for protection, which she receives; yet ladies simultaneously figure also as jousting prize and object of barter. Courtly love offered both threat and opportunity to women – or rather to 'ladies', since courtly love took little account of women from the lower ranks of society.

And the lady who is the object of a courtly writer's obsessive regard can herself be curiously underidentified, as if the writer's own dilemmas, his emotional development, preoccupied him more urgently. One noble troubadour, Raimbaut d'Aurenga, compares himself to Narcissus, who fell in love with his own reflection. As if, indeed, the honour he could win in loving were not in the end more important than the lady . . .[*]

But there was one noble lady without whose patronage, and that of her family, the courtly love story would never have found its voice.

Much is uncertain about Chrétien's text, but one thing he makes crystal clear. His introduction to his *Lancelot* declares the 'matter and meaning', the '*matiere*' and the '*san*', had been suggested to him by his patroness Marie, Countess of Champagne, daughter of Eleanor of Aquitaine by her first husband, Louis VII of France. In best courtly

---

[*] As Reay Tannahill put it: 'If some mischievous nineteenth-century time traveller had whisked the Lady away and replaced her with the Regiment or the Flag, the medieval knight would probably not even have noticed.'

style, in the prologue to his *Lancelot* Chrétien figures himself obedient to the commands of Marie (*'ma dame de Champaigne'*) 'as one who is entirely hers'.

Born in 1145, the young Marie had been left in the custody of her father when her parents' marriage was dissolved. Louis's need to assure the alliance of the powerful county of Champagne saw her betrothed to Count Henri 'the Liberal', whose terrain was increasingly important for the exchange of goods like cloth and dye; of luxuries like furs, spices, drugs, coinage – and ideas. Marie was sent to Champagne to be educated at the convent of Avenay and, in 1164, became its countess.

The court at Troyes was emerging as an important literary centre. Like her husband, Marie was a patron of letters: his preference, however, was for religious texts in Latin while she was more interested in the vernacular. Gace Brulé, one of the first and most noted *trouvères* to sing of courtly love, did so at the Champagne court.

Just before Marie's husband Henri went on pilgrimage to the Holy Land in 1179, the court was visited by the Welshman Walter Map. He had come from England, where he was credited with having written or translated, at the king's request, a prose *Lancelot*. He could certainly have disseminated the Arthurian tales. In Henri's absence Marie was left as regent: a role she would once again fulfil on behalf of their young son (Henri having died shortly after his return in 1181).

Chrétien's poem was probably composed just before or during Henri's pilgrimage but there is a lot we don't know about Chrétien, including his relation to Marie. She instructed him to write the *Lancelot*: the fact that after having written some six thousand lines he abandoned it, leaving another writer to finish the last thousand, is often taken to suggest he found the topic offensive. There may just conceivably be another reason.

Marie had an English half-brother, Henry, son of her mother Eleanor's second marriage to Henry II of England. Known as 'the Young King', he died before he could come to England's throne. He is remembered chiefly as the high-profile star of the new-fangled knightly tournaments – and as a footnote to the tale of his great knight, William Marshal: described by his biographer Thomas Asbridge as 'Lancelot come to life'; and elsewhere, in that old 'push me pull you' between fact and fiction, as inspiration for some of the Lancelots now reaching the page.

Marshal was a landless younger son who (as in so many of the Arthurian stories) had risen through his valour, his honour and, yes, his ambition to become, in the end, the right-hand man of five kings. And Marshal was said to be sleeping with Marguerite, the Young King's queen. There is no surviving evidence for this, and indeed we know of the stories only through the angry refutation of them in a biography commissioned by William's descendants. But there did come to be a bitterness between the Young King and his erstwhile friend; while Marguerite was, in the spring of 1183, just before her husband's early death, sent away to France.

Is it possible Chrétien abandoned his subject (or edited it, and invented a colleague on whom to cast the blame) less because of distaste than because it had suddenly got too hot to handle? He wrote several other Arthurian stories and in two of them Guinevere appears as an eminently courteous and conformable queen, devoid of any controversial adulterous elements. Chrétien's *Yvain* or *Le Chevalier au Lion*, in which the hero abandons and then wins back his wife, can be interpreted as subverting the ideas of courtly love: his Arthurian romance *Cligès* contains an explicit rejection of adultery.

Yet Chrétien's lovers in the *Lancelot* think and speak through the tropes of troubadour song. And Lancelot's actions have the force of moral weight behind them. When he rescues Guinevere simultaneously from a (false) accusation of adultery and from captivity in Logres, the act means he also sets all of Arthur's subjects free.

But does Chrétien also show a trap for women here? Though much is made of the protection of ladies, the custom of the land of Logres decrees that any knight can take – rape! – a lady if he can defeat the knight escorting her. And, again, the devotion he depicts in his Lancelot is so abject that critics have asked whether Chrétien was elevating courtly love to its ultimate form – or whether he was, rather, making fun of it.

The same doubt applies to the other great writer of courtly love whose career depended upon Champagne's Countess Marie.

The signature of one Andreas, a court official, appears as witness to nine charters at Marie's court in 1182–6. We cannot be sure that this is the 'Andreas Capellanus' (Andrew the Chaplain) who wrote what has since become known as *De Amore* (On Loving) or *De Arte Honeste Amandi* (The Art of Courtly Love); but the frequent references in the book to Marie and her circle – the fact that the author would be regularly described as a royal chaplain over the centuries immediately following – suggest it as a strong possibility, and generations of scholars have taken it as such.

Andreas envisages Marie, with her mother Eleanor and other ladies of note, presiding over actual 'courts of love'. In a slightly later work by another author, *Meraugis de Portlesguez*, Guinevere will tell her husband that 'all judgements in matters of love are mine'.

These famous courts of love, however, probably existed only as a literary conceit. (And no evidence actually places Eleanor in Marie's company at this time.) But in Capellanus's fantasy the lady judges are called on to give judgement on knotty points such as whether love, as understood by the courtly creed, is even possible between husband and wife. Marie's judgement was that – since true love must be given freely, rather than constrained by duty – it is not: but Ermengarde de Narbonne, judging another case, declared more tactfully that 'feeling in marriage and true love between lovers' are simply two different things.

Five judgements were attributed to Ermengarde, heiress to the Narbonne viscountcy, a powerful political and cultural player who numbered the Viking prince and later saint Rognvald II among her admirers. Rognvald was also a poet, writing of her:

> Golden one, Tall one
> Moving in perfume and onyx
> Witty one, You with the shoulders
> Wrapped in long silken hair

Another adjudicator was Eleanor of Aquitaine's niece Isabelle, Countess of Flanders and (in tandem with her husband Ralph) the ruling Countess of Vermandois. But Isabelle's life illustrates the different treatment of adultery meted out in literature and in life.

A twelfth-century chronicle describes how, when Ralph discovered Isabelle was having an affair, he had her lover beaten to death and seized control of her lands: this, only a few years before the probable date of Andreas's writing. Did the very power of courtly literature derive from an attempt to restore to women in fantasy what reality denied them?

Andreas based the first two parts of his book upon the *Ars Amatoria* (The Art of Love), written by the Roman poet Ovid almost 1,200 years before. Throughout the Middle Ages – and well into the Tudor age – Ovid was very frequently cited, copied, commented upon. Indeed, the amorous imagery he uses is still in currency: arrows, wounds, flames of desire. The enduring common sense of much of his advice on love (don't ask how old she is, he tells his male readers, and don't forget her birthday) should not make us forget that Ovid is remembered as a cynical writer with an eye for comic effect. The advice Andreas gives is so extreme, the dilemmas he poses so recondite, that, as with Chrétien, doubt has likewise been cast on his seriousness. Was he really trying to satirise/critique the extremes into which love can lead?

It is in this context that we have to read the actual 'rules' with which Andreas decorates what is in effect an instruction manual. From Book One:

5. Remember to avoid lying completely.
6. Do not have too many privy to your love.
7. Be obedient to mistresses' commands in all things, and always be eager to join the service of Love.

It was, after all, Andreas who ruled that:

12. When practising the consolations of love [i.e. sex] do not go beyond the wish of your lover.

But that lover, whose body was her own to give or withhold, could only be a lady, or someone of a certain rank. Andreas also wrote that the courtly lover who found himself enamoured of women of the lower orders should 'not hesitate to embrace them by force . . . use a little compulsion as a convenient cure for their shyness'. Along with love at first sight – love as ennobling, love as pain – the idea that there are people (women) who matter and those who don't is another belief enshrined in the courtly code, and since absorbed into our very bloodstream. And that door, once opened, could never be pushed shut. Later medieval literature at once exploring and exposing the courtly tradition would see cases – like the collection of texts which make up the *Carmina Burana* – where even the adored beloved (once forced, resisting, into sex) would prove to have enjoyed it *really*.

It was Andreas who tackled head-on the question of whether courtly love involved sex at all. Chaste love, he says, 'goes as far as kissing on the mouth, embracing with the arms, and chaste contact with the unclothed lover, but the final contact is avoided, for this practice is not permitted for those who wish to love chastely'. By contrast, 'compounded love' – still worthy, but one step down from chaste – allowed outlet 'to every pleasure of the flesh, ending in the final act of love'.

It is indeed possible that Andreas Capellanus in the latter half of the twelfth century was making as sophisticated a riff on an established idea as *Camelot* librettist Alan Jay Lerner in the latter half of the twentieth. But the often-made, always worth repeating, point is that satire requires an accepted belief of which to make mockery. If no one recognised what was being held up to laughter, the joke could only fall flat. Moreover, the Arthurian myths that walked hand-in-hand with the dream of courtly love were about to take on another identity: as tools in the real world of Plantagenet propaganda and popularity.

In 1190 monks digging in the grounds of the abbey at Glastonbury in Somerset – the 'summer country' of Arthurian myth – claimed to have identified the grave of King Arthur and Guinevere. Inside the grave was a large stone cross which, said Gerald of Wales, 'I have seen'. On it was carved: 'Here lies buried the famous King Arthur with Guinevere, his second wife, in the isle of Avalon'. The male skeleton was said to be of gigantic size; the female to retain some trace of lost beauty. Gerald described how a lock of golden hair was found, but 'when a certain monk snatched it greedily with his hand and raised it up, at once all of it crumbled into dust'.

There was, of course, a backstory here. On the one hand Avalon (from the Celtic demi-god Avalloc, who ruled the underworld) was where in some stories Guinevere was imprisoned by King Melwas in his castle on Glastonbury Tor. Rising sheer from the Somerset Levels, the Tor still broods over the site where, legend says, Joseph of Arimathea buried the Holy Grail; a place of Celtic pagan worship targeted by the first Christian missionaries, and still the focus of awed talk about ley-lines and earth energies.

On the other hand, more prosaically, in 1184 the Norman abbey at Glastonbury had been consumed by fire. Of the magnificent structure completed just decades before, only one chamber and the bell tower remained standing amid the ashes. The monks had urgent need of money for a rebuild.

Gerald described how Henry II himself, shortly before he died in 1189, told the monks where to dig, based on 'some evidence from his own books'. Henry was second husband to Eleanor of Aquitaine and first king of England's new Plantagenet dynasty. What better propaganda coup to bolster his line than to link it to England's most enduring myth? (Three centuries later the same benefits would draw a visit from Henry VII.) The ever-troublesome Welsh, just across the water from Glastonbury, might also learn that the 'once and future king' of whom they boasted was safely dead and in no position to contest Henry II's throne.

Henry and Eleanor's son Richard 'the Lionheart' found yet another way to use the story, and the sword also found within the grave. Stopping at Sicily on his way to the Holy Land in 1191, he exchanged gifts with Sicily's ruler Tancred. Tancred gave him fifteen galleys and four transport ships; Richard gave Tancred 'Excalibur'. To contemporaries, it clearly seemed a fair exchange. It was certainly an extreme example of how fiction could be taken as – could be pressed into the service of – hard, cold political fact.

This would prove to be a game the Tudors in their turn would play with mastery.

2

Realpolitik and the *Roman*

13th century

THERE IS ONE queen whose name has already appeared here
several times – as mother, as wife, as patron and as aunt; and,
appropriately, as a figure of Andreas Capellanus's fantasy. But
Eleanor of Aquitaine certainly deserves better than to figure as a mere
adjunct to anyone else's story. A quarter of a century before Chrétien
de Troyes wrote for Marie de Champagne, the Jersey-born Norman
poet Wace, translating Geoffrey of Monmouth into the vernacular,
presented his work to Marie's more famous mother, Eleanor. She is
often credited with having brought the idea of courtly love to England
in her train; and credited, too, with having helped inspire the popular
portrayal of King Arthur's Guinevere. Chrétien's early works display
detailed parallels with her English court.

Eleanor's grandfather, William IX of Aquitaine, had been one of the
first troubadours, writing of how his lady's ('*midons*') wrath could kill,
her joy could make a sick man well. (He also wrote: 'God let me live
long enough to get my hands under her cloak!'; so much for the idea
that courtly love was always chaste and non-physical. His thirteenth-
century biographer wrote that he was 'one of the most courtly men in
the world as well as one of the greatest deceivers of ladies'.)

Much about Eleanor's life provoked controversy in her own day. Her
journey to the Holy Land with her first husband, King Louis of France,
provoked rumours she had had an affair with her own uncle along the
way. Her subversive desire, and her very presence, were linked to the
failure of the crusade; just as, in the same way, any involvement with

women could jeopardise the quest of an Arthurian knight. When Eleanor joined with her sons in rebellion against her second husband, King Henry of England, she was warned by the Archbishop of Rouen that she 'would be the cause of a general ruin'; much as Guinevere brought down Camelot. D.D.R. Owen noted 'a progressive degrading of Guenevere's [sic] character that seems to parallel the worsening of Eleanor's reputation in popular esteem'. And it was after Eleanor died in 1204 (following sixteen years' imprisonment, and adventures stretching into her old age) that the 'black legend' surrounding her really got under way.

It was the Minstrel of Rheims who, around 1260, invented an affair between Eleanor and the Muslim leader Saladin. (More plausible stories describe her having an affair also with her husband Henry's father, Geoffrey.) Elizabethan tale would even suggest that it was she – rather than her daughter-in-law – who had an affair with William Marshal, frenemy to her son the Young King.

Another wholly fictional story of Eleanor's murdering her husband's mistress, 'Fair Rosamund', first appeared in the fourteenth century, though the most famous version was not perfected until two centuries later: the one in which Eleanor tracks Rosamund through the maze at Woodstock and offers her the choice of dagger or poison. This Rosamund might consider herself lucky, at that. One fourteenth-century version, the French *Chronicle of London*, had her roasted naked between two fires, then left to bleed to death in a hot bath with venomous toads on her breast. Curiously enough, the fictional Guinevere was about to suffer the same technicolour violence.

It is possible Eleanor of Aquitaine had been initial patron and planner of a group of long French prose Arthurian romances composed at the beginning of the thirteenth century by an anonymous author, or authors, and known as the Vulgate Cycle.

By now, Arthur's queen had two possible faces: the dark and the light. The Vulgate's way of dealing with the problem was to have two Guineveres: the 'true and false Guinevere', the latter being an illegitimate half-sister of Guinevere's who seduces the king and makes false accusations against the real queen, whom Lancelot must defend.

The false Guinevere's accusations lead to the real queen being sentenced to having the skin of her scalp flayed off:

> because she made herself queen and wore a crown on her head that she should not have worn. And afterwards, she shall have the palms of her hands sliced off, because she was consecrated and anointed, as the hands of no woman ought to be unless a king has married her faithfully and properly.

When Guinevere and Lancelot are found together, Arthur sentences her to death at the stake. But this harshness meets with universal disapproval; Arthur himself, after all, had said that rather than see Lancelot depart from his court, he would allow him to love the queen. The virtuous real Guinevere – '*si douce, si debonnaire, et si franc*' – always forgives Arthur his harshness and unkind treatment; yet, though the different tales that make up the Vulgate Cycle do not always speak with one voice, it is definitely the adultery of Guinevere and Lancelot that prevents Lancelot's achieving the Grail, and indeed that brings down Camelot.

The idea of courtly love – the shadow, even, of Arthur's Guinevere – haunts English queenship. Another of Eleanor's daughters-in-law – wife to King John of Magna Carta fame – may have been a later patron of the Vulgate Cycle. Dark rumours would cling to the beautiful Isabella of Angoulême; though, as with so many youthful royal brides, it's hard not to feel she had excuse for any perceived transgressions.

Married to John in 1200 (at an age that might have been anything from fifteen down to nine), she was forced to lodge in the households either of one of John's mistresses or of his discarded ex-wife Isabella of Gloucester, who had been set aside on a pretext to open the way for a different political alliance.* Small wonder if the second Isabella felt the need of support. During her first pregnancy she requested the presence in England of her elder half-brother Peter de Joigny. The rumours would be that they were having an affair.

A contemporary chronicler would declare that Isabella 'has often been found guilty of incest, witchcraft and adultery, so that the king,

---

* With Alys, sister to the king of France. But that alliance had fallen through, not least because John's father Henry II had made Alys his mistress.

her husband, has ordered those of her lovers who have been appre-
hended to be strangled with a rope in her own bed'. This report should
be taken less as signifying Isabella's certain adultery (for which there is
no real evidence), than the blurring of fact and fiction in these reports
– or rather, the way in which fact could be given the probably fictional
but ever-credible gloss of a woman's blame.

That said, when John died in 1216, Isabella not only decamped back
to France, but there married a man engaged to her daughter . . . Her
son Henry III's wife Eleanor of Provence would not be the last royal
bride to be accused of excessive promotion of her relatives and plump-
ing of her own purse. Hated by many of her husband's subjects, a focus
for howling discontent during the rebellions of the 1260s, she was
nonetheless sufficiently trusted by her husband to be left as his regent
when he was abroad.

The well-educated Eleanor had grown up familiar with the literature
of the Provençal troubadours, of which her father was a patron, and
would herself purchase expensive volumes of romance. Her daughter-
in-law and successor as queen of England – another Eleanor, but this
time of Castile – likewise came from a deeply literary court; she would
be a patron and promoter of books, Arthurian romance included. (She
was, however, also another queen who loved money even more than
myth.) Her husband Edward I, the 'Hammer of the Scots', who took
away their Stone of Scone, took also a keen interest in Arthur: he wrote
to the Pope urging his claim to be ruler of all the British Isles as his
'ancestor' had been. In evidence he cited Geoffrey of Monmouth.

In 1278 Edward and Eleanor travelled to Glastonbury for the
reopening of the much-disturbed grave of Arthur and Guinevere,
which they would have relocated to a site near the High Altar. Edward
took back 'Arthur's crown' from the defeated Welsh king Llywelyn, and
may have drawn on the Roman link to King Arthur in the siting and
design of the castles he built to keep Wales subdued. But with the
succession of his son Edward II in 1307, and Edward's marriage to
Isabella of France, English royal life – and the interest of the royal
family in the Arthurian myth – would take a sharper turn.

This Isabella would subsequently be blamed as 'the She-Wolf of France',
but was arguably forced into violent action by her husband's thraldom

to a succession of favourites. Married as a twelve-year-old to a husband in his twenties, she saw the property and position that should have been hers bestowed by the infatuated Edward on Piers Gaveston, a star of the tournament Edward arranged to display Gaveston's prowess.

When Gaveston was murdered by her husband's enraged lords in 1312 the stage seemed set for Isabella, still in her teens, to take her rightful place at his side: mother of Edward's son; living pledge of his relationship with France; diplomat between her natal and her marital country. But when Edward fell instead under the sway of the powerful and brutal Despensers, father and son, Isabella found herself once again sidelined and under threat, her lands confiscated, her children taken from her care.

Edward then made the strategic mistake of sending Isabella on an embassy to France, accompanied by their young son, England's heir. From France, Isabella wrote to Edward an extraordinary letter: 'I feel that marriage is a joining of a man and a woman, maintaining the undivided habit of life, and that someone has come between my husband and myself trying to break this bond.' She took to wearing a luxurious version of widow's weeds and declaring that her husband's deeds meant their marriage was ended as definitively as though he were dead. Invoking the help of her French family, Isabella – in her son's name – offered herself as figurehead to the many outraged by the Despensers' rule. She did so with the backing of one particular disaffected lord, Roger Mortimer, who, it soon became clear, was now Isabella's lover.

In the name of the young prince, Isabella and Mortimer swept through England carrying all before them. As the prose *Brut* chronicle put it: 'folk of this country had to her consented'. Alas, with Edward II imprisoned (to be murdered, it was said, by means of a red-hot poker), it soon became clear that the rule of Isabella and Mortimer was as rapacious as that of the Despensers had been. Peace was eventually restored to the country only when the seventeen-year-old Edward III staged his own coup against his mother's lover. Mortimer went to the gallows at Tyburn, but Edward declared that his mother had merely been deceived by Mortimer's wiles. Isabella enjoyed an extravagant lifestyle for almost three more decades before her death in 1358.

Chronicler Geoffrey le Baker recorded Isabella as a *'ferrea virago'*, 'a woman who aped a man', abandoning her female virtues to become as hard as iron. But this may not be how she saw her role in fact and fantasy. She was fascinated by the Arthurian stories: in Paris, her mother's books had included a number of romances and a volume of Arthurian legends beautifully bound in white leather. Many years later Isabella would be able to lend the French king two romances, of the Holy Grail and of Sir Lancelot. Equally fascinated was Isabella's lover Mortimer: a year before his fall he had played King Arthur to Isabella's Guinevere at a spectacular tournament, celebrating afterwards at a Round Table. It would, however, be Isabella's son Edward III who, swearing to institute a new Round Table, in 1348 set up the chivalric Order of the Garter.

The romantic preoccupations of Isabella's family would have dreadful consequences in reality. It was said to be Isabella herself who, on a visit to Paris in 1313, told her father the king that she thought she detected signs of adultery in two of her brothers' wives. The wife of a third brother, indeed, had been guilty of concealing the assignations they had enjoyed with their lovers in the Tour de Nesle. The two royal ladies had their heads shaved and were immured in underground dungeons. Their lovers were castrated, flayed alive and broken on the wheel before being decapitated. In France, it has been said, both the public credit given to women and the popularity of courtly literature underwent a sharp decline after the Tour de Nesle affair.

Courtly love was by now being mocked in the *fabliaux*, the comic and often scurrilous songs sung by jongleurs in the marketplace, not troubadours in the castle. Here women might be portrayed as lewd, lazy, lustful . . . Less serious a condemnation than that made by the Church, maybe, but as enduring.

But the thirteenth century had seen another major new player in town – and the greatest, to go by sheer popularity in its day. The *Roman de la Rose*, topping even Geoffrey of Monmouth's *History*, survives in some three hundred manuscript copies in different languages (a few of them created after the advent of printing, in the Tudor era). This was a book-length poem of around twenty thousand lines; the first four thousand or so written by one Guillaume de Lorris by 1230, and the subsequent sixteen thousand or so by Jean de Meun more than forty years later, in the 1270s. Or so says Jean de Meun in the text, anyway.

We have no other information concerning de Lorris; nothing, even, to confirm his existence.

The story – told in the first person – is an account of a dream the narrator had a few years before, in the month of May. Walking through a beautiful garden he comes across the wellspring of Love and sees therein the reflection of a perfect rosebud. As he gazes he is shot by the god of Love, 'the arrow passing through the eye and into my heart'. Surrendering himself to Love's domination, he becomes obsessed with plucking the rose. The allegory is obviously the courtly lover's pursuit of his lady.

But upon this slight framework – as de Meun took up the tale – was plastered an enormous weight of discourse on a range of subjects from science to philosophy. The volume of information is such that the *Roman* may have been used by readers almost as an encyclopaedia. It covers, particularly, the nature of women, of whom de Meun took a more jaded view than courtly predecessors had done. The dreamer gets advice from Nature and from Genius; help from Fair Welcome; impediments to his progress from Rebuff, Fear and Shame. The latter part of the poem even includes translations of part of the sixth-century Christian Boethius's *Consolation of Philosophy* (later translated also by Elizabeth I). Three centuries later Thomas Middleton wrote in his play *The Changeling* that Love 'has an intellect that runs through all . . . brings all home into one mystery'.

Less certainly, it has been suggested that the Middle Ages saw desire itself as in effect a sixth sense. The 'Lady and the Unicorn' series of tapestries from around 1500 adds to five tapestries representing the five senses an infinitely debated sixth, which sees the Lady in front of a tent, emblazoned with the words '*Mon Seul Desir*'. And indeed the whole tradition of – the value perceived in – courtly love makes more sense if it is viewed as a medium for other perceptions about the world.

But scholars cannot agree on the *Roman's* meaning. Was Guillaume de Lorris writing a straightforwardly courtly text? Did Jean de Meun merely continue the lover's journey in the more worldly spirit of later decades, or was he actually writing against the whole concept of courtly love, undermining the earlier part of the work, for all he claimed to be its continuator?

Or, even, was de Lorris himself poking a little fun, with his bizarrely explicit instructions for the lover, as explicit as those of Capellanus? Instructions, like those of Capellanus, echoing Ovid: 'Beautiful garments and adornments improve a man a great deal . . . You should have fine laced shoes and small boots and get new ones often, and you must see that they are so close-fitting that the vulgar will go around arguing over the way you are going to get into or out of them.'

De Lorris described his poetical dreamer challenged by Lady Reason, who came down from her tower to defend chastity and try to dissuade the dreamer from plucking the rose at all. In the thirteenth century there was a great debate over chastity. The Church's scholars could not agree. Was fornication necessarily a sin, since without it mankind would die out? Was it permissible, but only for procreation – or might (as the thirteenth-century theologian Richard Middleton put it) 'moderate pleasure' be allowed? In the *Roman*, Nature complains that man was failing to use the 'tools' he had been given for the purpose she intended: fathering children to continue the human race. But all the contradictions of the debate are there. 'Love is hateful peace and loving hate . . . a sin touched by pardon but a pardon stained by sin . . .'

Whereas de Lorris was writing about how to gain the love of a lady, de Meun wrote of how to gain what you want (i.e. sex) from a lady without yourself being caught in love's trap. Significantly, perhaps, Cupid is envisaged from the first not as a plump infant, but as a young man, a hunter, whose arrows pose a greater threat. Perhaps, indeed, the difference between the two sections of the *Roman* reflects the increasing suspicion with which women, and sex, came to be viewed in the course of the thirteenth century.

Guinevere's love made Lancelot the knight he became, but prevented his attaining the ultimate knightly goal. In the Grail volume of the Vulgate Cycle, the women who tempt the purer knights Perceval and Bors prove to be devils who, when rejected, disappear in a puff of smoke. Galahad, the purest knight of all, is seen consorting only with virgins; the ones he rescues and the one who leads him to the right path, representing probably the virtuous souls, and the figure of Christ himself. (Well, the authors of the Vulgate stories were probably monks: the last time the Arthurian tales would be left to religious hands.) The only good woman was now an untouched one, in contrast to some earlier moralities. In the last decades of the thirteenth century the Pope ordained an investigation into dangerous opinions – and the Bishop of Paris, Étienne Tempier, issued a series of 'Condemnations' that found it necessary officially to declare against the writing of Andreas Capellanus.

After the expansion of the twelfth century, the thirteenth saw an increasingly rigid climate, a bleaker view of the human condition itself. The historian Johan Huizinga, in his 1919 classic *The Waning of the Middle Ages*, described the *Roman de la Rose* as 'the breviary [i.e. prayer book] of the aristocracy' – adding that the wonder was that a Church so intolerant of dissent should allow its influence to continue for so many years. Was it because de Meun's jaded view of women – unstable and unworthy, at once deceitful and easily duped – increasingly corresponded to the Church's own? Perhaps courtly love could have died here and now, impaled on the tedium of the Scholastic debate (which did indeed argue whether several angels could be in the same place, if not how many could dance on the head of a pin).

But a very different impetus for the old ideal would soon be making its way northwards from Italy. The galvanic effect of the new humanist studies that came in with what we know as the Renaissance would reinvigorate the literature of courtly love – and give it a new moral dimension.

3

The *Commedia*, Chaucer and Christine

14th century

THE NEW TURN in the fortunes of courtly love began in the closing years of the thirteenth century – in 1284, in Florence, with an eighteen-year-old poet standing on a street corner, watching the girl of his dreams go by. His name was Dante Alighieri, a scion of minor Florentine nobility. He had first seen her at a May Day party nine years earlier, when she was eight ('an angel child, dressed . . . in a decorous and delicate crimson') and he just a year older. She has since been identified – by Dante's first biographer Boccaccio – as Bice Portinari, of rather higher rank than he. Dante called her Beatrice. 'Her image, always in my mind, inspired Love to take control of me.'

Beatrice, dressed in white, and with two older women, was passing along one of the streets that border the muddy waters of the Arno. Her eyes falling upon the quaking poet, she greeted him sweetly – 'so graciously that at that moment I seemed to experience absolute blessedness'. He had to retire to his room; and, as he slept there, he had a dream.

A giant figure, the Lord of Love, was coming towards him, carrying a woman, naked under a blood-coloured cloth. It was Beatrice. In one hand he held an object all on fire, and said to Dante: 'behold your heart.' The god woke Beatrice, and forced her to eat the flaming object. Literary critics today (and Dante's friends then, the group of poets he called the *Fedeli d'Amore*, the Followers of Love) are still trying to work that one out. But he and Beatrice were embarked on a journey during which they would ascend into Dante's *Paradiso* – and into literary history.

In the *Vita Nuova* Dante describes how he had been struck straight as an arrow by the Force of Love; how he became ill for love of Beatrice; how (in best courtly tradition) he nonetheless preserved the code of secrecy. He even set up another lady-love as a kind of stalking horse, much to Beatrice's displeasure. Dante was married; but that relationship – from their betrothal when he was ten through the birth of the couple's children – seems never to have caused anyone any jealousy. His love for Beatrice was 'so noble' that, unlike mere sexual desire, it could never lead him astray.

Just as the Virgin leads mankind to God so – controversially – Beatrice would lead Dante: Beatrice, whose very name means blessed. Her appeal would be the more powerful for the fact that in 1290 – a decade before vicious Florentine politics brought Dante's exile from his city; a decade before the fictional beginning of the *Divine Comedy* – the real Beatrice was dead.

'*Nel mezzo del cammin di nostra vita*', in the middle of our life's path, he had wandered from the true road: away from Beatrice and towards a corrupt and confrontational public life. Beatrice will show him the way home. In the *Divine Comedy* it is she who, at the behest of the Virgin Mary, sends the classical poet Virgil to be Dante's guide as he descends into Hell. In the second level – still in the area of the lighter punishments – they find the lustful: Cleopatra, Dido, Helen of Troy.

One particular couple catch his eye: pressed naked together as they float, weightless (and though they *are* in Hell, the image is a beautiful one). Paolo Malatesta and Francesca da Rimini died in Florence, in Dante's teenage years: killed by Francesca's husband, Paolo's brother, for whom a harsher place in Hell is being kept. Francesca tells Dante what brought them to this fate, circling endlessly on the viewless winds. They were reading *Lancelot du Lac*, the tale of Guinevere and Lancelot 'who loved illicitly'. When they read how Lancelot kissed Guinevere, Paolo kissed Francesca, and 'we did no more reading that day'.

But Dante's own love is not illicit. Cleansed of sin, he travels up through Purgatory, and at the hill at the very top – the Garden of Eden, close to Heaven – is hailed by his lost love. Shining like the sun, in a rain of white petals, Beatrice appears in a chariot drawn by a mythological beast and escorted by a gang of religious worthies. His reaction is not joy but shame: shame for the years when he was seduced away from Beatrice's pure image by other thoughts – and other women? She, tough as any courtly lady could be, tells him his estrangement is a sin; though now, of course, it is not the god of Love he has sinned against, but the all-high. We are relieved when at the very end of his journey Dante is forgiven, to soar with Beatrice through the stars. Her smile reflects the joy of God, her beauty transports Dante into the Empyrean. She then moves away from him, to take her place higher in the Celestial Rose.

The idea that a pure earthly love could act in the service of the pure love of religion was not new. Neoplatonic currents of thought, with their belief in the ennobling effects of love and beauty, were – thanks to Arab scholarship – reaching southern France in troubadour times. It was this implication – that a pure courtly love could act in the service of religious zeal – which would make it acceptable to one of the most morally aspirational of monarchs: Henry VIII.

Dante's central image of Beatrice, her Heaven-turned eyes leading his upwards, impacts even on those who never read Dante. Drawing from the image of the Virgin Mary, it led on to, for example, the Victorian picture of Woman as carrying (whether she wished to or not) responsibility for the moral tone of society. But it would be fellow-Tuscan Francesco Petrarca (Petrarch), and another woman who could not return a poet's love, who would frame the lyric poetry of many years to come.

Petrarch's Laura is a figure at least as elusive and allegorical as Beatrice a generation earlier. (As feminist critics note disapprovingly, like Beatrice, she was also dead.) In fact Laura may or may not have existed in real life; but the sonnets in which Petrarch wrote of her would shape the poems of Elizabeth I herself, and those Thomas Wyatt wrote to her mother.

Laura's relation to Petrarch is less wholly beneficial than that of Beatrice to Dante. But Petrarch became an international celebrity, his work set to music, and his determination to study 'what is to be found only within' would play a major part in forming even the new Renaissance sense of personal identity. One of the most famous portraits of Elizabeth I is informed by Petrarch's *Triumph of Chastity*, which praises the Vestal Virgin Tuccia who proved her disputed chastity by carrying water in a sieve. Elizabeth would join the already long and honourable list of those who translated his work.

Another name on that list was Geoffrey Chaucer who, in *Canticus Troili*, posed some of the central dilemmas of romantic love:

> If no love is, O God, what feel I so?
> And if love is, what thing and which is he?
> If love be good, from whence cometh my woe?

Indeed, there is a tempting theory that Chaucer may have met Petrarch on one of his journeys to Italy, and perhaps it hardly matters if this is just another story.* What matters is that Chaucer was deeply entwined both with European literary tradition and with England's royal family. And Chaucer also translated the *Roman de la Rose*, or the first 1,705 lines of it, anyway.

Geoffrey Chaucer, the son of a vintner, was probably born in London around 1340: a decade after the young Edward III seized power back from his mother Isabella and her lover Mortimer. During Chaucer's childhood the Black Death ravaged Europe, killing perhaps a third of the population, but many of those who survived thrived in an age of new opportunities for the literate layman, and bold new thought to which his education and reading gave him every access.

In 1357 household accounts of the Duchess of Clarence, one of Edward III's daughters-in-law, record one Galfridus (i.e. Geoffrey) Chaucer, clearly a page, being given a paltock – short cloak – and a pair of red and black breeches. Less than three years later he was recorded as going abroad on military service, being briefly captured, and ransomed, along with other imprisoned yeomen, by the king or John of Gaunt. But this marked only the start of his connection with royalty.

Edward III had in 1328 married Philippa of Hainault, who brought her continental culture to the English court. Her father's library boasted several Arthurian romances; Philippa had *chansons de geste*,

---

* '*Se non è vero, è molto ben trovato*', as the sixteenth-century philosopher Giordano Bruno would put it. This would appear to be the equivalent to what used to be known in journalistic circles as a fact too good to check.

romance and chivalry among her books and she gave her husband a silver cup and ewer decorated with worthies including Arthur and Lancelot. A good many of her countrymen followed her to England – chronicler Jean Froissart was only one who relished an impressive and artistic court. It was Froissart who imagined Edward, in the old courtly extra-marital fashion, wooing the Countess of Salisbury, whose wisdom, nobility and beauty 'hath so enraptured my soul, that I cannot but love you; and without your return of love, I am but as dead'. In the countess's honour, one story said, he founded the Order of the Garter; another tale, describing how his passion led him to rape her, was possibly set about by his enemies.

Edward seems to have been unusually prepared to indulge his children romantically – seems, moreover, to have partaken to some degree of the new interest in love within marriage. He is said to have written verse for his eldest son the 'Black Prince', urging him to

Love ladies and maidens
And serve and honour them in thought, word, and deed . . .
For we hardly ever see a valiant man
Who does not or has not loved.

The Black Prince, unusually, made his love match with the beautiful young widow Joan of Kent – a marriage ultimately accepted by his parents, though the prince's early death meant neither would come to the throne. And in a favourite story, Edward III allows his cherished eldest daughter Isabella to call off her arranged marriage, even as the ship ready to carry her abroad was about to set sail. It is possible, however, that a gloss of romance was being given to a political decision: Isabella's proposed match had suddenly become less advantageous to Edward.

Edward's third son John of Gaunt had married Blanche of Lancaster in 1359, and through her he inherited her father the Duke of Lancaster's title and lands. But this also became a love match. John of Gaunt was one of the most interesting figures of his age: intellectually adventurous as well as militarily successful; loving Arthurian literature; interested (until they became linked to political rebellion) even in the Lollards, whose yearning for a reformed Church and an English Bible foreshadowed Protestantism.

Gaunt came as close as any to fitting the bill for Chaucer's 'parfit gentil knight' – 'a lion on the field, a lamb in the hall'. It has been suggested, albeit without evidence, that it was Gaunt who commissioned *Sir Gawain and the Green Knight*, which, with *Pearl*, was one of the flowers of fourteenth-century literature. When Duchess Blanche died in 1368 it plunged her husband into grief. But it also almost certainly inspired Chaucer, by now an Esquire of the King's Household, to his first important poem.

The Book of the Duchess begins with the poet himself, sleepless and sick. The first lines are borrowed directly from Froissart (himself drawing on French poet and composer Guillaume de Machaut), and in Froissart's work the poet is lovesick. It is even possible Chaucer was figuring himself as – in the most courtly, the most respectful, the most platonic way possible – lovesick for the dead duchess. He sits up in a bed, and a servant brings him a book, a romance, 'to read and drive the night away': the legend, from Ovid, of a wife who died of grief after the loss of her husband. The grim story soothes him enough that he falls asleep and dreams.

It is (of course!) a lovely May morning, and he is in a room painted with the text of the *Roman de la Rose*. He hears outside the noise of a hunt and, following it, finds himself in a flowery wood where he meets a young knight in black, lamenting the death of his lady. The fact that the lady's name is 'White' (Blanche), and a series of puns on John of Gaunt's titles, suggests that Gaunt is the knight in black. The knight's lengthy exposition of his love places him firmly in the courtly tradition: after he 'chose love to his first craft' he begs his lady's 'mercy', tries his hardest 'to do her worship'.

In the real world, however, only limited indulgence could be given to a royal prince's sense of loss: John of Gaunt had to marry again, and swiftly. In 1371 he did indeed marry Constance of Castile through whom he could – unsuccessfully, as it turned out – claim the throne of Castile; but this marriage seems not to have proved personally happy. Chaucer's wife Philippa and her sister Katherine, wife to knight Hugh Swynford, went to serve Constance. They were daughters of Paon de Roet, a Hainault knight who had come in Queen Philippa's train. Katherine was governess to Gaunt's children by Blanche, and they soon began an affair.

In 1377 Edward III died, his son the Black Prince having died the year before. This left the prince's ten-year-old son to inherit the throne as Richard II. Richard was hailed – by no less a person than Christine de Pizan, of whom more anon – as a 'true Lancelot'. In a sense, she was right. The ideals of chivalry did not (as might easily have happened) vanish under a child-king. Nonetheless, events would prove Richard a spectacularly unsuccessful monarch. And meanwhile, the advent of an underage king, never a happy situation, thrust John of Gaunt into edgy prominence: suspected of wanting his nephew's throne. During the 1381 Peasants' Revolt a mob terrorised London for three days, burning Gaunt's Savoy Palace to the ground.

Yet these troubled years were very productive for Chaucer both in terms of his public career – trusted on a good deal of the king's business – and poetically. He would translate Boethius's *Consolation of Philosophy* and embark on those of his works that most directly confront the changing face of courtly love.

Chaucer's *Troilus and Criseyde* drew on Boccaccio's *Il Filostrato*, which in turn drew on earlier medieval sources. Troilus, a prince of Troy, is struck by love for Criseyde (Cressida): so struck as to swoon, lovesick, that sure test of a true lover. She returns his feelings, their affair facilitated by her uncle Pandarus. But when her father, who has defected to the Greek side, arranges for her to be sent after him, Criseyde allows herself to be seduced by a cynical Greek, Diomede, betraying Troilus's love.

But where Chaucer broke ranks with most of those who had come before him is to paint his Criseyde as a three-dimensional woman: a young widow who, certainly, is initially flattered by the princely hero Troilus's lovesick passion, but uncertain she wants to surrender her autonomy:

I am mine own woman, well at ease
I thank God – as after mine estate
Right young, and stand untied in lusty lees [pleasant pastime]
Withouten jealousy or such debate
Shall no husband say to me: 'Check mate'.

She accepts Troilus's love only on the understanding she can keep 'my honour and my name'. Troilus yields himself to her 'governance'. But

Criseyde's honour will be very much the question; not lost, in the story's eyes, when she sleeps with Troilus without marriage, but lost if he should reveal the fact. Lost for sure when she betrays the all-consuming love that alone had sanctioned her conduct . . . But Chaucer displays an unusual sympathy for the disgraced Criseyde.

Perhaps Chaucer's great appeal for contemporaries was that he managed to marry the new Italian humanist consciousness of the individual to the old Anglo-French romance. And Chaucer did not stand alone. His trusted friend, the poet John Gower – another Londoner, another who at least brushed against royal circles – is remembered chiefly for three works, of which the most famous, the *Confessio Amantis* (The Lover's Confession), in a sense combines the tropes of conventional Christian morality and courtly love. Probably written around the time Chaucer was beginning *The Canterbury Tales*, it is likewise a collection of stories, drawing heavily on Ovid, and framed around the Seven Deadly Sins.

The sins Gower's Lover has to confess, however, are sins against Love – and yet, at that, his penitent can show a streak of rebellion. The old theory of courtly love, and the desperation of the courtly lover, had effectively cast onto the woman the onus of response. (It was in effect a stalker's charter.) Gower is having none of that. If a man bewilders himself for love of a woman, he says crisply in the first volume of the *Confessio*, 'I can certainly acquit the woman', who may indeed know nothing of it. Do we blame the water if a man throws himself in it to drown? And though Gower's reputation has suffered by comparison with his more famous contemporary, the forty-nine surviving manuscripts of the *Confessio* suggest it was certainly popular in its day.

Was something new entering the equation? A new resistance to the old idea of love as suffering – and as something distinct from and in many ways antagonistic to a fruitful, if prosaic, marriage? Chaucer's *The Legend of Good Women* features a cast of heroines, from Cleopatra to Lucretia, all betrayed through their love; but a love which equates to marriage or the promise of it.* He wrote at a time when the Anjou

---

* Scholar of medieval literature D.W. Robertson deplored the ridiculousness of the whole concept of courtly love. By its supposed rules – he wrote, in a conscious *reductio ad absurdum* – he would be expected to love someone else's wife. Unless he lived in England, where he might occasionally be allowed to practise the art with his own . . .

nobleman the Knight of la Tour Landry had just produced the immensely famous manual of instruction for his daughters, the *Livre pour l'enseignement de ses filles*. In it he wrote of service to Love – and of the first wife ('of all good was she bell and flower') who had inspired his deeds of arms and his poetry. But the second wife he married when this paragon died warns the girls that such words, which all men use, are 'but sport . . . for to get them the better and sooner the grace and goodwill of their paramours'. In the kaleidoscope that is *The Canterbury Tales*, Chaucer was about to display marriage, love and, indeed, lust in all their varied hues.

Of course it had to begin on a vividly realised spring day, the kind when 'small fowls' seem to sing for joy; both practical for pilgrims preparing to travel the muddy roads of the Middle Ages, and replete with poetic significance. Of the storytellers and the tales they tell, three stand out in this context. *The Knight's Tale* – the most classically courtly, and told by a genuinely courteous teller – is essentially Chaucer's already-written *Palamon and Arcite*, about two knights contending for love of the same lady. (Note that she wants neither of them and would much prefer to continue her favourite pastime of hunting: like Diana, like Elizabeth Tudor in the years ahead, maybe.) The tale of the drunken, belligerent Miller which follows it is like one of the *fabliaux*, those ribald ripostes to the courtly story: the tale of an old husband, his young wife and his young clerk which winds up as an extended riff on the still-current injunction to 'Kiss my arse'.

The five-times-married Wife of Bath, Chaucer's most memorable creation, has her genesis in the Old Woman (a former prostitute turned bawd who gave the lover advice) of the *Roman de la Rose*.

> Experience, though no authority
> Were in this world is right enough for me
> To speak of woe that is in marriage

It speaks straight to us now and taps into a then-current debate. The Wife acknowledges virginity as the most virtuous way of life, but declares it can never be for her: 'Alas, alas that ever love was sin.' She quotes misogynistic tracts stretching over a millennia (quoted to her, perhaps, by her fifth husband, a handsome young clerk); refutes them with unabashed conviction no whit lessened by the fact that with every word, every recollection, she is painting herself as exactly what the misogynistic texts and the *fabliaux* alike condemned women as being. Earthy, greedy for life, for sex and for power.

Of all the pilgrims it is the Wife – not the dainty prioress, with her brooch reading *Amor Vincit Omnia* (Love Conquers All); not the man of law nor the Franklin; not even the Knight – whose tale is an Arthurian one. But what is its conclusion? The knight despatched by Guinevere to discover what it is women most want comes back with the answer that they want mastery over their husbands . . . Just like the Wife herself.

The 'fragments' that make up *The Canterbury Tales* as we know it today were probably assembled from the time when, in the late 1380s, Chaucer gave up his post as Comptroller of Customs and moved to Kent, though he continued to be employed in positions of trust about King Richard II's business. In 1387 his wife's pension seems to have come to an end: perhaps because in the taut politics of these years her husband was less in favour; or simply because Philippa Chaucer died. In 1394 Philippa's former mistress, Constance of Castile, also died, leaving John of Gaunt free to marry his long-time mistress, Katherine Swynford, Chaucer's sister-in-law, two years later.

It would be a reach to present theirs as a courtly love story. But it is remarkable that Gaunt chose to take this step, and to have the children of their affair legitimated.[*] Gaunt's first and third marriages saw romantic love located within marriage. But early in 1399 John of Gaunt died. Some eight months later John's son Henry of Bolingbroke deposed the ineffectual Richard II to make himself Henry IV: founder of the Lancastrian dynasty that would rule England for the next sixty years. The following year, 1400, Chaucer himself was dead.

It would be left for a woman, writing within a couple of years of Chaucer's death, to make the first explicit refutation of the ideal of

---

[*] There would be contradictory evidence over whether that legitimation did or did not allow rights to the crown, but in the event practical politics triumphed over legal propriety, since John and Katherine's great-great-grandson would be Henry VII.

courtly love; and not from either the masculine or the specifically Christian standpoint but from what one can only call the feminist one. Christine de Pizan – an Italian-born scholar's daughter whose father's success took her to the French court – had married a secretary of the French king. But his early death left her a young widow with a family to support, and Christine became the first woman in Europe to make a living by her able and ready pen. In 1399 she wrote a *Letter to the God of Love* complaining that many authors – including the author of the famous *Roman de la Rose* – were unfairly critical of women. Needless to say, the god is convinced, and bans such slanderers from his court.

She stuck with the subject. *The Debate of the Two Lovers*, in which a disappointed knight and a youthfully optimistic squire argue as to whether love brings unhappiness or the reverse, was followed by *The Duke of True Lovers*, which, while celebrating married love, so far subscribed to courtly lore as to focus on the platonic romance between a married woman and a younger man. But Christine was finding her voice, and it was not that of a woman constrained within the courtly story.

With *Le Dit de la Rose*, written in 1402, she jumped into a debate between two male authorities as to the morality or otherwise of the *Roman*. (Then as now, for Christine – the fifteenth-century equivalent of a modern newspaper columnist, writing on subjects from her own mental development to military tactics – there was cash in controversy.) She claimed that de Meun's work was unfair in its blanket denigration of women; that he disrespected marriage and advocated promiscuity. Her open letter drew a response from no less a person than the king's secretary, statesman and humanist Gontier Col, who described de Meun as his 'master teacher'. Christine's opinions could not be hers alone, he wrote, but those of satellites who would not dare attack de Meun themselves but 'wanted to use you as their rain cloak'. Nonetheless, she should 'withdraw and unsay what you have dared to charge'. Two days later he wrote again, begging 'you to correct and amend yourself from the manifest error, folly and madness that has come upon you through presumption and overweening pride, like a woman governed by emotion'.

Christine wasn't having any of it. If Col alleged 'the littleness of my faculties', on the grounds that she was a woman, 'then know for a truth that I do not consider this a crime or the least reproach, because of the comfort of the noble memory and continual new experience of the most wise and valiant ladies that have been and are fully worthy of praise'. A mouse, she wrote, can attack a lion; and whatever good things were to be found in the *Roman*, 'I say that it can only cause wicked and perverse exhortation to abominable morals, encouraging a dissolute life with doctrines full of deceit'. As the debate picked up strength, Christine sent a copy of the correspondence to the French queen, Isabeau; and eventually the chancellor of the University of Paris, Jean Gerson, weighed in on Christine's side, writing a treatise condemning the *Roman*.

But perhaps in the end the most important thing about the debate would be that through it Christine found her great mission: to defend the reputation of women from the clerkly misogynists who had held history in their hands until now. (Something the Wife of Bath, far more crudely, had also tried to do.) A famous illustration in one of Christine's works shows her writing in her study, half-finished book open in front of her, pen in hand and a small dog alert at her feet, amid the folds of her trademark blue robe. That rich blue, painted in the viciously expensive ultramarine pigment and repeated in numerous images of Christine throughout the text, suggests her status, as does the horned white headdress an aristocratic woman would wear. The writing pose had reinforced the authority of medieval male thinkers from St Luke in the Lindisfarne Gospels on. But Christine later described how in that study she picked up a volume of classical poetry (though books were still a rarity, she now had the run of the royal library) and was shocked at the hostile portrayals of women she found there.

The result was *The Book of the City of Ladies*, published in 1405, in which Christine gave a list of notable women from the Amazons to one Anastaise, the female illustrator who may have painted Christine herself; from the biblical Judith and Esther and the female saints to contemporary lady aristocrats. The book became an icon of feminist thought right through to the sixteenth century and beyond. There would be a copy of Christine's works in the Tudor royal library, and Elizabeth I had on her walls a set of tapestries drawn from *The City of Ladies*. That said, some of the advice in Christine's follow-up manual,

The Treasure of the City of Ladies, might well have appeased her harshest critic. Love and honour your husband, whatever he may be. Perils and dangers follow 'illicit love', and suspicion of wrongdoing is almost as destructive as the deed itself.

'Do not put trust in vain fancies, as many young women do, allowing themselves to believe that there is no harm in loving with a tender passion provided that it is not accompanied by any sinful act . . . Being merely suspected of such a love, the truth never really known, [such noble ladies] lost not only their honour but their lives'. Do not think you can make a man valiant, do not promote him at the risk of your reputation, do not tell yourself you are gaining 'a true friend and servant'. 'Some men say they serve their ladies when they do great deeds of arms. But I say they serve only themselves.' You could hardly have a more explicit refutation of the courtly love theory – or, as the next century would prove, one with more relevance for England's royal ladies.

It might have been easy, coming fresh from the all-encompassing humanity of Chaucer, to feel that Christine was tilting at windmills. To feel that the ideal of courtly love had on the one hand been subsumed into a broader and more realistic goal of love within marriage; or, on the other, been relegated to its appropriate place as a recherché literary game. The heat and publicity of the debate around Christine de Pizan's work give that comfortable theory the lie.

Charles VI – husband to Queen Isabeau who was Christine's patron – had recently founded a *Cour Amoureuse*, a court of love, the charter of which survives in the Bibliothèque Nationale de France. Male participants were to bring a love song they had written in praise of ladies. There is no evidence to suggest the court ever achieved the monthly meeting proposed in the charter. There may have been an element of fantasy in the concept, invented to provide distraction from a particularly virulent outbreak of the plague (and challenges in this context may have been used to mask others on the political stage). But the eventual list of members numbered some six hundred of the highest men in the land.

It was, moreover, a royal physician, Evrart de Conty, who wrote *Le Livre des Échecs Amoureux Moralisés* (The Edifying Book of Erotic

Chess) in around 1400. The analogy between the game of chess and that of courtly love had long been sufficiently popular for a chess match – often featured in a manuscript's illustrations – to signify that erotic content was to follow. Lancelot and Guinevere both played chess, as did Tristan and Iseult; the *Livre* takes place in a garden analogous to that of the *Roman de la Rose*.

In the course of the fifteenth century, images of the game of chess – like that of courtly love itself? – would indeed come to take on an increasingly domestic tone. But any change would be gradual; and the English royal library gives evidence that the old stories had by no means died away. Edward III passed on to his grandson Richard II several Arthurian volumes including, probably, Chrétien's *Conte del Graal*, the Vulgate *Mort Artu*, and the *Roman de la Rose*. Thomas Woodstock, Edward's son and Richard's uncle, had eighty-four volumes of romances and histories in his collection, including a French *Lancelot*, the *Roman de la Rose* and two books on Merlin.

In the last part of the fourteenth century there had been a burst of Arthurian literature: *Sir Launfal*, based on Marie de France's twelfth-century romance *Lanval*, which (unusually for its day) cast Guinevere as a sexual predator, pursuing the knights of her husband's court; the Alliterative *Morte Arthure* and the Stanzaic *Morte Arthur*; the *Awntyrs off Arthure at the Terne Wathelyne* (The Adventures of Arthur at the Tarn Wadling), in which the ghost of Guinevere's mother appears to tell of the penance she is having to do for her sins, and warn her lax daughter to be chaste, merciful and meek. That was exactly the model men were wishing on their real wives, too often in vain. And as several English queens would find in the years ahead, courtly love and the Arthurian myth alike remained spectres with every intention of joining in the feast. Ghosts who had never agreed to lie down and die.

4

Lancaster

1400–1461

W HEN, IN 1399, John of Gaunt's son deposed Richard II
to make himself the new Henry IV, it brought to England's
throne the fruits of a different branch of the Plantagenet
tree. (The branch would come to be called the Lancastrian line, after
Gaunt's title, Duke of Lancaster.) And, as we have already seen, a
newcomer grasps any weapon at hand to affirm his legitimacy . . . A
fine foreign marriage, maybe?

Henry IV's first wife was dead before he seized the throne, having
given him a quiver-full of children, but in 1403 he married the wealthy
and well-connected widow Joanne of Navarre. Joanne had been
governing Brittany as regent for her eldest son, experience which qualified her to play an active part in the governments of her husband and,
when the time came, of her stepson Henry V. The romantic story says
Henry and Joanne had already become close during his exile on the
Continent. Less romantically, the very generous financial provision
made for her provoked widespread resentment.

Before his death in 1413, Henry IV sought a daughter of the French
king for his heir, but the likelihood of a marriage between Prince
Henry and Katherine de Valois ebbed and flowed with hostilities
between the two countries, and it was several years after his victory at
Agincourt that Henry V finally met his future bride, near Paris.

It may be only legend that Henry V was struck by Katherine's beauty,
but contemporary reports do suggest that from the time of his accession,
he remained chaste until his marriage day. Chastity of course was an

attribute of the perfect knight – it was lack of chastity that cost Lancelot success in the quest for the Holy Grail – and Henry was obsessed by chivalry. He commissioned several chivalric epics from the monk and poet John Lydgate, whose *Complaint of a Lover's Life* was based on Chaucer's *Book of the Duchess*. Though chivalry only went so far ... Planning how best to make financial provision for his bride, Henry allowed his stepmother Joanne to be arrested on suspicion of 'sorcery and necromancy'; though the comfortable terms of her imprisonment in lovely Leeds Castle suggest that the confiscation of her lands was the real objective. Sensibly, Joanne seems not to have contested the accusation. Doing so could have brought her, like Guinevere, to the stake.

Henry's bride was a daughter of that Queen Isabeau to whom Christine de Pizan sent her *Querelle du Roman de la Rose*, and Charles VI who founded the *Cour Amoureuse* – but their life was far less elevated than their literary interest might suggest. Stories of promiscuity (and avarice, profligacy and sorcery) clustered like a flock of vultures around Isabeau: of affairs with her own brother-in-law the Duc d'Orléans – who in 1407 was murdered, it was said, to avenge her honour – and with another leader of strife-torn France's factions, Bernard d'Armagnac. More certainly, d'Armagnac held her captive for six months, to be rescued through the auspices of the man who had killed Orléans ... But modern scholarship suggests the stories were put about by her enemies. (And she might, in any case, have found some excuse in the fact her husband Charles was plagued by bouts of insanity.) But the nature of the slurs is nonetheless interesting, as established precedent for the best way to get rid of a queen.

Katherine's marriage to Henry V would last little more than two years. She gave birth to a boy in December 1421, with Henry away in France at the wars. But the following August, still in France, her husband died of sickness, leaving their nine-month-old son to inherit as Henry VI, and government in the competitive hands of the baby's two surviving uncles, the Dukes of Bedford and of Gloucester.

There seems to have been no thought of Katherine playing a significant part in that government. Instead there was scandalous talk of an affair with Edmund Beaufort, a grandson of John of Gaunt and Katherine Swynford. There were even stories (without evidence) that she was pregnant with Beaufort's child, and needed quickly to be married, when her eye fell on Owen ap Maredudd ap Tudor, a member of her household.

Owen's position may have been as high as keeper of her wardrobe (rather grander and more responsible than it sounds to modern ears) or as low (claimed one sixteenth-century Welsh chronicler) as the 'sewer' who placed her dishes at table. One story claims him as no Tudor at all, but the bastard of an innkeeper.

The family we know as the Tudors were prominent in medieval Wales, serving the princes of Gwynedd – descended, indeed, from a daughter of the house. But Welsh rank did not count for much at the English court; the more so since the family lands had been confiscated after Owen's father and elder brothers had taken part in Glendower's unsuccessful recent rising against English rule. A distant relative, however, introduced Owen to the English court, and one story has him, still in his teens, knighted by Henry V in the field after Agincourt.

The more probable story of Katherine's first interest in Owen has him accidentally collapsing into her lap while dancing too vigorously at a ball. Another sees her spying him swimming naked and, in best romantic tradition, arranging a disguised love tryst. The long-running chronicle written by the monks of Croyland Abbey noted disapprovingly that she – a queen of England – had been 'unable to control her carnal passions'. Though the pair went on to have children, their marriage – assuming such a ceremony did take place – was kept quiet until after Katherine's death in 1437. When Owen – no longer protected by the need to safeguard her reputation – tried to flee to Wales he was hauled back to Westminster to face an inquiry and (despite his pleas that he 'had nothing done') imprisonment on a trumped-up charge. Within a couple of years, however, he had been released; and Henry VI, as he came to manhood, welcomed his half-brothers Edmund and Jasper Tudor to his side.

At the age of fifteen, Henry VI was declared fit to rule – but in fact it is unclear how fit he would ever be. One papal envoy dismissively described him as more like a monk than a king. Henry hastily left the room when a courtier brought in dancing girls; he hearkened to a spiritual counsellor who preached celibacy . . . His marriage in 1445 was arranged to cement a peace in England's ongoing disputes with France, but it came decked in the trappings of chivalry. His fifteen-year-old bride Marguerite of Anjou was not only niece to the French king but daughter of René, Duc d'Anjou (and claimant to the crowns of Naples, Sicily, Jerusalem and Hungary), an accepted authority on the finer points of the tournament, and the author of the *Livre du Coeur d'Amour Épris* (Book of the Love-Smitten Heart).

The fifteenth century saw an extraordinary revival in the cult of chivalry – in England at least perhaps a response, just as in the twelfth century, to the disorder of the times. Tournaments were modelled on those read about in the prose romances, which themselves were enjoying a surge in popularity. Noblemen set up their shield at the crossroads, waiting for it to be struck by a challenger. The Burgundian Jacques de Lalaing went further by roaming Europe searching for chivalric combats.[*]

On Marguerite's marriage, her father organised a tournament featuring knights dressed up as Round Table heroes, and a wooden castle called Joyeuse Garde. A bound volume of Arthurian romances was presented to the bride. Marguerite had already won an admirer at her uncle's French court, Pierre de Brézé, to carry her colours at the joust. The Burgundian chronicler Barante wrote that she 'was already renowned in France for her beauty and wit and her lofty spirit of courage'. That courage would come to be both a blessing and a curse.

One Italian contemporary reports a story that when Marguerite landed in England, Henry VI secretly took her a letter, having first dressed himself as a squire: 'While the Queen read the letter the King took stock of her . . . she never looked at the King in his squire's dress, who remained on his knees all the time.' The disguised encounter was a favourite trope of the romantic story – the knight supposed to recognise the inner beauty of the woman who, as in the Wife of Bath's Tale, enchantment had turned into a 'loathly lady'. True love should see through any disguise. But *this* Henry (unlike, as we shall see, Henry VIII) seems not to have blamed the lady for being deceived.

Her kinsman the Duc d'Orléans wrote sympathetically that Marguerite seemed 'formed by Heaven to supply her royal husband the qualities which he required in order to become a great king'. But others saw those qualities very differently. They suggested, even, that

---

[*] Crucially, he was admired rather than mocked as Don Quixote's comparable effort would be, however gently, in the early seventeenth century.

Marguerite had become too close to her escort from France, the Duke of Suffolk. Suffolk – a man entering his fifties, but sufficiently enamoured of the chivalric tradition, in the course of the long French wars, to have once knighted a brave young French squire who captured him – wrote verses playing on the queen's name of marguerite or daisy:

For wit thee well, it is a paradise
To see this flower when it begins to spread
With colours fresh enewed, white and red.

In spring 1453 Henry and Marguerite were able at long last to announce a pregnancy, but that summer the king fell into a stupor, incapable of action for weeks and then months. When, in October, Marguerite – after so long a barren marriage – gave birth to a son, there were rumours about the baby's paternity. Henry recovered his senses, but his weakness had given a rival sight of an opportunity. The old 'Yorkist' line, displaced half a century before, had never gone away. Richard, Duke of York, was descended through his father from Edward III's fourth son, and through his mother from Edward's second, which arguably gave him a better claim to the throne than Henry. For the next few years Richard would contend control of the country against Henry – or rather, against Marguerite, acting in her husband's and her son's names, but with a band of knights called the 'queen's gallants'.

A 'great and strong-laboured woman', a 'manly woman, using to rule and not be ruled', was how contemporaries described her. Marguerite's transgressive political prominence was tied to spreading rumours of a relationship with her second great ally the Duke of Somerset . . . Which is where the name 'Tudor' re-enters the story.

This Duke of Somerset was killed in what most of us know as the 'Wars of the Roses' – though the alternative name of the 'Cousins' War' is a more accurate description. But he left behind him a niece, daughter of his elder brother – Margaret Beaufort: heiress, important conduit of the Lancastrian bloodline, and thus from birth a political pawn. In 1455 the twelve-year-old Margaret was married off by her kinsman Henry VI to Edmund Tudor, son of Katherine de Valois and Owen Tudor; elder of the two half-brothers the king had promoted to his side.

Twelve was the age at which a girl was legally considered ready to consummate a union. Margaret was particularly small for her age, but Edmund was too impatient (probably for her lands, rather than her person) to wait. In January 1457 Margaret, still only thirteen, dangerously and painfully gave birth. She did so in the care of her brother-in-law Jasper Tudor, her husband Edmund having died of plague during her pregnancy. It seems likely she was damaged physically or psychologically by the experience of her first delivery: Henry Tudor, the future Henry VII, would prove her only child.

Though Margaret was quick to marry again, this was probably a matter less of personal preference than of security. The choice fell on Henry Stafford, a mild-mannered Lancastrian some twenty years older with whom Margaret seems to have lived in harmony, if, perhaps, also celibacy.

Meanwhile, after a brief and fragile truce, the war between Lancaster and York was breaking out again, with success first for the one and then the other. In the summer of 1460 a Yorkist victory at Northampton was decisive enough to send Queen Marguerite fleeing to Scotland, but soon she was sweeping back southwards with a Scottish army. One anecdotal report of a speech Marguerite made to her men is as heroic in its way as Elizabeth I's at Tilbury. 'I have often broken the English battle line. I have mowed down ranks far more stubborn than theirs are now. You who once followed a peasant girl [Joan of Arc] now follow a queen ... I will either conquer or be conquered with you.' At Wakefield Marguerite's forces killed the Duke of York, but just days later York's eighteen-year-old son Edward was advancing on London. At the dreadful Battle of Towton in March 1461 Edward scored a bloody triumph, allowing him to be acknowledged as King Edward IV.

Owen Tudor became another victim of the Yorkist takeover when he was captured and executed in 1461. But his surviving son Jasper – who fled into exile, like the Lancastrian king and queen themselves – would never cease to fight a rearguard action on behalf of the Lancastrian cause. His little nephew Henry Tudor, meanwhile, was being brought up by a staunch Yorkist supporter, though in comfort and safety.

The new Yorkist regime got successfully under way, the golden eighteen-year-old Edward advised and bolstered by his mentor the Earl of Warwick and his forceful mother Cecily. But one pressing question remained: who should the new king marry?

5

York

1461–1485

I T JUST HAD – so story said – to happen on a May Day: 'the day of love *per eccellenza*' in courtly theory; the day on which the lover's quest in the *Roman de la Rose* began. The day on which, for almost a century and a half now, Toulouse had celebrated the Floral Games, a contest of troubadour poetry. As Thomas Malory would put it, 'all ye that be lovers, call unto your remembrance the month of May, like as did Queen Guinevere'.

This would be the other marriage that made the Tudor dynasty, and (unlike poor Margaret Beaufort's) it was a marriage perhaps not courtly, but nonetheless unusually romantic in its way.

A fragile dynasty like the new King Edward's needed to be bolstered by the powerful political marriage alliance that was in any case the norm for royalty. But instead – so the romantic popular version of this first meeting goes – the king's eye was caught by a beautiful young English widow, waiting underneath an oak tree near her family's home of Grafton to intercept him as he passed by.

Different versions of this story set it on May Day 1461, just weeks after eighteen-year-old Edward captured the throne; or, more probably, on the same day three years later – or even at a later season of the year. But if May Day's pagan origins are about love rather than marriage, this tale was about both; and perhaps all the more transgressive because of it, by the standards of the day.

The young widow's name was Elizabeth Grey (born Elizabeth Woodville), whose husband had died fighting on the Lancastrian side.

Now Elizabeth's best hope for the inheritance of her two little boys lay in pleading with the Yorkist king. And Elizabeth Woodville, said the historian Edward Hall in the sixteenth century:

> found such grace in the King's eyes that he not only favoured her suit, but much more fantasised her person . . . For she was a woman . . . of such beauty and favour that with her sober demeanour, lovely looking and feminine smiling (neither too wanton nor too humble) beside her tongue so eloquent and her wit so pregnant . . . she allured and made subject to her the heart of so great a king.

After Edward, Hall said, 'had well considered all the lineaments of her body and the wise and womanly demeanour that he saw in her', he tried to bribe her into becoming his mistress (under the more flattering courtly appellation of his 'sovereign lady') in the hopes of later becoming his wife. Whereupon she answered that 'as she was unfitted for his honour to be his wife then for her own honesty she was too good to be his concubine', an answer that so inflamed the king to a 'hot burning fire' he determined indeed to marry her.

The contemporary chronicler Robert Fabyan describes a marriage made at Grafton early in the morning of May Day: 'at which marriage no one was present but the spouse, the spousess, the Duchess of Bedford, her mother, the priest, two gentlewomen and a young man to help the priest sing. After which spousals [the king] went to bed and so tarried there upon three or four hours.' He returned to join his men some distance away as though he had merely been out hunting, but returned to Grafton where every night Elizabeth to his bed 'was brought, in so secret manner that almost none but her mother was council'.

Thomas More, working from Hall, would describe the same scenario: the king struck by this woman 'fair and of good favour, moderate of stature, well-made, and very wise' who claimed that if she was too 'simple' to be his wife she was too good to be his concubine . . . As one of Andreas Capellanus's Rules had laid down: 'One should not seek love with ladies with whom it is disgraceful to seek marriage.' More describes Elizabeth virtuously refusing Edward's advances, but 'with so good manner, and words so well set, that she rather kindled his desire than quenched it'. The same technique, of course, worked again when Anne Boleyn practised it on Elizabeth and Edward's grandson Henry VIII. Henry, when the time came, would be very visibly an echo of Edward, right down to his huge red-blond good looks. The story suggests another similarity.

Other late fifteenth- or early sixteenth-century writers described a more melodramatic version of the scene. One of the most dramatic versions, Antonio Cornazzano's *De Mulieribus Admirandis*, written in Italy soon after the event, has Elizabeth holding the king off with a dagger. The Italian Dominic Mancini, writing in 1483, reverses the tale to have Edward – 'so the story runs' – holding a dagger to Elizabeth's throat: again, as More and Hall would have it, 'she remained unperturbed and determined to die rather than live unchastely with the king. Whereupon Edward coveted her much the more, and he judged the lady worthy to be a royal spouse.'

Hearne's *Fragment*, written in the early sixteenth century by someone who was probably at Edward's court in its later years, similarly recorded that Edward 'being a lusty prince attempted the stability and constant modesty of divers ladies and gentlewomen' but after resorting at 'diverse times' to Elizabeth, became impressed by her 'constant and stable mind'.

What all these stories have in common is that they suggest a nobility of virtue in Elizabeth, as a viable alternative to the blood nobility she did not possess (much as the theory of courtly love opened heady vistas of nobility of virtue to a number of younger sons). Andreas Capellanus, after all, had decreed that: 'Honesty of character alone makes a man worthy of love.' Or a woman, presumably. But would that be enough to impress Edward's family and supporters? It was not until September 1464 that, in the face of mounting rumours, Edward admitted to his council that he *had* married Elizabeth Woodville, secretly; albeit (said Waurin, the medieval French chronicler) in a 'right merry' way that suggests embarrassment.

There is a less dramatic possibility for the whole encounter. In 1463 the male Woodvilles had been restored to royal favour and it is possible Elizabeth simply met Edward at the royal court. Caspar Weinreich's contemporary *Chronicle* claims that: 'The king fell in love with [a mere knight's] wife when he dined with her frequently.' This would fit with the fact that, in the first years of the 1460s, Edward seemed quite content that foreign marriages were being negotiated for him – but it is not the most agreeably romantic version of the story.

Whenever it happened, the wedding ceremony *was* sufficiently covert that it could later, under Richard III, be denounced as an 'ungracious pretensed marriage' by which 'the order of all politic rule was perverted'. One which had taken place privately 'and secretly, without Edition of Banns, in a private Chamber, a profane place'. Secrecy did not itself make the marriage illegal; but it was hardly the way kings normally did things. Elizabeth's mother Jacquetta would later be accused of having made this marriage by sorcery.[*]

If so, she had made it well: Elizabeth was presented to the court on 30 September, Michaelmas Day, in the chapel of Reading Abbey, in a ceremony that replaced the usual big public royal wedding. Led in by Edward's brother, the Duke of Clarence, and the Earl of Warwick ('the Kingmaker'), she received homage offered on bended knee. They made a stunning couple: Edward startlingly tall and fair – well over six feet – and Elizabeth (if her portrait is to be believed) conforming to the contemporary ideal of smooth pale skin, golden hair and slender rounded limbs.

But Edward's dramatic act of independence came as a shock to his former mentor Warwick. Another nose put abruptly out of joint was that of Edward's formidable mother Cecily, who had likewise played a crucial role in the very first years of his reign. But Edward answered his mother (More says) 'that he knew himself out of her rule'. This was the crunch – that the king would no longer be subject to anyone. And as for Warwick, Edward added that he could hardly be so unreasonable as 'to look that I should in choice of wife rather be ruled by his eye than by my own, as though I were a ward that were bound to marry by the appointment of a guardian'.

The Italian visitor Mancini would later claim that Cecily declared her son Edward was illegitimate: his choice of a woman of lower rank proved

---

[*] The romance of May Day is ushered in by Beltane, an important date in the witches' calendar. The question of a royal marriage made by witchcraft would be heard once more in the days of Anne Boleyn.

he could not be of the blood of kings. But how unsuitable was Elizabeth, really? She brought no great foreign alliance and would be the first English-born queen since the Conquest. But though her father had been merely Sir Richard Woodville, her mother Jacquetta came from the cadet branch of the Luxembourg family that gave her connections with the emperors of Germany and the kings of Bohemia. Jacquetta had briefly been the wife of the Duke of Bedford, Henry VI's uncle, before falling in love and making a secret marriage with Sir Richard, the young knight sent to escort her to England after Bedford's death.

According to legend, the house of Luxembourg was descended from the water spirit Melusine, a woman – like a mermaid – scaled and tailed from the waist down. Henry II, like his son Richard I, was said to claim Melusine as his ancestress. The story echoes those which had cast Guinevere as an otherworldly creature, a *fée*. Moreover, Melusine's royal or knightly husband met her in a forest and was too struck by her beauty to enquire into her origins: an echo of Elizabeth Woodville's own romance.

Much play would be made of her connections with European royalty, when the time came for Elizabeth's coronation. Conversely, however, there may have been some popularity value in Elizabeth's very Englishness – at least her connections would never drag England into costly foreign wars! – and even a reconciliatory value in her family's previous attachment to the Lancastrian cause.

But Elizabeth's widowhood was a potential problem, to say nothing of the fact she was five years the elder. Custom suggested the king's bride should be a virgin, not a widow; at least if (unlike, say, Joanne of Navarre) she was to provide the children who would inherit the throne. Thomas More, in describing Edward's mother, declared that 'it is an unfitting thing, and a great blemish to the sacred majesty of a prince . . . to be defiled with bigamy in his first marriage'.

More gives whole pages to Cecily's arguments against Elizabeth, urging the vital importance of marrying for foreign alliance, and 'that it was not princely to marry his own subject . . . only as a rich man would marry his maiden only for a little wanton dotage upon her person'.

But just how scandalous was marriage for 'wanton dotage'? In any age there are probably as many different deals and compromises made as there are individual marriages. But for the fifteenth century, the private letters of the gentry Paston family do give us some insights, albeit often contradictory.

When in 1469 Margery Paston made an unsanctioned love match with the family's bailiff, her mother Margaret was so disgusted as to urge her son to remember 'that we have lost of her but a brothel [older transcriptions say 'a worthless person'], and set it less to heart'. Margaret's own marriage had been an arranged one but, crucially, an arrangement where liking was taken into account. Letters from Margaret to her absent husband John vibrate with tenderness: her heart in 'no great ease' until she hears details of his health, her appetite for news of him inexhaustible.

Before their wedding ceremony, John's mother Agnes had written complacently of how well an initial meet and greet had gone, and how she hoped there would be need for 'no great treaty' between the well-matched pair. John would write of Margaret as 'my own dear sovereign lady': so far down the social scale had the language, and by implication the ideal, of courtly love reached. Their son, the upwardly mobile Sir John Paston, included several Arthurian and other romances among his books, and was a friend of the queen's brother Anthony Woodville, taking part in a great tournament at Eltham alongside Edward IV.

Of course, setting the fantasy of courtly love aside, love consequent on an approved marriage was the pattern sanctioned by Church and state. But perhaps that explains why women from the very top rank of society were seemingly the least ready to set that fantasy aside, since their marriages were the most likely to be made without thought for age or taste, to a man or boy they had never met.

For a king to marry for love or lust – for 'blind affection', as the Tudor historian Polydore Vergil would put it at the beginning of the sixteenth century – was so odd as to amount almost to an indecency. Yet here was Edward telling his mother, in More's version, that surely, 'marriage being a spiritual thing' and made for the respect of God, the parties ought to 'incline to love together' rather than to seek temporal advantage.

Certainly the couple seemed happy. Elizabeth was crowned the spring after the acknowledgement of her marriage, in a magnificent ceremony for which Edward had been ordering up jewels, gold and silks from abroad. Everything was done as custom and ceremony dictated: the queen spending the night before the coronation at the Tower; the procession to Westminster behind the blue and white splendour of several dozen new-made Knights of the Bath; the 'reverence and solemnity' of the anointing in the Abbey; the banquet, and the tournament the next day. Tournaments would feature largely in the ascendancy of the Woodville family.

As queen, there is no evidence of Elizabeth exercising overt political influence: something that would have seemed wholly in her favour to an aristocracy still reeling from the impact of Marguerite of Anjou. She was beautiful, a patroness of arts and industry, and a gracious presence at ceremonies. But there were, as contemporaries saw it, certainly charges to be brought against Elizabeth: notably the way the Woodvilles and their connections sucked up positions and advantageous marriages. The king's fool came into court in high boots complaining that he needed them, since the rivers (Elizabeth's father was now Earl Rivers) had grown so high. One of her brothers, aged around twenty, married the Duchess of Norfolk, in her sixties; a Milanese envoy reported that the Woodvilles 'had the entire government of the realm'. But in an age when kin were key, King Edward himself may have raised the Woodvilles to strengthen his own power base. And the Woodvilles did bring something else to the party. Theirs was a deeply cultured family: one Woodville especially. In a time when the notion of chivalry itself was changing, Anthony Woodville, Elizabeth's eldest brother, was at once a scholar and a star of the tourney.

Anthony seemed to look forward to Baldassare Castiglione's *Book of the Courtier* (published in Venice in 1528) as well as backwards to Chaucer's 'parfit gentil knight'. He translated from the French the *Dictes and Sayings of the Philosophers*, and William Caxton, who printed it, noted his surprise that Anthony left out the complaints about women attributed to the Greeks, speculating that he had forborne for love of, or at the request of, 'some noble lady'. Anthony also translated the *Moral Proverbs* of Christine de Pizan.

When the time came to escort Edward IV's sister Margaret to marry the Duke of Burgundy, Woodville star power would be particularly evident. The event was bookended by legendary tournaments. At

Smithfield in London in June 1467 Anthony – his train of horses variously decked out in white cloth of gold; in damasks of purple, green and tawny; blue velvet and crimson velvet; and crimson cloth trimmed with sables – fought the 'Bastard of Burgundy', the duke's half-brother, in a genuinely bloodthirsty battle carefully brought to an end by the king before the knights could do too much damage to each other, or to his diplomacy. Anthony made a courtly tale of how the queen's ladies had pounced on him and fastened to his leg ('nearer my heart than my knee', he said) a band of gold and pearls, with a jewel dangling from it, and a letter telling him he could win the jewel by challenging a nobleman to the fight. Visitors from all over Europe came to watch the fray.

Though the tournament tradition had never disappeared, it was Edward IV who brought it back to England in a major way, evoking his inheritance from his ancestor Edward III a century before, and himself often riding in the lists. The great Bohemian jouster Leo von Rozmital, touring Europe in search of fresh knights to conquer, had visited England, and declared that Edward had 'the most splendid court that could be found in all Christendom'. Other writers made a point of comparing this court to that of Arthur's day, delighting the king who relished a fine collection of beautifully bound and lavishly illustrated books of romance and chivalry.

The tournament that greeted the new Duchess Margaret in Bruges a year later was no less splendid than the one at Smithfield. The Tournament of the Golden Tree was built around a specially created fantasia with all the tropes of quests and mysterious ladies so beloved of chivalry, part of the nine-day celebrations that included feasts where unicorns bore baskets of sweets; where monkeys threw trinkets to the company; and a court dwarf on a gilded lion competed for attention with a wild man on a dromedary. The eldest Paston sons made part of the retinue and, as one of them wrote, 'As for the Duke's court as of ladies and gentlewomen, knights, squires and gentlemen I heard never of none like to it save King Arthur's court.'

In one sense, however, Edward's own court was unlike King Arthur's; and happily so. The stories do not describe Arthur and Guinevere as having children. It was February 1466 before Elizabeth Woodville first gave Edward a child – a daughter, Elizabeth of York – but then others came swiftly; albeit by the end of the decade they had still no boy. But despite dissent between Edward and his brother Clarence, the Yorkist dynasty seemed there to stay when, in 1470, fickle Fortune, in whom the fifteenth century so devoutly believed, gave events a dramatic turn.

Though Henry VI had spent the near-decade of Edward's reign first in exile and then in captivity, his exiled wife Marguerite was living abroad in bitterly impoverished liberty. She who had once had literally hundreds of attendants – for whom the English palaces had been redecorated, to please her sophisticated taste – had been forced to share with husband and son a ration of bread and 'one herring between three'; or so the Burgundian chronicler Chastellain claimed, anyway. But she had never ceased to campaign and, in the summer of 1470, in France, struck a deal with those who had once seemed her implacable enemies.

It was an alliance of the dispossessed. Those Yorkists disaffected by the Woodvilles' rise – Edward's former mentor Warwick and his brother Clarence – promised to help Marguerite to seize back control of England. Warwick's elder daughter Isabel was already Clarence's wife. Now, to seal the bargain, Marguerite's son, the Lancastrian prince, married Warwick's younger daughter Anne Neville.

Their forces landed in the West Country in September, and advanced on London. Edward, away in the north putting down a rebellion organised by Warwick's brother-in-law, had already moved his pregnant wife and family into the Tower of London for safety, but soon it became apparent that too would fall to the invaders. A vivid word picture describes Queen Elizabeth clutching a chest of jewels as she fled, while her daughters dragged bedsheets stuffed with clothing to the waterside, where boats carried the family upriver to Westminster Abbey and surer sanctuary. There, on 2 November, Elizabeth at last gave birth to a son and heir.

But would the Yorkist prince have any kingdom to inherit? His father Edward (with his own brother Richard, and Anthony Woodville) had fled abroad to Burgundy to take refuge with Duchess Margaret.

Something else happened over that patch of time, in the course of what the participants dubbed the Lancastrian 'Readeption'. In 'the ninth year of the reign of King Edward the Fourth' Thomas Malory finished writing his definitive *Le Morte d'Arthur* or *Darthur* (The Death of Arthur). He did so in or near Newgate gaol; or so, at least, we believe: when the book was printed by Caxton some years later, it was put out as the work of Sir Thomas Malory, 'knight prisoner'. We have no more certain information as to his identity. And yet Malory's work has proved the enduring embodiment of courtly love as seen through the prism of the Arthurian stories.

In the twentieth century, T.E. Lawrence kept a copy in his saddlebag during the Arab Revolt; John Steinbeck spent months in a medieval cottage in Somerset, rewriting Malory into modern English with a biro refill stuck into a goose quill. Yet Malory's Arthurian world is very much that of the late fifteenth century, not least in the fact that his Round Table finally falls to factional fighting. If the heroic Arthur of Malory's first two books was modelled on Henry V, then, it has been suggested, the hesitant later king drew on Henry VI. Malory's is a world where Lancelot swims across the Thames from Westminster Bridge to reach Guinevere, where Guinevere feasts the London merchants – and where the actions of Malory's legendary queen find echoes in the powerful women of his own day.

Guinevere has around her a body of 'young men that would have worship; and they were called the Queen's Knights'. Marguerite of Anjou likewise had a company of knights who wore her badge. Elizabeth Woodville's seeking refuge in the Tower had been foreshadowed by Guinevere's flight there, in her determination to escape Mordred.

Malory's family may have known the Woodvilles; for we believe the likeliest candidate for the author's identity is Thomas Malory of Newbold Revel in Warwickshire, a professional soldier in his fifties, a Justice of the Peace and Member of Parliament who had become embroiled in the tangled politics of the century. (It has been suggested that, once a Yorkist, in 1468 he became embroiled in Warwick's efforts to overthrow Edward IV.) But there are many anomalies to any version of his story.

This Malory, author of a book most see as reflecting the flower of chivalry, had repeatedly seen the inside of various gaols, charged with extortion, robbery, and even rape. We may hope, though, that this was 'rape' in the sense of abduction – one of the senses in which the age understood the term – or even of consensual sex with a married woman, the offence being against her husband rather than herself. Once Malory escaped from gaol by swimming a moat, once perhaps by bribery. This Thomas Malory died in March 1471 and his burial in the church of a monastery beside Newgate gaol does not suggest he was enjoying liberty. The legacy of London's late mayor Richard ('Dick') Whittington meant favoured prisoners were allowed to use the monastery's library, which could have allowed access to the various texts Malory drew together to make his vast story comprising eight different romances; twenty-one books; 507 chapters.

Malory's version of chivalry, as it applied to Guinevere, is contradictory. The Round Table, in Malory's tale, itself comes as dowry from Guinevere's father, King Leodegraunce. Hers and Arthur's seems a solid partnership, albeit with little heat in it. She is, before the arrival of Lancelot, a good wife: instructor and judge of knights, brave and beautiful. And yet, when the fellowship is broken because of Lancelot and Guinevere's love, Malory's Arthur can say he is more sorry for loss of knights than of his queen; 'for queens I might have enough, but such a fellowship of good knights shall never be together in any company'. Malory's Arthur three times condemns his wife to death; and when, on one of them, she is revealed to have been falsely accused, he nonetheless blames her for not having handled the situation more tactfully.

When Meligaunt seizes her as she and her knights come back from gathering May blossom in the woods, her concern is more for her men than herself – and yet she is a real woman, suffering bitter pangs of jealousy when Lancelot shows signs of interest in anyone else. Her love for him is not chiefly portrayed as sexual. Their one certain night of adulterous love is enough to prevent Lancelot from attaining the Holy Grail, but it is not (as their far more frequent adultery had come to be in other versions) necessarily what brings down Camelot. Aspects of Guinevere's position may reflect popular doubt about certain forceful real-life queens, as when she has difficulty finding a champion to defend her against a false charge of poisoning. (Indeed, the very title of that section of the book, 'The Poisoned Apple', may reflect older doubts about women, the daughters of Eve.) But Malory can write of Guinevere that 'ever while she lived she was a true lover, and therefore she had a good end'. Saying she will never again see Lancelot with her mortal eyes, she dies half an hour before he comes to find her in the nunnery where she has retired and he, having himself taken holy orders, is able to bury her.

Reading of Merlin trying to dissuade Arthur from marrying Guinevere, it is hard not to think of Edward and Elizabeth Woodville:

> as of her beauty and fairness she is one of the fairest alive. But an [if] ye loved her not so well as ye do, I should find you a damosel of beauty and of goodness that should like you and please you, and your heart were not set. But there as man's heart is set, he will be loath to return.

In March 1471 Elizabeth's husband Edward returned to seize back the English throne. And when Edward landed on the Yorkshire coast – a pattern of usurpation and reclamation so often seen in the Arthurian story – Thomas Malory, the man who wrote the tale, had died the day before.

The first of the great battles following Edward's return saw the death of the Earl of Warwick. (Margaret Beaufort's husband Henry Stafford had fought on the Yorkist side, and died of his wounds sometime after.) Marguerite of Anjou's son, the Lancastrian prince, was killed in or after the last of them, while the fuddled Henry VI died in the Tower 'of pure displeasure and melancholy', it was unconvincingly said. Marguerite was taken captive, paraded in triumph, to live out an inglorious existence in poverty, first in England and then in France.

One branch of the Lancastrian line had ended – but that only made the other more important. Lancastrian royal blood still ran in the veins of Margaret Beaufort – and of her thirteen-year-old son Henry, whose uncle Jasper now swept him away to Brittany where they would live for another fourteen years in Breton care or custody, their status somewhere between guest, state prisoner and international political pawn.

By contrast, as the ballads celebrated Edward's triumphant return to the arms of his wife and to his new son, the Yorkist king and queen settled into a life of increased security. The bogey had come out of the closet, and had been vanquished. In August 1473 a second son was born, a spare to follow the vital male heir, and the Croyland chronicler could describe a court filled with 'those most sweet and beautiful children'.

Of course there were flies in the ointment, notably the continued disaffection of Edward's younger brother Clarence, whose open rebellion finally ended in his execution: drowned, famously, in a butt of malmsey in 1478. And Clarence left behind him a poisonous legacy. It seems likely that in his discontent, he had been dropping hints about a lady called Eleanor Butler to whom, it was alleged, Edward had been pre-contracted or indeed actually married when he wed Elizabeth Woodville. Eleanor – a widow of rank and notable piety – had died in 1468, so no one could ask her, but Philippe de Commynes, the Burgundian courtier and historian, says that Edward 'promised to marry her, provided that he could sleep with her first, and she consented': the same technique Edward practised on Elizabeth. This story – with the corollary that the children of Edward's 'marriage' to Elizabeth were thus illegitimate – would resurface in the next reign, with serious consequences.

Edward was known now to be having affairs with other women. Mancini wrote that:

He was licentious in the extreme: moreover it was said that he had been most insolent to numerous women after he had seduced them, for, as soon as he grew weary of dalliance, he gave up the ladies much against their will to other courtiers. He pursued with no discrimination the married and unmarried, the noble and lowly: however, he took none by force. He overcame all by money and promises and having conquered them, he dismissed them.

That, however, could be seen as a norm for the fifteenth century; albeit that one of Edward's relationships could not be so easily dismissed. His affection for the so-called Goldsmith's Wife, Jane Shore (in fact herself born 'Elizabeth') lasted until his death. She was a beautiful and amiable woman in her twenties: 'worshipfully friended, honestly brought up, and very well married', wrote Thomas More, who admired not only her looks but her 'pleasant behaviour' and 'proper wit'. But whatever Jane's appeal, it was nonetheless inevitably Edward's 'dearest and most entirely beloved wife Elizabeth the Queen . . . our said dearest Wife in whom we most singularly put our trust' who was named first of ten executors in Edward's will when in the mid-1470s he went to war in France.

But Edward's inordinate appetites were not only for women. 'In food and drink he was most immoderate,' Mancini wrote: 'fat in the loins' and lazy. Various reports suggest that it may have been apoplexy following a surfeit that caused him to fall ill in the spring of 1483; others say it was an old ague, or a damp fishing trip on which he caught a serious cold. On 9 April he died.

A ballad pictured Elizabeth's grief:

O lady Bess, long for me may ye call!
For now we are parted until doomsday;
But love ye that Lord that is sovereign of all.

But for the immediate future, Elizabeth Woodville had no time to grieve.

What came next has its own body of story: as bloody and dramatic as the usurpation of Mordred at his uncle Arthur's court. Except that in real life – so the majority of historians have believed – the uncle was the villain. We all know how Richard III seized the crown from the young nephew who should have been Edward V; how the boy-king and his younger brother were taken into the Tower, never to be seen again. How Elizabeth Woodville's brother Anthony was executed on Richard's orders, while she and her daughters fled once more into sanctuary in the precincts of Westminster Abbey.

Richard's brief reign of barely two years is to a marked degree the story of women, and of women's perceived frailty. His seizure of the throne had been justified on the theoretical grounds of adultery and bigamy. Alongside the story that Elizabeth Woodville's marriage to Edward had been invalid, a new *canard* was added – that Edward IV himself had been illegitimate: born of his mother Cecily's liaison with a lowly archer. But the importance of women does not end there. With her husband dead and her sons lost to her, in the summer of 1483 Elizabeth Woodville (like Marguerite of Anjou before her) struck a deal with an unlikely ally.

After the failure of the Lancastrian 'Readeption', Margaret Beaufort seemed to have come to an accommodation with Edward IV's regime. Her son Henry Tudor was still in exile abroad, and she had made a final marriage to the rich Lord Stanley whose position in Edward's household and Woodville connections might be trusted to keep her in line. This chance, however, was too good to miss. She and Elizabeth Woodville joined forces, together with the Duke of Buckingham, to foster a rebellion against Richard, and though their 1483 uprising failed, its central premise – a marriage between Elizabeth Woodville's eldest daughter Elizabeth of York, and Margaret's son Henry Tudor – would prove the foundation of Britain's most famous dynasty.

The one woman of whom there is little to be said is Richard III's unhappy queen, Anne Neville. Though Warwick's daughter had been married off to the Lancastrian Prince of Wales just before the Lancastrians briefly regained the throne, his bloody death had left her a youthful widow. Richard (snatching her away from the custody of his brother Clarence) had married her for the sake of her vast northern lands – 'by force', one report said. We know little of their marriage, but she was crowned alongside her husband.

When, however, their only child died unexpectedly in the spring of 1484 it became clear she would not long outlive him. Anne died in March 1485, and there is some evidence that her husband had not awaited the event before casting his eyes another way.

In the course of 1484, Elizabeth Woodville had been forced at last to let her daughters leave the sanctuary of Westminster Abbey, trusting to Richard's promises not to detain them; to protect them from 'ravishment or defiling contrary to their wills'. The elder girls were indeed welcomed to their uncle's court (the court of the man many believed had killed their brothers!) and the warmth with which the eldest of them, particularly, was received by Richard soon gave food for scandal. There was talk in the winter of 1484 when the buxom eighteen-year-old Elizabeth of York appeared in much the same dress as the ailing Queen Anne. It 'was said by many that the king was bent, either on the anticipated death of the queen taking place, or else, by means of a divorce . . . on contracting a marriage with the said Elizabeth'.

With the Lancastrians still lurking in Brittany, Yorkist forces were now split between Richard's own adherents and those who believed he had unjustly usurped Edward's line. Marriage with his brother's daughter would reconcile the doubters. But was marriage between uncle and niece legal, never mind decent? With a papal dispensation – possibly.

The anonymous author of the Croyland chronicle records how Anne fell sick; how 'the king entirely shunned her bed, declaring that it was by the advice of his physicians that he did so'. Several chroniclers would report rumours that he had poisoned her. The marriage between Richard and his niece never took place. Public opinion would not stand for it: indeed, Richard was forced to make a public declaration that he had never thought of such a thing. But there have since been suggestions that the hope existed in the mind not only of Richard, but also of Elizabeth. One, unverified, seventeenth-century record pictures Elizabeth as eager to fall in with her uncle's plans. There was, after all, enough uncertainty over her brothers' fate for her perhaps to have been persuaded Richard did not murder them.

It was most likely at this time that Elizabeth wrote an inscription on a copy of Boethius's *Consolation of Philosophy* – 'Loyalte mellye', loyalty binds me. It was Richard's favourite motto. There is another inscription, on a copy of the French prose *Tristan* (dating originally from the thirteenth century but still a bestseller in the late 1400s): a collection of stories about an Arthurian knight fatally in love with a lady whose uncle he has unfortunately killed.* Above her signature, 'elyzabeth', the princess wrote '*sans re[mo]vyr*', 'without changing': and she wrote on the page with the mark that showed it was Richard's property.

Certainly Henry Tudor across the Channel heard the rumours and – says Polydore Vergil – they pinched him 'by the very stomach'. It was now he made his move. The previous Christmas, at Rennes Cathedral in Brittany, he had publicly declared his intention to marry Elizabeth, and it had brought a good many of the divided Yorkists to his side. Men and money had been gathered. War was on the way. On 7 August

---

* Tristan has been sent to win Iseult as bride for *his* uncle, and does so, despite the fact that their own passion eventually becomes clear. It is, you might say, a prime example of complicated relationships given the sanction of story. Medieval sources would readily have allowed the use of Tristan – or Tristam – and Iseult, rather than Lancelot and Guinevere, as a thread through this book. But the latter are far more widely known today.

1485 Henry landed on the Welsh coast and began the long march towards Bosworth Field, and the battle that would change the course of English history.

Henry Tudor has gone down as one of the least romantic of figures. The question is, why? Hindsight, and the mental picture we have of him in age, maybe. But here was Henry as a young man, with his way in the world to make, sailing in to seize his kingdom and even, it would be suggested, rescue its princess.

And Henry was well aware of the mythological potential. Before Bosworth he took as his standard the 'Red Dragon Dreadful': the dragon of Wales, yes. But Malory's *Morte* also described how King Arthur once had a dream, of a fight in the sky between a dragon and a boar; the dragon victor over the boar, a tyrant. (The boar, of course, was Richard's symbol.) The red dragon fluttered above his head as Henry, landing on the Pembrokeshire coast, knelt down and prayed.

The virtuous stranger from across the sea, the 'fair unknown', was a favourite figure of romance. But when his forces met those of Richard III, Henry's victory was very far from a foregone conclusion. In the best tradition of lost causes his troops, says Polydore Vergil, numbered less than half Richard's forces. Bosworth has bred its own legends – spread even before William Shakespeare's day – of Richard's forebodings before the fight, and his frantic charge towards Henry's position, determined to force the Tudor to single combat and finish the fight that way. Maybe that's why Henry did not here achieve the status of a figure of story. Perhaps it was because, in the face of Henry's cooler practicality, it was Richard who harked back to the older world of chivalry.

There were tales of Richard's final beleaguered end, hacked down by his enemies; of how, it would later be said, the crown of England was found hanging on a thorn bush – a may bush – and placed on Henry Tudor's head . . . Romance enough there to make a hero, surely?

Especially since, appropriately enough, just weeks beforehand William Caxton had finally amended and printed the *Morte d'Arthur*, Thomas Malory's story, written some fifteen years before. Caxton did so, he claimed, at the request of 'many noble and divers gentlemen'. Some believe it was actually at the request of Anthony Woodville (who, it has been suggested, may have given him the manuscript).

But however the tale of Arthur reached the page, Henry Tudor, now Henry VII, would seize upon it, gratefully. After the long years of watching and waiting – after the bloody victory – he had won. Richard's battered corpse, brutalised and reviled even after death, had been slung naked across a horse and carried away, to be buried without ceremony.

But there was another battle Henry had still to fight – a battle for hearts and minds. It remained to find a language, a *story*, to make Henry's new dynasty palatable to a divided country.

PART II

1485–1525

Bon Saber: 'good knowing', or insight into proper procedure in love

Though that men do call it dotage,
Who loveth not wanteth courage
And whosoever may love get
From Venus sure he must it fet
Love maintaineth all noble courage
Who love disdaineth is all of the village
Forwhoso loveth should love but once
Change whoso will, I will be none.

Attributed to Henry VIII

6

'nothing uxorious'

1485–1502

THE NEW TUDOR dynasty was forged on a battlefield – and in a bed. We have the four-poster bed itself; discovered ten years ago, overlooked and dismantled, in the car park of a Chester hotel.* Sometimes called the 'Paradise Bed' for its depictions of Adam and Eve – or of Christ and the Virgin Mary working to undo the harm Adam and Eve had wrought; and perhaps bring a Paradise also to England – its dark carving boasts symbols of fertility and of royalty; grapes and strawberries, lions and shields.

It boasts, too, the single roses of York and of Lancaster: not yet combined into the double 'Tudor rose'. This, however, was a situation the new king moved swiftly to rectify. The Lancastrian Henry VII was crowned at the end of October 1485 – and in early December Parliament begged him to 'unify two bloods' by marrying Elizabeth of York.

But who were the two people thrust together in the vital alliance that did indeed follow, the next month? We know comparatively little about the formation of Henry Tudor. The outlines are there, but the blank space within them leaves space for question – for new conjecture, maybe.

The facts – and Henry's later comportment, his wariness – suggest that the dramatic events of his early life had not been without effect.

---

* Thinking of Richard III, it is hard not to feel that car park discoveries feature unusually strongly in the post-Bosworth story!

But his childhood as such seems to have been comparatively tranquil. Polydore Vergil, historian at Henry's court, who may well have had information from the horse's mouth, reported that the young Henry was 'kept prisoner, but honourably brought up', raised by the Yorkist William Herbert of Raglan with the Herberts' own young family: the more so, since the Herberts planned to marry him to one of their daughters.

The year 1461 saw young Henry Tudor briefly taken to the restored court of his kinsman Henry VI, proudly presented by his mother Margaret Beaufort as a sprig off the Lancastrian tree. With the return of the Yorkists, however, thirteen-year-old Henry was hastily snatched abroad for safety by his uncle Jasper. The death of both Henry VI and his son had left Henry Tudor as the only surviving Lancastrian heir.

Jasper and Henry were heading for France, but were blown off course to land in the duchy of Brittany, whose Duke Francis received them both gladly and honourably. Fate had, after all, just handed Francis an invaluable pair of pawns to be tendered or traded in the great game of European diplomacy. In 1476 Duke Francis succumbed to pressure and handed Henry Tudor over to Edward IV's envoys, but the nineteen-year-old was by then savvy and bold enough to feign illness, escape from his escort, and take refuge in a church at Saint-Malo, where the Anglophobe townsfolk refused to hand him over.

We know the names of the châteaux where Henry was held over the years – but not what he was doing in his long days there. It is a safe bet that from the time of Edward IV's death and Richard III's controversial takeover in 1483, his sights were set on, and his thoughts occupied by, England. The conspiracy between his mother and Elizabeth Woodville that summer prompted Henry to sail towards England with an army, only to be turned back by foul weather before they reached shore. But before that? There were a dozen years between 1471 and 1483: years usually skimmed over by his biographers. Henry would have been allowed to engage in some of the pursuits customary for young aristocratic men, but not in all of them. Not war; not making a family; not even risking his useful life in the tourney. We know that he was later a patron of scholars and had a particular taste for music. Is it too fanciful to suggest that (like other prisoners before and since) he whiled away his time in reading? He had, after all, grown up in Wales, whence sprang many of the Arthurian legends; and in the French territories, where Chrétien de Troyes had first given voice to the courtly fantasy.

And Elizabeth of York? The early sixteenth-century *Ballad of Lady Bessy* (believed to have been written by an adherent of Henry's stepfather, Lord Stanley) imagined her as being in Stanley's London house early in 1485. There, as the spring begins to ripen, she waylays Lord Stanley in the palace corridors, and asks him to send a message to his stepson Henry Tudor, promising she would marry him and thus greatly strengthen his cause.

> For & he were King, I should be Queen;
> I do him love, & never him seen

The ballad has Elizabeth tearing her long fair hair in rage when Stanley refuses to commit, and sinking into a swoon. She would, she says, never be queen . . . Marriage to Henry – as to Richard – would indeed give her position, would be a way back out of the political wilderness. Ambition cannot be discounted in the wife, any more than in the husband. Indeed, 'Lady Bessy' shows a certain spirited practicality, detailing the Stanley military strength and volunteering herself to write the letters to Stanley's adherents: she was chief promoter of Henry's coup, in fact, and one who sees Richard as her 'mortal foe'. Henry, in the poem, responds to his 'lady bright' with his own verse:

> Commend me to Bessy, that Countess clear, [or Clare, a family
>   title]
> & yet I did never her see,
> I trust in god she shall be my Queen,
> For her I will travel the sea.

Once into the Tudor age, of course, everyone had an interest in presenting Henry's alliance with Elizabeth as desired by both parties, making it clear that the rumoured alliance with her uncle Richard had been none of her choosing. Polydore Vergil gives her 'a singular aversion' to that idea: 'Weighed down for this reason by her great grief she would repeatedly exclaim, saying, "I will not thus be married, but, unhappy creature that I am, will rather suffer all the torments which St Catherine is said to have endured for the love of Christ than be united with a man who is the enemy of my family."'

In fact, Henry Tudor, the Lancastrian, could as well be described as the enemy of Elizabeth's Yorkist family as could her uncle Richard. But Elizabeth's feelings for either man at this stage were an irrelevance. She was an essential part of the Tudor plan.

What did Henry expect of a wife? On a personal level, probably that she should be beautiful, compliant and fertile. But Elizabeth's most important contribution was the one that could not be spoken – that vital bloodline. To former Yorkists and Lancastrians alike, any child of these two would have an irrefutable claim to the throne.

Early stories of Arthur and Guinevere may refer to a time when rights in the crown and the land descended in the female line, and a successful war leader could claim them by marriage. But this is just what Henry was determined *not* to seem to do. He had won the throne of England in three ways: through victory in battle (which was, after all, the way in which God could show his will most clearly); through the acclamation of the people, or at least the nobility; and through his blood right via his mother, a blood right which, however, was both distant and tainted with illegitimacy. He needed to bolster his own claim through that which Elizabeth of York might be presumed to have inherited – but he did not wish to signal the fact too clearly. Francis Bacon, in the early seventeenth century, would write that he 'could not endure any mention' of it.

Across the Channel, Henry had grown up with an awareness of the potential of female power: Brittany's Duke Francis, in 1488, would be succeeded by his daughter. It had, moreover, been the formidable Anne de Beaujeu, acting effectively as regent of France on behalf of her younger brother Charles VIII, who had provided the soldiers who tramped with Henry to Bosworth. This seems, however, to have provided him chiefly with a model to be avoided in his marriage. After all, he already had a powerful woman in his life: and one who, unlike Elizabeth of York, had always been wholly allied to his interests. His mother, Margaret Beaufort.

Margaret's marriage to the powerful Lord Stanley had served its purpose. She had been able to sail through the second reign of Edward IV as an apparently willing adherent of the Yorkist regime. It was only when Richard III's usurpation split Yorkist loyalties that her real interests – her son's prospects – began to show. Even then, after her attempted coup of 1483, she suffered no worse a penalty than to have custody of her person and her lands handed over to Stanley. And he, ever adept at playing both sides against the middle, may have connived at her efforts to smuggle money and information to her son Henry in Brittany. It had been Stanley family forces that ultimately won Henry Tudor the day at Bosworth. Now, with her son on the throne, Margaret would reap her reward.

She was a lady of noted piety; but there is another side to her formidable scholarship. It was she who commissioned Caxton to publish *Blanchardin and Eglantine*, the romance of a noble lady and the royal knight who saves her city: a romance which casts the marriage her son Henry was about to make – the marriage Margaret herself had long arranged – as a romantic rescue fantasy. But perhaps it was unclear quite where the ardour in Henry's relationships lay. Margaret, the mother to whom he owed everything, was little more than a decade older than he. She would, in many important ways, be closer to him than his wife.

Certainly Margaret's emotional force would be directed towards her son rather than her husband. Her marriage to Stanley, however useful, had always been a matter more of business than of pleasure and her son's reign would see her amicably separate herself from him: first assuming the legal status of a feme sole, and then taking a vow of chastity. Her letters to Henry, by contrast, are addressed to: 'My own sweet and most dear king and all my worldly joy', her 'dearest and only desired joy in this world' and her 'dear heart'. It sounds a little like the tropes of courtly love albeit with the roles reversed so that she, not he, was the suitor. Henry's 'faithful true bedewoman', she would call herself. A beadsman or beadswoman, one who used their rosary beads to keep count as they prayed for their patron . . . As the Elizabethan poet George Peele would put it, declaring that in age his knightly helmet was turned into a hive for bees, his 'lover's sonnets turn to holy psalms':

Goddess, allow this aged man his right
To be your bedesman now that was your knight.

One of the first things Henry did after Bosworth was to make an extended stay with the mother he had not seen for more than a decade. We do not know in what emotional climate he first met his bride-to-be, Elizabeth of York. But when the two were married on 18 January 1486 the ceremony was greeted, said Bacon, with 'greater joy and gladness' in the streets than Henry's coronation, something 'the King rather noted than liked'.

It is possible that Henry slept with Elizabeth before their marriage. If not, their first child born on 20 September was a whole month premature, and there is no evidence of haste in the preparation for the birth. Henry had ushered his pregnant wife to Winchester: England's ancient capital, identified as Camelot by Thomas Malory.

And when the baby was born a boy, he was named Arthur. Malory had described how the Latin words meaning 'the once and future king' were inscribed on King Arthur's tomb. It would be useful to figure the baby Arthur Tudor as a returned King Arthur – a way to legitimise a dynasty with very little real claim to the English throne.

The marriage of Henry and Elizabeth had not been a love match, but there is every sign that over the years they grew to love each other, in an appropriate way. Their relationship was after all soon tested, in the cauldron that bubbled somewhere between the realms of fantasy, of self-invention, and of cold hard political fact. The continued uncertainty as to the fate of the 'Princes in the Tower', Elizabeth's brothers, and the continued imprisonment in the Tower of Clarence's son Warwick, had left the way open for pretenders – claimants – to Henry's vulnerable throne, and the first of them came early.

Even before the birth of Prince Arthur there had been rumours of one Lambert Simnel, claiming first to be the younger of the princes, and then to be the imprisoned Warwick. In May 1487 Simnel landed with an army (there would always be powerful figures, at home and abroad, prepared to lend their support to any pretender) but they were defeated in the Battle of Stoke, and Simnel himself, in a humiliating act of mercy, was sent to work in Henry's kitchens.

That autumn, at last, Elizabeth of York was finally crowned queen: in celebration, maybe. The motto she chose was 'Humble and reverent'. Broadly speaking, she lived up to it. Bacon said she was 'depressed' in status; the Spanish ambassador that she was beloved 'because she is powerless'. There was always that formidable mother-in-law, so close to her son, to take into account. Bacon saw Henry as 'nothing uxorious, nor scarce indulgent' but 'companionable and respective, and without jealousy'; this last was not necessarily good news, in the courtly love story.

But at least there were more children. In the autumn of 1489 Elizabeth gave birth to a daughter, Margaret, and eighteen months later Prince Henry was born, in June 1491. (Though other pregnancies would follow, only one more baby survived into anything like adulthood – Mary, born some five years later.)

The autumn of 1491, however, brought another threat: a pretender far more dangerous than Lambert Simnel. Indeed, even today no one can say with absolute certainty that Perkin Warbeck's claims to be Richard, Duke of York, the younger of the Princes in the Tower, were false. Margaret of Burgundy, sister of Edward IV, claimed to have recognised her nephew immediately, and with great emotion, 'as easily as if I had last seen him yesterday'; albeit that this could only be the supposed recognition of true identity, true royalty, beloved of the courtly love story, since Margaret had last seen the real Richard as a young child, some dozen years before. But the childless Margaret nonetheless gave Warbeck not only money but international credibility.* In autumn 1494 Henry VII created his own son Henry as Duke of York – by implication, the only real such duke.

The three-year-old Henry rode through the London streets on a tall horse, though he had to be carried in to receive his title. Invested as a Knight of the Bath the day before the ceremony, he had solemnly sworn to be a 'manly protector' to widows and oppressed maidens.

---

* Warbeck, under interrogation, would later confess to being the son of a Tournai trader. Many, however, continue to doubt. It has been suggested that Warbeck was actually Margaret's natural son, though an illegitimate son of Edward IV seems a likelier possibility.

(Malory had based the oath taken by his Knights of the Round Table on the oath taken at this ceremony.)

The jousters in the three-day tournament that followed wore the queen's crest as well as the new duke's livery, while his elder sister Margaret presented the prizes at the end of the first two days' jousting. The third day began with a pageant, four knights led by four ladies, in honour of this 'redoubted lady and fairest young princess'. Heady stuff, for a princess who had not quite attained her fifth birthday but whose attendants, if not her mother, had surely told her the tales from whence came this whole delicious conceit.

Perkin's first invasion attempt, in June 1495, failed, and he made his way to Scotland. There, in the young King James IV, he found a man happy to subscribe to a glamorous fantasy. (It didn't hurt that this one also embarrassed the English king.) James had come to the throne, aged fifteen, after the murder of his father some seven years before, inheriting the ever-fraught relationship with England, and the old alliance with France. Probably he genuinely believed Perkin's story, for he not only maintained the pretender and his army, but found him a bride of Scottish royal blood, Lady Katherine Gordon, and the couple married in a splendid ceremony.

A significant part of Perkin's claim, after all, lay in the fact that he *seemed* like a prince: another example of the compliance of fact to fiction. (Seemed too, as Henry VII himself had once done, like the legendary stranger knight from over the sea.) And someone had coached Perkin in at least an assumption of the courtly graces. He would write to Katherine of her 'eyes, so brilliant as stars . . . your neck which outshines pearls'. She was the 'most noble lady, my soul' and he her 'slave'. He would 'in all things cheerfully do your will' as long as his days should last.

'Love is not an earthly thing, it is heaven born. Do not think it below yourself to obey love's dictates. Not only kings, but also gods and goddesses have bent their necks beneath its yoke.'

The first bloody skirmish Scots king and pretender made across the border did little more than satisfactorily prove their valour, but in 1497 Warbeck was back, this time by sea. Landing in Cornwall he was declared 'Richard IV' on Bodmin Moor; but his forces proved no match for those Henry sent against him. Captured, and paraded through London streets lined with jeering citizens, he at first (after confessing to being an imposter) received surprisingly lenient treatment. His luck would run out, ending with execution at the end of 1499; but more interesting is Henry's treatment of Katherine Gordon.

Warbeck's wife had accompanied him to Cornwall, and after Perkin's capture Henry sent down to see after her welfare with the most assiduous care. His gifts were enumerated in his accounts – satin dress, riding cloak, hose, shoes: all the necessities, right down to sanitary cloths – with matrons to accompany her and protect her virtue. Henry's poet Bernard André records that when the famously beautiful Katherine was brought into Henry's presence 'in an untouched state', there to confront her disgraced husband, the king made her a long speech, telling her that life ahead would have 'many possibilities'. He had, so chronicler Edward Hall puts it, 'began then a little to fantasy her person'.

Fantasy was where it remained: Katherine was given an honourable place among the queen's ladies. Henry presented her to his wife as 'a true and undoubted token of his victory'. But the gifts of lavish clothing he continued to make Katherine cast another light on his feelings. Even after Elizabeth's death, he kept her so close by there would be stories that she and Henry had married – though in fact, Katherine's long and successful career included marriage to three other English gentlemen.

Henry and Elizabeth, after all, had other concerns: notably the perpetuation of their dynasty.

The question of a marriage between Henry VII's heir Arthur and a daughter of the great Spanish monarchs Isabella of Castile and Ferdinand of Aragon had been under discussion since the very first years of the reign. In 1498 matters were sufficiently advanced that the Spanish ambassador could report home that the queen and the king's mother wished the twelve-year-old Catherine of Aragon to learn French so that they could converse with her. Furthermore, she should learn to drink wine. 'The water of England is not drinkable, and even if it were, the climate would not allow the drinking of it.'

In the spring of 1500 Henry and Elizabeth crossed the Channel to the English-owned port of Calais to meet with a representative of

Catherine's family and ratify the marriage treaty. The celebratory tournament was based on the legendary Tournament of the Golden Tree at Bruges that had celebrated Margaret of Burgundy's marriage more than thirty years before. Copies of the challenge were issued in the name of Elizabeth's kinsman the Earl of Suffolk, and sent to Spain, and to the kings of France and Scotland. There was a special point in doing things correctly, since Europe's eyes would be on the conduct of the new Tudor dynasty.

In 1501 Catherine of Aragon finally arrived in England, after the stormy voyage that seemed to have become traditional for royal brides. Henry took his son Arthur and rushed to intercept Catherine on her journey, insisting on seeing her for himself, against Spanish etiquette and the protests of her scandalised staff. On 12 November Catherine entered London, with an escort of lords: a fifteen-year-old with 'fair auburn' hair, wearing 'rich apparel on her body after the manner of her country', and 'a little hat fashioned like a cardinal's hat of a pretty braid with a lace of gold'. The wedding in St Paul's Cathedral two days later was purposely public: this signified the ultimate acceptance of the Tudor dynasty into the European club. Ten-year-old Prince Henry – dressed like bride and bridegroom in white satin – led Catherine in to face the three-hour ceremony. Needless to say, King Arthur too was featured in the pageantry that followed.

There was Solemn Mass the next day, Tuesday, and a move to Westminster. On Thursday, the tournaments began: a deliberately resplendent re-creation of the great days of chivalry. There were more pageants on the next day – reluctant ladies successfully assaulted by Knights of the Mount of Love – and afterwards the company danced.

On the morning after his wedding Prince Arthur emerged from his chamber demanding drink – so a courtier would later recall – boasting of his thirst since he had 'been this night in the midst of Spain'. Any such words would be obsessively examined almost thirty years later. Then, famously, Catherine would maintain in the face of every pressure that she emerged from the nights she spent with Arthur a virgin – as 'intact and uncorrupted', she would say vividly, as when she came from her mother's womb. But as the newly married couple left together for their life as Prince and Princess of Wales in Ludlow, on the Welsh borders, no one seemed to consider that anything was wrong. Perhaps royal wedding nights – so often between very youthful strangers – must sometimes have resulted in a measure of uncertainty, a sense that there would, after all, be plenty of nights ahead?

But that would not be the case. Less than five months after his wedding, in distant Ludlow, on 2 April 1502 Prince Arthur died following an illness that has been tentatively identified as tuberculosis. It may, alternatively, have been testicular cancer, which might explain the information Catherine's Spanish doctor gave her parents: that 'the prince had been denied the strength necessary to know a woman, as if he had been a cold piece of stone'. Catherine's duenna Dona Elvira would likewise tell Ferdinand and Isabella that their daughter 'remained as she was when she left here' . . . But they (like the Tudor courtiers who thirty years later reported Arthur's brags to the contrary) were saying what their employers wanted to hear.

It took more than two days for the news of Arthur's death to reach his parents at Greenwich. But their reaction on hearing the dreadful tidings is the best evidence we have that this relationship – however begun – had achieved the contemporary, the Christian, goal of marital affection and harmony.

When his Grace understood that sorrowful heavy tidings, he sent out for the Queen, saying, that he and his Queen would take the painful sorrows together . . . she with full great and constant comfortable words besought his Grace, that he would first after God, remember the weal of his own noble person, the comfort of his realm, and of her. She then said that my Lady his Mother had never no more children but him only, and, that God by his Grace had ever preserved him, and brought him where that he was. Over that, how God had left him yet a fair Prince, two fair Princesses, and that God is where he was and we are both young enough [to have more children] . . .

After that she was departed and come to her own Chamber, natural and motherly remembrance of that great loss smote her so sorrowful to the heart, that those that were about her were fain to send for the king to comfort her. Then his Grace of true gentle and faithful love, in good heart came and relieved her, and showed her how wise counsel she had given him before . . .

Elizabeth sent a black velvet litter to carry her daughter-in-law Catherine of Aragon back to court – but back to a future of painful uncertainty.

7

'to marry whom he choose'

1502–1509

PRINCE HENRY, JUST turning twelve, was now – after a month's wait to be sure Catherine was not pregnant – acknowledged as his father's heir. We know considerably more about the formation of the future Henry VIII than about that of his father. And – unusually for a future king – it was a woman who took a leading role in that early moulding.

Elizabeth of York's eldest son Arthur had been taken away from her care to be educated as befitted a Prince of Wales, taking his seat at Ludlow on the Welsh borders. By contrast, there is evidence Elizabeth played a strong role in educating not only her daughters but their brother Henry, that second son who was never expected to inherit the throne. In 1497 the Venetian ambassador, visiting the royal family at Woodstock, was received first by the king, with his eldest son Prince Arthur; and then by the queen, with Henry by her side. The divisions were clear.

David Starkey suggests that from certain similarities of handwriting, it was Elizabeth who taught her second son and her daughters to write – but it is likely also to have been Elizabeth of York who gave to her children the strong romantic streak that came from her own forebears. In her youth, she had the chance to pore over the lovely manuscripts in the royal library, and read the kind of books which, declared a contemporary, caused 'weak-breasted women to fall into libidinous errors'. An early fourteenth-century manuscript of an Arthurian romance bears the signature 'E Wydevyll' on the back and the signatures 'Elysabeth, the kyngs dowther' and 'Cecyl the kyngs daughter' (her next sister Cecily) on the flyleaf. The two sisters also wrote their names on a French story of the world and an account of the funeral rites of a Turkish emperor. As queen, Elizabeth would commission from Caxton a collection of English and Latin prayers and she would own or use several beautifully illustrated Books of Hours.

Elizabeth had always ensured that the old Yorkist establishment was by no means forgotten in the upbringing of her children. Back in spring 1488 when a Lady Mistress was chosen for Prince Arthur (at a sizeable salary of more than £26 a year) the choice fell on Elizabeth Darcy, who had presided over the nursery of Elizabeth's brother Edward V. In 1501 Elizabeth welcomed into her household Arthur Plantagenet, her illegitimate half-brother – one of her father's bastards.

Sometime in the late 1490s John Skelton was appointed to be Henry's tutor. Poet laureate and scholar, Skelton was nonetheless a cheerful self-promoter who owed a good deal to his success with the ladies of any household, who wrote poems inspired by the mothers of two of Henry's wives: Anne Boleyn and Jane Seymour.

Skelton would later boast in verse of having taught Henry 'to spell'; his most important task would have been to teach him to do so in Latin. But Skelton's own eclectic interests make it likely that to some degree he also shared with the young and presumably impressionable boy his enthusiasm for subjects as diverse as mathematics (at which Henry was apt), the English and French chronicles, and English verse from the days of Gower and Chaucer. In an age that loved manuals of instruction, and was particularly assiduous in thrusting them on royalty, Skelton in 1501 penned the *Speculum Principis*, the 'first mirror' of maxims for Henry. Among all the instructions to 'lead in learning and virtue' and 'peruse the chroniclers' is one precept that stands out: 'Choose a wife for yourself; prize her always and uniquely.'

There was another important influence on the young prince, introduced as mentor by Queen Elizabeth. William Blount, Lord Mountjoy, was just turned twenty, and from a wealthy family with an impeccable history of Tudor support; his stepfather was the queen's chamberlain.

These years saw an ever-growing tension between the old aristocratic ideals of the chivalry that masked militarism, and the new Renaissance learning of the classics, the new humanist ideals of what a ruler should be. It was the difference between Geoffrey of Monmouth's old Arthurian *History of the Kings of Britain* and the new history commissioned by Henry VII from the Italian humanist Polydore Vergil, who could barely hide his contempt for Geoffrey's 'fable'. The humanists were disinclined to subscribe to the courtly creed. Erasmus himself (in an English translation published by Edmund Beck in the 1540s) declared it:

> a mad thing, to love, to wax pale, to be made lean, to weep, to flatter and shamefully to submit thyself unto a stinking harlot most filthy and rotten, to gape and sing all night by her chamber window, to be made to the lure & to be obedient at a beck, nor dare to do anything except she nod or wag her head, to suffer a foolish woman to reign over thee ... to give thyself willingly unto a Queen that she might mock, knock, mangle and spoil thee.[*]

But Mountjoy (like Anthony Woodville before him) managed to excel in both the old world and the new; and both would have their influence on his pupil Henry.

As Skelton was replaced by John Holt, a friend of Thomas More, the young prince would have been given the classical curriculum laid down for his brother Arthur: Homer and Virgil, Caesar and Livy; the *Stoic Paradoxes* of Cicero and the observations of Pliny. But there was also Giles Duwes, who taught Henry both the lute and the French language, and who at Richmond Palace had been librarian of the (largely French) collection of books built up by Edward IV and Henry VII.

The death of her eldest son Prince Arthur had given Elizabeth of York a new challenge – England still had an heir in the shape of Henry, but (since a third sibling, Edmund, had died while his parents were on the way back from Calais) now no spare. By the summer she was pregnant again.

Her accounts show, in December, a reward to a monk who brought 'Our Lady girdle' to the queen: to be worn by women in childbirth. Elizabeth visited the Tower to inspect arrangements for her delivery: a 'rich bed' decorated with red and white roses and with clouds, new

---

[*] Beck was, however, an intensely Protestant cleric whose own prejudices – as well as his passion for hawking! – may have coloured his translation.

linen, childbed attendants. After a comparatively cheerful Christmas at Richmond, with card games and music (and an astrologer's hopeful prophecy that Henry would father many sons, and Elizabeth live until she was eighty), she went to the Tower at the end of January. Just a week later she was delivered of a baby girl.

But then the records of Elizabeth's Privy Purse expenses take an ominous turn. They show payment for 'iii yards of flannel bought for my Lady Katherine', the daughter who would live only a matter of days. But then comes 'Item to James Nattres for his costs going into Kent for Doctor Hallysworth physician to come to the Queen by the King's commandment'. Boat hire from the Tower to Gravesend and back (3s 4d); horse hire and guides 'by night and day'. This was an urgent journey. But the doctor's efforts were unavailing. On 11 February 1503 Elizabeth of York died. Her husband was distraught enough to become seriously ill; his mother moved into Richmond Palace to nurse him. And Elizabeth's son, that other Henry, would years later remember his mother's death bitterly enough to recall that 'hateful intelligence' as a standard for melancholy. A contemporary illustration shows a small boy, believed to be him, kneeling by his mother's bed, in tears.

There was of course the thought that Henry VII might marry again. He had briefly mooted, indeed, the idea that he might marry his dead son's bride, Catherine of Aragon, but that was rejected with horror by her mother Isabella: 'a very evil thing – one never before seen, and the mere mention of which offends the ears – we would not for anything in the world that it should take place.' Instead, negotiations for Catherine's marriage to Prince Henry would go ahead. By the end of June, they were betrothed. Matters could go no further for now, given Henry's youth – and in the meantime, one thing did have to be sorted.

A papal dispensation would be needed, given that Catherine had been married to Henry's brother. But a dispensation to cover what set of circumstances, exactly? A mere formal, unconsummated marriage, such as might easily be set aside; or a full and consummated union?

Amid the welter of diplomatic speculation there is no record (at this time) of any statement from Catherine herself. The bickerings over her marital status were a matter of political expediency, dwelling as much on money as on maidenheads.

If the marriage had been consummated, and Catherine had become fully Arthur's wife, then her parents owed Henry VII the unpaid remainder of her dowry. And, until he got it, he had no obligation to bestow on her the income to which she would be entitled as Princess Dowager of Wales. This, broadly speaking, was the English view.

If the marriage had not been consummated – the Spanish view – then unless another English marriage were on the cards, Catherine should be returned intact to her parents . . . along, of course, with that portion of her dowry that had already been paid. The draft treaty mentioned the need for a dispensation since the marriage had been solemnised 'and afterwards consummated'. The Spanish rulers insisted this was not the case but – as Ferdinand's ambassador in Rome was instructed to tell the Pope – they were prepared to give way to the English on the wording.

The Papal Bull finally sent towards the end of 1504 had one crucial word inserted into the original phraseology. Catherine's marriage to Arthur had been consummated . . . *'forsan'.* 'Perhaps'. But by that time something else had happened – Catherine's mother, too, had died, and Queen Isabella's kingdom of Castile was inherited not by her husband but by their eldest daughter Juana. A match with Ferdinand of Aragon's daughter Catherine suddenly seemed a much less attractive proposition. Truly, it was not easy to be a sixteenth-century princess.

Another newly motherless princess, the thirteen-year-old Margaret Tudor, had already been sent north to cement her marriage to the thirty-year-old King of Scots. When the match had been mooted five years before, her mother Elizabeth and grandmother Margaret Beaufort, in a rare but telling moment of unity, had combined forces to urge she should not be sent until fully mature for 'fear the King of Scots would not wait, but injure her, and endanger her health'. (Just so had another mother and daughter-in-law, the Eleanors of Provence and of Castile, joined forces to prevent another such early marriage, more than two centuries before.) Margaret Beaufort – whose husband had not 'waited' to consummate the marriage and possess himself of her lands – knew what she was talking about.

But the proxy celebration of this marriage in January 1502, at Richmond – the ceremony that officially made Margaret a queen and her mother's equal – had stipulated that she should be sent to Scotland only eighteen months later, and in June 1503 Margaret set out on her journey.

She travelled north accompanied by a large retinue, and care was taken to make a resplendent business of it, with ceremonial entries into the towns she passed along her way. And James IV – the man who had been so happy to shelter the romantic pretender Perkin Warbeck – tried, too, to make a courtly business of their meeting. The official known as the Somerset Herald records how, when Margaret had crossed the border and been welcomed to Haddington Castle as its 'Lady and Mistress', James came to meet her there, and having kissed, they went aside 'and communed together by long space'. In the best style of chivalric fantasy, he came lightly disguised in a huntsman's outfit, with a lyre on his back.

If the Herald is to be believed, James continued to do everything right. His experience as a womaniser, his brood of illegitimate children, seems to have taught him something. That, or his experience as a noted patron of the arts and sciences. James was a polyglot and builder; a consciously Renaissance prince whose court poets or *makars* – men like William Dunbar, Robert Henryson and Gavin (or 'Gawain') Douglas – explored both old and new traditions. Douglas's now-lost *Palice [sic] of Honour* is believed to play on the old conceit of the courts of love, while Dunbar's *The Thistle ['Thrissil'] and the Rose*, written in honour of this marriage and set in a Maytime garden, features Tudor Margaret as the red and white rose, and James variously as the Lion, the Eagle or the Thistle. Margaret had come to no uncourtly wilderness: James's great-grandfather James I is credited with being the author of *The Kingis Quair*, an early fifteenth-century poem, dedicated to Chaucer and to Gower, which casts the poet's own adventures in courtly form. (Indeed, the Arthurian legends took on their own form in Scotland. The *Historia Gentis Scotorum* (History of the Scottish People), first written and published by Hector Boece in 1527 but later extended, had Guinevere fleeing north after the discovery of her adultery, and Arthur ordering her to be dragged to death by wild beasts.)

This later king James IV played the lute and the clavichord for the music-loving Margaret and came instantly to commiserate when a fire killed her favourite horses (something with which James could have sympathised since he had a passion not only for hunting, but for riding in the tournament). He even insisted that she took his own, high-status, chair at supper since the stool where she was seated, he said, was not comfortable enough. More importantly, it seems probable he may indeed have 'waited', since Margaret did not become pregnant until three years after the marriage, though then pregnancies came quickly. The new bride would nonetheless write miserably to her father: 'I would I were with your Grace now, and many times more.' The instant closeness between her husband and her escort the Earl of Surrey, a former Yorkist and expert soldier, left her out in the cold. (Surrey – later Duke of Norfolk – would be the grandfather of Anne Boleyn.) Nonetheless, as the marriages of royal princesses went, perhaps she had been lucky.

Luckier than her sister-in-law Catherine of Aragon, anyway.

Catherine's prospective bridegroom Henry was now England's heir. In February 1504 he was formally created Prince of Wales, but there seems to have been no thought of his following the normal pattern, and being sent away. That summer he moved not to Ludlow, but to join his father's court. Ambassadors noted that he was kept with his father, himself the young prince's 'governor and steward', in order to 'improve him'.

In June 1505, as Prince Henry was about to turn fourteen (the age at which a marriage contract might be considered indissoluble), he was summoned into the presence of his father and his father's counsellors to make a formal declaration that he considered the child marriage he had made with Catherine to be 'null and void'. It was, however, perfectly apparent that the statement Henry read was his father's doing, and one which, since the younger Henry's declaration was never made public, left all the elder's options open. Officially, the marriage was still on; and the Bishop of Winchester, who was present, recalled many years later that the king had no particular objection to his son making 'signs of love' to the princess (all the easier for the fact that the prince's governor Mountjoy was wooing one of Catherine's ladies).

For the next four years, Catherine's position in England would improve or worsen according to the utility or otherwise of an alliance between England and Catherine's family. Caught between her father and her father-in-law as they tried to outfox each other, her life would become a living hell. Her plight was certainly enough to make a mute appeal to a chivalrous young man.

As young Henry grew, it was evident he was besotted with the chivalric tradition beloved of the Yorkist side of his family – of the grandfather, Edward IV, he so resembled. His enthusiasm was further kindled when, in the first weeks of 1506, chance brought a glamorous visitor to England's shores. The new sovereign of Castile, Catherine of Aragon's sister Juana, and her husband Philip of Burgundy were sailing towards Spain to claim Juana's inheritance when storms swept them, instead, onto the Dorset coast.

Juana has gone down in history as Juana 'the Mad' – probably unfairly, though she was undoubtedly obsessed by both love and hatred for her husband. More interesting to young Prince Henry – while his father set about wringing an advantageous treaty out of the guests so unexpectedly delivered into his hands – was that husband Philip: Philip 'the Handsome', international star of the tourney. And even King Henry took care to ensure Philip visited Winchester on his way to their summit meeting at Windsor. How better to impress the flower of European chivalry than by reminding him the Tudors were King Arthur's heirs?

At Windsor, itself still resonant with the chivalric dreams of Edward III, King Henry made Philip a Knight of the Garter and Philip made Prince Henry a Knight of the Golden Fleece, a Burgundian order founded three quarters of a century before. As they dined together afterwards Henry VII spoke of the Round Table, saying he hoped the table at which they dined would itself be worthy of display, for the part it had played in friendship between two countries.

As Philip and Juana – King Henry's treaty signed – were allowed to resume their journey, Prince Henry sent after them a letter in his own hand (and in French: the language he would choose for many of his letters to Anne Boleyn). With 'all my heart' he desired Philip's health; he begged Philip to write 'from time to time'. The letter breathes the spirit of a crush. Alas for Henry's desires, Philip died of fever that September. His wife refused to be parted from his body, but the young prince's reaction was as extreme, in its way. Nothing, he wrote to Erasmus, had distressed him so much since his 'dearest' mother's death: indeed, this seemed 'to reopen the wound'.

Henry VII's first thought was that Juana was now free to marry again. He had been struck, on her visit to England, by her exotic beauty (as well as her inheritance). The ambassadorial report that Henry had been moved to 'incredible love' may have been a tad more than the usual diplomatic flummery. Less romantically, the ambassador said the English appeared not to be concerned by Juana's reputed insanity – especially since it would not affect her ability to bear children.

Poor, isolated Catherine of Aragon was drawn into the courtship, her letters to Juana describing Henry as 'a very passionate king'. Henry's pursuit of Juana gave Catherine a new importance. She had, moreover, successfully persuaded her father Ferdinand that rather than rely on a series of ambassadors she felt were doing nothing for her – her household, she claimed, were now dressed in rags – she should herself be given the diplomatic codes to understand his letters. She would act as her father's ambassador, effectively. But she was caught between her urgent desire to have a sister and ally at the English court, and Ferdinand's determination that he, rather than any second husband, should now control Juana's lands.

In the end, however, Henry VII would not remarry. His health was by now giving cause for concern. Instead, he seemed to grow more sour as the years went by – more secretive, more reclusive, more obsessed with money, and more alienated from the ever-disaffected Yorkist aristocracy. But those Yorkist aristocrats his father was so keen to extirpate looked very different to the younger Henry.

It was increasingly with the younger generation that any thought of romance lay. It was the Yorkist lords who were the stars of the tournament, and Prince Henry longed for nothing more than to compete in the jousting arena. Allowed, reluctantly, to test his prowess 'running at the ring', he was, however, denied the chance to risk himself in combat.

Yet neither his father nor his grandmother, that power behind the throne, were indifferent to the opportunities the tournament offered: for spectacle; for validating the Tudor regime; for confining the impulses of the warrior class within the code of chivalry. On the occasion of Philip of Burgundy's visit, when England's jousters would have a chance to go up against Europe's finest, Margaret had given her grandson a new horse, and a saddle trimmed with cloth of gold, with which to cut a figure at the tournament. And prominent among those jousters were the 'spears', the bodyguards cum companions-at-arms the king recruited to be around his son. Jousting offered now, as it had centuries before, a way for a brave and ambitious young outsider to make his mark.

There was an element of the subversive about any joust – even its association with the flourishing month of May. And throughout May 1507 there was a veritable festival of jousting, presided over by Prince Henry (almost sixteen, but still not allowed to compete) and by his eleven-year-old sister Princess Mary. She had early begun to prove herself as an adept and courtly figurehead, dressed in green festooned with flowers to represent 'Lady May' as she presided over the festivities as their 'sovereign lady'. In a tournament themed on new love, her challengers wore her green favours, and beside the prince and princess stood a blossoming may tree hung with coats of arms. Perhaps participation in such tournaments would teach Mary something as well: the opportunities, the liberties, that the chivalric code might offer women.

But as these jousts went on from May into June, the mounting violence of the spectacle had begun increasingly to alarm the authorities: breaking the chivalric bounds. Dressed now in white and blue, wearing a white enamelled heart between the letters R and H (for *Roy Henry*, King Henry), the jousters were forced to protest their loyalty in poetry, declaring they had only been emulating the example of King Arthur and his knights. The courtly culture which had begun to cluster around the young prince and princess could only be allowed to go so far. But one conspicuous presence in this as in every other joust was Charles Brandon – now in his early twenties, favoured as the son of a man who gave his life at Bosworth as Henry VII's standard-bearer – who would later feature as an important and disruptive presence in both royal brother and sister's story.

Prince Henry was also collecting musical instruments, songs of courtly love and of old adventure. He especially liked the stories of Robin Hood. But there was a split between the fantasy presentation of Henry's life as the chivalric prince and the reality: just as between his father's increasing avarice and Robin Hood's bold generosity.

It would be surprising if Catherine of Aragon did not play some part in this chivalric fantasy. In that fan letter to Philip of Burgundy young Henry had written of her as his dear and well-beloved wife ('*compaigne*'). On New Year's Day 1508 he gave her 'a fair rose of rubies set in a rose white and green', clearly symbolising Henry himself. Was there a rescue fantasy, a sense of the unattainable *princesse lointaine*? Or was there the sense that both Henry and Catherine were prisoners in a tower?

Nothing in Catherine's life had improved. As Ferdinand still failed to produce the rest of her dowry, even the food and lodging she was accorded by the English went from bad to worse, and the worry told on her health. There had long been concerns over her 'excessive religious observances', as the Pope put it in a letter forbidding the fasting which Catherine saw as a manifestation of piety but to modern ears sounds much like anorexia. Squabbling in the ranks of her Spanish attendants complicated her situation and now she had fallen under the influence of a confessor, Fra Diego, whose hold over her began to spark scandal.

She could sound a note of defiance: 'They tell me nothing but lies here, and they think they can break my spirit. But I believe what I choose and say nothing. I am not so simple as I seem.' But another letter breathes desperation. Henry VII had told her, she wrote to Ferdinand in the spring of 1508, that 'as long as he is not entirely paid, he regards me as bound and his son as free. [Prince Henry] is not yet so old that delay is disagreeable. Thus mine is always the worst part.'

Henry VII was retreating into premature old age. His former counsellors were increasingly dismissed from his confidence, to be replaced, as the last years of his reign drew in, with new men whose strength was their ability to squeeze money from his subjects: Richard Empson and Edmund Dudley. Ferdinand's ambassador described how the younger Henry was kept 'like a girl', hardly speaking in public except in response to his father.

At Christmas 1508 the proxy marriage took place of Princess Mary to the seven-year-old son of Philip of Burgundy and Juana 'the Mad': the boy who as Charles V would inherit both Spain and the Netherlands, as well as the Holy Roman Emperor's crown, bringing together the vast Habsburg territories. The official account declared this 'the most notable alliance and greatest marriage of Christendom'. Events would prove there could be many a slip . . . But at the time, it could only have seemed to Prince Henry (and, Heaven knows, Catherine of Aragon) as though both Tudor sisters were going on to glory. Catherine's situation was growing ever worse, with King Henry railing at her for her father's iniquities. The Spanish ambassador had described her despair. But events would soon release both Catherine and the younger Henry.

Henry VII had been believed to be at the point of death before, and yet recovered, but this time it was certainty. As the first months of 1509 wore on, King Henry himself knew it. So did the mother who hurried to his bedside. Yet on 21 April, when Henry died, there was no public outcry, no call for mourning. Instead, the event was masked in secrecy, his counsellors conspiring with Margaret Beaufort to deny all knowledge of it for more than two long days: days spent in the placing of soldiers, the suppression of any possible controversy. On 24 April 1509 Henry VIII was proclaimed king, still weeks short of his eighteenth birthday.

In the years ahead it would be characteristic of Henry always to throw himself into any role he assumed, whether of Christian king or chivalric lover. Now the Spanish ambassador was told by the royal councillors that in a last deathbed conversation, father assured son that the new Henry VIII would be 'free to marry whom he chose'. Henry himself would give a different story: writing to Margaret of Austria, the Netherlands regent, at the end of June, just weeks after the death, that his father on his deathbed, 'among other good counsels', charged him 'to fulfill the old treaty with Ferdinand and Isabella of Spain by taking their daughter Catherine in marriage'.

By that time he and Catherine of Aragon were already husband and wife.

8

'Sir Loyal Heart'

1509–1515

T HERE IS AN image of King Arthur dating from 1509, the year of Henry's accession. Grey-bearded, but nonetheless resplendent in elaborate armour, vivid with jewels and gilt with all the emblems of chivalry. It is not an English image: the wonderfully illuminated manuscript of the *Livro do Armeiro-Mor* was created in Portugal, whose king Manuel I had already married two of Catherine of Aragon's sisters.* But this – rather than the father who had come to define himself by the depth of his purse – was the king Henry wanted to be. One of his first acts would be to order the arrest, and eventual execution, of his father's money-extracting machines, Empson and Dudley.

The romantic ideal, in one form or another, would dominate Henry VIII's marital alliances – and the pattern stamped his reign from the very start. Catherine's father had written that things might be better for his daughter when Henry VII was dead: 'Please God they may, but I see no likelihood of it,' replied his pessimistic ambassador. But as April turned to May, and he was in the very act of arranging to have Catherine's goods shipped across the Channel, he was summoned by

---

* Manuel first married Catherine's eldest sister Isabella; but when Isabella swiftly died in childbirth, he married her sister Maria. He would – when Maria died in 1518 – go on to marry their (and Catherine's) niece Eleanor. One cannot but feel that this family history must have coloured Catherine's attitudes, when the time came for Henry to tell her of concerns about the fact she had been married to his brother!

Henry VIII's council to be reproached for slowness in arranging her marriage to the new king . . . They say good news never kills a man. But it would not be surprising if the ambassador saw his life passing before his eyes.

What caused the new king's urgent desire to marry Catherine of Aragon? He may have been eager to prove his independence by making a decision of such magnitude alone. Perhaps the younger brother saw her – 'Arthur's' bride – as a token of regal legitimacy; one, moreover, with more experience of the world than he. Henry was in many ways a young eighteen-year-old, by the standards of the day, who came to the throne without having been on the battlefield, or knocked around the courts of Europe, like Henry VII, Edward IV, or indeed Richard III.

There could be real political advantages in the match. In the world-view to which Henry VIII subscribed, the first item in the job description of an English king was to win famous victories in France, as Henry V had done. This, in the European dynamics of the early sixteenth century, meant allying England with the Spanish kingdoms from which Catherine came, or the Holy Roman Empire with which she also had familial links. A letter from Ferdinand to his daughter before the marriage had urged her to use 'all your skill and prudence' to 'close the deal'; and it would not be the first nor the last time the glow of courtly love had served to mask – even in the eyes of the lovers themselves – a more pragmatic reality.

But we may indeed see this as a gesture from the realm of fantasy. The prince, in best tradition, rescuing at a stroke the Spanish princess who had spent seven years in penurious uncertainty. There was no reason Catherine would not love the tall, fair young giant who saved her from an uncertain and humiliating future, and whose looks foreign envoys noted in almost erotic terms. His face was so beautiful it would become a pretty woman, one wrote; while in Flanders they would hear that the young king's 'nobleness and fame' was 'greater than any prince since King Arthur'. The king of Camelot was still in currency at the English court: Henry would have read Caxton's preface to *The Order of Chivalry*, beseeching contemporary knights to return to the virtuous old days and 'read the noble volumes of the holy grail, of Launcelot, of Galahad, of Tristan'.

But there is little doubt Henry, too, at least persuaded himself into love with the attractive strawberry-blonde 23-year-old from a far more established royalty than the Tudors. Her own interest in the game of courtly love would be limited. Perhaps a childhood watching her mother Queen Isabella exercise real power had given her less taste for a game that allowed women a simulacrum of it; perhaps her impoverished young womanhood had given her no chance to play. But Catherine's well-known virtue, her staunchness and her loyalty provided the moral example that had always been one province of the courtly lady. As a poem of Henry's own composition put it:

I hurt no man, I do no wrong,
I love true where I did marry

Even Catherine's father wrote to the new couple on the blessing of a happy marriage. 'To be well married is the greatest blessing in the world . . . God shows favour to good husbands and wives.'

Henry wrote to Ferdinand praising Catherine's virtues and boasting of his love: 'If I were still free, I would choose her for wife before all others.' Catherine's confessor Fra Diego wrote: 'The king my lord adores her, and her highness him.' A Spanish traveller visiting England a year into Henry's reign recalled later that 'King Henry loved the Queen his wife greatly . . . stating publicly in French [the language of courtly love] that his highness was happy because he was owner of such a beautiful angel and that he had found himself a flower.'

In short, if the brutal practical truth was clearly that Henry bestowed a huge favour on Catherine when they married – if there were cold hard reasons on both sides for the match – the emotional dynamics might still play out rather differently.

The wedding took place fast and privately. The joint coronation ceremony less than a fortnight later was, by contrast, huge and public. It was held on Midsummer Day, though – unlucky omen? – a sudden squall forced the queen to shelter under the awning of a draper's stall, and continue to Westminster Abbey with her fine robes drenched. Observers nonetheless remarked the 'beautiful and goodly' spectacle of her long hair hanging down her back.

At the jousting, two days later, the leader of one team approached Catherine to declare that 'his knights were come to do feats of arms for the love of ladies'. It set the tone for the first part of the reign. The stand where the royal couple sat was fashioned as a castle ('Cast'ile), slathered with Henry's roses and Catherine's pomegranates, whose multiple seeds seemed fitting for her fertile family.

Catherine wrote to her father that their time was 'spent in continual festival'. Besides his passion for sport, Henry loved the fantasy element of masques and disguises. The king and his friends might appear as outlaws, Muscovites, wild men, Saracens, and whenever they burst incognito into Catherine's rooms, she and her ladies were careful to be astonished. May Day, so important in the courtly calendar, was celebrated with new enthusiasm; it might see the royal couple, all in green, partying in a bird-decked woodland. In May 1510 the Spanish ambassador noted Henry's endless tournaments 'instituted in imitation of Amadis and Lancelot and other knights of olden times, of whom so much is written in books'.

Taking its tone from the king and queen, this was a cultured court. Henry was described as spending his time (besides shooting, wrestling and jousting) 'singing, dancing . . . playing at the recorders, flute and virginals, and in setting of songs and making of ballads'. Learned men had every hope of patronage: without them, Henry said to Lord Mountjoy, 'we could scarcely exist at all'. The new learning went hand in hand with an antiquarian interest and a fresh appreciation of the old: poems like the early-fifteenth-century *The Court of Love* or the Middle English *Ten Commandments of Love* were once more in currency; and courtiers wrote love letters using stanzas from Chaucer's *Troilus and Criseyde*. Titles of lyrics (many written by Henry himself) in the songbook known as Henry VIII MS, now in the British Library, read like a litany of courtly concerns: 'Alas what shall I do for love', 'Though that men do call it dotage', 'Departure is my chief pain', '*En vrai amour*'. (One song – 'Yow and I and Amyas', by William Cornish, Henry 's Master of the Children of the Chapel Royal – would reference the pageantry of the Siege of the Château Vert described in the Prologue.)

Catherine too was a major patron who gathered humanists about her. 'Astonishingly learned', Erasmus called her. And Castiglione in his *Book of the Courtier* wrote (plausibly or otherwise) that her mother

Isabella had set lovers at the forefront of her armies, and made sure that the ladies they adored were there to watch them, and inspire them to great deeds.

One beneficiary of the educated atmosphere was Henry's younger sister Mary. In 1512 John Palsgrave, a scholar of French language and literature, was hired to teach Mary, using a number of courtly texts as tools and examples. One such was *La Belle Dame Sans Merci*, written in 1424 by Alain Chartier and provoking a '*Querelle*' almost as vehement as that around the *Roman de la Rose.*

Chartier's poem featured the usual Lover pleading for the favour of a Lady who, however, rejects the notion that his passion gives him a claim. Instead, she declares her right to live and love as she pleases – lessons Mary, it would transpire, had taken to heart. The story ran that Chartier – accused by a group of courtiers of portraying women as cruel – had been formally summoned by the ladies of the French court, who threatened to have their lawyers charge him before the God of Love. It was a typical piece of courtly play, possibly initiated by a rival poet, Pierre de Nesson. But the key was the suggestion that the Lady was cruel to refuse the Lover's advances – a charge gaining new impetus in courtly literature. Somewhere along the line, the original courtly ideal of love reciprocated had taken on a new dimension: something in the nature of a double-edged sword. The lady was now compromised if she responded to her lover's advances; cruel if she did not. The *Querelle* had been one of those public spats highly enjoyable to the literary ladies and no doubt highly profitable to the professional poets; but the central subject was still being debated a century on.

No wonder, in this emotive climate, that Henry wore Catherine's favours in the lists, allegorically proclaimed his devotion; as well as hastening to share books and musicians with her. Perhaps her role in Henry's games was that of an admiring audience: as much an object as the lady in any courtly lyric. But the entertainments he devised were described in the accounts as being 'for the Queen's pleasure'. And everything was the sweeter since Catherine swiftly became pregnant. Nothing was too good for Henry's 'most dearest wife, the queen'.

* * *

In January 1510, however, Catherine suffered what would prove the first of many miscarriages. This was far from an unusual occurrence at the time: it has been estimated that any pregnancy had only a fifty per cent success rate (to say nothing of the perils of infancy). When in 1512 Margaret Tudor in Scotland gave birth to the baby who would become James V, she had already seen her first three children die early (one of them another 'Arthur' who would not live long enough to inherit a throne).

But a bizarre and worrying twist with Catherine's miscarriage came when her doctors convinced her she was still pregnant with the second of what had been twins (though the Spanish ambassador reported she had resumed her menstrual cycle). As late as March, Henry was ordering goods for a christening; it was late May before Catherine acknowledged the mistake. By that time, however, she was able to announce that she was pregnant again.

But while Catherine had been secluded, awaiting birth, there had been stories that, as the Spanish ambassador reported, one of her ladies was 'much liked by the king, who went after her'. This was Lady Anne Hastings, a sister of the Duke of Buckingham, in her late twenties and recently married for the second time. It appeared that Anne had been having secret trysts with . . . somebody. Sir William Compton, Henry's Groom of the Stool, was found in her room; but he might have been carrying messages for another. Compton was close enough to his king to share the same disguise in the masques or jousts Henry adored. Certainly Anne's relatives intervened, and whisked her away to a convent. Certainly Henry spoke angrily against them, and against 'tale-bearers'. And certainly 'almost all the court knew that the Queen had been vexed with the King, and the King with her, and thus this storm went on between them'. Catherine had shown 'ill will' towards Compton, reported the latest Spanish ambassador.

History has Henry down as uxorious rather than broadly amorous. He is not known to have had as much truck with mistresses (in the conventional, sexual sense) as some contemporaries. He was at least unusually discreet – anxious, perhaps, to protect the image he so valued, of the faithful courtly lover. As one of Andreas Capellanus's Rules put it: 'The man affected by excessive sensuality is not usually in love.' And Thomas More had written, adapting the work of the late

Italian philosopher Pico della Mirandola into *Twelve Properties or Conditions of a Lover*:

The first point is to love but one alone,
And for that one, all others to forsake
For whoso loveth many, loveth none

But there are reports that suggest otherwise. The French ambassador said that Henry 'cared for nothing but girls'; his doctor described him as 'overly fond of women'. And Catherine of Aragon would, over the years ahead, be repeatedly pregnant: this at a time when sex in pregnancy was discouraged, both for fear of harming the foetus, and because this could only be sex for pleasure rather than procreation.

Theoreticians might denounce what one fifteenth-century manuscript described as using your spouse 'as your sweetheart in intent, only for lust . . . not for love, nor the fruit of wedlock, nor to be honest, but as an unreasonable beast'. But in practice, it was accepted that a royal wife's pregnancy meant her husband might look elsewhere.

Catherine's prime function as queen was to give her husband an heir. When, later in 1510, she once again took to her chamber in preparation for giving birth, Henry placed her in his own seat at the banquet which preceded the confinement, and himself acted as master of ceremonies, showing ladies to their seats at the feast.

The birth of a healthy baby boy, on New Year's Day 1511, was welcomed ecstatically, and the celebratory jousts were the most elaborate England had ever seen. Henry rode as 'Sir Loyal Heart', the words '*Cure loial*' embroidered in gold on the blue he wore. As he passed the specially built stand where Queen Catherine was sitting he made his horse cavort and beat the wooden barrier with its hooves and, as he left the field, made her a 'lowly obeisance'. As the chronicler Hall put it, he had made the world 'of Lancelot, and other knights of olden times, of whom so much is written in books' to live again. But, tragically, the little prince died at less than two months old, leaving the parents distraught.

Catherine's role, at this stage of Henry's reign, was not confined to the birthing chamber. Her husband listened to her advice and received ambassadors in her rooms. She had written to her father that, among the many reasons for her to love Henry, 'the strongest is his filial love and obedience to Your Highness'; Ferdinand's Iberian agenda would indeed, for Henry's first five years, set the direction of England's foreign policy.

In 1511 the Pope organised a Holy League to wage war on an expansionist France, to which he recruited Ferdinand; the Holy Roman Emperor Maximilian; and, inevitably, Henry. As the Venetian ambassador wrote: 'the King is bent on war, the Council is averse to it; the Queen will have it, and the wisest councillors in England cannot stand against the Queen'. In the 1512 armed sally England suffered a hugely embarrassing loss of men and money, but Henry seems not to have held Catherine responsible. (A Spanish delegation who saw the couple at Winchester in 1512 'were amazed at the great love that the King professed towards the Queen'.) She was soon actively involved – looking into the price of galley-hire, checking lists of equipment – in readying for a new anti-French campaign the following year. So too was that new voice on the council, the king's busy almoner, one Thomas Wolsey.

England was in fact being manipulated by Ferdinand (who was quietly concluding a private treaty with the French) and Maximilian: two wily and ruthless elderly foxes up to every trick in European diplomacy. But at the end of June 1513, Henry set off across the Channel in a whirl of horses, armour, and troops clad in silver-spangled Tudor white and green. Catherine was made 'Regent and Governess' of England, and captain-general of the forces left behind to guard the realm.

Henry met with glamorous success, taking Thérouanne and Tournai (in modern-day France and Belgium) and sending home the captured Duc de Longueville as a somewhat embarrassing present for Catherine, whose letters declared she was 'without comfort or pleasure' unless she heard her absent husband was well. Henry's allies too could play the chivalric game: Maximilian declared he would act as a volunteer in the English army. But the English expedition was about to offer an exemplar in what could be a yawning gulf between game and reality.

The Netherlands were governed by Maximilian's daughter Margaret of Austria, on behalf of her nephew (Maximilian's grandson), the future

Charles V. In her early thirties, and already twice widowed, she was capable, forceful, educated – and becoming something of a fixer in European diplomacy. Her one-time father-in-law Ferdinand of Aragon declared that Madame Margaret was the person upon whom all depended.

But the cultured, music-loving Margaret had also a more sensual side. She took zestful part in the weeks-long celebrations that followed the fall of Tournai. Perhaps both pleasure and political savvy led her to respond to the advances of one of the men who accompanied the English king.

We last heard of Charles Brandon in the previous reign, as one of the 'spears' placed around Prince Henry. Since Henry's accession, that closeness had increased. Indeed, one of Margaret's agents informed her that Brandon was 'a second king'. Around thirty, he had a chequered marital history, having early made one of Elizabeth of York's gentlewomen pregnant before repudiating their match, to marry her wealthy widowed aunt instead. Having sold many of the aunt's lands, he then succeeded in having the marriage declared void, and returned to the younger lady, who, however, died in 1510. Henry had sanctioned his betrothal to the eight-year-old heir of the Lisle barony, and made him a Knight of the Garter and Viscount Lisle. He had also handed him the keys to a surrendering Tournai. Henry and Charles could be found joining forces to answer all comers in the joust, or dressed identically in gold-trimmed purple velvet. Margaret would not be the last royal lady to see him as almost a kind of alter ego for Henry.

The scandal at Tournai (for such it became) started with a piece of pleasurable, probably wine-fuelled, courtly play. It centred on a ring, appropriately. As Margaret told it later – in a frantic, self-exculpatory letter – one night 'after the banquet [Brandon] put himself upon his knees before me, and in speaking and him playing, he drew from my finger the ring, and put it upon his, and then showed it to me and I took to laugh'. Margaret told Brandon he was a thief, and begged him to give the ring back, 'because it was too much known'. She gave him one of her bracelets instead. But there was a later episode when Brandon regained the ring and would not give it back, saying he would give her other, better, rings . . . He 'would not' understand her protests. All she could do was to beg that it might not be shown to anybody.

Secrecy was a prime duty of the courtly lover. But, by the time Margaret described the incident, Brandon had been displaying it openly, and Margaret was caught up in 'all the inconveniences of this thing'.

Margaret's warmth towards Brandon was being spoken of – at home, abroad, even in Germany – 'so openly as in the hands of merchant strangers'. Some dared make wagers upon it. 'A woman,' Baldassare Castiglione wrote, 'has not so many ways of defending herself against false imputations as has a man.' Now Margaret saw 'the bruit [rumour] is so imprinted in the fantasies of people . . . [that] I continue always in fear'. And Henry VIII had been a very active participant in Brandon's dangerous games: had indeed, 'many times' suggested Margaret might marry his friend. He urged that this (a love match, a woman making her own choice?) 'was the fashion of the ladies of England, and . . . was not there holden for evil'.

Brandon for his part, late one night in Margaret's chamber, told Margaret he would never marry, nor yet take 'lady nor mistress, without my commandment, but would continue all his life my right humble servant'. She promised 'to be to him such mistress all my life as to him who me seemed desired to do me most of service'. So far, so courtly. But what game were the two men really playing? Back home, Henry took the unprecedented step of creating Brandon Duke of Suffolk; and suggestions spread he had done so to make him a more suitable match for the Netherlands regent.

Was Henry simply trying to help his friend to a good, a stupendous, marriage? Had it been a joke that turned sour, albeit one more likely to damage the woman than the man? Was there even an attempt to discredit Margaret, whether for political manoeuvring or personal sport?

Margaret had been raised partly in the care of the powerful French regent Anne de Beaujeu, who had written a manual of instruction for aristocratic ladies. It contained an uncomfortable warning: 'There is no man of worth, however noble he may be, who does not use treachery, nor to whom it does not seem good sport to deceive or trick women of rank . . . there is no man so perfect who, in matters of love, is truthful or keeps his word.' Margaret might have added Christine de Pizan's advice into the mix: as part of the celebrations at Tournai, she had been presented with a six-piece tapestry depicting Christine's *City of Ladies*.

Small wonder Margaret in her turn wrote a poem for her young attendant ladies, warning them against taking the game too seriously.

Trust in those who offer you service,
And in the end, my maidens,
You will find yourselves in the ranks of those
Who have been deceived.

It is likely that one of those maidens in Margaret's train that summer she met Brandon was Anne Boleyn. Just thirteen years old, she had been sent to Margaret's court to further her education. Her stay in the Netherlands would be just the start of her continental training – and the lessons she learnt during this period would change the course of history.

Meanwhile, however, the quarrel between France and its neighbours was also being fought out on another front. And that, too, began with a gesture from the world of chivalry. France had not hesitated to demand collaboration from Scotland, its traditional ally and England's traditional enemy. The French queen, Anne of Brittany, sent James IV her glove and ring and begged him to be her champion: with Henry absent abroad, Scotland should invade across England's northern border.

James's pregnant wife, Margaret, was one Tudor who knew the difference between fantasy and reality. A later report has her asking: 'Should the letters of the queen of France – a woman . . . who ye did never nor shall ever see – prove more powerful with you than the cries of your little son and mine?'

Margaret was filled with forebodings (or so later stories reported): she dreamt of seeing James hurled over a cliff, of her jewels turning to widow's pearls. Scotland's declaration of war on England, moreover, sounded as the death knell for what she sincerely believed was her life's work: the maintenance of friendly relations between the country into which she had been born, and that into which she had wed. Her marriage had been made to seal the 1502 Treaty of Perpetual Peace between them. Now, peace and marriage were alike in jeopardy.

In England her sister-in-law Catherine of Aragon's marriage was displaying a new strength as England prepared to face down the

Scottish threat. Catherine's commission from the king had empowered her 'to fight and wage war against any of our enemies' in his absence; to summon troops, 'to station, prepare and lead them'. While she wrote coyly to Thomas Wolsey that she and her ladies were 'horribly busy' making banners and badges, she was also, more seriously, organising troops, money, artillery for the north. And though England's first wave of defence was led northwards by the veteran Earl of Surrey, Catherine was herself preparing to command one of the lines further south, despite perhaps being in the early stages of another doomed pregnancy. She may or may not actually have made the rousing speech reported for her, urging Englishmen to defend home and hearth; but there is no doubt she was wholeheartedly ready to follow in her mother Isabella's footsteps and embrace the role of warrior queen. It may have been more naturally congenial to her than that of courtly lady.

In the event, her courage was unnecessary. The Battle of Flodden on 9 September brought Scotland's army not merely defeat but annihilation by the English; and death to James IV, Margaret Tudor's husband. Catherine wrote exultantly to Henry that she thought of sending James's corpse to him as a trophy, except that 'our Englishmen's hearts would not stomach it'. Tactfully, however, after the initial brag, she was careful to make it clear she regarded the victory as belonging to her absent husband.

By late September, he was taking ship back to England in advance of his army and galloping to her at Richmond Palace for, says Hall, 'such a loving meeting that every creature rejoiced'. Catherine's star was high. But in an era deeply familiar with the concept of the Wheel of Fortune, it would have come as no surprise to contemporaries that from a position of height, the only way was down.

There were now two challenges for the English royal marriage to confront. One was political: forced to realise her father's continued manipulation of herself and her husband, Catherine, so Ferdinand's ambassador complained, had been persuaded to forget Spain, 'and everything Spanish, in order to win the English king's love and the love of the English'.

More fundamentally, the lack of children was becoming an issue. In the summer of 1514 there were reports in Europe that Henry was planning to divorce his wife because of her failure to produce an heir. They are unlikely to have been true, especially since Catherine was pregnant at the time they were recorded. But that winter, to 'the very great grief of the court', she once again lost a (premature, male) baby – because, they heard in Spain, Henry had been upbraiding her with her father's misdeeds. But an end of the once-dream marriage was evidently regarded as a possibility. And Catherine had yet another difficulty to face.

'Bessie' – Elizabeth – Blount may have caught the king's eye as early as the start of 1514, when she partnered him in a masque. This was no casual fling. Bessie – who exceeded all others in singing, dancing and 'goodly pastimes' – probably owed her place in the queen's household to her kinsman, Lord Mountjoy. She herself was a woman of some culture, who at a time when books were still a rare luxury owned, and was interested enough to make notes in, a copy of John Gower's *Confessio Amantis*. Henry's Elizabethan biographer Lord Herbert of Cherbury wrote that Bessie's 'rare ornaments of nature and education' made her 'the mistress-piece' of her time; and that the king was bound to her by 'chains of love'.

Nor did Catherine still hold quite the place she had as Henry's adviser in matters of state. The rise of Thomas Wolsey in the eighteen months after Flodden was extraordinary: archbishop of York and lord chancellor, and cardinal too. As his contemporary biographer Cavendish put it, Wolsey 'ruled all under the king'.

That 1514 peace Ferdinand and Maximilian had both struck with France had repercussions; not least on the long-agreed marriage of their joint heir Charles, and Henry VIII's younger sister Mary. The match had been in the planning for years, and Mary herself had gone as far as writing to Margaret of Austria to discuss the local fashions she should wear.

But now, Charles's wily grandfathers had proved dilatory (to the anger of teenage Charles himself, who had heard much of Mary's lively beauty). Now they hoped to break that match, and instead betroth Charles to the French king's three-year-old daughter; while the newly bereaved Louis XII himself could choose between Charles's sister and his aunt Margaret of Austria. But England, making their own peace with Louis, made the French king a more tempting offer – and so Mary Tudor, aged eighteen, was to be married to the 52-year-old Louis, who seemed far older even than his years.

It was framed as Mary's own choice. On 30 July 1514 she summoned the leading English peers to inform them she had resolved not to marry Charles, and had never had 'marital affection' towards him. She was speaking of her own sole mind 'and of her own accord' . . . It was as implausible a statement of independent judgement as when a twelve-year-old Henry had renounced his contract with Catherine of Aragon. But perhaps that very positioning – that idea that Mary's marital choices were hers to make – would have consequences in the months ahead.

Mary understood the political stakes – but she also had her own agenda. As she would later remind her brother, he wished her to marry Louis 'for the good of peace and for the furtherance of your affairs'.

> Though I understood that he was very aged and sickly, yet for the advancement of the said peace, and for the furtherance of your causes, I was contented to conform myself to the said motion, so that [as long as] if I should fortune to survive the late said king [Louis] I might with your good will marry myself at liberty without your displeasure. Whereunto, good brother, you condescended and granted, as you well know

Perhaps Henry never envisaged being held to such a promise – or had any idea of just how soon he would be called on to make good his word. But all the same, Mary's demand, and her victory, are notable.

Ferdinand and Maximilian both spoke out – perhaps with slightly forked tongues – about how disgraceful it was that 'such a fair and virtuous princess' should be tied to 'an impotent, indisposed and so malicious' a man as Louis. But the lavish arrangements, designed to flaunt the grandeur of both parties, went ahead, and in August, dressed in ash-coloured and purple satin and chequered cloth of gold, Mary underwent a proxy wedding ceremony at Greenwich, with the Duc de Longueville standing in for Louis. (Longueville's role-play extended to the bedroom, where Mary was formally undressed and ushered into bed and, after Longueville had touched her with his naked leg, the marriage was deemed to have been consummated.) The royal couple exchanged several letters, ritually expressing their married affection, their burning desire to see each other. And on 2 October – furnished, as Henry instructed his ambassadors, 'with all things appertaining to so great a princess' – Mary set sail from Dover.

She was greeted, at every town she passed, with immense public pageantry – and greeted with a private piece of make-believe, too. There might be, as a leading French courtier called Fleuranges claimed, two thousand mounted Englishmen riding with her, but her encounter with Louis was staged as a matter of romantic simplicity. Approaching Abbeville, Mary dutifully lingered while a forewarned Louis came out of the town with a hawk on his wrist so that he might meet her 'accidentally', while out hunting. Just so had James, in Scotland, met her sister Margaret.

The French king seemed enchanted with his new bride. He had reason to be: one dazzled observer described her as 'a nymph from heaven', another as 'a paradise'. And, after their wedding night, Louis claimed to 'have done marvels' in the bedroom. 'Thrice last night did he cross the river, and would have done more had he so desired.' But it may have been mere boasting; Louis's existing heir was relieved to be told that (presumably because of Louis's aged debility) 'the King and Queen cannot possibly have children'. This was the future François I, both a distant relative of Louis and his son-in-law. It might, indeed, have been François and Mary who were getting too close: his ambitious mother Louise of Savoy was warned to take care, lest François father the male baby who would supplant him.

But Mary as well as Louis put on a convincing show of marital harmony. Henry's ambassador reported that the pair shared 'as good and perfect love as ever two creatures can be'; and Charles Brandon wrote that there was 'never queen in France that demeaned herself more honourably, nor wiselier' – and as for the king, there was 'never man that set his mind more upon [woman] than he does on her, because she demeans herself so winning unto him'.

Brandon had been the other starring figure of Mary's arrival in France; he and the other leading jousters (in one report) having come to France disguised, in grey cloaks and hoods, in the best tradition of romance. They made sure the honour of England was more than upheld at the jousts to celebrate the wedding: jousts in which Mary stood alone on 'a goodly stage' to welcome the knights as they 'wondered at her beauty'. Her husband 'was feeble, and lay on a couch for weakness'.

Soon Brandon would play a more invidious role in Mary's story; but here that 'weakness' of Louis's recorded by Hall is the key. Generations of writers, both factual and of fiction, have seen Mary as wholly a victim; in fact there is every sign that she relished both the privileges and the responsibilities of queenship. But she was not to enjoy them long. The young men about town were saying that the king of England had sent a filly to the King of France to carry him swiftly to Heaven or to Hell. It proved all too accurate a prophecy. Less than three months after Mary Tudor was married, on 1 January 1515, her husband Louis was dead.

9

'mine own heart and mind'

1515–1525

TRADITION PRESCRIBED THAT the young widow went into forty days' seclusion: dressed in the white of royal mourning; secluded in a darkened chamber lit only by candlelight. Underneath the picture of mournful tranquillity, however, currents ran fast and deep.

There was a practical point to the term of forty days, more than a month. That time would tell whether or not the dowager queen was pregnant. The question was of urgent concern to Louis's existing heir, François, whose rights to the throne would be superseded by any son of Louis. No wonder he visited her daily; even that, as she would shortly write, she was persuaded to disclose to him 'the secret of my heart'. For those long days in the darkened chamber gave Mary time to consider her own desires.

Any of the men around her might now try to marry her off again, for their own political advantage. It might be her brother Henry, seeking to forge a Habsburg alliance. It might be the French, anxious to keep her dowager queen's revenues within the country. There were rumours of the Duc de Lorraine – or even of King François himself putting his wife Claude away to marry her. Wolsey – whose star was ever more in the ascendant – urgently warned Mary to give no heed to any new 'motion of marriage' that might be made to her. 'I trust the King my brother and you will not reckon in me such childhood [childishness],' she replied. She had her own ideas instead.

The promise Mary had extracted from her brother was a comprehensive one. Henry had guaranteed (she now had occasion to remind him) that in any question of her marrying again, 'you would never provoke or move me but as mine own heart and mind should be best pleased; and that wherever I should dispose myself, you would wholly be contented with the same'. And where Mary's own heart and mind took her was to none other than Charles Brandon, her brother's friend.

Brandon had been sent back to France to escort the widow home. Before he set out, Henry extracted from him a promise that he would bring Mary back unmarried. Marriage between these two had clearly been already in the air. As Mary told her brother, she had always 'been of good mind' to Brandon, 'as ye well know'. It sounds as if the idea *might* have been mooted that Henry, duly consulted, would in time give his consent ... But perhaps other, more pragmatic, concerns supervened. And Mary, probably wisely, was taking no chances.

As soon as the hapless Brandon saw Mary, she said she would be short with him [get straight to the point]; that she wished to show 'how good a lady' she was to him and how, if he did as she wished, she 'would never have none' other. A rattled Brandon wrote to Wolsey on 5 March: 'The Queen would never let me be in rest till I had granted her to be married, and so, to be plain with you, I have married her heartily and lain with her in so much I fear me she may be with child.'

The pair had not acted in isolation; nor was their marriage conducted in complete secrecy. King François had actively encouraged them. He and Brandon admired each other; and this marriage ensured Henry could not marry Mary off contrary to France's interests. But from the viewpoint of the English king it was *lèse-majesté* almost to the point of treason; and a betrayal, moreover, of his and Brandon's knightly bond. The couple made every effort to stress that Mary, not Brandon, was the prime mover: that the match had been made, as Mary wrote, 'without any request or labour on his part'.

When Brandon wrote to Wolsey that he had been driven to the altar by Mary's storm of tears ('I never saw woman weep so') it has been taken by generations of historians as evidence of her fragile femininity. That she was either a fool for love or, alternatively, a romantic heroine adrift in an unfeeling age. But recent scholarship has considered, instead, how Mary crafted her letters to produce a desired effect – as the king's beloved sister, she was never likely to suffer the same penalties Brandon might do – and how hers was almost certainly the creative voice behind missives from the comparatively unlettered Brandon, too.

Here, as in his relations with Mary's brother, Brandon can look like a man who has wandered onstage into the wrong play. Hero of the tournament he may be, but there is no sign of his having much truck with the more romantic elements of the courtly fantasy. By contrast, Mary's education in chivalry, in courtly love, had taught her how to use its tropes – the woman seeking protection, as well as the woman exercising power – to bolster her own position.

Perhaps she had learnt two lessons; one was, indeed, that in matters of the heart a woman might have agency. But another was that with the personal went the political: Guinevere's sexual choices, for better or worse, had implications for Arthur's kingdom and a knight might win a kingdom by winning its lady. There would, indeed, be concern that Brandon hoped, by marriage with Mary, to position himself as heir to the still-childless Henry. But conversely, Brandon's knightly prowess might sanction what would otherwise seem a political mismatch. While the *Journal* of Louise of Savoy, King François's mother, noted that Mary had married 'a person of low estate' – while others expressed similar disapproval – Mary's dead husband Louis had himself written to Henry that Brandon's 'virtues, manners, politeness and good condition' deserved 'even greater honour'.

Mary's letters to her brother pulled out all the stops. She urged that she had sought Brandon 'not carnally, or of any sensual appetite'. That she was afraid François would arrange another marriage abroad, and that she would never see her brother again. That François himself had been making suggestions against her honour … The picture she painted had its effect. Wolsey had written furiously to Brandon: 'Cursed be the blind affection and counsel that have brought ye to this.' He warned that Brandon was in 'the greatest danger that ever man was in'. But Wolsey, in the end, suggested Henry might be placated: by a combination of letters from the French royals and the promised handover of a large part of Mary's jewels, and her revenues as France's dowager.

On 2 May the newlyweds sailed back to England and another ceremony, a public English wedding, attended by both Henry and
Catherine. It was summer before the Venetian ambassador felt it safe
officially to congratulate Brandon (on allying himself with Henry, as
well as with Mary). But by that time it was clear Mary was once again
to be regarded as an asset to the English court, where she and Brandon
spent much of their time. At the jousts of July 1517 the king and his
followers, decked in his initial and that of the queen, competed against
Charles Brandon's side, wearing C and M, for Charles and Mary.

The role Mary resumed in courtly play was one Catherine was prob-
ably increasingly ready to cede. The two were closer to each other than
to Margaret, thanks to that decade they had spent together while
Margaret was far off in Scotland. (One letter from Mary to Henry
describes Catherine as 'my most dearest and best beloved sister' and
Margaret merely as 'my wellbeloved sister'.) But neither had forgotten
Margaret; and letters show Mary using the weight of her influence as
France's dowager to solicit protection for her sister in the turmoil of
Scottish politics.

The Battle of Flodden had not merely left Margaret a 23-year-old
widow, and a pregnant one. It had left her with the urgent problem of
trying to hold the country for her eighteen-month-old son James, now
James V. Too many of the nobles who might normally have helped her
were dead; and she was, moreover, in an invidious position: widow of
the dead Scottish king but sister of the English one whose army had
killed him. Nonetheless, the remaining quorum of the Scottish council
approved James's will, making her (subject to conditions) regent
during the minority of their son James V.

The Scottish nobles tolerated the peace with England that Margaret
managed to force through in February 1514. They supported her as, in
April, she prepared to give birth to what would prove a second son
(while Henry's continued childlessness left her line heirs to England).
That July, after she emerged from the confinement of childbirth, they
signed a joint statement of support for her role. But six weeks later, the
situation changed, dramatically.

The problem was that perennial source of Tudor dramas: matrimony. On 14 August, Margaret made a secret marriage with Archibald

Douglas, 6th Earl of Angus: an accomplished young widower of her own age, 'very lusty in the Queen's sight', in the later words of Scottish chronicler Robert Lindsay, who added that she 'thought him most able'. The Earl of Angus was an ambitious scion of the Douglas family, whose power had almost rivalled that of the crown; and nephew of Gavin Douglas the poet, or *makar*, previously mentioned; who, however, in the weeks after Flodden, had abandoned his literary pursuits to become one of Margaret's advisers.

It seems probable there was a political element to Margaret's choice of husband: the Douglases were, like her, associated with the pro-English party in Scotland. She may also have been afraid her brother would try to marry her off again for England's ends. But if it had been political security she sought, it would swiftly be shown her hopes were misguided.

Scotland's pro-French party believed much of the power onto which she clung should be in the hands of James IV's cousin, the Duke of Albany. (Margaret would at one stage suggest she had been under pressure to marry him: a suggestion all the more odd for the fact he was married already.)

All that said, however, later evidence shows that Margaret (by birth a Tudor, after all) also sought a personal element in her marriage. It had been in a second or third marriage that earlier royals like John of Gaunt had felt able to consult their own pleasure; to say nothing of Margaret's sister Mary. Were the rules different, however, for a woman? Contemporaries like Bishop Leslie, in a world that saw women as sexually voracious, grumbled that Margaret had married the Earl 'for her pleasure': lust rather than love.

Less than a fortnight after her marriage to Angus, the council demanded that Albany should be summoned from France to become Governor of Scotland in her place. (Albany's father had been exiled to France after an attempted rebellion.) Her late husband's will made her power dependent upon her not remarrying and, the lords protested virtuously, they had honoured that will: 'contrary to the ancient law and custom of this kingdom. We have suffered and obeyed her authority the whiles she herself kept her right by keeping her widowhood.' But now 'she has quit it by marrying, why should we not choose another to succeed in the place she has voluntarily left?'

Both the rash Angus and his relatives made the situation worse by physical violence against the nobles they felt were impeding them. But so did Margaret herself, by attempting to nominate her new husband as her co-regent.

The outraged nobility invited Albany to return to Scotland. Margaret's 'party-adversary', as she put it, blocked her receiving the revenues from her dower lands. As they took possession of Edinburgh Margaret and Angus sought refuge, with her all-important sons, in the security of Stirling Castle. This was civil war, with Margaret and the Douglas family isolated in Scotland, but backed by Henry VIII. The impasse was broken, in May 1515, with the arrival of Albany, who, by force of arms and the will of the council, took charge of the small James V. At the end of August Margaret retired to her own property of Linlithgow, ostensibly to give birth to the child she was carrying. Her real purpose (once the baby's father Angus had been allowed to join her) was to flee south, to the protection of her brother Henry.

Under cover of darkness, she and Angus slipped away towards the border, and it was in England, on 8 October, that the dowager queen gave birth to a daughter, Margaret Douglas. She was ill for many weeks after the delivery (too ill for anyone to dare break the news that her younger son had died). It was April 1516 before she set out for her brother's court; and then she did so 'in much heaviness'. Rather than lose all his vast Scottish lands, her husband Angus was preparing to strike a deal with Albany.

There had in the autumn of 1515 been three pregnant queens in England: Margaret of Scotland (now delivered); Mary of France, pregnant with Brandon's child; and England's Queen Catherine herself. This time the latter pregnancy would – in a sense – be successful: on 18 February 1516 Catherine was safely delivered of a daughter, another Mary.

The Venetian ambassador wrote home bluntly that the birth of a mere girl 'has proved vexatious, for never had this entire kingdom ever so anxiously desired anything as it did a prince, it appearing to every one that the state would be safe should his majesty leave an heir male, whereas, without a prince, they are of a contrary opinion'.

But Catherine of Aragon was triumphant, and Henry convinced that a living daughter was at least promise of better to come. As he told Giustinian, the Venetian ambassador: 'We are both young. If it was a daughter this time, by the grace of God the sons will follow.' Some three weeks after Catherine, Mary Tudor gave birth to a short-lived son, named Henry for his uncle.* All of May was party time, with a tournament at which Henry and his men were decked out in purple velvet, embroidered with golden roses.

Mary, with Brandon, was living as sumptuously as their shaky finances allowed. And beyond them – they were in perpetual negotiation over Mary's dower revenue from France, and their debt to Henry. But perhaps Brandon, some seven years older than his king, was beginning to find Henry's affections shared with younger 'minions' like Henry Norris and Nicholas Carew. Catherine of Aragon, meanwhile, seems to have taken the birth of her daughter as an excuse to retreat into a more private life; the Venetian ambassador said she was seen 'but seldom' over the next few years. Though still barely thirty, foreign visitors commented she was losing her looks. Her closest friends, on the 'queen's side', were now women rather older than she.

But Catherine, like Mary, was there to greet Margaret as she arrived at the English court, on the white palfrey Catherine had sent. The Scottish queen, says Hall, was 'highly feasted' – but the Venetian ambassador reported that Henry refused to acknowledge her marriage to Angus (who himself refused any invitation to come south on a visit, something that caused Margaret 'much to muse'). Wolsey took over negotiations with Albany and the Scottish lords to get Margaret safely back north again, and her finances secured.

That summer, Margaret was persuaded to return to Scotland again. Angus, with several other lords, met her at the border. With Albany back in France (where he had left a wife behind), and in no hurry to return, there was some question of the dowager queen resuming her

---

* Another son Henry, born some seven years later, also died early. Had either of the boys survived, the course of the English succession might have been very different. Since they did not, it was Mary's daughters Frances and Eleanor – born 1517 and, probably, 1519 respectively – who would be canvassed as alternative conduits of inheritance to the throne: Frances would be the mother of Lady Jane Grey.

regency. Margaret soured any chance of that by suggesting that her husband, with whom she appeared reconciled, should be her deputy governor: an idea with which other councillors were never likely to agree. But soon, Margaret had reason to be grateful for their recalcitrance. While she was in England, Angus had been living with Lady Janet Stewart of Traquair, to whom he had formerly been betrothed, and he had been doing so on the rents from Margaret's lands – Methven and Ettrick Forest. Nor was he prepared to refund the revenues he had seized, or to abandon his claim, as Margaret's husband, to enjoy her property.

Just three months after she had arrived back in Scotland, Margaret was writing to Henry begging to return to England and to separate from Angus. Henry's response was to send north a friar to impress on her the sanctity of marriage. The Scots lords agreed with English observers that she was being badly treated, with 'no promise kept to her', as Henry's representative Lord Dacre reported. But while the Scots, she complained, gave her 'nothing but fair words', Henry likewise put her feelings second. He now had every reason to prefer a pro-English Angus over a pro-French Albany as the leader of Scotland's government.

Henry and Catherine were both horrified to hear that Margaret now sought a formal separation. By October 1518 Margaret could write to her brother that she and Angus had not been together 'this half year'. 'I am so minded that, an [if] I may by the law of God and to my honour to part with him, for I wit well he loves me not, as he shows me daily.' Her son was kept apart from her; she was personally humiliated and forced to pawn her jewels and silver. In 1519 she and Angus could be seen riding into Edinburgh together, to the relief of everybody. But the rapprochement was brief. By the summer of 1520, as armed conflict broke out again, Margaret would be taking the part of her husband's enemies.

In England Catherine had her problems too, albeit of a less dramatic nature. The huge (in every sense) red-robed figure of Cardinal Wolsey was now *alter rex*, the other king. Ambassadors reported that Henry 'is away hunting, while everything here is managed by the Cardinal'; 'the King takes his pleasure and leaves to the Cardinal the whole government of the realm'. The death of Catherine's father Ferdinand, while she was awaiting the birth of her daughter in 1516, had perhaps made the need to promote a pro-Spanish policy less pressing; and when, in the summer of 1518, Wolsey negotiated the betrothal of two-year-old Mary to the infant son of the King of France, Catherine did not oppose it. She was pregnant again, but in November lost the baby. It had in any case been a mere girl. It would be her last pregnancy.

By painful contrast, in the summer of 1519, Bessie Blount gave birth to a boy. The child's name – Henry FitzRoy ('Henry, Son of the King') – made it clear the king was happy to acknowledge paternity. Here, after all, was the proof of his virility. Bessie was married off to a young man in Wolsey's household; but though the king had no further personal interest in her, he kept her son closely under his eye.

But even if Catherine was somewhat down, she was never out. The summer of 1520 saw several different pieces of diplomatic pageantry. The kings of France and England were to meet, near the English-owned French town of Calais. It was the party-of-the-century that became known as the Field of Cloth of Gold. But it was Catherine – publicly falling on her knees before Henry, and begging to see her nephew Charles – who ensured that the Anglo-French meeting would be bookended, before and after, by two meetings with Charles V, recently elected as Holy Roman Emperor and thus combining in his physically unimpressive person the might of all his grandparents: the Austria-based Holy Roman Empire; Burgundy; and Spain, with all its growing power in the New World.

Perhaps the manoeuvring around Henry's French jaunt showed both Catherine of Aragon's influence, and the limits of it. He and François had sworn a jovial oath not to cut their beards until they met. When Henry had himself shaved, 'by the queen's desire', the French king's mother pointedly asked the English ambassador whether Catherine of Aragon was enthusiastic about this meeting, or not . . . But though everyone knew the answer was 'not', she had to go through with it anyway. She had to order vast stocks of luxurious fabrics and select her best-looking ladies (as Henry's ambassador begged she should do) to make a good show.

The diplomatic encounters of that summer were to be carried out on a high note of presentation and fantasy. When Charles V and his huge retinue arrived in England and were entertained at Canterbury, one Spanish noble went so far as to swoon away at an English lady's beauty and to have to be carried out by his hands and feet. When, just a few days later, Henry and Catherine set sail for Calais, they found the French side a village of tents whose humdrum canvas was covered with silk or velvet in glowing colours, while the English boasted a *trompe l'oeil* temporary palace of real foundations topped with canvas painted to look like brick. (The four suites in the English temporary palace were for the king; the queen; Wolsey; Mary and Brandon.) Strategically placed between the two camps was a tournament ground, with a decorated artificial tree of honour on which challengers could hang their shields. Here – in jousts organised by Charles Brandon – the two enemy nations could act out their conflicts in comparative safety. King Arthur was among the worthies impersonated in the masques by the English party. Nothing was left to chance. It was the ladies of the opposite camps who feasted each king, to avoid awkward questions of precedence should the two rulers sit down to eat. When each king left his own lodging a gun fired, so the monarchs' meeting in the middle could be timed precisely. But who were the ultimate winners?

After the fabulous Field of Cloth of Gold was over, the English once again met Charles V, just along the coast at Gravelines, with his aunt Margaret of Austria. And there twenty-year-old Charles was betrothed to England's heiress, four-year-old Princess Mary.

In Scotland, Margaret Tudor was having a less festive time, making formal suit to Rome to be separated from her husband Angus. In this she was supported by Albany – to the fury of her brother, who accused Albany of 'inciting and stirring Margaret to be divorced from her lawful husband for what corrupt intent God knoweth'.

Henry and Catherine sent another friar north to describe to Margaret the 'divine ordinance of inseparable matrimony first instituted in paradise between man and woman, now for no cause to be sundered'. The suggestion was that Margaret had merely been persuaded by the evil councillors always blamed for royal misdeeds to seek an 'unlawful divorce'.*

Henry's representative in the north, Lord Dacre, wrote urgently to Margaret to the same effect, albeit in less religious and more political terms: that Angus and his Douglas kin were England's allies. But Margaret's reply to Dacre was blunt:

> As to my lord of Angus if he had desired my company or my love, he would have shown him more kindly than he hath done. For now of late, when I came to Edinburgh to him, he took my house without my consent and withholding my ferms [rents] from me . . . I had no help of his Grace my brother, nor no love of my lord of Angus and he to take my living at his pleasure and despoil. Methink my lord, ye should not think this reasonable, if ye be my friend.

She concluded significantly: 'I must cause me to please *this* realm, when I have my life here.' It was perhaps a decision every princess had to make: one Catherine had confronted when she chose her husband's interests over those of her father. And Margaret's decision went the same way. In November 1521 Albany returned to the Scotland he had left four years before, to be welcomed by Margaret with a cordiality that set the rumour mill grinding. It was now Angus's turn to flee to France.

The rumours were serious enough to rattle Dacre, who sent Henry stories that Albany might (having murdered little James V) make himself Scotland's king by marriage to Margaret. For more than two years Albany and Margaret managed to some degree to work in tandem, although Margaret was always under pressure to abandon Albany and ensure that her son was brought up with England's interest at heart.

In May 1524, however, it was Albany who would abandon Scotland, leaving never to return. Margaret now suggested her twelve-year-old

---

* In 1521 – in the teeth of a new threat to the Catholic Church by the renegade monk Martin Luther, whose attacks on its corruption were beginning to spread with alarming speed – Henry would write a defence of the sacraments, the *Assertio Septem Sacramentorum*, which caused the Pope to dub him 'Defender of the Faith'. So Margaret's tussle with one of those seven sacraments was particularly embarrassing.

son might assume the reins of government, with his mother's help. But Angus, hearing the news, broke loose from the hospitality/captivity of France and made his way to the English court.

Margaret was incensed to receive a letter from her brother announcing the arrival of Angus; 'whom we find to be your obedient, loving, and faithful servant and husband', and who wished nothing more than to return to Scotland, planning 'first to reconcile himself unto your [Margaret's] grace and favour'; and secondly to restore English influence there. Margaret huffily replied that since Angus 'hath not shown, since his departing out of Scotland, that he desired my good will and favour, neither by writing nor word', she hoped her 'dearest brother' would not ask her to compromise her own interests.

The prize the English dandled was that young King James might be allowed to marry his cousin Princess Mary, England's heir; and at one moment Margaret seemed provisionally to agree to Angus's return, though stipulating that she would not 'be familiar' with him again. The next moment she would declare her son the king would prevent his stepfather coming anywhere near her; that she would turn to France for help; that Angus's return would create 'great jealousies'.

But Margaret's moral position, as dowager queen and James's mother, was not improved by the fact that she had embarked on another relationship. An attractive young man called Henry Stewart seemed to be rising up the ranks. In September 1524 he was appointed Carver to James V, Master of the Artillery, director of Chancery . . . And this time, there was little doubt that Margaret's interest was personal, not political.

Scotland was accustomed to feuding. But the row that ensued when Angus came northwards in the autumn nonetheless caused a scandal. As Angus and his followers approached Edinburgh, Margaret closed the city gates. As they tried to scale the walls, she had the castle cannons trained on them. A pro forma deal was struck, in which both Margaret and Angus appeared to concur. But in 1525 Angus would succeed in seizing the person of his stepson, holding the young king in care or custody for the next three years.

Early in 1525 Margaret sent fresh pleas to the Pope for a divorce from Angus (on the grounds that her first husband James IV might have survived Flodden, and been still alive on her remarriage!). Her relationship with her young Stewart lover was now so open that Henry VIII told the French ambassador 'it was impossible for anyone to live a more shameful life'. The young King James (probably influenced by Angus) seemed to agree. But Henry's opinions on marital fidelity would soon look less than convincing.

South of the border, in England, the first half of the 1520s look in retrospect like the calm before the storm in the life of the royal family. Mary Tudor's marriage to Brandon seems to have been harmonious, to judge by his concern over her frequent ill health. The Anglo-Habsburg rapprochement signalled by the meetings before and after the Field of Cloth of Gold had been cemented, in January 1521, by confirmation of Charles V's betrothal to little Princess Mary, and a brooch bearing his name was pinned onto the six-year-old's dress that Valentine's Day. But however pleased Catherine was, this was less her triumph than a shift in Wolsey's foreign policy, now geared towards an invasion of France ... and Henry, of course, would soon be talking quietly of betrothing his daughter, instead, to her cousin, the Scots king.

Still, Charles made a second trip to England in the summer of 1522, and visited Winchester on his way back to the coast. Henry VIII had the table in the Great Hall of Winchester Castle repainted with the Tudor rose at its centre, and himself depicted in the place of King Arthur. He was as much in thrall to the courtly ideal as ever – and that spring had seen the pageantry of the Siege of the Château Vert, which marked Anne Boleyn's first recorded appearance at court.

Nothing happened immediately after that springtime masque – or nothing of consequence, anyway. It was possibly around then that a Boleyn entered Henry VIII's bed: this, however, was not Anne, but her elder sister Mary. Mary Boleyn had gone to France as one of Mary Tudor's attendants, stayed on, and may while there have become the mistress of François I. In 1519, however, she was back in England, to be married, in February 1520, to one William Carey. In 1522 Carey was suddenly given lands and offices, and it seems possible that this marks the start of the relationship of Carey's wife with the king. Over the next few years Mary Boleyn bore children (Catherine and Henry Carey) who may have been fathered by her husband, or by King Henry.

Queen Catherine's attention was now focused on her daughter Mary, whom Catherine – unlike, perhaps, her husband – regarded as a viable heir to England's throne. As such, Mary's education was a matter of prime importance; and while the little girl would be trained in the conventionally feminine arts, both courtly and domestic, Catherine also commissioned the Spanish-born humanist Juan Luis Vives to lay out a programme of schooling for her. But Vives's book *The Education of a Christian Woman*, published in 1523, gave some very mixed messages. On the one hand Vives (sometimes known as the father of modern psychology) did not necessarily perceive women's brains as being inferior, and did recommend a measure of classical reading; but on the other he declared they should 'know only what pertains to the fear of God'.

Vives was, however, both coherent and vehement in his condemnation of the games of courtly love: of masques and disguises, which allowed women 'to say fearlessly what they would not dare to think if they were recognised'. 'From meetings and conversations with men, love affairs arise. In the midst of pleasures, banquets, dances, laughter and self-indulgences, Venus and her son Cupid reign supreme.' To some, that would have sounded like a promise, but Vives clearly meant it as a threat.

He was even more hostile to romances. Better a young woman should lose her eyes than read those, he declared. 'In the education of women the principal and, I might say, the only concern should be the preservation of chastity.' A woman's obedience to her husband should be complete, for 'who can have respect for a man who he sees is ruled by a woman?'

These cannot have been the only lessons given to a child whose mother hoped she would reign over her country – but they must have coloured the terms in which Princess Mary perceived her own capabilities; the more so since Mary's mother Catherine was being increasingly sidelined by Wolsey. Catherine's hopes, for her daughter and perhaps herself, were pinned on Mary's future marriage to Charles V. But 1525 – a pivotal year in several ways – brought an end to that possibility.

When, at the end of February 1525, Charles scored a great victory over the French at the Battle of Pavia, taking François I captive, it looked at first like great news for Charles's friends and allies. In fact, it meant that Charles no longer needed England to keep the balance of power in Europe. Conversely, his wars had been enormously expensive, and he was in urgent need of cash. That summer, he declared that either the nine-year-old Mary, with her dowry, should be sent to Spain immediately, or he would instead marry another cousin, Isabella of Portugal, who would not only bring him nine hundred thousand golden ducats but who, at twenty-one, was mature enough to act as regent while he was away. Charles struck a peace with France. So too, separately, did Henry and Wolsey. But this time, a humiliated Henry did show signs of blaming Catherine for her family's perfidy.

In June 1525 Henry FitzRoy, the king's illegitimate son by Bessie Blount, was knighted in a hugely public ceremony attended by the leaders of the nobility. Conducted by England's two dukes, Norfolk and Suffolk (Brandon), he was created a third: the 'right high and noble prince Henry, Duke of Richmond and Somerset'. The six-year-old became Lieutenant-General of the North, Lord Admiral of all King Henry's realms (among a host of other resounding titles), and England's premier peer. The name of his dukedom was particularly suggestive: Henry VII had been Earl of Richmond before he ascended the throne. The implication of future possibilities seemed clear. (In the same ceremony, Mary Tudor's surviving son was created Earl of Lincoln.)

When Catherine spoke out against FitzRoy's elevation, three of her Spanish ladies, blamed for having encouraged her, were dismissed: 'a strong measure', noted the Venetian ambassador, 'but the Queen was obliged to submit and have patience'. The all-powerful Wolsey, who pressingly desired a French alliance, would not even allow Catherine to be alone with the new Spanish ambassador. The ambassador wrote that the queen 'will do her best to restore the old alliance between Spain and England, but though her will is good, her means are small'.

Yet the signals were unclear. Henry could still be found receiving envoys in his wife's chamber. And just weeks after FitzRoy's astonishing rise, as if to keep the balance, Princess Mary was sent to Ludlow as nominal Governor of Wales. It was the traditional training for England's heir and, as such, welcome to Catherine; but it deprived her of her daughter's company. As mother wrote to daughter: 'the long absence of the King and you troubleth me . . .'

Catherine of Aragon might at this time have found some of the Rules of Andreas Capellanus all too telling. 'If love diminishes, it soon fades and hardly ever gains strength.' And, perhaps: 'No one can be bound by two loves.'

At the end of the year Catherine would turn forty: past the usual age of childbearing. Two years earlier, indeed, she had been reported as 'beyond the ways of women'. In that summer of 1525, by contrast, Mary Boleyn was pregnant, and would next spring give birth to a boy, Henry Carey. Henry VIII was ever the serial monogamist, and to his ever-more-demanding ego it might seem as though both his wife and his mistress had abandoned him. Both politically and personally, the scene was set for another player to move centre stage.

PART III

1525–1536

Fin amor: true love, as opposed to *fals amor*, impermanent
or superficial love

Whoso list to hunt, I know where is an hind,
But for me, helas, I may no more.
The vain travail hath wearied me so sore,
I am of them that furthest come behind.
Yet may I by no means my wearied mind
Draw from the deer, but as she fleeth afore
Fainting I follow, I leave off therefore
Sithens in a net I seek to hold the wind.

Thomas Wyatt

'My Mistress and friend'

1525–1527

W HO WAS THE Anne Boleyn recently appeared at the English court? She exercises more fascination than almost any other character in English history, yet we have comparatively little evidence as to her real nature. That fact has itself enabled a huge body of fantasy to accrue to her figure.

We have few letters, and almost none that actually express her feelings. No prayers or poems such as her daughter Elizabeth wrote; no memoirs or manuals of instruction such as were authored by or on behalf of other contemporary royal ladies. In a century when royal women were beginning to express themselves with greater freedom her silence might seem baffling.

Perhaps, in the decade Anne spent in the public eye, she was simply too busy living her extraordinary life to record it; perhaps her time as queen was too brief and too contentious for her ever to let down her wary guard into something more revelatory . . . Though in fact, her few recorded comments could be inflammatory. Perhaps the truth is that most of the reported conversation we have for Anne consists of those fragments that would be weaponised against her.

The result can be to leave the much-adored, much-disputed Anne as inscrutably undifferentiated a figure as the lady in any old courtly poem. Though almost uniquely proactive in her day, she exists in posterity only to be loved or loathed; human only in certain sharp-edged aspects of what was surely a complex personality.

There are many incarnations of, and views on, Anne: many of them opposed with binary simplicity. Was she primarily a victim, destroyed for crimes she did not commit; and if so, was she also coerced into her relationship with Henry, whether by him or as pawn to the ambitious plans of her family? Was she, by contrast, the prime mover in the affair, cleverly manipulating Henry from lust into all-consuming love? 'Le temps viendra / je anne boleyn', she wrote in one of the three Books of Hours that bear her inscriptions, below a miniature of the Second Coming. 'The time will come – I, Anne Boleyn.' But was it a statement purely of religious faith; of identity; or of intent?

To see her as prime mover in her relationship with Henry offers its own binary: of an Anne either to be condemned as a heartless schemer, or admired as a quasi-modern woman daring to shape her own, ambitious destiny. Or was she a hardy crusader campaigning for a higher religious cause? One long-popular fictional story sees her as a romantic victim, hardened by the thwarting of her love for Harry Percy; but there could be another tale – alas undocumented – that sees her quite simply in love with Henry.

Today's favourite version – the feminist version – is the Anne who had ambitions of her own (with the rider: and why shouldn't she?). This, on the whole, is the one celebrated on countless social media sites, where knotty points of her life are debated with highly varying degrees of information and accuracy, and where the icons of Anne's life are celebrated in everything from cake to Christmas bauble.[*] And this version inevitably gives rise to the compelling question: what gave her the sense of entitlement that allowed her to dream so high?

We know that Anne would become a multi-faceted figure of story; indeed, that she was so even in her own century, whether to hostile Catholic commentators or Protestant propagandists. More recent fictions have seen her as a vampire and a werewolf, a time traveller and ghost. But to what stories did Anne herself listen? What were the perceptions of women's place that formed her imagination, and paved the way for her rise (and perhaps fall)? The lessons she learnt during her foreign education may offer an alternative prism through which to view her and Henry's story.

*   *   *

---

[*] This is the version, too, that sees Anne adopted by fans of Meghan Markle: another – as followers see it – bold and brave outsider done down by the royal family.

Neither the date nor the place of Anne Boleyn's birth are entirely certain, but it was likely Blickling Hall in Norfolk, and 1501. Some historians hold by a date at least five years later, but when our first clear sight of her comes in 1513, it comes from the Netherlands court whence Margaret of Austria wrote thanking Anne's father for having sent her 'so bright and pleasant' a companion; and twelve is the youngest age at which a girl was likely to take up a maid of honour's duties.

The popular perception of Anne as a girl from nowhere on the make is a mistaken one. It was the diplomatic work of her father Thomas, a rising man, that won her the foreign post; but her mother Elizabeth was born into the powerful Howard family – daughter to the 2nd Duke of Norfolk, sister to the 3rd: one of England's premier peers and a leading figure of Henry's reign.

The time of her arrival makes it likely that Anne was in Margaret's train at Tournai, where the Netherlands regent received the double-edged attentions of Charles Brandon. It represented a compelling lesson in the powerful, problematic weapon that was love. It would not be the only one. Margaret herself had extensive youthful experience of life around the courts of Europe, raised partly in France in the care of its powerful regent Anne de Beaujeu, who penned a manual of instruction for aristocratic girls. The passionate and cultured Margaret was aware of love's pleasures; but a powerful woman must be careful 'because you can be blamed even for something very slight', Anne had warned sternly.

> Suffer no man to touch your body, no matter who he is – not one in a thousand escapes without her honour being attacked or deceived, however 'good' or 'true' her love. Therefore, for the greatest certainty in such situations, I advise you to avoid all private meetings, no matter how pleasant they are

Anne would be in the Netherlands little more than a year before her father arranged for her to move to France, where Mary Tudor was newly installed as queen. But there she would take in more powerfully mixed messages.

When Mary Tudor's elderly husband Louis died, and she returned to England with Brandon, Anne stayed on at the French court for almost seven formative years, internalising its culture to the point where the French diplomat Lancelot de Carles would later write that she seemed 'a Frenchwoman born'.

Queen Claude, wife to King François who replaced Louis, was demure, slightly deformed and almost permanently pregnant: never herself a participant in the courtly dance. But she was a cultured as well as a deeply religious woman who enjoyed and commissioned romances, and employed the poet Anne de Graville as one of her ladies.* And François's court knew another powerful influence in the shape of his sister Marguerite, whom Anne Boleyn much admired.

Marguerite of Navarre, as she is best known, was an eager participant in the so-called *querelle des femmes* (the woman question), a debate running roughly from the fifteenth to the eighteenth centuries that discussed women's position in society, and whether or not it appropriately reflected their abilities. She was moreover a prolific and published author – yet her most famous work, the *Heptameron*, harps almost obsessively on the theme of women betrayed by men; of seduction or even rape taking place under courtly guise. It is possible that, as Anne Boleyn arrived at the French court, Marguerite herself was abused by one of her brother's gallants, a man called Bonnivet – France's answer to Charles Brandon. It is possible, too, that Anne received another lesson, closer to home, when her sister Mary (who had likewise been sent to join Mary Tudor's court) had a brief affair with King François, repeatedly described as 'clothed in women' – as 'young, mighty and insatiable'.

It would later be said that François ungallantly described Mary Boleyn as 'a very great whore and infamous above all'. This was, however, reported by a hostile source in 1536, when nothing about any Boleyn was too bad to say; and Mary's biographer Alison Weir argues that on this slight foundation alone has been built the image of Mary as (in twentieth-century words) the original 'good time who was had by all': seduced by the sensuality of the French court; cast off by François and passed round among his courtiers; sent back to England only to fall into King Henry's arms. On this image rests the idea of an

---

* Among Anne de Graville's works are translations of *Palamon and Arcite*, the basis for Chaucer's *The Knight's Tale*, and Alain Chartier's *La Belle Dame Sans Merci*.

Anne whose own determination to resist Henry was fuelled by observing her sister's fate.

In fact, Anne may have learnt a rather different lesson at the French court. Above the band of casual flings to which Mary Boleyn reputedly belonged sat the *maîtresse-en-titre*, the king's acknowledged and respected mistress. (Diane de Poitiers would, in François's reign, be the best-known occupant of this role; at the time of Anne's sojourn in France, it was occupied by Françoise de Foix.) It is possible that this more nuanced conception of the mistress's role opened up in Anne's mind a vista of opportunities; albeit that she would take them further than any had done before.

At the beginning of 1522, and in a climate of mounting hostility between France and England, Anne Boleyn's family summoned her home. But how much of this complicated baggage did she carry with her?

Anne was recalled because her marriage was being arranged. It was an advantageous match for her family: with her kinsman James Butler, whose disputed Irish earldom of Ormonde the Boleyns sought to claim. It is unclear why that marriage never took place; but certainly, from Anne's viewpoint, a more tempting one soon offered.

Sent to the English court, attendant on Queen Catherine, Anne met Henry Percy, heir to the great earldom of Northumberland and part of Wolsey's household. Percy

> would fall in dalliance with the Queen's maidens, being at the last more conversant with Mistress Anne Boleyn than with any other, so that there grew such a secret love between them that at length they were ensured together intending to marry.

This information comes from Wolsey's gentleman and later biographer George Cavendish, who described a contemptuous Wolsey – when the 'secret love' was discovered – lambasting the hapless Percy for his 'peevish folly' and putting an end to the couple's hopes. From this tale comes the story of Anne, whether from disappointed love or thwarted ambition, swearing that 'if it lay ever in her power, she would work the cardinal as much displeasure'.

But Anne may have had, to some degree, a third emotional involvement: with the poet Thomas Wyatt, through the prism of whose verse we come closest to a sense of her allure.

Wyatt – besides his career as courtier and diplomat – was revered as the poet who introduced the sonnet into English. He translated Petrarch but also experimented with verse forms himself, bringing the style of Italy to the spirit of England – marrying Petrarch and Chaucer, you might say. His work would be both popularised and debased by posthumous publication. *Tottel's Miscellany* (1557) slapped onto his poems titles the poet may never have approved, effectively turning them into a 'how to' lover's manual. But the real Wyatt was a deeply ambiguous poet; uncertain in his allegiances, unclear in his self-identification; exploiting the conventions of courtly love even as he complained of them. 'It is but love. Turn it to a laughter,' he wrote, in a cynical poem urging every courtier to pimp out his pretty womenfolk advantageously.

When Wyatt writes 'I' in a poem, it would be unsafe to assume that this is indeed the man born in 1503, at Allington Castle in Kent. When he writes that 'naught availeth faithfulness / To grave within your stony heart', he may indeed be complaining of a typically ungrateful courtly lady. But he may also be exploiting the convention by which apparently romantic verse could be used to voice criticisms it would have been unwise to utter more directly. He could have been writing less of an Anne-figure than of King Henry.

The nature of Thomas Wyatt's relationship with Anne Boleyn is unclear. It rests largely (though not entirely) on hindsight: on the fact he was one of the men implicated in her fall. Their childhood homes were close; but Thomas was only ten when Anne went abroad. Any intimacy more likely began only in the early 1520s, when they were both stars of Henry's court (and Wyatt had been unhappily married for several years). Peer pressure from the clever, courtly group to which both he and Anne belonged might well have forced them into at least the appearance of some sort of power couple – but did it? The only honest answer is that we are not sure.

It has often been assumed that many of Wyatt's poems were 'about' Anne, so well do they seem to fit the Anne we think we know. Anne would epitomise the kind of contradictory dazzle Petrarch had hymned, and Wyatt half recognised, half mocked:

Alas, I tread an endless maze
That seek to accord two contraries.

And though overidentification is dangerous, a few poems do give more specific reason to think of Anne. When Wyatt wrote of 'Brunet', the description is all the more suggestive for the fact that in the same short poem he first described the dark-haired girl (Anne was famously dark) as 'her that did set our country in a roar'; and then replaced the words with the less riskily specific her 'that set my wealth [estate] in such a roar'.

There may be an element of sexual suggestiveness in that poem; but another is more specific:

They flee from me that sometimes did me seek
With naked foot stalking in my chamber.
I have seen them gentle, tame, and meek
That now are wild and do not remember
That sometimes they put themselves in danger
To take bread at my hand; and now they range
Busily seeking with a continual change.
Thanked be fortune it hath been otherwise
Twenty times better, but once in special,
In thin array after a pleasant guise,
When her loose gown from her shoulders did fall
And she me caught in her arms long and small,
Therewithal sweetly did me kiss
And softly said, 'Dear heart, how like you this?'
It was no dream: I lay broad waking.
But all is turned through my gentleness
Into a strange fashion of forsaking.
And I have leave to go of her goodness
And she also to use newfangledness.
But since that I so kindly am served
I would fain know what she hath deserved.

The poem is interesting firstly for where courtly love now stood. This was not, Wyatt assures the reader, one of the dream experiences beloved of courtly literature. And it shows an element of detachment from that ideal; of protest that the forsaken poet's 'gentleness' has not met with a similar fidelity. Wyatt's biographer Nicola Shulman perceptively declares that 'a courtly lover in full plain can sound not so much heartbroken as gazumped . . . This ringing of tills is particularly loud in the poetry of Wyatt and his contemporaries.' But this perception may fit better with what courtly love had become, than as it had once been written by Chrétien de Troyes.

But *could* this poem have been about Anne? There are two stories that suggest she and Wyatt could have had a sexual relationship, though they have to be treated with extreme caution.

A piece of Catholic propaganda, circulated in the reign of Anne's daughter Elizabeth, claimed that Wyatt (according to an Italian merchant then around the court) approached the king in the early days of his relationship with Anne, and warned that she 'is not meet to be coupled with your grace, her conversation hath been so loose and base; which thing I know not so much by hear-say as by my own experience as one that have had my carnal pleasure with her'.

The Elizabethan Catholic propagandist Nicholas Sander would elaborate the same story to have Wyatt declaring Anne's looseness to the council, and Charles Brandon urging it on an incredulous king. The Spanish *Cronica del Rey Enrico Otavo de Inglaterra* is more graphic still, having Wyatt later describe how he had gone up to Anne's bedchamber to tell her of his suffering heart, with the assumption that it was her responsibility to ease the pain she had caused. 'And I went up to her as she lay in bed and kissed her, and she lay still and said nothing. I touched her breasts, and she lay still, and even when I took liberties lower down she likewise said nothing.'

Suddenly, however, she leaves the room by a secret staircase, returning an hour later in a far less yielding mood. Wyatt, in this scurrilous version, recalls the tale of a lover in a similar situation, who followed the lady only to find her in congress with a groom . . . Women *were* often seen as sexually voracious; with not only lusty widows like the Wife of Bath but even the most seemingly innocent young girl hungry for the seed that would let her empty womb bear fruit. But so crude a picture nonetheless comes from the world of the *fabliaux* rather than from that of *fin'amor*.

As with the scandal stories about Anne at the French court, this latest version is clearly propaganda; but all the Wyatt stories are highly unlikely. Not only would it have been a huge risk crossing King Henry this way, but Henry would hardly have continued his own chaste pursuit of Anne, regardless.

Another tale, however, is at once more plausible and more courtly, set down by Wyatt's grandson George who wrote *The History in Defence of Anne Boleigne* in hopes of pleasing Anne's daughter Elizabeth. It evokes memories of Brandon's dangerous play with Margaret of Austria; but also of Chaucer's *Troilus and Criseyde*, in which Troilus sees the brooch he had given Criseyde worn by her new lover and realises her infidelity.

Here Wyatt, having been struck by the new arrival at the English court and her 'witty and graceful speech', one day playfully snatched a small jewel hanging by a lace out of her pocket. The king, meanwhile (hiding his thoughts of marriage under pretence of 'an ordinary course of dalliance'), was secretly wearing Anne's ring.

When the king was playing bowls with some of his courtiers, Wyatt among them, he claimed the winning throw. Wyatt protested, at which Henry pointed meaningfully at Anne's ring on his own finger and said, smiling, 'Wyatt I tell thee it is mine.'

Wyatt, perhaps misled by the smile, said that if the king would 'give him leave to measure it, I hope it will be mine'. He pulled out the lace to measure the throw, which meant that Henry saw Anne's jewel and then kicked away the bowl in a temper. 'It may be so, but then I am deceived,' the king said.

Though all these stories walk the tightrope between fact and fiction, there may well be truth in the idea that an element of competition spurred Henry on. But to position yourself as the king's rival in love was at once glamorous and dangerous. In a court of perhaps twelve hundred people, only some two hundred of whom were women, the currents of sexual frustration were always going to run high. As the French regent Anne de Beaujeu had written some twenty years before: 'suppose a castle is beautiful and so well-guarded that it is never assailed – then it is not to be praised ... the thing most highly commended is that which has been in the fire yet cannot be scorched'. This, however, as events would prove, was inviting Anne Boleyn literally to play with fire.

Where did Anne's powerful allure lie? Not primarily in her looks. She would be described by a Venetian diplomat as not one of the handsomest women in the world: 'a swarthy complexion, long neck, wide mouth, bosom not much raised'. Unremarkable, in other words, save for her eyes, which 'are black and beautiful', and, tellingly, 'invited conversation'. Lancelot de Carles called her 'beautiful, and with an elegant figure', but others found it easier to praise her style. Anne's early biographer George Wyatt would write that she was 'in beauty inferior' to many at court, 'but for behaviour manners, attire & tongue she excelled them all'.

Nicholas Sander's description of her as 'rather tall of stature, with black hair, and an oval face with a sallow complexion, as if troubled with jaundice' in some ways echoes that of the Venetian. But Sander continues with what is surely fiction. 'She had a projecting tooth under the upper lip, and on her right hand six fingers. There was a large wen under her chin'. George Wyatt too would mention that Anne had a vestigial sixth fingernail; a sixth finger, however, could be the sign of a witch. A minor deformity is said also to have inspired in her a taste for long, hanging sleeves. Legend credits these sleeves with inspiring the song 'Greensleeves', that lament addressed to a fashionably cruel lady, written anonymously but sometimes attributed to King Henry (though in fact the musical style probably places it later in the sixteenth century):

> Alas my love you do me wrong
> To cast me off discourteously;
> And I have loved you so long
> Delighting in your company.

Even the hostile Sander goes on to describe Anne as 'handsome to look at, with a pretty mouth, amusing in her ways, playing well on the lute, and was a good dancer. She was the model and the mirror of those who were at court . . .' Here, surely, was the key.

*   *   *

It is unclear precisely when Henry's interest in Anne began; during the latter part of 1525 (when her sister Mary fell pregnant), or during 1526. At the Shrovetide jousts in February 1526, Henry rode under the device 'Declare I dare not', which has often been seen as an approach to Anne; but at the banquet which followed, in his capacity of courtly admirer as well as loyal husband, he waited on Catherine. It is possible – probable – that his first plan was simply to use Anne to replace her sister Mary in his bed. If so, the surprising thing seems to have been how quickly his goal changed. But to trace the relationship with any certainty is impossible.

Seventeen letters from Henry VIII to Anne Boleyn survive, written during their courtship, and preserved in the unlikely setting of the Vatican archive, where they were presumably taken by a spy. Anne's replies are missing, along with the insight they might have given us into her personality.[*]

Henry's letters are all undated (and only a few can be placed by reference to external events): a common problem, but here more than usually vexatious. Without dates, it is hard to be sure – eyeing Henry's desire for Anne and his desire to be rid of Catherine – which was the chicken and which the egg. There are as many different chronologies suggested as there are historians – but tonally and perhaps chronologically the bulk of the letters seem to fall into three distinct phases.

The first and by far the largest group of letters – mostly written in French – are exercises in the rhetoric of courtly love. This was an important arena and one in which Henry – pleased to have found so discriminating an audience – was delighted to display his prowess. When Troilus was first described to Chaucer's Criseyde, one of her first questions was: 'can he speak well of love?' So in one early letter

---

[*] Two letters have in the past sometimes been printed as written from Anne to Henry, and one pre-dates their marriage: thanking Henry in the most effulgent terms for the warrant of maid of honour to Queen Catherine, and expressing 'the joy that I feel in being loved by a king whom I adore'. But there is a huge question mark over it; as over the second, discussed in the next chapter. It was published, in Italian, by the seventeenth-century historian Gregorio Leti, who claimed while in England to have seen the original: since, suspiciously, lost. Translation from English to Italian and back again means no certain conclusion can safely be drawn from its style, but its authenticity seems unlikely.

Henry chides 'my mistress' with having failed to write as she promised; yet 'to acquit myself of the duty of a true servant' he nonetheless writes, and sends her a buck (hart – heart) 'killed late last night by my own hand, hoping that when you eat it you may think of the hunter'. The letter is 'written by the hand of your servant, who very often wishes for you instead of your brother'. Her brother George and other members of Anne's family were clearly representing Anne's interests at court. With every desire to promote the relationship, they would continue to feature in the correspondence: with Henry once grumbling that her father Thomas was being too slow 'to do the lover's turn'.

Another letter addresses the supposed abasement of the courtly lover before his mistress more directly: 'Although it doth not appertain to a gentleman to take his lady in place of a servant, nevertheless, in compliance with your desires, I willingly grant it to you . . .' Anne had evidently – and reasonably – protested that the real difference in their rank belied the courtly ideal. Would Anne's letters, if we had them, show her as in some ways courting Henry? Even Henry's male servants used the language of love to their monarch. 'There was never lover more desirous of the sight of his lady than I am of your most noble and royal person,' Wolsey once wrote.

Anne, in the early stages of Henry's courtship, withdrew herself, presumably to the family home of Hever Castle in Kent. It has often been assumed this was a tactical withdrawal, designed to inflame the king's passion but it may, instead, have been a genuine attempt to escape so problematic a wooing. Henry (who signs himself off as 'your entire servant') expresses concern that:

> since my parting from you, I have been told . . . that you would not come to court either with your mother, if you could, or in any other manner; which report, if true, I cannot sufficiently marvel at, because I am sure that I have since never done anything to offend you, and it seems a very poor return for the great love which I bear you to keep me at a distance both from the speech* and the person of the woman that I esteem most in the world.

---

* *Parrolle*, in the original French, carries a sense of discourse or teaching.

If Anne felt as much love for him, surely the distance between them would be 'a little irksome' also to her . . . 'though this does not belong so much to the mistress as to the servant', Henry adds, tardily recalling the rules of the game.

In Henry's early letters, the ritual humility of the courtly lover runs side by side with the conscious status of the king. In another letter – addressed to 'My Mistress and friend', and signed 'from the hand of your loyal servant and friend, H.R.' – Henry may declare that 'my heart and I surrender ourselves into your hands'. But he grumbles (several times) that 'it would be a great pity to increase our pain', of which Anne's absence already produces 'enough and more than I could ever have thought could be felt'. Henry was in love – so deep in love, an ambassador would write later, as to be unable to see clearly. But one suspects that so far, for all the talk of pain, he was rather enjoying his enthralment; or, at least, not viewing it as something to affect the main course of his life.

Henry's view of Anne, and her place in that life, may have shifted in stages. One letter is particularly interesting in this context.

> Debating with myself the contents of your letter, I have put myself in great distress, not knowing how to interpret them . . . praying you with all my heart that you will expressly certify me of your whole mind concerning the love between us two.

He has been now 'above one whole year struck with the dart of love, not being assured either of failure or of finding place in your heart and grounded affection'.

It is the last point, he says, that prevents him 'from calling you my mistress, since if you do not love me in a way which is beyond common affection that name in no wise belongs to you, for it denotes a singular love, far removed from the common'.

> If it shall please you to do me the office of a true, loyal mistress and friend and to give yourself up, body and soul, to me . . . I promise you that not only shall the name be given you, but that also I will take you for my only mistress, rejecting from thought and affection all others save yourself, to serve only you.

The letter was 'Written by the hand of him who would willingly remain yours'; and the first point was often stressed: Henry usually avoided the messy manual labour of putting pen to paper himself.

We cannot, as always, be certain precisely when this letter was written, but surely sometime between the latter months of 1526 and the summer of 1527. By this time Henry had thought of seeking a degree of nullity for his marriage to Catherine; there was, however, as yet no suggestion that this was to free him for a marriage to Anne.

Through the course of 1526 Catherine became ever more isolated at court. Henry's letters to Anne probably began later that year. But (though the double sense of mistress is of course confusing) Henry seems in the letter above to be offering Anne the position not of wife, but of *maîtresse-en-titre*; better than the position Mary Boleyn had held, but still problematic. But the last letter in this group suggests things were getting ever more serious.

At some point in 1527 Anne Boleyn sent Henry VIII a gift, a jewel, encompassing a 'fine diamond' and the image probably cast in silver of a 'ship in which the solitary damsel is tossed about'. Henry's enthusiasm dwelt less on the jewel's beauty than on the 'fine interpretation and the too humble submission' that came with it. Submission to what, precisely? To Henry's passion, to a proposal of marriage? Or, crucially, to Anne's own feelings? Was that what produced the ecstasy of a Henry 'who in heart, body, and will, is / Your loyal and most assured servant'?

The damsel was clearly Anne, Henry presumably her refuge from the stormy seas. Perhaps the unyielding diamond is the steadfast heart: Henry would sign several of his letters with a heart drawn around Anne's initials. But the literature of courtly love had repeatedly made a connection between seasickness and love sickness: Wyatt translated one of Petrarch's *canzoni* which publisher Richard Tottel would later gloss as 'the love compareth his state to a ship in a perilous storm tossed on the sea'. Was Anne indicating that she was now the lover – that she had fallen in love with Henry?

As Henry enthused: 'The demonstrations of your affection are such, the beautiful mottoes of the letter so cordially expressed, that they oblige me for ever to honour, love, and serve you sincerely, beseeching you to continue in the same firm and constant purpose.' If she does, Henry will 'surpass it rather than make it reciprocal'.

And as lust in courtly guise developed ever further into an overwhelming love, another element was entering the picture: the equation of a personal, a courtly, passion with religious fervour. If the king had in any way offended Anne, he begged 'that you would give me the same absolution that you ask, assuring you, that henceforward my heart shall be dedicated to you alone. I wish my person was so too. God can do it, if He pleases, to whom I pray every day . . .' The courtly lady was supposed to lead by moral example.

In another of Wyatt's poems, the one quoted at the top of this section, which pictures the poet as hunter and the woman as the hart (heart), the elusive quarry, the references are complex:

Whoso list to hunt, I put him out of doubt,
As well as I may spend his time in vain.
And graven with diamonds in letters plain
There is written her fair neck round about:
'Noli me tangere, for Caesar's I am,
And wild for to hold, though I seem tame.'

The penultimate line reflects both the words of the risen Christ to Mary Magdalene and the suggestion of rendering unto Caesar what is Caesar's – which inevitably allies Henry's claim to Anne with his claim to sovereignty over what would soon become the English Church. But there are other evocations, too. The deer in the wood was a quasi-mystical beast in both folklore and Christian writing: often a guide for the human wanderer. And, 'Gwenhwyfar of the deer's glance', Guinevere had been called, in a twelfth-century Welsh poem.

One way and another, when Henry hailed Anne Boleyn as his new partner in the game of *amor purus* – the game of love that was itself supposed to make the lovers more virtuous – he could feel himself part of a long and honourable tradition, and proceed with a conscience burnished as a shield.

11

'our desired end'

1527–1533

ENRY HAD NOW determined to move. Around Easter
1527 he informed Wolsey he had serious 'scruples' about his
marriage to Catherine of Aragon. But this was the king, who
could do no wrong; in his own eyes, never mind those of the world. It
was, accordingly, Wolsey who in May summoned Henry VIII to appear
before an ecclesiastical court, to discuss matters affecting the 'tranquillity of consciences'.

Wolsey had recently sponsored the Treaty of Westminster between
England and France against Catherine's nephew Charles V. But he had
probably as yet no idea that it might not be sealed, once Henry was
freed, by the king's marriage to a French princess.

The court was held at Wolsey's residence and, officially, in secrecy. But
Charles V's ambassador was sending reports from the first day; and
Catherine too knew that the first official salvo had been fired in a long
war of attrition. 'Spanish ladies spy well', as Anne's kinsman Francis Bryan
once said. The Imperial ambassador told Charles V that though the
queen maintained a discreet silence, 'all her hope rests, after God, on your
imperial highness'. And Charles would – without even any very active
involvement – remain the strongest weapon in Catherine's armoury.

The debate before the cardinal – Henry's qualms – focused first on
biblical interpretation. The book of Leviticus warns that: 'If a man shall
take his brother's wife, it is an unclean thing: he has uncovered his
brother's nakedness. They shall be childless' – which, in Henry's terms,
meant without male child.

Under debate also was the validity of the original dispensation granted for Henry to marry Catherine; and by implication the then-Pope's right to grant it. But this was a political as well as a religious issue: and politics was about to intervene in a dramatic way.

On the Italian peninsula, where Charles V had long been attempting to pursue his territorial claims, some thirty thousand of his troops, many of them unpaid German mercenaries, had been advancing steadily southwards into the Papal States. On 6 May (though the English would not know it for several weeks) the furious soldiers surged into Rome itself, committing what Charles's own horrified envoy described as 'unparalleled atrocities', and forcing the Pope to flee.

It has been estimated that, during ten days of hell, as many as twenty thousand died; but the political upshot was that Charles had the Pope at his mercy . . . Which made it very unlikely Henry would get papal authority to proceed against Charles's aunt. When the news arrived in England, Wolsey's inquiry was abruptly broken off.

On 22 June Henry VIII at last confronted Catherine directly, and told her he wanted an annulment. He seems to have been positively taken aback by her storm of tears: perhaps the way their relationship had morphed from courtly to quasi-mother-and-son had led him to expect she would see things his way. Catherine's reaction was to deny that her marriage with Arthur had been consummated; and this would remain the core of her case. In the investigations ahead, hearsay from twenty years before would be hauled out into the light of day, as Tudor courtiers (Charles Brandon prominent among them) dutifully recollected everything Arthur had said that post-wedding day.

In fact, no one can be certain whether her marriage to Arthur was consummated: the participants themselves included, maybe. Catherine was capable of fudging facts in what she undoubtedly saw as a good cause; but it is entirely possible that a measure of sexual interaction took place which could or could not be considered full consummation.

To add to the confusion, Catherine would continue for another four years after this confrontation officially to retain her place as queen, and her queen's apartments, where, according to Cavendish, she would sometimes detain Anne, in order 'that the King might have the less her company'. Thence comes the famous story of the card game which saw Anne, as Catherine pointedly said, 'have the good hap [luck] to stop at a king, but you are not like the others, you will have all or none'. It was an accurate summation of Anne's personality. Catherine clearly knew her enemy.

That Henry VIII and Anne Boleyn had agreed to marry is clear from the terms in which, in September 1527, a dispensation was requested from Rome. It did not name Anne, but it did pointedly seek permission for Henry to marry a woman 'in any degree [of affinity], even the first, arising from illicit intercourse [ex illicito coito]'. The Latin has variously been translated as referring to Anne's sister Mary – or to Anne herself. It is possible that Henry and Anne did have sexual relations at the beginning of their affair; more interesting is why, and how, they decided to stop.

The traditional picture sees Anne holding Henry at bay, the better to increase her market value: just as Elizabeth Woodville had held off Edward IV. One of Andreas Capellanus's Rules decreed that love easily obtained is of little value (Book Two, Rule 14: 'An easy conquest makes love cheaply regarded: a difficult one causes it to be held dear.')* And indeed, the idea of Anne as Henry's mistress in the courtly sense would be all the stronger if it were she who refused to become his mistress in the sexual one.

But the request to Rome suggests a different scenario. During the summer of 1527 Henry decided that Anne might be not only the object of his private passion, but his wife, and mother of his son. In which case, it was essential that any child they conceived should be a legitimate one. To make things easier, the theory of courtly practice (and Anne and Henry were both people who lived by theories) sanctioned a certain level of physical intimacy. And restraint would be the easier for what would at the time have seemed the obvious assumption that they would be able to marry soon.

---

* As Freud put it: 'An obstacle is required in order to heighten libido; and where natural resistances to satisfaction have not been sufficient men have at all times erected conventional ones so as to be able to enjoy love.'

In September 1527 Wolsey, returning from a mission abroad, found himself summoned by Anne into the king's presence – a sign of how power was shifting. In October Henry asked Thomas More his opinion on that passage in Leviticus; in November he invited a number of scholars to Hampton Court. Wolsey's pressure on the Pope persuaded the latter to issue permission for Henry to marry Anne if his marriage to Catherine were once dissolved, albeit that it failed to say how that dissolution might be attained.

A letter to Anne – written in English, unlike the courtly French of the first group – conveys Henry's sense of a goal ahead, and perhaps of a new intimacy. 'As touching our other affair, I assure you there can be no more done, nor more diligence used, nor all manner of dangers both foreseen and provided for, so that I trust it shall be hereafter to both our comforts . . . thus for lack of time, darling, I make an end of my letter . . .'

Their relationship was now an open secret. The French envoy that winter reported from Greenwich – where Wolsey's good offices secured Anne apartments close to Henry – that: 'Open house is kept by both the King and Queen, as it used to be in former years. Mademoiselle de Boulan is also there, having her establishment apart, as I imagine, she does not like to meet with the Queen.'

Anne needed now to appear the unobtainable lady to others than just Henry. In February 1528 new envoys were sent to Rome, with instruction to call, on their way, on Anne, who had withdrawn herself to Hever. A letter from Wolsey (now enlisted to the cause) would declare that: 'the approved, excellent virtuous [qualities] of the said gentlewoman, the purity of her life, her constant virginity, her maidenly and womanly pudicicity, her soberness, chasteness, meekness, humility, wisdom . . . be the grounds on which the King's desire is founded.' A Book of Hours now at Hever is graffitied with an exchange of jingles between Henry and Anne. Anne's ditty:

Remember me when you do pray
That hope doth lead from day to day

is written opposite an image of the coronation of the Virgin. Another Book of Hours belonging to her contains an exchange of verses with Henry. Anne's was written below an image of the Annunciation:

By daily proof you shall me find
To be to you both loving and kind

Implicit promise that her 'kindness' will bear fruit – Anne too will deliver a son – but linking her also with Mary's virginity.

As Henry wrote: 'Darling, these shall be only to advertise you that this bearer and his fellow be despatched with as many things to compass our matter, and to bring it to pass as our wits could imagine or devise; which brought to pass, as I trust, by their diligence, it shall be shortly, you and I shall have our desired end . . .' It seemed a reasonable hope that things were moving ahead.

Margaret Tudor in Scotland had, after all, early in 1527 finally been granted the annulment of *her* marriage to Angus, on the grounds of his pre-contract to Lady Janet Douglas. The following spring she married her lover Henry Stewart. Her brother, somewhat ironically, wrote ordering her to: 'Relinquish the adulterous company of him that is not, nor may not be, of right, your husband.'

Angus, still in control of the young King James V, succeeded in getting Stewart hauled out of Stirling Castle, where the newly married couple had fled, and clapped in prison. But in that summer of 1528 James escaped Angus's custody to begin his personal rule, aged sixteen, and celebrated by creating Stewart Lord Methven 'for the great love that he bore to his dearest mother'. (It would be as late as 1529 that Charles Brandon – the first of whose previous discarded wives was still living when he married Mary Tudor more than a decade before – received final confirmation of a Bull declaring the children of his marriage to the dowager queen unquestionably legitimate.)

But in the summer of 1528 it looked briefly as though events might overtake Anne and Henry; and those events give us a third group of letters, which can be dated. The sweating sickness broke out with dreadful virulence, sending Henry and Catherine to the comparative safety of the country, and Anne to Hever. One letter reflects Henry's concern about her health; something she had said 'disturbed and alarmed me exceedingly'. (He ended by saying that 'I wish you in my arms, that I might a little dispel your unreasonable thoughts': had she objected to being sent away?) The next letter reported with horror that he had in the night received 'the most afflicting news that could have arrived . . . the illness of my mistress, whom I esteem more than all the world, and whose health I desire as I desire my own, so that I would gladly bear half your illness to make you well.' Anne had indeed fallen ill but – under the ministrations of the physician sent by Henry – survived. A letter to 'mine own darling' lamented her absence, but urged her to follow her instincts as to how long she should recuperate at Hever: 'you know best what air doth best with you'.

And there was more news, by which to date more letters. The Pope had been persuaded to send a legate, Cardinal Campeggio, to look into the royal marriage; and Henry's missives to Anne impatiently pace his journey. In one: 'the legate whom we most desire arrived at Paris this Sunday or Monday last past'. Henry trusted soon 'to enjoy that which I have so long longed for, to God's pleasure, and both our comforts'. In fact, the gout-stricken Campeggio arrived in October, ill, which caused further delay. Reporting 'the unfeigned sickness of this well-willing legate', the king was relieved at Anne's 'conformableness' – 'and of the suppressing of your inutile and vain thoughts with the bridle of reason'. He urged that his 'good sweetheart' should display the same reason in all her doings hereafter. Was the strain beginning to show?

Two other letters may likewise suggest the relationship was chang-ing. In one, the king makes a point of sending her 'some flesh, repre-senting my name, which is hart flesh for Henry', wishing they 'were together of an evening'. This may tentatively be dated to 1528 by a reference to Anne's sister's trouble: Mary's husband William Carey died from the outbreak of sweating sickness that summer, the outbreak Anne had survived.

In another, undateable, letter Henry writes to tell Anne of 'the great elengesse' – loneliness? – he felt since she went away. 'I think your kindness and my fervency of love causeth it; for otherwise, I would not have thought it possible that for so little a while [that so short a time since her departure] it should have grieved me.' He writes only briefly because of 'some pain in my head' – clearly they were past the stage of wishing to appear perfect to each other – and wishes himself 'in my sweetheart's arms, whose pretty dukkys I trust shortly to kiss'. 'Dukkys' was slang for breasts. But the physical closeness is not the only significant thing. The letter's sign-off is a statement of intent:

'Written by the hand of him that was, is, and shall be yours by his own will.'

The idea urged on Catherine by everybody, from Campeggio down, was that she might honourably retire to a nunnery. Henry would then be free to marry again since Catherine might be regarded as dead to the world. (And, crucially, their daughter Mary might still be regarded as legitimate, her place in the succession unaffected.) The cardinal cited the example of the first wife of Louis XII: 'a queen in France who did the same and is still honoured by God and that kingdom'. He suggested this solution would appeal to Catherine's 'prudence'. But Catherine saw her situation – her crusade – in personal as well as prudential terms.

She surely regarded it as her duty to protect her husband from Anne's pernicious influence; and her husband's country from the heretical beliefs making their way across Europe. She had been raised all her life to regard her destiny as that of Queen of England. She had, in youth, had a long and disagreeable experience of life in an anomalous position between wife and widow, and she had no wish to experience it again.

But perhaps, too, Henry had made a rod for his own back. If he had never made his marriage to Catherine so personal – if it had been the usual working partnership between nations, thrust together into a brief alliance just as the married strangers were thrust together into the nuptial bed – perhaps Catherine would have reacted differently.

The next day Catherine saw Henry to demand some more 'indifferent' [impartial] counsel than she could find in England. To Campeggio, she declared 'on her conscience' that her marriage to Arthur had left her a virgin, and that they could tear her 'limb from limb' before she altered her intention 'to live and die in the estate of matrimony'. She had, moreover, a weapon in her hands, in the shape of a document found among the papers of the late Spanish ambassador: a copy of the one the then-Pope had sent to Ferdinand and Isabella sanctioning Catherine's marriage to Henry, whether or not she had slept with Arthur; in which, declared Charles V's current envoy, 'consists the whole of the Queen's right'.

On 31 May 1529 Campeggio's summons went out. King and queen should make their first formal appearance at a legatine court at

London's Blackfriars monastery on Friday 18 June. This was to be presented wholly in terms of the king's conscience, his concern not from 'any carnal concupiscence, nor for any displeasure or dislike of the queen's person, or age'.

While Henry sent proxies, Catherine herself unexpectedly made an entrance surrounded by advisers, four bishops and a swarm of her ladies. 'Sadly and with great gravity' she read an appeal that she had recorded and had notarised two days before – an appeal that her case would be heard in Rome, and not be subject to the dubious mercy of an English court.

This appeal would be rejected by Campeggio and Wolsey – but when, a few days later, she and her husband met in court, it was clear Catherine had become a true Tudor in her ability to use dramatic tropes. Rising from her seat, she crossed the floor to kneel at her husband's feet. 'Sir, I beseech you for all the love that hath been between us, and for the love of God, let me have justice.'

> Take of me some pity and compassion, for I am a poor woman and a stranger born out of your dominion. I have here no assured friends, and much less impartial counsel. Alas! Sir, wherein have I offended you, or what occasion of displeasure have I deserved? I have been to you a true, humble and obedient wife, ever conformable to your will and pleasure . . . I never grudged in word or countenance, or showed a visage or spark of discontent.

She had borne the king 'divers children, although it hath pleased God to call them out of this world'.

> When ye had me at the first, I take God to be my judge, I was a true maid without touch of man. And whether it be true or no, I put it to your conscience.
>
> If there be any just cause by the law that ye can allege against me, either of dishonesty or any other impediment to banish and put me from you, I am well content to depart to my great shame and dishonour. And if there be none, then here, I most lowly beseech you, let me remain in my former estate.

As she finished her peroration she rose off the knees from which Henry had twice tried to raise her, made a low curtsey, and moved towards the door. Though the crier called her back, she moved on: 'it is no indifferent court for me, therefore I will not tarry.'

Catherine had presented herself as much a lady-in-distress as any of the done-down demoiselles who appeared at Arthur's court. But there was a sharp point under the pathos: Henry and his ministers should consider the reputation 'of her nation and her relatives'.

And in effect, she won. On 23 July, the day the cardinals were to have given their verdict, Campeggio, instead, formally referred the case to Rome. The result would be a tussle of authority between King and Pope that would shape England's destiny for centuries.

Anne had no doubt who to blame for the difficulties: Catherine herself. When, that autumn, Henry was unwise enough to be lured into direct confrontation with his wife, Anne (so Charles V's new ambassador Eustace Chapuys reported) lashed out with the hysteria of insecurity. 'Did I not tell you that whenever you disputed with the Queen she was sure to have the upper hand? I see that some fine morning you will succumb to her reasoning and that you will cast me off . . . alas! Farewell to my time and youth spent to no purpose at all.'

Catherine had one new ally close at hand: the ardent partisanship of the diplomat and humanist Chapuys would be a support to Catherine for the rest of her days (and, after her death, to her daughter Mary). But though she had won the battle, the forces ranged against her were varied enough to ensure she could not win the war.

If evidence were needed of how serious matters had grown, it could be found in the fate of Cardinal Wolsey, who, having failed to deliver for Henry, lamented that 'none dare speak to the King on his part for fear of Madame Anne's displeasure'. In the autumn that followed the Blackfriars hearing, Henry's once-almighty minister was charged with *praemunire* (asserting the Pope's authority over that of the king) and stripped of his government offices, his powers and his properties. Forced to retreat to York, of which he was still archbishop, failing to garner support from the foreign allies who had once been happy to make use of him, his ruin, the Venetians reported, 'may be said to exceed his late fame and elevation'. The following October, arrested and brought southwards, Wolsey died on the journey to London.

There had at this stage – still little more than a decade after Martin Luther first nailed his criticism of papal practice to a church door – been no overt suggestion that the alliance of Henry and Anne was tied to a break with Rome. After all, to invoke the Pope's judgement, as had been done at Blackfriars, was implicitly to acknowledge his authority. But now, with Rome seemingly recalcitrant over 'the King's Great Matter', things were about to change.

It would at all times be impossible to disentangle personal or political ambition from religious passion, and both would be inextricably bound up in Anne's story. On 3 November 1529 Henry opened what would come to be known as the Reformation Parliament which, over more than five years, would debate the position of the king in relation to his Church. A month later Thomas Boleyn was made Earl of Wiltshire, and at the banquet which followed the ceremony, his daughter Anne was given precedence over all other ladies (even the king's sister Mary).

One of the few things we do know for sure about Anne Boleyn is the importance of her religious convictions. But it can be hard after almost five hundred years of a Protestant England to distinguish Anne's effect from her intent. Chapuys would excitably declare that the Boleyns were 'more Lutheran than Luther himself', and in the reign of Anne's daughter *Foxe's Book of Martyrs* would portray her as a Protestant heroine (an early example of her transformation into story).

But a number of great ladies had been interested in the reform – with a small 'r' – of abuses in the Catholic Church while remaining its loyal daughters (just as great ladies had once also been promoters of the Cathar creed). Prominent among their number – seeking a more spiritual and less ritualistic model of Christianity than had been coming out of Rome – was François I's sister Marguerite of Navarre. Her writings would, in the early 1530s, be condemned as heretical, but Marguerite would in the end reaffirm her ultimate loyalty to the Catholic Church. Indeed, the crusading fervour with which Anne would prosecute what she saw as corrupt or detrimental practices should not obscure the fact that she practised her faith according to Catholic form to the end of her life.

Yet it was Anne who, even before the Blackfriars showdown, presented Henry VIII with useful passages in an illicit book, *The Obedience of the Christian Man and How Christian Rulers Ought to Govern*, published by the exiled William Tyndale. Questions of religion might combine with those of politics and practicality, for the book queried whether the Pope should be regarded as the ultimate religious authority in every land. It suggested instead that the subject was accountable to the ruler, and the ruler to God alone.

Anne had used a courtly game with one of her ladies to bring the forbidden work to Henry's attention while allowing him to think he had discovered it for himself. She lent it to her gentlewoman, whose lover snatched it from her 'among other love tricks', and read it publicly enough to get it confiscated and handed to Wolsey, which allowed Anne to go to Henry and complain . . . Her efforts paid off. 'This book is for me and all kings to read,' Henry said.

Soon after the hearing at Blackfriars the Cambridge scholar Thomas Cranmer was introduced at court, having made the useful suggestion that the universities of Europe should be canvassed on whether there was any theological backing for the Pope's right to dictate to princes. Through the spring of 1530 one institution after another – Paris, Orléans, Bologna – gave Henry the answer he wanted. In June he was handed the *Collectanea Satis Copiosa*, a compendium of biblical and historical material confirming that the Pope was not necessarily supreme. Charles V's horrified ambassador Chapuys warned that if 'the Earl [of Wiltshire] and his daughter' – Anne Boleyn and her father – remained in power, they would 'entirely alienate this kingdom from its allegiance to the Pope'.

The words intended as an indictment were in fact prophetic. In February 1531 Henry VIII demanded that the Church authorities recognise him as 'sole protector and supreme head of the English church and clergy'. Anne Boleyn, Chapuys reported, made 'such demonstrations of joy as if she had actually gained Paradise'.

The question of religious reform tied into Henry VIII's desire for – conviction that he was entitled to – an empire of the sort King Arthur once had. In January 1531 the Duke of Norfolk defended the king's actions to Chapuys on the grounds of Arthur's precedent: Arthur, whose seal (Norfolk said) described him as '*Britanniae, Galliae, Germaniae, Daciae Imperator*': emperor of Britain, Gaul, Germany and territories east. (The ambassador sniffed that it was a pity they hadn't called him Emperor of Asia as well.)

The latest developments of Henry's reign had given him a fresh reason to cast himself as Arthur's heir, for had not Arthur defeated the Roman Empire? This victory was a frequent element in the Arthurian story (albeit one of which we've rather lost sight today), but Malory had given it a new prominence in his version of the tale; linking it, moreover, to the more recent victory of Henry V. The humanist scholars had been inclined to dismiss the Arthurian legends beloved of earlier chroniclers: Polydore Vergil, whose *Anglica Historia* was finally published in 1534, discounted all but the very barest bones of the Arthurian story. (And in the years ahead they would find little favour with the new Protestant moralists: Roger Ascham, Elizabeth I's tutor, would complain that in Malory's *Morte*, the noblest knights were considered to be those who 'commit foulest adulteries by subtlest shifts'.) But over the next few years the antiquary John Leland, patronised by the king himself, wrote several angry refutations of Vergil's dismissal.

On the political weight of Henry's break with Rome, however, the messages continued to be mixed. In January 1531 Chapuys, who hated her, nonetheless described Anne as 'braver than a lion' in speaking openly of her contempt for the Spanish queen. Yet in that spring of 1531, even as Henry was declaring his religious supremacy, Catherine's daughter was brought to court and shown off by her proud father. The ambassadors of her Habsburg relatives were reassured to feel that Henry would not proceed to any extremity.

At the end of May 1531 another attempt was made at persuading Catherine of Aragon to go quietly. Made – and failed. One of the nobles sent to persuade her was Charles Brandon, Duke of Suffolk, who, as a king's man, had supported Henry's attempt to assert his own authority but whose wife, the former French queen, was wholly on Catherine's side. Indeed, the Suffolks displayed a hostility towards Anne Boleyn marked enough to make a breach between royal brother and sister. This fight would get dirty: while Brandon sought to rake up stories about Anne's earlier life, she accused him of having 'criminal intercourse' with one of his daughters by a former marriage.

Catherine still officially retained her place as queen, moving around the country at the king's side, even though Anne might also be one of the party. Early in July 1531 they were all three at Windsor. But on the 14th Henry and Anne rode away to hunt at Chertsey Abbey, with Catherine ordered to remain behind. As summer drew to an end, she was sent away to the More in Hertfordshire, while her daughter Mary was ordered to Richmond. They would never be allowed to live together again.

Christmas saw Anne with Henry at Greenwich, lodged in the queen's apartments and attended by a great train of ladies. Henry returned the gift Catherine sent him but delightedly accepted the set of ornate foreign boar spears from Anne. He gave her in return a room hung with cloth of gold and silver. But 'all men', Edward Hall recorded, declared there was 'no mirth' with Catherine and her ladies absent.

The following spring, May 1532, England's clergy formally submitted to Henry as head of their Church. The submission was delivered up to the king by a former servant of Wolsey's who, with this ultimate proof of usefulness, seemed ready to step into his old master's shoes. His name was Thomas Cromwell. (In 1534 Cromwell would be appointed the king's principal secretary, and Chapuys would write that he had 'risen above everyone, except it be the Lady [Anne] . . . Now there is not a person who does anything except Cromwell.')

That month, Thomas More resigned his position as lord chancellor, unable as he was to sanction Henry's usurpation of the Pope's authority. John Fisher, Bishop of Rochester, was only the most prominent of the clergymen preaching against the king's actions. In August the archbishop of Canterbury, the old and weary William Warham, died, to be replaced, that winter, by the evangelical Cranmer. Bonds were being broken, decks were being cleared, dies being cast. And (to complete the slate of clichés!) something had to give.

Malory in his *Morte d'Arthur* had grumbled that 'nowadays men cannot love a sennight [week] but they must have all their desires . . . But the old love was not so. For men and women could love together seven years, and no licorous [lecherous] lust was betwixt them.' Ironically, seven years was almost exactly the length of time for which Henry VIII and Anne Boleyn probably kept consummation of their love at bay before, in 1532, they began – or resumed – full sexual relations.

Perhaps Anne felt that only a pregnancy would push Henry to take the final steps towards severing himself from Rome and from Catherine; perhaps both were aware that time was getting on. Anne was, after all, now past thirty; comparatively old for childbearing by the standards of the day. Typically, however, the next stage of the game was played out with a mixture of secrecy and ceremony.

In October, in pursuance of an Anglo-French alliance, Henry travelled to Calais for an encounter with François I. So too did Anne. While France acknowledged her as their most effective voice at the English court, France's backing made her a more credible player in the international game that was royal marriage. The Venetians reported as fact a rumour (believed by Catherine, for one) that they would be married in Calais, perhaps with François present at the ceremony and effectively giving his blessing. (The Venetian envoy also reported rumours that Catherine's sister-in-law Mary 'adamantly refused' to attend; as, to Anne's disappointment, did the French royal ladies.)

For the visit Anne, newly created Lady Marquess of Pembroke, was decked out in the royal jewels wrenched from Catherine of Aragon, who had protested it was against her conscience to hand them over to decorate a woman who was 'the scandal of Christendom'. (Unfairly, the haul even included some jewels Catherine had brought with her from Spain.) Anne and her ladies made a masked entrance into a dinner of the two kings, warmly welcomed by the men of the French court. And – either in Calais itself or on the protracted, storm-delayed journey home – she may at last have slept with Henry. Hall and Sander both report that on the very day of their return, at Dover, the couple underwent a private marriage ceremony.

At the end of January – quietly, in London – Henry and Anne underwent another wedding ceremony. Possibly the earlier one at Dover was no more than a rumour put about to ensure no one questioned the legitimacy of the child Anne now suspected she was carrying. By the end of February word of her pregnancy had spread. In April four of Henry's senior men – among them a deeply embarrassed Charles Brandon – visited Catherine in her country confinement to inform her she would no longer be called queen; that many of her servants and much of her money would be stripped from her. In May, Cranmer – in his new capacity as leading prelate of the English Church – pronounced Catherine's marriage to Henry null and void, and Anne's legitimate.

On 1 June Anne would be crowned queen: the same pattern of a small wedding followed by a splendid coronation that Catherine of Aragon had experienced almost a quarter of a century before. Though no one could have guessed it then, it would not be the only similarity between the two.

At the end of June, Mary Tudor died. Letters from her husband Charles Brandon had long reflected concern about her health. And Anne's rise had seen Mary increasingly withdraw to their estates, ever more vocal in her dislike of the newcomer: the previous year, the Venetian ambassador had reported her 'insulting words'. Some ten weeks after Mary's death, Brandon married his ward, the youthful heiress Katherine Willoughby.

In Scotland Margaret Tudor would accommodate herself to the idea of England's new queen. She had never been as close to Catherine as Mary had. With Catherine herself essentially now a prisoner, the way seemed clear for Anne's queenship: the queenship that famously would last little more than a thousand days.

'the most happy'

1533–early spring 1536

THE FOUR-DAY CEREMONIALS for the coronation of Anne Boleyn might have been exhausting for anybody, let alone a woman moving into the second half of her pregnancy. But this was Anne's triumph; and indeed the pageantry celebrated her fertility as well as her chastity. The two faces of Christian womanhood – and what would prove to be two of the most contentious aspects of Anne's persona.

On the first day, Anne was escorted to the Tower (as tradition dictated) with a water pageant, the likes of which the Thames had hardly seen – or heard. The fifty great barges of the London livery companies, glittering with gold foil and hung with tinkling bells, were crammed with squalling musicians. The floating procession was led by a mechanical dragon belching flame and rounded off by the royal barges and those of the courtiers: more than three hundred vessels in all.

On the third day, after forty-eight hours of rituals in the Tower, for the procession back to Westminster Abbey Anne was dressed in silvery white, travelling in a white litter drawn by palfreys draped in white damask; her emblem the white falcon. Verses composed for the occasion stressed the point.

Of courage halt
No manner fault
Is in this Falcon White,

In chastity,
Excelleth she,
Most like a virgin bright

She proudly displayed, however, her swollen belly; queens, after all, often represented Mary, the Virgin Mother. The pageantry recollected the 'fruitfulness' of the Virgin's own mother, St Anne. 'Queen Anne, when thou shalt bear a new son of the King's blood; there shall be a golden world unto thy people!'

It may have been in gesture towards the son the pregnant Anne was presumed to be carrying that the crown of St Edward, hitherto used only for monarchs, was briefly placed on her head, before being replaced by something lighter. But this did represent an upping of the stakes; almost as though Anne's potent persona of the courtly lady had given her male agency. It was only the start of the mixed messages that would plague Anne's queenship.

Anne chose the motto 'The most happy': recognition of all Henry had done for her, perhaps, but alternatively a kind of triumphalism perhaps born of insecurity. Ambassador Chapuys reported that the crowd lining the streets for her coronation were sullen – though his missives (while one of our chief sources for Anne's queenship) were coloured by his and his master Charles V's hostility.

It was undoubtedly a disappointment for the parents when, on 7 September, Anne gave birth to a girl, rather than the longed-for boy. But both parents put a good face on it: a healthy daughter would surely be followed by healthy sons, and the baby was named Elizabeth after Henry's mother (and Anne's). The tournament that would have greeted a prince was cancelled, but the pre-written letters of announcement were sent out with 'prince' altered to 'princes'[s], and the French ambassador was guest of honour at the christening.

It seems Anne miscarried in the summer of 1534, though (as with some of Catherine's pregnancies) there is an element of uncertainty. In spring her pregnancy had been common knowledge: the nursery at Eltham was being readied, and up until June she was described as having a 'goodly belly'. There was, however, no report of the occasion of her miscarriage, and in September Chapuys sent a strange letter to his master Charles saying Henry was beginning to doubt Anne's pregnancy:

Since the King began to doubt whether his lady [Anne] was *enceinte* or not, he has renewed and increased the love he formerly had for a very beautiful damsel of the court; and because the said lady wished to drive her away, the King has been very angry, telling his said lady that she had good reason to be content with what he had done for her, which he would not do now if the thing were to begin, and that she should consider from what she had come, and several other things.

To which, Chapuys said, realistically, 'it is not well to attach too much importance, considering the changeable character of the said King and the craft of the said lady, who knows well how to manage him'.

But it was in the understanding of Anne's pregnancy that in March 1534 Parliament passed the first Act of Succession, to which everyone of consequence would be asked to swear, declaring Anne Boleyn Henry's lawful wife and their children the heirs to the throne. The former princess Mary would be asked to renounce her title, although the displaced Catherine had not abated one jot of her conviction that she was Henry's wife, writing in the month of Anne's coronation of 'the great love that hath been betwixt him and me ere this . . . the which love in me is as faithful and true to him . . . as ever it was'.

Anne swore she would have Catherine's daughter Mary as her maid or see her married off to 'some varlet'. 'She is my death, and I am hers,' Anne is reported to have said – but, though history has censured her vindictiveness, Henry similarly refused to endure any defiance of his authority. Catherine of Aragon wrote to her daughter in terms that reflect her belief their very lives might be in jeopardy.

Daughter, I heard such tidings today that I do perceive, if it be true, the time is come that Almighty God will prove you; and I am very glad of it . . . If any pangs come to you, shrive yourself; first make you clean; take heed of His commandments, and keep them as near as He will give you grace to do, for then you are sure armed . . . we never come unto the kingdom of Heaven but by troubles.

That November, the Act Respecting the Oath to the Succession required swearers 'to be true to Queen Anne, and to believe and take her for the lawful wife of the King and rightful Queen of England, and utterly to think the Lady Mary daughter to the King by Queen Katherine a bastard, and thus to do without any scrupulosity of conscience'. It also required that they abjure any 'foreign authority or potentate'.

Thomas More and Bishop John Fisher both refused to sign and were sent to the Tower and, early in 1535, Henry passed the Act of Treason, which made 'maliciously denying' the royal supremacy a capital offence. More and Fisher were executed in the summer of 1535; More's death, in particular, was a scandal that resonated down the centuries.

Anne's relationship with Henry had, in some ways, continued along its old lines: intense in its moments of both heat and chill. Even Chapuys described many of their squabbles as mere 'lovers' quarrels', over as soon as they began. There were, however, two new factors with which they would have to contend.

Anne's status had, of course, in the public sense been massively raised by her marriage. She was now Queen Consort of England. But as wife, it was hard for her to play the courtly trick of unavailability, while pregnancy opened the way for other women to take her place. When Anne confronted Henry with his interest in another woman, he angrily told her to 'shut her eyes and endure', as 'more worthy persons' – Catherine – had done. She might well have retorted with one of Andreas Capellanus's Rules: 'The person who is not jealous cannot love.' But Anne had effectively fallen foul of the situation described almost four centuries later: that the man who marries his mistress creates a job vacancy. 'Marriage does not constitute a proper excuse for not loving', Andreas had written. But he envisaged the object of that love as being *outside*, distinct from, the marriage.

At the end of February 1535 Chapuys was writing that Henry was now enamoured of 'a cousin of the concubine, daughter of the present governess of the princess [Mary]'. Mary's household was at this time being run by Thomas Boleyn's sister, Anne Shelton, who had, we *think*, two daughters in Anne's service: Margaret ('Madge') and Mary. Which of them was reputed Henry's mistress depends on a single, carelessly written, letter that could read either 'Marg' or 'Mary'. It has indeed been suggested they were actually the same person, though it is Mary of whom we shall be hearing more shortly. It is possible that Anne had once again become pregnant, and that the Howard clan were actively promoting Henry's liaison with a Shelton girl, just to keep things in the family.

These affairs did not necessarily matter; they were within the tradition of courtly behaviour. But they do show Anne was having difficulty in accommodating herself to her changed circumstances, and the rules prescribed by that very tradition. Only Henry's love, after all, had made her queen; thus, unlike previous consorts, she was in no position to rise above any fling on his part. Perhaps both she and Catherine of Aragon had suffered from the confusion caused by the intromission of courtly rules into royal marriage.

But the difference in status between Anne and Catherine was made clear when, in 1535, the swelling belly of Anne's sister Mary Boleyn led to the revelation of her secret marriage to the comparatively humble courtier William Stafford. For a woman often regarded as a simply physical creature in contrast to her cerebral sibling (the 'Other Boleyn Girl', in the title of Philippa Gregory's novel, and the subsequent film), Mary's long letter to Thomas Cromwell, whom she hoped would intercede on her behalf, is remarkably expressive:

> he [Stafford] was young, and love overcame reason; and for my part I saw so much honesty in him, that I loved him as well as he did me; and was in bondage, and glad I was to be at liberty . . . Well might I have had a greater man of birth, and a higher, but I assure you I could never have had one as should have loved me so well

Mary would, she said, perhaps somewhat pointedly, 'rather beg my bread with him than be the greatest queen christened': is it fanciful to imagine that the transgressive marriage of Anne and Henry had opened up all other sorts of possibilities? But in so far as Anne was now queen, at the very top of the social hierarchy, her sister's marriage to a man of low rank was an embarrassment. Mary's actions reminded the world that the Boleyns – who promptly cut off their errant daughter – were not royalty.

All the same, Mary was safer out of the queen's chambers, in the months ahead.

Far from having abandoned her religious reformism, Anne insisted her ladies attend divine service every day, reproving one of her Shelton cousins for scribbling verses in a religious text. She supported the candidacy of evangelical churchmen when natural wastage (alongside the execution of Fisher) vacated a number of bishoprics. There was, however, obviously motive to exaggerate her zeal – on both sides of the religious divide. The Scottish reformer Alexander Ales would tell Anne's daughter Elizabeth that: 'True religion in England had its commencement and its end with your mother.' Chapuys likewise perceived the heretical doctrines and practices of 'the Concubine' (as he called Anne) to be 'the principal cause of the spread of Lutheranism in this country'.

Anne was, in truth, no follower of Martin Luther, but she did support study and dissemination of Bible texts and exposing the superstitions of the old papal priesthood. Queenship gave her new opportunities. We see Anne actively sponsoring the investigators who discovered that the ever-liquid 'Holy Blood' at Hailes Abbey was in fact the blood of a duck; herself visiting the nuns of Syon and reproving their moral decline and continued use of the Latin psalter.

The year 1535 saw a general inspection ('visitation') of the monasteries, with some smaller institutions already scheduled for suppression. And those who hated to see the old ways go had a scapegoat close at hand. To blame the woman was a familiar trope: just so had King John's wife been blamed for his failings, and Marguerite of Anjou for those of Henry VI.

And elsewhere in Europe, a backlash against change had already begun. The reforming nature of *their* beliefs put pressure on Marguerite of Navarre in France, and, in the Netherlands, Mary of Hungary, who had succeeded her aunt Margaret of Austria as regent. Both hastily made clear that they had never left the Catholic fold. For Anne there could never be any such option: her position as Henry's lawful wife depended on the rejection of papal authority. In any case, there is little doubt she saw herself as fulfilling a moral imperative by giving a lead in religious matters – fulfilling the queenly *and* the courtly role of exemplar. Castiglione had written that, without women, not only would life lack 'charm', would be 'uncouth', but that 'if we really consider the truth, we shall also recognise that in our understanding of great issues, far from distracting us, they awaken our minds'. But in other ways the anomalies of Anne's position were becoming harder to reconcile.

As well as religion, Anne's court would have relished discussion of the games of love in their more intellectual aspects. Awareness of French courtly literature was given a boost in 1530 when John Palsgrave, once tutor to Henry's sister Mary, published his mighty guide to the language, using literary examples. And in 1532 a courtier called William Thynne published (with Henry VIII's active approval) *The Workes of Geffray Chaucer Newly Printed: With Dyvers Workes Whiche Were Neuer in Print Before*. This included not only Chaucer's *Romaunt de la Rose*, but Richard Roos's translation of *La Belle Dame Sans Mercy* [sic], erroneously believed to be Chaucer's. The following year Thynne was recorded as one of Anne's treasurers.[*]

Anne's chamberlain wrote that: 'as for pastime in the queen's chamber, [there] was never more. If any of you that be now departed have any ladies that ye thought favoured you and somewhat would mourn at parting of their servants, I can no whit perceive the same by their dancing'. Anne was particularly skilled as a musician, playing the lute, flute and rebec, a skill she would first have learnt at the court of Margaret of Austria, who was a major patron of music. Even the unsympathetic George Cavendish would write that: 'when [Anne] composed her hands to play and her voice to sing, it was joined with that sweetness of countenance that three harmonies concurred'.

An unsympathetic account by the Catholic Jane Dormer would later describe the 'masques, dancing, plays and such corporeal delights, in which [Anne] had a special grace, temptations to carnal pleasures and invitations to disgrace' of the queen's chambers. And with hindsight the games played there do seem deadly: the more so since we know of them largely from reports made later, after Anne's fall. But were the signs already there to read?

---

[*] Thynne's nephew would be the builder of Longleat.

Anne might have remembered Castiglione's declaration that the courtly woman's contradictory task was to 'come just to certain limits, but not to pass them'. The rules of courtly love laid down back in the twelfth century by Andreas Capellanus were equally paradoxical. On the one hand they seemed to give licence to flirtations by which, perhaps, Anne had hoped to spark Henry's jealousy. (Book Two, Rule 22: 'Once suspicion about a lover is entertained, jealousy and the feeling of love grow.') Yet those very Rules offered stark warnings, had Anne only read them:

17. A new love forces the old to give place.
28. The slightest supposition forces a lover to entertain dark thoughts about his beloved.

There is another, little-discussed, text dating from Anne Boleyn's queenship that reflects the degree to which it – like Henry's kingship – was founded on notions of (hi)story. But it reflects, too, the degree to which success for a queen lay ultimately in one thing: the production of an heir. *The Black Book of the Garter*, laying down the regulations and ceremonies of the Garter knights, and held in St George's Chapel, Windsor, was created in 1534, probably by the Flemish artist Lucas Horenbout. It displays, prominent among the knights, the king who founded the order – Edward III – and his queen, Philippa, presiding over the ceremonies.

For heretofore when jousts, tournaments, entertainments and public shows were made, in which men of nobility and valour showed their strength and prowess, the Queen, ladies, and other women of illustrious birth with ancient knights, and some chosen heralds were wont . . . to see, discern, approve or disapprove what might be done . . . to encourage and stir up bravery by their words and looks.

One of the kingly figures depicted in the *Black Book* to illustrate the Garter's history boasts the red-gold beard and recognisable features of Henry VIII, cast as the king and knight Henry V, the victor of Agincourt. But the queenly figure? Recent study has shown that the figure presumably depicting Queen Philippa wears a pendant with the letters 'AR' – *Anna Regina* – while she and her attendants wear the fashions of the 1530s.

Philippa of Hainault is remembered in English history for the gentleness and courtesy Froissart praised – for her famous intercession on behalf of the condemned burghers of Calais. And, of course, for her fertility – that roster of eight surviving children whose own progeny would provide most of the players of the 'Wars of the Roses'. Something there for Anne to live up to, clearly.

At some point early in 1535 Anne may have miscarried a pregnancy that facilitated the rise of her Shelton cousin into the king's affections. To Henry, the pattern was hideously familiar. Earlier that year, a French envoy had reported Anne confiding to him that she feared finding herself 'ruined and lost'. That she could not speak freely, dared not express her fears in writing . . . 'the lady is not at her ease'.

Yet when, on summer progress, the royal couple visited Thornbury Castle in 1535, they were still described as being 'merry'. It could, of course, have been merely a good façade. The progress also included a week-long stay at Wulf Hall, home to Sir John Seymour, and his daughter Jane. But by the autumn of 1535 Anne was once again pregnant. In other words, it is far from clear whether Henry and Anne's marriage was already in serious trouble, or whether the staggering events of the following year came out of a clear blue sky.

In the first weeks of 1536, ironically, it was the death of Catherine of Aragon that provided one context for Anne's fall. It was disease – probably a cancer – that killed her; but there were inevitably rumours. She had long insisted on having her meals prepared by the few old servants she trusted, for fear of poison: confining herself to one room; disdaining the new servants Henry had put about her as 'guards and spies'. Her life had, as in her youth, become the stuff of dreary nightmare; but this time there would be no prince to rescue her. Her prince was her gaoler.

Aware she was dying, Catherine wrote Henry an uncomfortable last letter. Her 'most dear lord, king and husband' should prefer the 'health and safeguard of your soul' to worldly matters, and to 'the care and pampering of your body'. She pardoned him everything, and prayed that God would do the same. 'Lastly, I make this vow, that mine eyes desire you above all things'. She signed herself, defiantly, as 'the Queen'. Henry and Anne celebrated her death together. But Anne had second thoughts: Chapuys reported that she 'frequently wept, fearing they might do with her as with the good queen'. Indeed, Catherine's death would prove to have the rippling effect of a stone thrown in a pond.

On the very day of Catherine's funeral – 29 January – disastrously, Anne miscarried again. The foetus was a boy. Five days beforehand, Henry had fallen injured in the joust and some historians suggest that a possible bruise to the cerebral cortex caused a major change in his reign and his personality; though the pain of another injury, to his leg, which never entirely healed may be as responsible. Anne blamed the shock of hearing the news for this latest tragedy; that, and her distress over Henry's interest in another lady. (Catholic propagandists would write that she had found Jane Seymour on Henry's knee.) But whatever the cause, all knew she had 'miscarried of her saviour', as Chapuys reported.

'I see that God will not give me male children,' Henry (Chapuys said) told Anne ominously. The invocation of the deity, in this context, was all too significant; and too reminiscent of the ending of his marriage to Catherine. Anne's moral worth was compromised: not, after all, a woman good enough for God to give her sons.

If the history of English queenship offered Anne a choice of role models – one chain of apparently meek and maternal wives, and another of witches and bitches – Anne's temperament, and her route to the throne, ensured she would be grouped with the latter . . . literally. Henry (someone told Chapuys) told a male courtier that he had been 'seduced by sortilèges' into this marriage. There is some question over whether the word should be translated as sorcery, or merely as prophecy, i.e. Anne's promise to bear sons. But, as we have seen, other royal women in the last century had been accused of witchcraft.

Anne clearly knew she was vulnerable. In January, in a complete change of tack, she had sent orders that the former princess Mary should no longer be pressured to acknowledge her half-sister Elizabeth as her superior in rank. Anne must, moreover, have been aware that (while she herself had been, as George Wyatt put it, 'waxing great again and so not fit for dalliance') Henry had become attracted to Jane Seymour, one of her own ladies-in-waiting. A French visitor to the

English court in October 1535 had reported that Henry's feeling for Anne was 'less than it has been, and diminishes day by day, because he has new amours'.

Anne had sowed the seeds of her own abandonment. The same change of rules that had made possible her own queenship would open the way for Jane Seymour, Katheryn Howard, Katherine Parr . . . So much for courtly love: ironically, the very creed that was supposed to exalt women had ultimately helped to make them replaceable.

13

'the spotted queen'

April/May 1536

THE TROPES OF courtly love, with its notional insistence on a woman's dominance, had masked the sheer affront of Anne's transgressive rise. But for Anne's fall, as for that rise, courtly love provided the means through which other forces could operate.

And Anne's fall was likewise assisted by the shifting international climate. With Catherine dead, her nephew Charles V – as Henry, rather brutally, had earlier suggested to Chapuys – had no cause to trouble himself about English affairs. Henry could once more open diplomatic relations with Charles, without having to renew his relations with Charles's aunt. It was, if anything, the Francophile figure of Anne who was now the difficulty.

The idea of France had long both lured and repelled the English. There had, a few years before, been concern that a number of Henry's 'minions' – gentlemen – were unhealthily aping French ways, and the result had been a cleansing of the court. It is even possible that concern over a Frenchified Anne was coloured by memories of those dominant French queens – Isabella, Marguerite – who had come before.

But France had not been as wholly supportive of Anne's queenship as she might have hoped. At the end of the day she was simply not royal. Unwilling to tackle the Pope on the subject of Henry's annulment, they also (to Anne's dismay) still apparently rated the officially illegitimate Princess Mary – who they suggested might marry their dauphin – higher than Anne's baby Elizabeth. The French had been lukewarm about the suggestion Elizabeth might marry even one of

François's younger sons. By the spring of 1536, a vulnerable Anne herself found it politic to make gestures of support for a pro-Imperial policy. On 18 April Charles V's representative Chapuys was manoeuvred into doing what he had long avoided and acknowledged Queen Anne as she passed through the chapel – exchanging the 'mutual reverences required by politeness'.

But the signals were contradictory. On 24 April Henry signed a commission for Cromwell to investigate 'unknown treasonable conspiracies'. It is possible he had already earlier enquired as to the prospect of ending his marriage. But the day after signing that commission, he was writing to a representative abroad of the 'likelihood and appearance that God will send us heirs male . . . through our most dear and entirely beloved wife, the Queen'.

It is, in other words, unclear whether Henry was tiring of Anne, or whether the problem was just the opposite: that his enduring commitment to her threatened others at the English court. Over the next week, however, things would move at speed.

The very weeks that saw Anne's troubles gather pace saw the legislation that would confiscate the wealth of the lesser monasteries. But Anne clashed with Thomas Cromwell over where the proceeds of the confiscations should go.

So far, her interests had run in tandem with Cromwell's; but now there came a parting of the ways. Anne's interests lay in education and social reform, Cromwell's in the strengthening of the monarchy. And diverting the wealth of the monasteries into the king's coffers would buy a lot of strength.

One of the great debates about Anne's fall is whether Cromwell or his king was the chief agent of it. Chapuys would later report Cromwell as having said he had 'set himself to devise and conspire the said affair', but in a context that perhaps suggests Henry had licensed him to do it. If Cromwell now perceived Anne as his enemy, he would see her as a dangerous one: the woman many thought had brought down his old master Wolsey. As her great biographer Eric Ives memorably put it, Anne 'became the leader of the opposition'. But Anne's fall would save Cromwell only if it also brought down others of the Boleyn faction. And, as so often in court politics, two very different interest groups found themselves briefly fellow travellers. Edward Seymour had been appointed to the Privy Council on 3 March: he (and thus his sister Jane) now had rooms with easy access to Henry's own.

On 2 April 1536 Anne's almoner John Skip preached a sermon in front of the king's councillors, describing how King Ahasuerus was almost persuaded to the massacre of the Jews by his evil counsellor Haman, and was saved only by his wife Esther. Haman was easily identifiable as Thomas Cromwell. Anne obviously knew there was a danger to avert, and it was not in her nature to back off from any confrontation. But this time it didn't serve her well.

It was, with a horrible appositeness, the last day of April – the eve of May Day – that saw events pick up terrifying speed. There was a confrontation between Anne and Henry: Alexander Ales would later describe to Elizabeth I 'your most religious mother carrying you, still a little baby, in her arms and entreating the most serene King, your father, from the open window . . . the faces and gestures of the speakers plainly showed that the King was angry.'

On the same day, Anne begged the courtier Henry Norris to swear before her chaplain that she 'was a good woman'. Why the need? Norris ('gentle Norris', Wyatt would call him) made himself felt as a quietly significant figure at court: at once one of Anne's inner circle, and the king's Groom of the Stool – one of the men Henry most trusted. He was also a leading member of the Boleyn faction, and thus a potential target for Cromwell.

Just the day before, Anne had been speaking to Norris about his dilatory courtship of Madge Shelton. 'You look for dead men's shoes; for if ought came to the King but good, you would look to have me,' she told him. Perhaps Anne was losing the lightness of her courtly touch. The anonymous medieval romance *Yder* has Arthur demanding to know who Guinevere would marry if he died. When she admits it is Yder, Arthur sets out to destroy him. More to the point, under Henry's Treasons Act of 1534 words which suggested harm to the king were treasonable.

Also on that crucial 30 April, Henry decided to postpone his planned trip to Calais with Anne. But yet, in a contradictory message, the jousts to celebrate May Day were still to go ahead, with King and

Queen presiding as usual. May Day, the festival of courtly love. As Wyatt put it:

You that in love find luck and abundance
And live in lust and joyful jollity,
Arise, for shame, do away your sluggardy,
Arise, I say, do May some observance!
Let me in bed lie dreaming in mischance
Let me remember the haps most unhappy
That me betide in May most commonly.
As one whom love list little to avance.

George Boleyn captained one team, and Henry Norris the other. In an account by Nicholas Sander, Anne tossed her handkerchief to wipe Norris's sweaty brow, thus convincing Henry of their adultery. Certainly something dramatic happened: halfway through, a message was brought to Henry, who abruptly left the festivities. Anne can have had no idea she had seen her husband for the last time.

It is possible Henry now, overwhelmingly, heard of the confession made by a court musician, Mark Smeaton. For yet something else had happened on 30 April: Smeaton had been taken to Cromwell's house for questioning and confessed to – or boasted of – having had sex with the queen three times.

Such an accusation was extraordinary; and it is one that Smeaton (more vulnerable than the higher-ranking gentlemen around Anne) may have been pressured, or tortured, into making. Obscure, possibly of Flemish origin, he was said to be the son of a carpenter and a seamstress.

Anne herself may inadvertently have launched the disastrous train of events that set her, and several of those closest to her, careening down the slippery slope towards disgrace and death. She would describe a recent exchange of words which seemed to show Mark languishing after her in courtly tradition, and her sharply reproving him that this was a game he, a mere servant, was not licensed to play.

The anonymous Spanish *Cronica* would invent a salacious tale which (as in the other pieces of Catholic propaganda) shows Anne as the sexual aggressor. It describes Mark being hidden naked in a closet off Anne's bedroom, used to store sweetmeats, and Anne calling for a little marmalade as the cue for an elderly attendant named Margaret to produce him.

Other spinners of songs and poems had languished respectfully after other ladies in the long artistic tradition of courtly love, without anyone thinking the worse of it. What had brought a dream of sighs in a rose garden down to sordid suggestions of bawds and doubtless bribes, of brutally swift secret couplings? Was it tiny points, to do with Mark's (or Anne's) precise degree of inappropriateness? Or was the whole fantastical game of courtly love losing its fragrance at last?

Other sources would describe other accusations against the queen, made by other members of Anne's household – even by Anne's sister-in-law Jane Rochford, George Boleyn's wife. A Lady Worcester who, when herself accused of lax morality, had exclaimed that her own faults were nothing compared to those of the queen; a Lady Wingfield who made a deathbed confession of what she had known. But it was Smeaton's confession that gave Cromwell what he needed. On 2 May, the day after the jousts, Anne was summoned to face inquiry by the Privy Council, presided over by her own uncle the Duke of Norfolk, and told she stood accused of adultery with Smeaton, Norris, and one other.

The king had already tackled Norris as they rode away from the May Day jousts, promising him clemency if he confessed: Norris offered to prove his innocence in trial by combat. Indeed, all the men who would be accused with Anne continued stoutly to declare their (and her) innocence, excepting only the hapless Smeaton. As Anne was taken by barge to the Tower, she clutched a vain hope that the king was doing this only to test – to 'prove' – her: a regular trope of courtly love. She had yet to learn that the third man with whom she had already been accused was her own brother George.

On the damp steps of the watergate, Anne dropped to her knees – 'Jesu have mercy on me.' The Constable of the Tower Sir William Kingston described her falling from 'weeping a great pace' into a 'great laughter'. She asked whether she would be placed in a dungeon; in fact, she was taken to the royal lodgings redecorated for her coronation. There she began frantically to canvass all her recent actions.

And she did so surrounded by ladies placed there to catch every damaging word.

Her wit did not desert her, but it took on a frenetic note. Asking about the men imprisoned for her sake, and who was making their beds for them, she punned that if they could not make pallets they could make ballads. As one of the spying ladies (her aunt Anne Shelton) told her sourly: 'Such desire as you have had to such tales has brought you to this.' Recklessly, desperately, she even risked giving credence to that hint of her witchcraft by predicting that if she died, there would be no rain for seven years: seven being a magic number.

Most historians see no reason to believe Anne guilty of adultery (let alone sorcery). Apart from anything else, she and her supposed paramours were simply not together at the times and in the places stated. But did Henry truly believe the accusations? The pattern of events does suggest a sudden and shattering revelation – but while it would be out of character for Henry cynically to tell Cromwell to invent evidence against Anne, it is easier to envisage him to some degree persuading himself into belief.

Once set on a mental trail, Henry's obstinacy would preclude further doubts. Wolsey had once warned another minister to 'be advised and assured what matter you put in his head; for ye shall never pull it out again'. But what was already lurking in Henry's psyche that allowed him to change his view of the woman he loved, so completely and so disastrously?

He had a pattern of suddenly rejecting former favourites – Catherine and Wolsey among them – along with, perhaps, a punitive impulse all the greater for his former affection. And for all history often condemns Henry VIII as heartless, his rejection of Anne was in the bitterest and most painful sense an affair of the heart. The very indictment against her would be couched in terms of a betrayal of love as well as of the laws of matrimony. It alleged that she had never wished to choose the king in *her* heart.

Yet perhaps in the end Anne's downfall exposes a different truth, about Henry and about courtly love too. Ultimately, the king's romance was with himself: just as had perhaps been true of all those literary lovers before him. The idea that the woman could hold the power in this relationship was nothing more than an illusion, insubstantial as a morning mist burnt away by the sun.

That said, however, romance legends may have played yet one more role here, paving the way for, and soothing the chagrin of, Henry's credulity. If Henry had been betrayed by his wife and his friend Norris – why, so had Arthur; and without its diminishing his prestige in any way. Perhaps Henry had morphed from Lancelot the wooer to Arthur the wounded . . . but there is another compelling lesson from the Arthurian story.

When his fellowship is broken because of Lancelot and Guinevere's love, Malory's Arthur regrets the loss of knights more than of his queen: he can, he says, always get another wife. In the case of Henry, with the knowledge hindsight gives, that sounds like a prophecy.

Other gentlemen of the court were now arrested. Francis Weston had been flirting with Anne's cousin Madge Shelton but, reproved by the queen, said that he loved another in Anne's chamber better. When she asked him who, he said: 'It is yourself.' This was well within courtly tradition – indeed, a virtually identical scene, with Queen Guinevere pressing a knight as to who in her chamber he loved, and receiving the same answer, appeared in the prose *Lancelot* several centuries before. It should have been uncontroversial – especially since Anne had 'defied' him, told him off. But read too literally, it could be turned against her. Courtly love had been a dream and a challenge; a joke and an opportunity. Now in Cromwell's hands it became a tool.

Joining Weston, Norris and Smeaton in the Tower were others of Henry's household: Groom of the Chamber William Brereton, Thomas Wyatt and Richard Page (both of whom would eventually be released without charge), as well as Anne's brother George. The theme of incest featured also in Arthurian legend: Mordred, who brought Camelot down, was the fruit of Arthur's unwitting incest with his half-sister Morgana le Fay – and was himself often written as guilty of incestuous approaches to Guinevere. But George's name both added to the horror of Anne's alleged crimes, and got another threat out of Cromwell's way.

One historian, Retha Warnicke, made a much-debated link between later Catholic reports that in January Anne had miscarried 'a shapeless mass of flesh', and contemporary beliefs that sinful practice such as incest – or witchcraft – could result in a deformed foetus. She suggested this as the cause of her rejection by Henry. Nicholas Sander would raise the idea of Anne's turning to her brother to father the baby that Henry could not provide. But Sander also upped the incest stakes beyond the point of credulity by declaring Anne to be Henry's own daughter by Anne's mother, Elizabeth Boleyn.

On 12 May Norris, Weston, Brereton and Smeaton were put on trial for high treason at Westminster Hall. Inevitably, all four were found guilty, and sentenced to a traitor's death. On 15 May Anne and George Boleyn came to trial before a jury of their peers.

Anne was charged with twenty acts of adultery, three of them also incest, and with the treasonous act of having plotted the king's death. The indictment drawn up preparatory to the trials said that she, 'following daily her frail and carnal appetites, did falsely and traitorously procure by base conversations and kisses, touchings, gifts, and other infamous incitations, divers of the King's daily and familiar servants to be her adulterers and concubines'.

More explicitly, she 'procured her own natural brother to violate her, alluring him with her tongue in his mouth, and his tongue in hers, against the commands of Almighty God and all laws human and divine'. But as even Chapuys put it, the incest charge rested only on 'presumption, because he had been once a long while with her, and certain other little follies'.

Anne's trial was held in the Great Hall of the Tower of London, packed with some two thousand spectators, and she entered it 'as though she were going to a great triumph', wrote one eyewitness. 'She made so wise and discreet answers to all things laid against her, excusing herself with her words so clearly as though she had never been faulty to the same', recorded the Windsor Herald Charles Wriothesley, usually far from sympathetic to Anne Boleyn.

The only crimes she did admit were jealousy, and that she had not always behaved towards the king with the humility she owed him 'considering his kindness and the great honour he showed me and the great respect he always paid me'. She was saying she had been a good courtly lover, but a bad wife. Inevitably, all twenty-six peers declared Anne guilty and she was sentenced to be burnt or beheaded at the king's pleasure. Anne once told her husband it was prophesied that a queen of England would be burnt, but that even a thousand such deaths would not abate her love for him. Did she remember Queen Guinevere, sentenced to the flames?

When it was George's turn, his blatant defiance dealt another blow to Henry's vanity. Handed a note, he was instructed to read it to himself before answering questions. Instead, he read it aloud. The note charged that Anne had said her husband was 'not skillful in copulating with a woman and had neither virtue nor potency' ('*vertu*' nor '*puissance*'). That Anne had laughed with George's wife Jane at his clothes and his poetry ('which was objected to them as a great crime', wrote Chapuys, with visible incredulity).

George too was found guilty and sentenced to death.

The verdict on Anne Boleyn was a foregone conclusion. The French swordsman hired to behead her was already on the way from Calais. A recently explored document shows that Henry laid down every detail of this execution; and there has long been discussion over precisely what motivated his unprecedented decision that Anne should die by the sword, not the axe. It could have been mercy: to give a swifter death to the woman he had loved. But it could also have been because the sword was the ultimate symbol of the chivalric code that had first bound, and then divided, them. Perhaps the powerful cultural echo of Guinevere's guilt played its own part in colouring Henry's thinking.

Did Anne hope that she might be saved at the last minute, as Guinevere had been? Sir William Kingston reported that for the first days of her imprisonment Anne seemed 'in hope of life', thinking she might be allowed to enter a nunnery. That was the fate Catherine of Aragon had refused – but Catherine, unlike Anne, had ultimately been protected by the spectre of her powerful family.

From the moment of her arrest, Anne had protested her innocence: 'beseeching God to help her as she was not guilty of her accusement'. 'I am as clear from the company of men, as for sin . . . as I am clear from you, and the King's true wedded wife.' But she had, she said, no way to prove her innocence – unless by opening her body and exposing her organs to the view. It is hard not to see a perverse parody of the 'blazon', the anatomising list with which the courtly lover detailed his mistress's beauties.

The night before her execution she again swore to her innocence 'on peril of her soul's damnation', before and after receiving the holy sacrament. She told the lords at her trial, after her sentence was pronounced, that she 'believed there was some other reason for which she was condemned than the cause alleged', and Henry's own later words of warning to Jane Seymour would suggest this was true.

On 17 May the five men charged with Anne were executed, and on the same day Anne's marriage was annulled and her daughter Elizabeth bastardised. She was told she would die the next day. She had been joking about the prospect with the hysteria of terror: that the swordsman was expert and she had a little neck. Kingston reported that this lady 'hath much joy in death'. But there was an excruciating delay of another twenty-four hours before, on the morning of 19 May, Anne – looking around her, as if she still hoped for a messenger bearing a royal pardon – walked out to mount the scaffold and face the watching crowd.

Her speech subscribed to the conventions of the day, which called for a dignified acceptance; an acknowledgement that all men and women were guilty in the face of God (if not necessarily of the crimes of which they had been accused). Is it fanciful to imagine there was a flash of Anne herself in the words?

'Good Christian people, I have not come here to preach a sermon,' she said. 'I have come here to die . . . And if any person will meddle of my cause, I require them to judge the best.' As she knelt upright in the straw, the executioner signalled his assistant to distract her attention, and, as she had fearfully hoped, the deed was swiftly done.

In all the care taken to arrange Anne's death, no one had thought to provide for her remains, which were unceremoniously bundled into an arrow chest and taken to an unmarked grave in the chapel of the Tower. It was elsewhere – in the vast body of legend accrued to her memory – that her real legacy would lie.

Lord Hussey, chamberlain to the former princess Mary, had written in the days before Anne's death that: 'if all the books and chronicles . . . which against women hath been penned . . . since Adam and Eve, those same were, I think, verily nothing in comparison of that which hath been done and committed by Anne the Queen'. Henry himself told his daughter Mary and his son FitzRoy they had been lucky to escape Anne's evil plans for their murder. He declared he believed Anne had been guilty with a hundred men: he took to carrying around a poem of his own composition on the subject.

This was the established legend of the 'unchaste wife, the spotted queen', as Wolsey's former man George Cavendish would describe her. But the reformer Ales would report a measure of sympathy growing for Anne, after her terrible death. As some spectators of the execution put it at dinner a few days later, it was after all no new thing 'that the King's chamberlains should dance with the ladies in the bedchamber', nor that a sister should kiss her brother. And Ales reported Archbishop Cranmer, wakeful in the early hours before Anne's execution, declaring with tears that 'She who has been the Queen of England upon earth will today become a Queen in Heaven'.

Perhaps in Anne's death as in her life, it was Thomas Wyatt who had the word for it, writing of what he had seen from his imprisonment:

These bloody days have broken my heart.
My lust, my youth did them depart,
And blind desire of estate.
Who hastes to climb seeks to revert.
Of truth, *circa Regna tonat* [thunder rolls around the throne].
The bell tower showed me such a sight
That in my head sticks day and night.
There did I learn out of a grate,
For all favour, glory, or might,
That yet *circa Regna tonat*.

Wyatt was released from the Tower in June; but he never forgot those who had been less lucky.

PART IV

1536–1558

Not: the pain of love

> . . . freely pardon my offence
> Since it proceedeth of lover's fervence
> And of my heart's constancy.
> Let [keep] me not from the sweet presence
> Of him that I have caused to die.

Margaret Douglas, the 'Devonshire Manuscript'

14

'My faithful, true and loving heart'

1536–1540

O N 15 JUNE 1536 King Henry rode with Jane Seymour in the procession to celebrate the feast of Corpus Christi. Riding as the first of the new Queen Jane's ladies was the king's niece, the only child of Margaret Tudor's unhappy marriage to the Earl of Angus. With the declared bastardy of Anne's daughter Elizabeth (and the similar disparagement of Catherine's daughter Mary) Margaret Douglas might well pro tem be regarded as her uncle's heir.

It was less than a fortnight after the execution of her former mistress that Jane Seymour became Queen of England: a queen, however, cast in a wholly different model from her predecessors. Nobody thought she had much beauty, said Chapuys who, since Jane was known to incline to the old religion, might have been expected to err on the side of generosity. The same had been said of Anne; but Jane was pale, Chapuys said, and lacking in wit.

As for Jane's trumpeted virtue, he suggested that 'being an Englishwoman, and having been so long at court' she might well 'hold it a sin to be *virgo intacta*'. Crudely, he suggested she might have 'a fine enigme' – which in Tudor times could mean secret place, or genitalia, as well as 'understanding'. But the lord chancellor assured Parliament that the king married 'not in any carnal concupiscence' but at the request of his nobility, and for the common good.

Even before Anne Boleyn died, Chapuys had described Jane as 'the lady who he [Henry] serves', and the king had been addressing Jane

Seymour as 'My dear friend and mistress', in a letter from 'thy entirely devoted servant'. Or from 'your own loving servant and sovereign', as he signed off. Servant *and* sovereign. He had not mentioned the latter in his letters to Anne. One might see this letter, this relationship, as a kind of halfway house between fantasy and reality.* Jane Seymour was no dazzling, dominant, courtly lady. But that fantasy would still have a role to play.

Henry would praise Jane's 'loving inclination, and reverend conformity'; the way she would 'in all things well content, satisfy, and quiet herself' with whatever he should decide. There is a story of Henry (while Anne was still his queen) sending Jane a full purse as a present. She kissed it before returning it to the messenger, with her own grateful but implacable message that the time for such a gift would be when God gave her a good husband ... It was personal, performative, unavailability, of the kind that puts the performer on a pedestal. Historians (like Jane's contemporaries) are still guessing as to whether this was the scheming act of a girl coached to snatch the king from her family's enemies, the Boleyns, or evidence of dutiful Christianity.

The very limited evidence we have as to Jane's character suggests that she would have had neither the education nor the inclination to indulge in the courtly fantasy. But then, no one wanted her to. As one minister put it, Henry had 'come out of hell into heaven, for the gentleness in this [i.e. his marriage to Jane], and the cursedness and the unhappiness in the other'. Inevitably, however, once queen, Jane was under some pressure to do, and not simply to be: Chapuys himself was not backwards in suggesting she should prove herself a peacemaker – Jane 'the pacific' – not least in reconciling the king with his daughter Mary.

Luckily, these were Jane's own inclinations. She had interceded for Mary before her marriage, daring to suggest (even in the face of Henry's snub) that this was the only way the royal family could be secure. The price of Mary's being received once again at court would

---

* If one seeks evidence of Henry's dwindling interest in courtly lore and legend, when the abbey at Glastonbury was dissolved in 1539, there is no sign of his having taken special care for the preservation of Arthur and Guinevere's supposed bones. Indeed, the execution of Glastonbury's venerable abbot, dragged on a hurdle to the top of Glastonbury Tor, would go down as a byword for brutality.

be her signature on the document declaring her parents' marriage invalid and herself a bastard. But that price once paid (at whatever cost to Mary's soul), she was reconciled to her father and received at court, when not sharing an establishment with the little half-sister Elizabeth for whom, now Anne's inimical influence was gone, Mary could allow herself to feel affection.

Almost the only record of Jane's intromission into public affairs records her fruitless pleading on behalf of the rebels who in the autumn of 1536 rose against the dissolution of the monasteries – which, whatever their faults, had provided a certain succour to the poor – and against the new men around Henry, notably Thomas Cromwell (who, though a layman, had that June 1536 been appointed vice-regent over ecclesiastical affairs).

First Lincolnshire and then the north rose in the 'Pilgrimage of Grace', one of the most threatening events of the Tudor age. A French agent described Jane throwing herself on her knees before her husband, at the beginning of the revolt, to beg that the abbeys might be restored. Intercession might have been seen as a queen's traditional duty; but it might also be seen as evidence of papist sympathies on Jane's part. Henry (so a French diplomat was told) warned her harshly to remember 'that the last Queen had died in consequence of meddling too much in state affairs' – a comment that seems to validate Anne Boleyn's own statement that she died for causes other than the crimes with which she was charged. The rebellion was put down, with savagery and a good deal of duplicity. And Jane had been given a lesson no Tudor woman could forget.

Jane's marriage was not necessarily the idyll hindsight would make it. It was reported that, only a week after the publication of his marriage, Henry was casting his eye elsewhere. But her queenship rested not on politics or personality, but on sheer physiology. News of her pregnancy, in spring 1537, would ensure there was no danger of her suffering Anne's fate.

It was, meanwhile, another royal woman who seemed in danger of inheriting Anne's bloodstained mantle.

Henry's had not been the only Tudor heart in turmoil at court in the early 1530s. Even as Anne Boleyn was unwittingly assembling the case against herself, another romantic love story had been unfolding within the dynasty. Henry's niece Margaret Douglas had been raised largely at her uncle's court, as a valuable pawn in the marriage market. But like her mother (and in the phrase of her future daughter-in-law Mary, Queen of Scots), this Margaret would regard her heart as her own. She had shared more with Anne Boleyn than just the queen's rooms, which had seen such dangerous games of love. Would they end as badly for Margaret?

Born in 1515, in the course of her mother's wild flight from Scotland and, crucially, just after her mother crossed the border into England, Margaret was an Englishwoman only by a bare week; but this was nonetheless a vital point. Foreigners, like Margaret's surviving half-brother the young Scottish king, were by common practice debarred from inheriting land in England – let alone, presumably, the land of England itself. So Margaret's English nationality shot her into edgy prominence with regard to succession to the English crown.

Margaret nonetheless spent her first decade or more receiving the upbringing of a Scottish princess. Aged five, negotiations for her own possible marriage, with a series of suitors, began. But everything changed when, in 1527, the Pope granted Margaret Tudor her long-sought annulment from Angus, albeit with the proviso that their daughter's legitimacy was not affected by the decree. Sometime around then, Angus seized the young Margaret Douglas from her mother's care. But in 1528 James V, Margaret's half-brother, escaped from his stepfather Angus's custody to assume rule himself.

Margaret was holed up at Tantallon Castle with her father as news came that Angus was now an attainted traitor. James was advancing on Angus with an army, and a reward was offered to anyone who would return the young Margaret (willing or not) to her mother's charge. In the best traditions of her family, there was a dramatic scene as Angus, shouting across the River Tweed which formed the Anglo-Scottish border, negotiated for his daughter to be admitted to England, out of her half-brother's reach. For some eight months she remained at her first place of refuge, Norham Castle in Northumberland, then for another year at Berwick under, effectively, the distant care – or protective custody, since there was fear she might be snatched back to Scotland – of her godfather Cardinal Wolsey.

Happily, by the time Wolsey died, Margaret's father had committed himself wholly to England's cause. Margaret came south to Henry VIII's court, her uncle marking the occasion by ordering a costly wardrobe for the notably good-looking fourteen-year-old; gowns of tawny velvet and of black satin, of black damask decked with crimson and white. Margaret was sent to join the household of her cousin and contemporary Princess Mary. But when, within a few years, Mary was stripped of her privileges, and even of her title of princess, Margaret was brought to court, first lady in rank of all those around the new queen Anne Boleyn.

Her allegiances must have been deeply divided. She would retain her friendship with Mary, and her Catholic religion. But perhaps Margaret's tumultuous early life in Scotland had taught her a thing or two. She seems to have kept a still tongue in her head and to have formed a strong connection with the literate, emotionally adventurous, group at Anne Boleyn's court. She also formed an attachment to Lord Thomas Howard, younger half-brother to the Duke of Norfolk, who had played so strange a part in Anne Boleyn's rise and fall.

Late in May, days after Anne's death, Margaret and Thomas made a secret marriage contract. In June or early July 1536, soon after that Corpus Christi procession, the king found out about the romance. This, at a moment when events had just thrust Margaret into the dubious distinction as her uncle's putative heir. And the Howard family, Anne Boleyn's maternal relatives, were a tribe prominent and thrusting enough that Thomas might be thought to be dreaming of a throne.

Henry had the couple thrown into the Tower, and his Act of Attainder would charge that Thomas, in marrying a girl 'which pretended to be the lawful daughter to the Queen of Scots, should aspire by her to the dignity of the imperial crown of the realm'. New legislation was brought in to ensure that unsanctioned marriage with any of the king's near relations might be considered treason. Thomas was sentenced to suffer a traitor's hideous death; and, the Act continued, 'be it enacted that the woman so offending shall incur like danger and penalty, and shall suffer such-like death and punishment as the man offending'.

The Imperial ambassador Chapuys wrote that Margaret might even suffer the fate of a female traitor – death by burning. Soon, however, he could send another bulletin: that Margaret had 'for the present, been pardoned her life considering that copulation had not taken place'. The intercessor on Margaret's behalf would appear to have been Thomas Cromwell, to whom she wrote frantic assurances 'not to think that any fancy doth remain in me' touching Thomas Howard. From Scotland her mother, Henry's sister, also pleaded that her daughter should be treated leniently. But Margaret's timing proved even more unfortunate when, on 23 July, Henry had to hear of the sudden death of his illegitimate son Henry FitzRoy whom many thought he might yet make his heir.

Chapuys said rather pointedly that Margaret should not be blamed too harshly, having daily seen examples of such behaviour 'in her own family circle'. But perhaps Margaret was following her family in another way – in eliding the dreams and desires of the real world with those of literary fantasy.

The so-called Devonshire Manuscript is one of the most striking arte-facts in the whole history of courtly love. The manuscript is a verse miscellany; a notebook, passed backwards and forwards between a clever, cultivated, glamorous young group who first clustered together in Anne Boleyn's rooms. The question of whether Anne herself made any direct contribution to the manuscript is a debated point; the answer is probably not. But she sowed the seeds of which it was the flower. The group transcribed verses that had impressed them (more than two thirds of the 190-odd items are by Thomas Wyatt); commented upon them; and added original verses of their own. Nicola Shulman memorably described the Devonshire Manuscript as the Facebook of its day. She wrote around 2010; were she doing so a decade later, a WhatsApp group might have been an even more apt analogy.

Margaret Douglas was one of the leading lights of the group – the one whose handwriting appears all over the manuscript – as were two friends. Anne Boleyn's cousin Mary Howard, daughter of the Duke of Norfolk, had been married to the king's illegitimate son Henry FitzRoy. Her initials, M.F., were on the cover of the bound manuscript, and a poem by her brother the Earl of Surrey is transcribed in her handwrit-ing. But more of the handwriting belongs to Mary Shelton, another of Anne's cousins, whose mother was Thomas Boleyn's sister, and whose surname (as Sheltun) is spelt out in the first letter of each stanza of one poem. Underneath that poem – a male lover's plea that he is 'suffering in sorrow' – Shelton wrote that 'undesired service requires no hire' (or, 'undesired favours deserve no hire': the writing is unclear).*

One particular handful of poems, seeming to address and answer one another, may represent Margaret Douglas and Thomas Howard's time in the Tower; were probably even written there and passed between the pair of them, by the connivance of their gaolers. Critics warn against too simplistic an identification of poetic posture with reality. Poetry, for the Tudor courtier, was essentially performative: a proof of wit, a tool of propaganda, designed to produce an effect. But here, the match of writing with real events is too close to be ignored.

Their plight – longing unfulfilled – was itself the very essence of the distant, the estranged courtly fantasy. As Thomas wrote:

Who hath more cause for to complain
Or to lament his sorrow and pain
Than I which loves and loved again
Yet can not obtain?

One of the poems they exchanged had, drawn underneath it, two barbed arrows – Cupid's darts. Love was supposed to hurt. But the poems in Margaret's voice proclaim enduring love and, by implication, trumpet defiance at those who had imprisoned them. Poetry could also be a means to express what could not safely be said elsewhere.

I may well say with joyful heart,
As never woman might say beforn,
That I have taken to my part
The faithfullest lover that ever was born.
Great pains he suffereth for my sake,
Continually both night and day.
For all the pains that he doth take,
From me, his love will not decay.

---

* Notes scribbled around that poem also have Margaret Douglas recommending 'Forget this', and Mary Shelton contradicting that 'it is worthy'. It sounds a curiously modern exchange.

The author declares that she, in turn, is doing right, according to the rules of love, in giving herself to this faithful lover:

> Who shall let [prevent] me then, of right,
> Unto myself him to retain
> And love him best both day and night
> In recompense of his great pain?

It was a proclamation in favour of love itself, setting the rules that had been laid down for courtly love above those of socially accepted reality. This was not the humble face Margaret showed her uncle Henry. Thomas's reply acknowledges the difference in rank that had been the cause of their troubles:

> Since ye descend from your degree,
> Take ye this unto your part,
> My faithful, true and loving heart.

But Margaret Douglas's real need was to prove to her uncle the king that her heart was faithful, true and loving towards Henry himself. It seems she succeeded: by the end of the year, the king had melted sufficiently to assure her mother Margaret Tudor that if his niece would 'conform herself to what is convenient henceforth', he would be good to her.

In Scotland, however, Margaret Tudor was finding her own third marriage her unhappiest yet: Henry Stewart, Lord Methven, was another husband sexually unfaithful and spendthrift with her money, while her son James V kept her estranged from power. In 1537 her complaints finally drew a magnanimous response from her brother. She should tell the English emissary the points wherein she found herself evil-handled by 'Lord Muffyn' (Methven, who was spreading rumours she would remarry Angus), and Henry would take up her cause.

Her dream of returning south once more would never be fulfilled. But the position of both Margarets, mother and daughter, could only be eased by Henry's pleasure in the news at the English court.

*   *   *

Above: The medieval cult of courtly love was all about the heart, as reflected in this illustration of Venus from a manuscript of Christine de Pizan's writings.

Below: The adulterous yet noble passion of Lancelot and Guinevere, from the popular Arthurian romances, came to embody *fin'amor*. The early fourteenth-century image from the Vulgate Cycle (left) shows Guinevere and Lancelot speaking of love; the other depicts the pair in fifteenth-century finery, embracing for the first time.

Above: In the early years of his reign Henry VIII, watched by his queen Catherine or Katherine, of Aragon, rode as 'Sir Loyalheart', his horse's trappings embroidered with her initial 'K'.

Below: The European court painter Michael Sittow depicted a young noblewoman variously identified as Henry VIII's sister Mary or his wife Catherine, and seems to have used the same model for Mary Magdalen (here). The Catherine of Henry's early reign was a figure with whom he could easily fall in love.

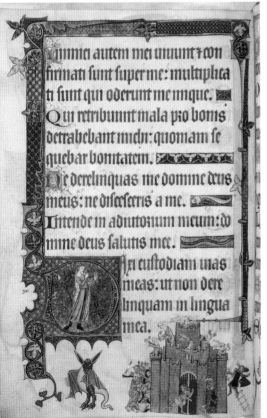

Above: The Henry who Anne saw in the 1520s was not yet the bloated figure of later years; while her appeal for him lay not in conventional beauty but in her force of character and cosmopolitan distinction.

Left: No illustration survives of the Siege of the Château Vert, where Henry first noticed Anne Boleyn, but we do have the kind of image Henry and his courtiers were looking at when they conceived it. The Luttrell Psalter two centuries before showed a Siege of the Castle of Love (bottom right), defended by ladies throwing roses.

The painting commemorating the coronation of Elizabeth I echoes the coronation portrait of Richard II, an earlier monarch famous for his chastity.

In the first half of her reign Robert Dudley, Earl of Leicester (*above left*) and Christopher Hatton (*above right*) cast themselves as worshipful courtly lovers as they competed for Elizabeth's favour. Later, Walter Ralegh (*below*) hailed her in verse.

Above: When the 'Armada Portrait' was painted Elizabeth was in her mid-fifties. The strategically placed pearl below her waist links her virginity to her nation's triumph.

Though the marriage of Margaret Douglas to the Earl of Lennox was originally arranged for political ends, they developed deep affection for each other, commemorated in the heart-shaped Lennox Jewel. Two hearts pierced by arrows are among the symbols of profane and sacred love inside.

Above right: Now believed to show the Earl of Southampton, Essex's friend and Shakespeare's patron, this miniature was once believed to represent a woman. Gender fluidity could be a characteristic of courtly love.

The 'Young Man Among the Roses' by Nicholas Hilliard may well be Elizabeth's last great favourite, the Earl of Essex. The black and white of his clothing are her colours; the wild rose her favourite flower; while the soaring tree trunk may represent either masculine strength or constancy.

Above: The 'Procession Picture' of Elizabeth apparently borne aloft by her courtiers is believed to have been painted by Robert Peake the Elder around 1601. It demonstrates not only the ritual adulation demanded by the queen, but the convention that gave her face a 'Mask of Youth'.

Left: Courtly love never entirely died out. Chivalry was at the heart of the Victorian dream, and 'The Accolade' (1901) was one of Edmund Leighton's best-known paintings.

The motto Jane Seymour took as queen was 'Bound to obey and serve'. In the summer of 1537 nothing was too good for the expectant queen – not even quails sent especially from Calais for which she had a pregnant woman's fancy – and in September the birth, at last, of Henry's longed-for son assured her position.

The christening of baby Edward seemed to promise, as Jane might have hoped, a reconciliation of old and new. One half-sister Mary was the baby's godmother, and the other, Elizabeth, carried the chrisom-cloth. Henry's (and Anne's) reforming Archbishop Cranmer officiated. But within days Jane sickened and died, leaving Henry sincerely to mourn her.

In his eyes if not those of posterity she would – as mother to his son – be remembered as his most significant queen; the one alongside whom he would be buried. Perhaps it is cynical to suggest, also, that, on a personal level, he had not had time to tire of her . . . But, had she lived, as the mother of Henry's son, Jane would have been unassailable.

If Jane's advent had heralded the disgrace and incarceration of Margaret Douglas, Jane's exit would see Margaret once more at liberty. The birth of Edward meant that she was no longer heir presumptive to the throne. In the autumn of 1537, when Margaret and Thomas both fell ill of an ague in the Tower, Margaret was sent to Syon Abbey to recover.

One of Thomas Howard's later poems borrows extensively from – figures himself and Margaret as – Chaucer's *Troilus and Criseyde*. Prophetically, it echoes Troilus's grief at the news Criseyde is to be sent away, and hints at a darker fate for himself:

But when you come by my sepulchre,
Remember that your fellow resteth there,
For I loved eke, though I unworthy were.

Thomas Howard was indeed less lucky than Margaret. As his nephew the Earl of Surrey wrote:

The gentle beast so died, whom nothing could remove,
But willingly to lose his life for loss of his true love.

When told he had died of the ague from which she recovered, Margaret took the news 'very heavily'. Within a year, however, her uncle was once more considering her potential marriage, like those of his daughter-in-law Mary FitzRoy and his young daughter Elizabeth, as part of his diplomatic plans. And King Henry himself had to start thinking of a fourth wife.

There was never any question but that Henry needed to marry again. He had an heir but no spare and – himself a second son – could hardly view that as a situation of safety. But this time, fate had caught him on the hop; after the shock of Jane's death it took more than eighteen months – long enough to cause considerable concern at court – before a suitable new bride could be agreed upon. Much of the delay was due to Henry himself, and his own oddly anachronistic attitudes.

There was talk of Christina, Duchess of Milan, the sixteen-year-old niece of Charles V. But the beautiful and educated Christina famously, if apocryphally, declared that if only she had two heads, one would be at the King of England's disposal. Henry liked the idea of that other young widow, Marie de Guise, a kinswoman of the French king, saying that he and Marie should suit well since they were both large in stature. Tall Marie is said to have added her *mot* to the Tudor lexicon by retorting that though she might be large in person, she had a little neck.

Marie would indeed be a significant player in English affairs; but not in the way Henry had planned. In May 1538, to Henry's fury, she married James V of Scotland, arriving in time to form a warm relationship with Margaret Tudor, the mother-in-law who might instead have been her sister-in-law. Margaret never made that journey back to her brother's court, dying in Scotland in 1541.

Any thought of an alternative French match for Henry foundered on his insistence on meeting the women concerned – his suggestion they might all be brought to Calais so he could see which one he liked best. The French envoy managed to shame him by asking pointedly whether he would like to try them all in bed – and whether this was how King Arthur, how the Knights of the Round Table, had behaved?

There remained the possibility of the political alliance Cromwell had always favoured – not with a leader of Catholic Europe but with the Protestant Germans to the north. An alliance with Anne of Cleves.

Her brother the Duke of Cleves was no part of the recent Protestant alliance called the Schmalkaldic League. But their elder sister was married to a Lutheran leader, the Duke of Saxony. It was good enough. But was Anne? The English envoy sent with private instructions from Cromwell to discover Anne's 'beauty and qualities . . . her shape, stature and complexion' reported back that 'for the face, as for the whole body' Anne surpassed Christina of Milan 'as the golden sun excelleth the silvern moon'. By March 1539 negotiations had begun.

This was the only one of his six marriages in which the king tried to follow the royal norm and make a match based on political expediency. Even so, he sent his painter Hans Holbein to the German court – but it was in Holbein's demure yet beguiling image, which purposely but disastrously concealed Anne's long nose, that the first seeds of trouble lay.

The next wave of English ambassadors pointed out that Anne (and her younger sister, an alternative candidate) were so thoroughly concealed by their bulky German court dress that little of them could be seen. 'What, would you see them naked?' countered the German envoy. Anne's lack of education was noted. She could read and write her own language but knew no other; spent her time sewing rather than in card games; had little interest in the 'good cheer' which was 'our English pastime'. In Germany, moreover, it was taken for 'a rebuke, and an occasion of lightness' that a great lady should have any knowledge of music, that important transmitter of the courtly love tradition.

But the spin perhaps sponsored by Cromwell emphasised that Anne was grave, good and gentle. It made her sound like . . . Jane Seymour, basically. Perhaps Cromwell should have remembered that Henry had already ricocheted from Catherine to Anne Boleyn to Jane – from grave to gay and back again. Perhaps he was ripe for another ricochet? Or perhaps, even, unconscious expectations were aroused by the idea of another queen called Anne; another (he might have hoped) bringing with her a waft of culture from beyond the sea.

In October 1539, Anne of Cleves began her slow journey towards England. From the moment of arrival on 27 December, however, it was clear things would not go smoothly.

The English courtiers sent to meet her repeated those words: good and gentle. And far from stupid, able rapidly to learn English ways . . .

Henry's hopes were high. Maybe that's why he took a decision, 'to nourish love', to surprise his bride along the way.

It is one of the minor debates of Tudor history, whether Anne of Cleves was or was not the bulky, unattractive Flanders mare Henry described. But certainly she failed to conform to the fantasy of the desirable, the courtly, lady for whose arrival Henry had prepared by polishing up his own musical skills, and ordering in stocks of artistic luxuries. Travelling down to Rochester, Henry – disguised, with a group of his courtiers around him – burst into Anne's presence, as she watched a bull-baiting from a window. He told her he had to deliver a present from the king, and tried to snatch a kiss. Anyone at the English court could (should?) have told Anne that Henry loved disguise, though in fact his height – and by now his bulk – made him easily recognisable. They might have explained that this was a trope familiar from the courtly love story. Henry was horrified when Anne repulsed him – when she failed to demonstrate love by penetrating his disguise. According to one witness he left abruptly, and without handing over the gift of bejewelled sables he had brought her.

Margaret Douglas, wholly rehabilitated now, had been appointed chief of the six 'great ladies of the household', attending the prospective queen. But as the royal group moved back towards Greenwich, Henry made his private views about the planned marriage known to the men around him: 'How like you this woman? Do you think her so fair and of such beauty as report hath been made'?

When Cromwell, maker of the match, asked eagerly how the king liked his bride, 'Nothing so well as she was spoken of,' Henry answered heavily. Already – though Cromwell may not quite have assimilated the fact – the king was looking for a way out. On 3 January he met Anne formally, on Blackheath, both dressed in cloth of gold. But the wedding scheduled for the following day did not take place.

Henry was thrashing like a fish on a line, summoning the council to find some legal way off the hook. The only possibility came from the question of whether Anne had been pre-contracted to the Duc de Lorraine's son. She would have to sign a solemn declaration that no such contract had taken place . . . She signed. Henry knew there was no way out without making such 'a ruffle in the world' as to push Anne's brother into the emperor's camp. 'Is there none other remedy,' he asked vainly, 'but that I must needs, against my will, put my neck in the yoke?' There was none, and on 6 January the two were wed.

The marriage celebrations followed the public celebratory royal pattern: banquets, masques and 'divers disports'. What came after, in the bedchamber, was as much of a failure as Catherine of Aragon claimed her disputed wedding night with Arthur had been, almost forty years before. The next morning Henry, asked by a quaking Cromwell how things had gone, replied: 'I liked her before not well, but now I like her much worse. For I have felt her belly and her breasts, and thereby, as I can judge, she should be no maid.' We can perhaps dismiss this, since any real suspicion as to Anne's virginity would have been a serious matter, and worthy of more mention. But the crux was what Henry said next. This conviction 'struck me so to the heart when I felt them that I had neither will nor courage to proceed any further in other matters'.

We should perhaps remember that Henry was an unfit and increasingly obese 48-year-old, his waist almost twenty inches larger than it had been; remember how scathingly Anne Boleyn and her brother had spoken of his virility some years before. But remember too that consummation was a crucial component in making a marriage. 'I left her as good a maid as I found her,' the king added, definitively.

Henry tried again on the third and fourth nights of the marriage, and consulted unattractively with his doctors, telling them that the 'loathsomeness' of Anne's body was such that he could by no means be 'provoked or stirred' to the act with her. (Though to prove it was not his potency at fault, he declared he had had *duas pollutiones nocturnas*, two wet dreams.) On this worryingly clinical note, Anne's career as queen began.

Anne sought to make a success of the role. She, like Jane Seymour before her, was prepared to risk Henry's wrath in order to invite his existing children to court. She, like Anne Boleyn, attended the May Day jousts with him; though perhaps it was not only his ulcerated leg, never healed from that old jousting injury, which prevented him riding in her honour.

But a very revealing conversation soon took place between Anne and her ladies. They had been primed to ask whether she might be with child; in response to their prodding, Anne told them that the king got into bed with her every night, kissing her in greeting and farewell. But there would, as her ladies declared, need to be more than that to make a Duke of York. Could Anne really be so naïve? It seems likelier that, in her untenable position, she was desperately groping after what best to say to whom – or indeed (given her lack of English!) that the whole conversation was a convenient invention of good Tudor courtiers, who had every motive to suggest no possible consummation had taken place.

As for the king, he heard some consolingly meant but ultimately unpalatable home truths from Anthony Denny, his Groom of the Stool and *ipso facto* confidant. 'The state of Princes . . . in matters of marriage [is] far of worse sort than the condition of poor men,' Denny sympathetically told his master. While 'poor men be commonly at their own choice and liberty', princes 'take as is brought to them by others'.

Or don't take, as the case may be. The painful process of Henry's ridding himself of the match Thomas Cromwell had made would cost Cromwell his head. In June 1540 the king's great fixer was attainted as 'the most false and corrupt traitor, deceiver and circumventor' of Henry's authority; and perhaps kept alive until the end of July only that he might perform one last service in helping to end the Cleves marriage.*

On 24 June Anne of Cleves was sent away from court. On 6 July (with the anti-Cromwell party now in the ascendant) she was told that the question of that pre-contract with Lorraine's son still concerned King Henry; that she was required to assent to an investigation into it. The decision was a foregone conclusion. By the end of 9 July Anne was no longer queen.

She had wisely done little to fight the proceedings, instead submitting herself to Henry's 'goodness and pleasure'. She had of course no weapons with which to fight; had, moreover, the memory of Anne Boleyn's fate; of how little Catherine of Aragon's struggles had availed.

By way of reward, Anne was left with honourable rank as the king's 'dear sister'. She had spirit enough, after writing to her brother in

---

* A near-casualty of Cromwell's fall was Thomas Wyatt who, the following year, would be back in the Tower. The charge was suspect dealing with Catholics abroad, but his real crime may have been his closeness to the disgraced minister.

Cleves to inform him the marriage was over, to send Henry back her wedding ring (the ring that celebrated their 'pretensed marriage'), 'desiring that it might be broken in pieces as a thing which she knew of no force nor value'. We like to imagine Anne of Cleves, in the years ahead, as happy doyenne of her own destiny. But the evidence suggests that she never ceased to mourn her role as queen.

Henry, meanwhile, was already deep in love – or lust, or infatuation – with one of Anne of Cleves's ladies: Katheryn Howard, young cousin to Anne Boleyn.[*]

Henry VIII's fifth marriage was undoubtedly a matter of emotion on his side at least. He was besotted with his 'jewel' – but he seems not to have felt the need to couch his fancy in courtly terms. If courtly love was in the end a fantasia performed upon the theme of power, then between the king and the pretty flirtatious teenager there was no question and no pretence as to how the balance of power lay.

All the same, in a different way, Katheryn would be as much a victim as her kinswoman Anne of that still-potent fantasy.

---

[*] The proliferation of C/Katherines in Henry VIII's marital history is a problem for the writer – never mind any confusion it caused in his own psyche! I shall therefore use Katheryn, one of the contemporary spellings, for Henry's fifth wife.

15

'it makes my heart die'

1540–1547

IT WOULD BE said that Henry, in the throes of his distaste for Anne of Cleves, 'did cast a fantasy' on Katheryn the first time that he saw her. She was promoted by her Howard relatives as an alternative candidate for Henry's fancy to the Cleves match arranged by Thomas Cromwell – and by the early summer of 1540 a full-blown affair had been under way for some time.

The Cleves match was formally annulled by Parliament on 12 July; Cromwell was executed on the 28th; on the same day, at Oatlands Palace in Surrey, Henry married Katheryn, his 'jewel'. The motto she took was 'Non autre volonté que la sienne' – no other will but his.

History has identified Katheryn Howard almost entirely through her sexuality – and through the extreme youth that has been invoked to excuse her seeming adultery. Youth, and perhaps silliness, since her relations with other men tend to be presented less as adult overwhelming grand passion than as a teenager's heedless inability to understand that actions have consequences. Even her notably tiny stature paves the way for patronage. Nonetheless, there is evidence that to some degree at least she tried to fulfil the requirements of queenship. She made efforts to draw Henry's children together with their father (despite some initial difficulty with Mary, the stepdaughter several years older than she). She exercised the queen's intercessory function on behalf of Thomas Wyatt, who was duly released from the Tower; albeit on the unwelcome and highly unusual condition he reconciled with his wife, Elizabeth Brooke, who was, however distantly, one of the

Howard kin. Wyatt died from sickness the following year, probably still in his thirties, having twice escaped the axe that had hovered over his head. But Katheryn's problem lay not in her good intentions, but in her past, which held secrets unknown to Henry.

The date of Katheryn Howard's birth is unsure. It would be good to know, since the vagaries of her dubious reputation depend in part on whether she married Henry as a teenager or as a comparatively mature – by Tudor standards – and therefore more responsible young woman. But dates as early as 1518 and as late as 1525 have been suggested, with the likeliest between 1521 and 1523. A niece, like Anne Boleyn, of the great Duke of Norfolk, Katheryn was, however, one of ten children, sprung from a very minor branch of the spreading family tree. She came to court in late 1539; 'glad and desirous' to do so.

She had spent eight of her growing years in the household of her step-grandmother the Dowager Duchess of Norfolk, at Horsham in Sussex or at Lambeth – where the duchess, as would later transpire, had exercised only a very casual chaperonage. There is little evidence of Katheryn's having had very much in the way of book-learning; but one thing was done, probably with the aim of fitting her for a court career. One Henry Manox was hired to teach her music and to play on the virginals.

Manox would later say he fell in love with her; but there are two ways of looking at what came next. One sees Katheryn as a flirtatious teenager; the other sees her as a youthful victim of abuse. There was a certain amount of sexual foreplay – Manox would later claim to 'have had her by the cunt, and I know it among a hundred'. When the duchess found out about it, she gave the girl 'two or three blows' and forbade them to be alone together. But Manox did not take Katheryn's virginity. That was left for a young Howard kinsman, one Francis Dereham, who came to join the duchess's household, and swiftly became an intimate of the maidens' chamber.

By night – as would later be revealed – a group of young gentlemen would enter the locked maidens' dormitory, by purloined key. They would bring 'wine, strawberries, apples and other things to make good cheer'. In the darkness, things went far beyond a dorm feast. Others present would later describe how Katheryn and Dereham, in one of the shared beds, would 'hang together by the bills [lips] like sparrows'.

Another described seeing Dereham lift Kat's clothes 'above her navel'. One Alice Restwold described the 'puffing and blowing' that went on. Katheryn herself would later admit that Dereham lay with her naked 'and used me in sundry sort as a man doth his wife, many and sundry times'. Indeed, the pair considered themselves, referred to each other as, husband and wife. A jealous Manox tipped off the duchess, but her grumbles at the couple's 'misrule' fell short of any real condemnation of their morality.

As Katheryn came to court, the affair seemed to have ended; nor did any of her relatives see it as a bar to putting her in the way of King Henry. But there were a number of people who knew about her past, if the king did not. And several of them pushed to join the court of the new Queen Katheryn, anxious to cash in; their whispering at worst attempted blackmail, at best loose-lipped folly.

Most dangerous among them, or so it seemed, was the braggartly Francis Dereham. When one of the queen's gentlemen ushers, Mr Johns, sent Dereham a rebuke for taking liberties allowed only to members of the queen's council, Dereham bragged: 'I was of the queen's council before he [Johns] knew her and shall be when she hath forgotten him.' But Katheryn was amassing far more serious evidence against herself.

Anything that happened with Manox or Dereham had happened before her marriage to the king; and failing to tell your future husband everything about your earlier life was not – yet – a crime. But before the court set off on progress northwards in 1541, Katheryn had become dangerously close to one of Henry's gentlemen (and yet another of her own distant kinsmen, on her mother's side), the handsome young Thomas Culpeper.

Now in his mid-twenties, Culpeper had risen high in the king's favour. One source would describe him as having succeeded to Henry Norris's place (hardly auspicious, given Norris's fate). But Culpeper himself may have had a dodgy past. A man of his name – a name he shared with his elder brother – had recently been pardoned after apparently raping the wife of a park keeper while 'three or four of his most profligate attendants were holding her at his bidding'. It is another instance of the strong class bias – only ladies counted – that underlay the code of chivalry.

That royal progress northwards would be remembered for giving occasion to several private meetings between Culpeper and Queen Katheryn. Up a backstairs to her bedroom at Temple Brewer; behind a bolted chamber door at Pontefract Castle; a four-hour conversation at Gainsborough Old Hall near Lincoln. Their meetings were facilitated and their privacy guarded by Jane, Lady Rochford, the widow of George Boleyn. The attainder against Katheryn would describe how 'that bawd the lady Jane Rochford' facilitated one meeting, from eleven at night till three in the morning, in 'a secret and vile place' – a privy.

The verdict of history depends less on reports of these meetings than on a letter Katheryn wrote to Culpeper. But there could be two ways of looking even at that.

The letter declares that Katheryn 'never longed so much for anything as to see you and speak with you'. It has been suggested, though, that this was less because of any passion, than that they had urgent business to settle – even that Culpeper was threatening to reveal the indiscretions of Katheryn's past.

Perhaps the same interpretation could apply to: 'my trust is always in you that you will be as you have promised me'. Even the letter's sign-off – 'yours as long as life endures' – was within the standard parameters of the day. And contemporary letters were often written as exercises in literary tropes, their exaggerated phrases of affection drawn from rhetoric or poetry. Both Katheryn Howard and Thomas Culpeper swore they did not consummate their relationship – though Culpeper would later admit he *intended* 'to do ill' with her, 'and that likewise the Queen so minded with him' – and historians have tended to believe them.

The life of a court, a teetering pyramid of influence and patronage, offered many reasons, sex apart, why a young man on the make would wish to get close to a queen. And of course Katheryn's higher rank – like the urging of secrecy; the use of the go-between, Lady Rochford; even the description of Culpeper as sick (lovesick) – fits within the tradition of courtly love. It might be said Katheryn Howard was insufficiently educated to be cognisant of the game, but that is to ignore how often courtly poetry took the form of song. And if there is one thing we do know about Katheryn, it is that she was (by Manox!) tutored in music.

But *if* the crucial letter from Katheryn to Culpeper is to be perceived as an exercise in the rhetoric of courtly love, it only shows how debased the dream had become. And one line is hard to reconcile with this theory: 'it makes my heart die to think I cannot always be in your company'. Was she just trying to play the courtly game, and doing it rather inexpertly? (But, four hours spent solely talking? In a privy? The conversation is hard to imagine.)

Lady Rochford seems to have played a curious role here: advising the young queen to 'give men leave to look on her' (since they were going to do so anyway); encouraging her to meet with Culpeper, who 'meant nothing but honesty'. And Katheryn does seem in a sense to have pushed the idea away: telling Lady Rochford to avoid any more meetings with Culpeper, that she had no wish for such 'light matters'.

It would not, however, be Culpeper or Lady Rochford, or even Dereham, who directly brought Katheryn into jeopardy. It was instead one of the girls who had shared the maidens' chamber in Katheryn's grandmother's house, and who sought a place in the queen's household that would allow her to share her former roommate's 'great destiny'. This girl spoke to her brother of the queen's former 'light behaviour'; and her brother (a religious reformer hostile to the conservative Howard faction) reported it to Cranmer. The horrified archbishop had no choice but to act.

On 2 November, as Henry went to Mass, he found a letter left by Cranmer on his seat, describing Katheryn's behaviour before her marriage. His first reaction was disbelief; but over the following days, subsequent revelations fell like a series of cards, albeit more slowly. Manox, brought in for questioning, described how he had urged Katheryn to 'let me feel your secret', and she had consented, if he would be content with that. Dereham, brought in likewise, revealed how they had often shared a bed – 'six or seven times ... naked'; and that, crucially, when he joined her royal household he had hoped to have relations with her again. On the night of 6 November Henry left Katheryn behind him at Hampton Court for a specially convened council meeting in Whitehall. He greeted the revelations there with tears, reportedly calling for a sword that he might kill Katheryn himself.

Worse was to come. On 11 November, probably under torture, Francis Dereham named Thomas Culpeper. Three days later Katheryn, with her household dismissed, was taken to Syon Abbey. Questioned, she admitted three secret meetings with Culpeper, though denying 'on her oath' that he had ever touched 'any bare part of her' beyond her hand, which he had kissed at the end of that meeting in the privy, saying he 'would presume no further'. The same day, Culpeper was taken to the Tower. Henry had once again been betrayed by one of the men closest to him, as Arthur had been betrayed by Lancelot.

But there were suggestions that Henry, once his first burst of rage was over, was inclined to mercy. Katheryn, accused, lamented that she had been too 'blinded with desire of worldly glory' to have told Henry of her 'former faults', but denied wrongdoing with Culpeper. And after all, if she had been married to Dereham (and promise and consummation would constitute a binding pre-contract) then she had never been married to – and could never have been unfaithful to – the king. Word was she might be let off with imprisonment; or with the annulment of her royal marriage; or even forgiven completely.

There had been little more than two weeks between Anne Boleyn's accusation and her execution: with Katheryn, it took two months. Dereham and Culpeper were executed on 10 December (Culpeper's sentence commuted to beheading but Dereham suffering the full horror of hanging, drawing and quartering). But it was late January before a Bill of Attainder against Katheryn Howard was passed; February before she, and Jane Rochford, were sentenced to death.

It may well have been the religious radicals dominating the council who pushed Henry to proceed against her and ensured, too, that she was never brought to actual trial. New legislation did now make it illegal for any woman to marry the king without disclosing the errors of her past. The lord chancellor noted with concern in Parliament that Katheryn had thus 'had not liberty to clear herself'; but in fact, she seems to have sought none – refused, even, an open trial. On 10 February Katheryn was taken from Syon to the Tower; and on 13 February 1541 was executed by the axe: no French swordsman here. Chapuys heard that the night beforehand, she asked for the headsman's block to be brought to her room, so that she could practise doing things properly. She did: an observer recorded that she made a 'most godly and Christian' end. It is only a myth, reported by the Spanish

Cronica, that she cried out – romantically, but damningly – that she died a queen, but would rather have died the wife of Culpeper.

Chapuys noted the depths of Henry's grief in the days before Katheryn's death – that he showed 'greater regret at her loss than at the faults, loss or divorce of his preceding wives'; possibly, as the ambassador perceptively noted, because (as with Jane) he did not already have another candidate lined up. But perhaps the king was mourning the death of love itself – mourning the loss of his role as the devoted lover.

Perhaps the brutality of Katheryn's fall and execution did, however, display once again how romantic love could turn sour – and how, in an age when real power was almost always vested in the male, it was then the woman who had to pay. And though it paled in comparison to her other offences, Katheryn Howard had been caught up in yet another potentially lethal love story: a drama, once again, with Margaret Douglas at its heart.

Margaret had been appointed to a prominent place in Katheryn's household and had been one of the four ladies attending her on that fatal northern progress. And Margaret had fallen in love again, while Katheryn was still perched unconvincingly on her throne. She had formed another romantic attachment to another Howard: Charles Howard, the brother of little Queen Katheryn (and nephew – though not necessarily much the younger – to that Thomas Howard with whom Margaret had intrigued before).

News broke in November 1541, in bizarre (or telling) tandem with the suggestion of Katheryn's adultery. On 10 November, just three days after Archbishop Cranmer questioned the queen, Chapuys was writing to Mary of Hungary that Charles Howard had been 'forbidden the King's chamber', the French ambassador chiming in the day after that he was 'banished from Court without reason given'.

Family history cannot have helped, given the king's bitter disillusionment with two queens from the Howard dynasty; but the real issue, again, was that of a potential heir to the throne contemplating marriage without sanction. Happily, contemplation seems to be as far as things had gone. While Charles fled abroad, Margaret was ordered out of the way to the Duke of Norfolk's house at Kenninghall, in company with her friend (and collaborator on the Devonshire Manuscript), Norfolk's daughter Mary. It was a light punishment. Perhaps Henry's distress and disillusionment over Katheryn encouraged him to mercy on the lesser fault.

The king's secretary instructed Cranmer that he should 'declare unto [Margaret] how indiscreetly she hath demeaned herself towards the King's Majesty, first with the Lord Thomas, and secondly with the Lord [*sic*] Charles Howard; in which part you shall, by discretion, charge her with overmuch lightness, and, finally, give her advice to beware the third time'.

In later life Margaret would indeed several times find herself confined on orders of the authorities; and over the question of unsanctioned marriage, too. But, unlike other women in the courtly story, she always bobbed up like a cork. The summer after next she was back at court to the household of Henry's sixth queen Katherine Parr – trainbearer, no less, at the wedding which took place quietly, in an oratory at Hampton Court, on 12 July 1543.

The child of a prominent courtier family, Katherine Parr had ancestors going back to both sides of the old York/Lancaster divide. Her father Thomas Parr had been sent to escort the fleeing Margaret Tudor south from Scotland, back in 1516; her mother Maud Green was heir to significant lands in the north.

Even more significantly, Maud had been one of Catherine of Aragon's ladies; and Henry's first queen was almost certainly godmother to his last. In 1517, when Katherine Parr was five, her father died of plague. Maud never remarried. Instead, while she remained close to her royal mistress, she developed something of a reputation as an instructor of the young in virtue and erudition, in languages and courtly polish. If Henry's first two wives had been women of intelligence and education, his last would make up the trio.

When she caught Henry's eye, Katherine Parr had not long turned thirty, and was not once but twice a widow. She had at seventeen been married to the well-born and well-to-do Sir Edward Burgh, but he had died after some four years of childless marriage. Within a few months she married again to John Neville, Lord Latimer, a widower with two children, twenty years older than she. His extensive family was one of the most powerful in the north – but John was about to fall foul of the challenging times.

Latimer took a leading role in the Catholic Pilgrimage of Grace. But he then quit the rebellion and returned to the royal fold, leaving Katherine to face down the rebels' wrath at Snape Castle, their Yorkshire home. Katherine herself may already have converted from the Catholic faith of her parents and royal godmother to an ardent Protestantism. In later life she vividly described the conversion of her 'obstinate, stony and intractable heart', without however suggesting the timing of it. But her Protestant connections may have been influential in sparing her husband the most serious penalty after the rebellion was put down.

In March 1543 Latimer died. Katherine had twice made what we may guess to be marriages of the head rather than the heart. Would it be third time lucky? The man on whom her fancy lit was not the ageing King Henry. It was Thomas Seymour, dashing brother to the dead Queen Jane. Though a mere fourth son, his sister's marriage to the king (and success in producing an heir) had ensured he rose swiftly, Henry himself merrily praising Thomas's 'towardness' and 'considerable merits', as well as his 'lust and youth'.

Later Katherine would write to Seymour that: 'My mind was fully bent . . . to marry you before any man I know.' But there was a force before which even the mind of a formidable woman must bend, and that was the royal will.

It had not been wholly a foregone conclusion that Henry's interest would turn Katherine's way. There had been talk of his taking up again with Anne of Cleves, of a lady called Anne Bassett, or of Thomas Wyatt's wife, soon to become widow, Elizabeth Brooke (though Chapuys's mention of her as a 'pretty young creature' suggests a possible confusion with her niece). We know almost nothing about Henry's courtship of Katherine Parr, if it can be called such. Her acceptance of the royal hand came from a conviction that it was God's will; a hope, perhaps, that her elevation could play a real role in promoting religious reform. She would write to Seymour of her tussles. But eventually 'Through His grace and goodness [God] made that possible which seemed to me impossible: that was, made me renounce utterly mine own will and to follow His most willingly.'

It would, in any case, have been very difficult to have said 'no'.

Just a few days after the wedding on 12 July, Henry's powerful secretary Thomas Wriothesley (a former satellite of Cromwell but a religious conservative) was writing that Katherine was 'for virtue, wisdom, and gentleness, most meet for his Highness and I am sure his Majesty had never a wife more agreeable to his heart than she is'. History has often pictured Katherine as more nurse than wife, to a king who on his worst days had to be lugged around his palaces in a carrying chair. But in fact she may have hoped even to bear him children. A foreign visitor would describe her 'lively and pleasing appearance', her magnificent dress of cloth of gold and crimson; financial records reveal her passion for shoes, flowers and sweet-perfumed oils.

There were no grand formalities to celebrate the union – no river procession such as Katheryn Howard had, and certainly no coronation – but there was (due in part to the plague in London continuing through the autumn) a very extended progress together: part of it involving also Henry's children. Mary was only four years younger than Katherine, and of a very different religious persuasion, but their shared tie to Catherine of Aragon made a bond between them. And Katherine succeeded in bringing about a happier relationship between Henry's whole family: not only Edward the cherished heir, being carefully reared in his own household, who wrote to Katherine as his 'most dear mother'; but Elizabeth, whose precocious love of learning Katherine encouraged. Elizabeth had so far been taught by a governess, Kat Ashley, with perhaps lessons from Edward's tutors when her establishment joined his, but now she – already becoming a fluent linguist – was given tutors of her own.

The start of 1544 saw a new Succession Act to replace that of 1536. It was, the Act acknowledged, 'in the only pleasure and will of Almighty God' whether the king would have any more children with his sixth queen, and likewise God's will whether six-year-old Edward would ever have children of his own. Failing any such, Mary and then Elizabeth were restored to their place after Edward in the succession.

Something else of moment happened in the spring of 1544. Just as at the start of his reign, Henry decided to go to war; once again in alliance with the Habsburgs and against the French. And, just as he had left Catherine of Aragon, he left his wife in charge of England. As the council of 7 July declared, 'The King's Majesty hath resolved that the Queen's Highness shall be Regent in his absence.' She would be advised by a council of five, but the king's business would pass in her name.

One of Katherine's letters to the absent Henry declares that: 'the want of your presence so much beloved and desired of me, maketh me that I cannot quietly pleasure in anything until I hear from your Majesty'. She wrote even that she made 'like account with your Majesty, as I do with God for his benefits and gifts heaped upon me daily'. It was the trope of courtly love, but with Katherine as the lover.

By contrast, a lengthy letter of his to her, written while he was away in France, speaks briskly of ambassadors and armouries ('no more to you at this time, sweetheart') before signing off 'your loving husband HENRY R'. No more talk of 'servants' – and he had been too 'occupied' to write most of the letter in his own hand – but it showed both respect and affection.

But Katherine had risen to prominence at a dangerous time for one of her religious convictions. In the months before her marriage there had been a reactionary revolt against reform – and particularly against the spread of religious books among the laity. It was in this climate that Queen Katherine set out not only to read, but to write several of them herself. Perhaps her taste of power as regent had made her bold; certainly time had seen a certain changing of the guard in her household, so that Katherine was now surrounded by women who shared her own passion for reform. There might be a surprise for Henry when at the end of September he returned home.

In June 1545 the royal printer published Katherine's *Prayers or Meditations* (*Prayers Stirring the Mind unto Heavenly Meditations*), snippets 'collected out of holy works', and the first book to be published under her own name by any woman in England. It did very well; her stepdaughter Elizabeth, who learnt much from her time at court with Katherine, translated it into Latin. Too well, perhaps? Katherine's husband Henry was growing determined (as he informed Parliament on Christmas Eve 1545) to rein back the use of a vernacular Scripture which was seeing God's word 'disputed, rimed, sung and jangled in every alehouse and tavern'. Two months later – and surely not coincidentally – the new Imperial ambassador who succeeded Chapuys reported that there were 'rumours here of a new Queen . . . Madame

Suffolk is much talked about and is in great favour.' In fact, Charles Brandon's recently widowed wife Catherine Willoughby was as great a reformer as Katherine Parr.

At one moment Katherine, visiting the sick and surly king in his apartments, had been unwise enough to turn the talk to religion. After she left, Henry complained: 'A good hearing it is when women become such clerks.' We have our account from the later Protestant writings of John Foxe and his *Book of Martyrs*; and Foxe says the conservative Archbishop Gardiner urged the king on to 'anger and displeasure'. Perhaps Henry was increasingly vulnerable to manipulation by the men around him. But certainly what followed – as Foxe tells it – was a bizarre and worrying game.

Henry gave Gardiner permission to arrest Katherine's crusading ladies, to seize their books and to convey the queen herself to the Tower. But the king confided the plan to his doctor; the doctor told Katherine, urging her 'humble submission' to the king; she went again to her royal husband. When Henry tried to provoke a discussion of religion, Katherine refused the proffered bait. She herself had no opinions; her husband in his wisdom was her 'only anchor . . . next under God'. If she had ever entered into argument with him, it was only to take his mind off the pain of his ulcerated leg . . . It was a denial both of her principles, and of the moral high ground she might have claimed as a courtly lady; but it may have saved her life. Was it, Henry asked, no more than this? Why then, sweetheart, they were friends again.

She was walking in the garden with the king next day when Wriothesley and a detachment of guards arrived with the warrant to take Katherine away. Henry stormed at him for a knave, beast and fool. Katherine had won the field . . . Or had she? Had Henry been playing with her, a perverted version of the test game so visible in courtly love? Was there, indeed, a streak of cruelty in the Tudors that responded to the exigencies of courtly role-play? (In the years ahead Elizabeth too would be figured as a cat.) But if so, on this occasion, both players won. Henry achieved Katherine's submission, and Katherine had to hold her tongue for only a limited time. On 28 January 1547 Henry was dead.

He died just days after his last execution – of the poet Henry Howard, Earl of Surrey, son of the Duke of Norfolk, on a treason charge that thinly concealed his real crime of being too close to the throne. The duke himself should have followed, but was spared by Henry's demise. But if the immediate future of England would lie with Henry's children, another of Surrey's surviving collaborators on the Devonshire Manuscript had yet a role to play.

Another story had run alongside that of Katherine Parr's queenship through the 1540s: Margaret Douglas had at last, after those turbulent love affairs, been married off, in the interests of her uncle's foreign policy. Her bridegroom was Matthew Stuart (or Stewart), Earl of Lennox, a noble with a claim to Scotland's throne who had been made into a significant player by the turbulent affairs of the Scots.

Scotland was once again a country torn by faction, reigned over by an infant. Overwhelming English victory at the Battle of Solway Moss in November 1542 had been followed by the death of Scotland's king James V, to be succeeded by his week-old daughter Mary. The pro-English faction among the Scottish nobility quickly arranged the baby queen's betrothal to Henry's young son Edward, with the country to be thrown in as her dowry; but her mother Marie de Guise instead sought an alternative, French, alliance for Mary. Henry predictably was furious, and the result was an English invasion: the so-called Rough Wooing in which swathes of Scotland were laid to waste.

But in Lennox Henry found another weapon; for Lennox was offering England his alliance. In the summer of 1543 Margaret Douglas learnt that, by way of confirming his allegiance, Henry had agreed to grant him her hand.

The issue was clouded by doubt on both sides. Henry had qualms about granting Lennox the dynastic importance Margaret represented; Lennox wondered whether a quicker route to Scottish power might not be to marry the widowed Marie de Guise herself. And in 1544, after hard bargaining on both sides, the deal was done.

A Scottish report declared that Lennox was 'far in love' with Margaret, whom he had never met. But perhaps, after all, there was to be some element of romance about the alliance. Henry's agreement that, if Lennox perform certain 'covenants', Margaret should be his, contained the following astonishing condition: 'forasmuch as we have promised unto our niece never to cause her to marry any but whom she shall find it in her own heart to love, and that, they never having one seen another, we know not how they shall like one another when they see together', the 'covenant cannot be easily now treated'.

Lennox had to win his fair lady by service to the said lady's uncle Henry, he had to agree a suitable dower, but it sounds very much as though he had also to win the lady's heart . . . Perhaps Henry was, on one level, seizing any excuse to keep Lennox dangling on a string; but it is nonetheless notable that this was the excuse he chose. Lennox's formal agreement with Henry in May 1544 still stipulated that, on meeting, he and Margaret should 'agree and well like together'.

Lennox was described as very good-looking, polished by a decade at the French court, and 'very pleasant in the sight of gentlewomen'. Both parties seem to have been delighted with each other when, in the summer of 1544, Lennox came to the English court, signing over his rights in the Scottish crown to King Henry. By way of 'an indissoluble knot-band', the marriage was agreed. Finally the tempestuous Margaret would at last find a socially sanctioned love – a partnership, as it would prove, that would endure for almost three decades (and would, through the marriage of their son Lord Darnley to Mary, Queen of Scots, help form the bloodline of the present British royal family).

It is tempting to feel that the centuries-old fabric of courtly love was at last wearing thin, rubbed bare by the long chronicle of Henry's wives. His repeated attempts to play the game in close cohesion with political reality had put an unbearable strain on both. But perhaps something else was happening here. Perhaps – jerkily, patchily – medieval courtly conventions were being subsumed into the broader sphere of what we call romantic love; something which could still be both transgressive and inconvenient, but was nonetheless more amenable to being pressed into the service of sustained marital life.

A feast at Whitehall Palace to celebrate Margaret's marriage may or may not have included Margaret herself (who perhaps was being entertained by Queen Katherine: their whereabouts are not recorded). But certainly present were Margaret's cousins, Henry's three children: Edward, Mary and Elizabeth. And if the reigns of two of Henry's children seem to represent something of a hiatus in the story of courtly love, it would nonetheless become apparent that romance still jerked the reins of the Tudor dynasty.

16

'shameful slanders'

1547–1553

HENRY VIII WAS succeeded by his nine-year-old son Edward. From the monumental figure of the old king, whose crumbling bulk seemed to embody his brutal authority even more than his splendid young manhood had done, to a pale slip of a boy. Henry's will decreed that should Edward VI die childless, Henry's elder daughter Mary should follow him. Should the same fate befall Mary, she should be succeeded by Elizabeth ... Provided, that is, that neither daughter married without the consent of the executors of his will.

Those sixteen executors – and the government of the country during the boy-king's minority – would be dominated by two men. The first to make himself felt – the young king's eldest uncle Edward Seymour – had at least the ties of blood and custom on his side as he swiftly created himself Duke of Somerset (and lord protector).

The other who came to the fore, as Edward's brief reign wore on, would be more surprising. John Dudley was the son of Edmund Dudley who, as scapegoat for Henry VII's money-grasping regime, had (with Richard Empson) been arrested and executed when Henry VIII came to the throne. After Edmund Dudley's widow had married Edward IV's illegitimate son Arthur Plantagenet, however, her son John found favour in Henry VIII's eyes: as soldier, royal servant and jousting star of the tournament. The last years of Henry's reign had seen John Dudley's talents carry him rapidly up the scale: heading the army that in 1544 crushed Scotland and then sweeping south to more success across the Channel. Dudley, even more strongly than

Seymour, was a religious reformer: all the better for closeness to the young king.

Nothing we know of the intensely Protestant schoolboy Edward VI suggests that, even had he lived longer, he would have had much time for the courtly fantasy. The first decades of the Reformation had seen a new enthusiasm for love and sex, a rejection of St Augustine's diktat that sex was necessarily sin – what Diarmaid MacCulloch calls 'a sexual revolution'. Sex safely enshrined, however, within the context of marriage . . . Protestants all over northern Europe had bought prints of Martin Luther, the former monk, and his wife the ex-nun Katharina von Bora, with whom he shared ardent after-dinner debates (he teasingly called her 'Dr Luther'), and produced six children in eight years. Even this domestication of love might well have been inimical to the courtly fantasy – but Luther died in 1546. And the advent of the Counter-Reformation, the Catholic fightback initiated by the opening of the Council of Trent in 1545, would come to see Catholics and Protestants competing as to who could exhibit a more stringent sexual morality.

As it is, Edward's romantic proclivities could never be established. For his sister Elizabeth, on the other hand, the first year of her brother's reign saw the start of an episode which might colour all her later relations with men.

Thirteen at the time of her father's death in January 1547, Elizabeth was sent to live with her stepmother Katherine Parr, who set up her establishment in Chelsea. But that spring, with scandalous speed, Katherine herself embarked on another, secret, marriage. Thomas Seymour was the man of whom she had dreamt before King Henry cast his eye upon her. He was, moreover, less than happy with the rise of his elder brother the lord protector, although as a sop he had been created England's lord admiral.* Rumour said he settled for the Dowager Queen Katherine only when baulked of his first hopes, to marry one of the two princesses, Elizabeth or Mary. And as he married Katherine – as they seemed, for that brief moment, happy;

---

* Rather likeably, describing the lord protector's evident disapproval of his younger brother's grand match, Katherine wrote that it was lucky they were not in the same place 'for I suppose else I should have bitten him!'

as she fell pregnant with his child – those hopes seem never to have gone away.

We know about the goings-on at Chelsea from the testimonies of Elizabeth's governess Kat Ashley and gentleman Thomas Parry, extracted under pressure. How the lord admiral would come bursting into her bedchamber early in the morning, pulling back the young girl's bedcurtains to 'make as though he would come at her' while she scooted away. If he caught her getting dressed, then he would 'strike her on the back or buttocks familiarly'. Next, he appeared 'bare legged', in his nightgown, and tried to snatch kisses from Elizabeth as she lay in bed.

Kat Ashley told him he went too far, for 'These things are complained of, and my lady is evil spoken of'. He answered hotly that he meant no evil – and indeed, as Kat told it, the dowager queen herself sometimes joined in Seymour's mock assaults on their stepdaughter, helping him tickle Elizabeth in bed, and once holding her when, in the garden, he cut her dress into pieces.

What was Thomas Seymour thinking? Was he thinking at all? As Sir Nicholas Throckmorton put it, neatly and damningly, he was 'fierce in courage, courtly in fashion, in personage stately, in voice magnificent but somewhat empty of matter'. It is equally hard to be sure of Elizabeth's feelings – frightened, tempted, longing? All at once, possibly. She tried (so her servants asserted) to hide, to avoid the man who stood in the position of a stepfather to her; to get away. When his name was mentioned, however, she showed 'a glad countenance'. She loved to hear him praised.

But in the spring of 1548 came a moment when the dowager queen 'suspecting the often access of the Admiral to my Lady Elizabeth's Grace . . . came suddenly upon them, where they were all alone, he having her in his arms. Wherefore the Queen fell out, both with the Admiral and with Her Grace also'. Katherine was by this time five months pregnant with Seymour's child, which provided a pretext for sending Elizabeth away to the household of Kat Ashley's sister. The letters between stepmother and stepdaughter give every future promise of a renewed closeness between them, but within a few days of giving birth to a baby girl on 30 August, Katherine developed puerperal fever. She died on Elizabeth's fifteenth birthday.

Elizabeth herself was ill at the time. She would throughout her life be plagued by nerve storms that exhibited themselves in migraine, panic attacks and menstrual problems. But some contemporaries drew a different diagnosis from the symptoms, whispering that Elizabeth had miscarried Seymour's baby. Elizabeth pleaded to be allowed to come to court to refute the 'shameful slanders'. Later there would be other tales of a country midwife summoned to attend to a very young and obviously noble lady; of a child born only to be killed at birth. For none of this is there any evidence – and improbable tales of secret pregnancies would continue to haunt Elizabeth's career.

Katherine's death left Seymour once more in search of a wife. He was, moreover, in ever more frantic search of some way to topple his brother from power and take what he considered his rightful place in the kingdom. It would not be the last time a man looked at Elizabeth and saw both personal appeal and political opportunity. But when in January 1549 Seymour tried also to seize the person of the young king, the authorities arrested him. Questioning of his known associates was bound to follow; and his treasonous ambitions for a royal marriage were by now an open secret.

Elizabeth's favourite servants were taken to the Tower, accused of having abetted Seymour, and her household taken over by Sir Robert Tyrwhit, with instructions from the Privy Council to obtain evidence of treasonable activity on Seymour's part – and on Elizabeth's, too? Tyrwhit had, he said confidently – and brutally – good hopes 'to make her cough out the whole'. But Elizabeth, metaphorically and literally, kept her head, denying that she or her household had any thought of her marrying without official approval. Her terrified servants supported her. They 'all sing one song', Tyrwhit reported disgustedly. It was only Thomas Seymour himself who, late in March, went to the block, charged with thirty-three counts of treason.

Events moved fast over the next months. That summer one Robert Kett led a rebellion against land enclosures and rural poverty. It was John Dudley who, on the instructions of Edward Seymour the lord protector, set out to quash the rebellion, which he did with ruthless efficiency. But somehow, before his forces were disbanded, in the autumn Edward himself followed his brother Thomas to the Tower, and Dudley (soon to be created Duke of Northumberland) moved to take charge of the government.

*   *   *

Elizabeth, meanwhile, had retreated into her own household (her beloved servants restored to her) and a carefully restrained life of study. Her tutor Roger Ascham described how the beginning of the day was devoted to the New Testament in Greek, followed by Greek literature and Latin literature, and by oral studies in modern languages. Kat Ashley's husband John later recalled the 'free talk' and 'trim conferences', the 'friendly fellowship' and 'pleasant studies' of the group that came to centre around Elizabeth. In truth, she must have learnt from recent experiences that talk had better not be *too* free. But what other lessons would she take away?

All her life, Elizabeth would be drawn to men with a swashbuckling streak. But the Seymour affair could only reinforce in her mind the link between sex and danger that started with the fates of her mother and stepmothers: a link which would have been apparent to many heroines of the courtly story. Small wonder if she now threw herself into the role of, as he called her, the king's 'Sweet Sister Temperance', Ascham praising not only her learning but the elegant simplicity of her dress. Perhaps the most useful lesson she had learnt, for her political future, was the art of performance on the brink of a precipice.

It worked: Elizabeth was at court for the Christmas festivities of 1549, preferred to her sister Mary by Edward's circle as being, in the words of the Imperial ambassador, 'more of their kidney'. The following year, he noted that the Christmas celebration of 1550 brought her to London 'with a great suite of gentlemen and ladies', escorted by a hundred of the king's horse and formally welcomed by the council. A parade was being made of the fact that she who had embraced the new religion had 'become a very great lady'. She had finally been granted possession of the huge land holding willed to her by her father.

The situation of Mary, by contrast, was worsening as her brother's reign wore on. Edward's accession had swiftly been marked by sweeping religious changes, carried out under the auspices of Archbishop Cranmer: the removal of images, of crucifixes, the destruction of stained glass windows and rood screens – a denial, even, of the 'real presence' of Christ at the Mass. Mary had written to her brother to express her consternation, insisting she would remain 'an obedient child' to the moderate reforms her father had laid down, until her brother should 'have perfect years of discretion'. On the extensive lands she too had inherited, her household practised according to the old religious forms.

So too did that of Margaret Douglas. Lady Lennox had soon become aware that, as a Catholic albeit not of the papal variety, she was out of favour with the new King Edward's regime, and retreated to family lands in Yorkshire. Her daughters had died early but her focus was her son Lord Darnley, already a year old when King Henry died. In Scotland her father Angus had gone over to the pro-French party, but her husband Lennox was supporting the English cause north of the border, and proving his use on the battlefield. One way and another, Margaret was sufficiently useful, sufficiently discreet, and often at sufficient geographical distance, for Edward's government to leave her alone. It was otherwise with Margaret's old friend, Princess Mary.

The new regime had at first been reluctant to challenge even Mary, tacitly allowing her to hear Mass in private, though they failed to deliver the written permission she demanded. Edward seems to have been torn between the reforming zeal urged by those around him and his affection for Mary. His council was conscious of her Habsburg relatives watching from across the sea. But as Mary's own court became a centre for disaffected Catholics, her opponents were pushing reform ever further. By 1550 she began to fear she might have to flee the country. Her kinswoman Mary of Hungary had three ships waiting off the Essex coast to aid her escape, should it be necessary.

When she came to London in March 1551, she, like Elizabeth, was accompanied by a great train of gentlefolk – but her attendants each carried a Catholic rosary. Soon Mary of Hungary was writing to the Imperial ambassador that if Mary were barred from having Mass celebrated even in private, she might have to endure it; but that if her brother's government tried to force her into 'erroneous practices . . . it would be better for her to die than to submit'.

Perhaps it was political considerations that prevented anyone proceeding to extremities. England and the Spanish Netherlands were alike dependent on the wool trade between their two countries. But soon another issue would come into play.

In the spring of 1552 (a spring that saw Elizabeth at court with an even greater train of attendants) Edward fell sick of measles, and then of smallpox. He seemed rapidly to recover; but would lapse back again.

As the autumn wore on it was obvious within court circles that the feverish and coughing boy-king was seriously ill, probably with tuberculosis. By the terms of Henry VIII's will, Mary was still her brother's heir. As he turned fourteen his councillors had begun to involve him more in matters of state – and as 1552 rolled into 1553 and his health worsened, it was Edward's own determination that his throne should not pass to Catholic Mary. It is less clear why he sought also to bar Protestant Elizabeth. One way or another, it is behind bedchamber walls that the answer may lie.

The official reason Edward gave to his agitated justices was that Elizabeth, like Mary, was a bastard. Was, moreover, the daughter of Anne Boleyn – Anne 'more inclined to couple with a number of courtiers rather than reverencing her husband, so mighty a King'. Elizabeth's feelings when she heard that can only be imagined. But the real reason is more likely to be Elizabeth's own unmarried state: the fear she might marry a Catholic prince, and England be forced back into Catholicism that way. The trouble for Edward, as for his father before him, was the absence of any male heir; neither susceptible to a husband's influence, nor inheriting Eve's sin.

The only solution – since all the candidates were women – lay in finding one already safely married, and to a Protestant. Edward had no hesitation in excluding the Catholic descendants of Henry's elder sister Margaret. (Henry in his will had taken the same decision, should all three of his own children die childless.) Mary, Queen of Scots had now been sent away to France, to be reared there as future consort to the next French king; and Margaret Douglas had, conveniently, in April been granted licence to visit distant Scotland and her relatives there.

That left the daughters of Henry VIII's younger sister Mary (who themselves had only surviving daughters). The 'Device for the Succession' Edward himself jotted down late in the spring of 1553 left the crown, first, to the 'heirs male' of Frances Grey, née Brandon, the elder of them. Failing the appearance of any such heirs, it went to the heirs male of Frances's own eldest daughter Jane Grey.[*]

Fifteen-year-old Jane was as ardent a crusader for the Protestant cause as her cousin King Edward, whom it had at one time been

---

[*] Jane's father was a descendant of Elizabeth Woodville, through Elizabeth's first marriage.

thought she might wed. But just days earlier Jane Grey had been married to Northumberland's son Guildford Dudley (a mere fourth son in the large Dudley family; but his elder brothers were married already). Her next sister Katherine married William Herbert, son of a leading English peer, at the same ceremony; while the youngest sister Mary was betrothed to another.

But soon it became apparent Jane's marriage had come too late for her to produce boys in time to inherit Edward's throne. His final scribbled correction to his 'Device', in June 1553, a month after the wedding, was an admission of defeat: the throne would go to 'the L. Jane and her heirs male'. But who – other than a vessel for the Tudor bloodline – was Jane Grey?

Few members of the English royal club can have less in common than Eleanor of Aquitaine and Lady Jane Grey. Yet both are creatures not only of history, but of legend. The image of Eleanor is of agency and controversy; that of Jane is above all that of a victim, and by implication a passive one. That has in the past made her all the more appealing, though we might seek a different coding today.

Our picture of the child Jane – nine years old when her great-uncle Henry died – comes largely from one reported conversation some three years later, with Elizabeth's tutor John Ascham. Ascham, visiting the Grey family home of Bradgate in Leicestershire, found Jane alone, and reading Plato 'with as much delight as if it had been a merry tale of Boccaccio'. Her parents were out hunting, but she was glad of it, for whenever she was with either of them:

Whether I speak, keep silence, sit, stand or go, eat, drink, be merry or sad, be sewing, playing, dancing or doing anything else, I must do it, as it were, in such weight, measure and number, even as perfectly as God made the world, or else I am so sharply taunted, so cruelly threatened, yea, presented sometimes with pinches, nips, bobs . . . that I think myself in hell, till the time comes when I must go to Mr Aylmer [her gentle tutor, Ascham's friend].

On this conversation was built the picture of her mother Frances Brandon as a cruel, hard-riding harridan, and of Jane as a pale, somewhat priggish, paragon of learning. A better scholar even than Elizabeth, hinted Ascham (who published the conversation in a book, *The Schoolmaster*, which aimed to inculcate more kindly teaching methods).

Modern scholarship has brought a more nuanced perception; though perhaps the basics remain in place. Jane's eighteen-year-old husband Guildford Dudley has often been cast as a thug but contemporaries described him as a 'comely, virtuous and goodly gentleman' and Jane seems, with whatever emotions, to have accepted him as her husband. But when, agonisingly, Edward died on 6 July, and Guildford Dudley's father Northumberland declared Jane queen, she burst into tears when she heard the news and sank to her knees. She cried out, even (so the papal envoy reported), that the Lady Mary, not she, was the rightful heir before, recovering, she prayed to God for 'such grace as to enable me to govern this kingdom with his approbation and to his glory'. To keep England in the Protestant faith, in other words.

But Jane, and those around her, had reckoned without the heir of Henry VIII's will. They had reckoned without Mary.

Even as the new Queen Jane was proclaimed, Mary – secretly warned of Edward's death before it was made generally known – had fled to East Anglia, where she had lands and supporters. On 10 July the newly declared Queen Jane was ceremonially taken to the Tower of London (not just a near-impregnable fortress but traditional lodging of monarchs before their coronation). But that evening the council, to their utter consternation, received a letter from Mary demanding 'your allegiance which you owe to God and us'.

And there were more problems for the new government. The people of London – informed in one breath of Edward's death and the accession of a virtually unknown Queen Jane – showed no sign of welcoming this deposition of Great Harry's daughters. Half a century on, it would be remarked that King James did not 'caress' the people as Queen Elizabeth had done. Perhaps Northumberland too had underestimated the resistance of those to be wooed – had failed to understand the difference between a romance and a rape.

Jane herself, within the Tower, had to be persuaded to try the crown for size. She had (according to Italian reports) already made clear her resistance to making her husband Guildford king. Others had assumed that king he would be: a despatch from the Imperial ambassador referred to 'the new King and Queen'. But Jane stood firm on the royal blood she had, and Guildford did not. There was trouble at the very heart of the London regime. In East Anglia, by contrast, hearts were high.

As Mary set up her standard at the mighty Framlingham Castle in Suffolk, many flocked to it. At sea, some of the royal ships had gone over to her cause. As the Genoese merchant Baptista Spinola reported: 'the hearts of the people are with Mary, the Spanish Queen's daughter'. On 20 July she rode down from the castle to inspect her forces (a scene which, with hindsight, evokes the later one at Tilbury). As Northumberland himself rode north to confront her, his own troops slipped away.

In London, meanwhile, the councillors turned the Tower over to Mary's supporters. Jane had been sending out – or, there had been sent out in her name – warrants proclaiming her 'title and dignity royal', demanding that her subjects resist the claims of 'the Lady Mary'. But it was an unconvincing clamour: unconvincing even to Jane herself, maybe. On the 20th Mary was proclaimed queen and for the next two days, the Imperial ambassador reported, the streets were filled with people 'mad with joy'. Jane's own father ripped down the royal canopy from above her head, and told her henceforth she should be content with a private life. Jane's answer was that in taking on the royal honours she had 'grievously sinned and offered violence to myself. Now I do willingly and obeying the motions of my own soul relinquish the crown . . .' She remained in the Tower: no longer potentate but prisoner.

Mary had followed in the footsteps of her grandmother Isabella, Spain's warrior queen; but also in those of her grandfather Henry VII. Like him, she had won a crown by right of armed victory, as well as blood and, importantly, the acclamation of the people. Like him, she would not, in later centuries, get appropriate credit for it. Robert Wingfield, in his *Vita Mariae Angliae Reginae*, wrote that her feat 'should have been judged and considered one of Herculean rather than womanly daring'. But it remained to be seen – as England's first queen regnant – what use she would make of mythologies.

'a husband may do much'

1553–1558

ON 3 AUGUST Mary formally entered London – and her
sister Elizabeth rode immediately behind her. Now, if ever,
was the time for a show of unity between Henry's daughters.
At the end of September, Elizabeth again rode behind her sister on the
way to her coronation. Mary would never make play with the tropes of
courtly love – she listened to the beat of a different drummer – but she
was aware of the need to get to grips with the chivalric aspect of
monarchy.

The ceremonies of her coronation sent a curious mixture of
messages. The day beforehand she was carried through the streets in a
litter, rather than riding as a king would do. Her hair was loose,
symbolising the traditional womanly qualities of chastity and fertility.
A male peer stood in for her at the ceremony which created fifteen new
Knights of the Bath: an important stepping stone of masculine chivalry. The next day, however, she proceeded to Westminster Abbey with
the sword of state carried in front of her by the Earl of Arundel and,
after being anointed and crowned, was presented with all the ceremonial regalia. But she merely touched the spurs, instead of attaching
them to her heels, and while she was given the king's sceptre to hold in
her right hand she also held in her left 'a sceptre wont to be given to
queens, which is surmounted by doves'.

There were two other factors with which Mary had to get to grips,
and swiftly. The first was the question of her marriage. In childhood
she had of course been betrothed several times – indeed, a Venetian

described the promise of her hand being used to make alliances as if she were a lure used to hunt birds. But later, the fact of their father's declaring them illegitimate had lost – or spared – both her and Elizabeth the arranged marriage that was the usual destiny of princesses.

Mary seems always to have assumed she needed to share her monarchy with a man; an attitude with which her contemporaries would wholeheartedly have agreed. As a private individual, she declared, she would have 'preferred to end her days in chastity', but she bowed to the opinion expressed by her cousin Charles V that 'a great part of the labour of government could with difficulty be undertaken by a woman'.*

The leading English candidate for the role of husband was Edward Courtenay, son of the Marquess of Exeter and a great-grandson of Edward IV. But the family's staunch Catholicism (and their royal blood) had caused them to fall from favour with Henry VIII. Courtenay, in his twenties, had spent all his adult life in the Tower. He was in no position to offer Mary any support in her rule.

The other leading candidate for Mary's hand suffered from no such drawback, though he too was a good decade younger than the 37-year-old Mary. Mary's queenship was hardly announced before the suggestion came that she should marry Philip of Spain, son to her former fiancé Charles V; and at the end of October, she accepted him. A fortnight later Parliament presented a petition that she would reconsider, and marry within the realm, but Mary's emotional allegiance had always been to her Spanish family. Notably – as one who was also a Tudor – her reply to Parliament's plea was couched less in political terms (the utility of a powerful Spanish alliance) than in those of her feelings. 'Where private persons in such cases follow their own private tastes, sovereigns may reasonably challenge an equal liberty,' she declared, controversially.

But from the start, the idea of the Spanish match drew deep public hostility. And within weeks of Elizabeth's leaving court in December 1553, her name was invoked as figurehead (to put it no higher) for a rebellion triggered by that hostility.

---

* Though the Habsburg regime was notable for its use of women as regents: see *Game of Queens*.

The Wyatt rebellion, aimed at replacing Mary with Elizabeth, was named for its instigator – son and namesake to Sir Thomas Wyatt who had written poems to Anne Boleyn. The rebels claimed their cause was to prevent England's 'over-running by strangers' – becoming a mere part of the vast Habsburg Empire – and the plan was for a series of coordinated risings around the country. But word reached the authorities, and only Wyatt's forces marched on London at the end of January 1554.

Mary rode out to address her troops. She had, she told them, been wedded to her realm at her coronation, 'the spousal ring whereof I wear here on my finger, and it never has and never shall be left off'. And though 'I cannot tell how naturally the mother loveth her children, for I never had any, but if subjects may be loved as a mother doth her child, then assure yourselves that I, your sovereign lady and your Queen, do earnestly love and favour you. I cannot but think you love me in return.'

She was, she added, 'neither so desirous of wedding, nor so precisely wedded to my will, that I needs must have a husband'. She would marry only if it were agreed to be 'for the singular benefit of the whole realm'. Mary's speech figured herself simultaneously in several different female roles. Addressing the soldiers guarding St James's Palace, she had couched her plea in chivalric terms, urging that they were the 'gentlemen in whom only she trusted'.

The soldiers stood; and London rallied to the queen. The armed rebellion was soon over. But it remained to be seen just how close to the throne the conspiracy had come. Two days after the collapse of Wyatt's forces, three Privy Councillors and a detachment of soldiers arrived at Elizabeth's house.

That show of unity between the sisters, in the first weeks of Mary's reign, had not lasted long. Marriage apart, the second issue with which Mary needed to get to grips was religion. She started out cautiously. A fortnight after her entry into London, she issued a proclamation that while she herself would always practise the [Catholic] religion 'which God and the world knoweth she hath ever professed from her infancy', nonetheless, because 'of her gracious disposition and clemency her highness mindeth not to compel any her said subject thereunto unto such time as further order by common consent'.

But Mary also wrote to the Pope, professing that 'his Holiness had no more loving daughter than herself'. She told one foreigner she wished to restore papal authority, but as yet such matters should not be spoken publicly. Elizabeth was likewise hiding her teeth. In September Elizabeth had an interview with her sister in which, 'having been brought up in the [Protestant] creed which she professed', she pleaded mere ignorance of, rather than hostility to, the Catholic faith. She had requested instructors and, a few days later, duly attended Mary's Chapel Royal, but with an ostentatiously 'suffering air' that gave a coded message to her supporters. But the path of compromise was becoming ever less viable as, in Europe, the Counter-Reformation gathered strength against a Protestantism in which Martin Luther's reforms were increasingly superseded by the harsher doctrines of Calvin and the Swiss reformers.

As a terrified Elizabeth was brought to court to face questioning, it became clear that all those who had ever tried to usurp Mary's place in the succession must now be deemed too dangerous to live. Though Northumberland had swiftly been executed on Mary's accession, no dreadful penalty – then – had been enacted against Jane Grey, the nine-day-queen he had hoped to make his puppet, nor against her husband. Now, that changed.

On the morning of 12 February, Guildford Dudley was beheaded. The papal envoy reported, in romantic vein, that Guildford begged to see Jane on the last night of their lives, wishing 'to embrace and kiss her one last time'; but that Jane had refused, saying it might damage their composure, and better to turn their thoughts to God.[*] Jane's voice sounded an increasingly religious tone as she neared the end of her life, sternly warning her young sister Katherine that death and judgement awaited; that if ever she compromised with the Catholic faith, 'God will deny you and shorten your days'. A last note to her father figures herself and her husband passing together from a mortal to an immortal life. She signed it 'Jane Dudley'.

Jane saw Guildford's lifeless body brought back, 'his carcass thrown in a cart and his head in a cloth'. An hour later it was Jane's own turn.

---

[*] In the Beauchamp Tower – those rooms in the Tower of London where the Dudley brothers were held – two carvings, presumably made by a prisoner, read 'JANE'.

On the scaffold the seventeen-year-old's dignified composure did crack at last as she struggled to adjust her clothing for the axe and, with the scarf tied round her eyes, groped blindly for the block. 'I pray you despatch me quickly,' she begged the headsman.

In Whitehall palace, meanwhile, the investigation went on – and on. There was in the end no evidence to prove Elizabeth had known of, had agreed to, armed rebellion. Nonetheless, on 17 March she was charged with conspiracy. The next day the councillors came to take her to the Tower of London, but she implored, first, to be allowed to make a written plea to her sister. That letter bought her the turn of the tide, and it was Palm Sunday, 19 March, before her boat set off downriver to the Tower. Physically, the terms of her imprisonment were not harsh. She had four rooms and a dozen servants. But those rooms were the ones rebuilt for Anne Boleyn's coronation – those in which she stayed before her execution.

Elizabeth's traumatic experience of confinement in the Tower may – importantly for the years ahead – have fostered her closeness to another who was being held prisoner there. Robert Dudley was – like his brother Guildford – a younger son of the executed Duke of Northumberland, imprisoned with his brothers for their part in the attempt to place Jane Grey on the throne. It is likely he and Elizabeth were already well acquainted, since Robert had attended her brother Edward.

Writers over the years have made much play with the idea of romance blooming behind the Tower's thick walls but actual trysts are unlikely. There may nonetheless have been a powerful pull in this common experience of danger and captivity. When Anne Boleyn heard that her brother George was also in the Tower she had said, 'I am very glad that we both be so nigh together.'

In the event, Elizabeth's own imprisonment would not last long. When Wyatt was executed on 11 April, his speech from the scaffold exonerated her completely. The terms of her captivity became lighter. When fresh guards appeared at the Tower early in May, she reacted with terror and asked whether Jane Grey's scaffold was still there. But the guards had come to escort her away. She left the Tower on 19 May, leaving behind the Dudleys.

It was not over, to Elizabeth's knowledge. As she lay at Richmond Palace after quitting the Tower she told her servants that, this night, 'I think to die.' There was real fear of assassination: her enemies at court had hoped to send her to Pontefract Castle, where Richard II had been murdered. In fact, she would be taken to Woodstock, and a not-uncomfortable house arrest. But the experience had helped forge her, both personally and politically.

One lynchpin of Elizabeth's identity throughout her life would be – whether or not she liked it – that of a Protestant heroine. It is one she was temperamentally inclined to resist; it showed every sign of bringing her into danger. If forced, she would, throughout Mary's reign, be prepared to attend the Catholic Mass. But – as Mary had Parliament declare valid the marriage of Henry and Catherine of Aragon – it was only by Protestant rules that Elizabeth was legitimate, and worthy a place in the succession.

The Imperial ambassador had early reported that Mary wanted to disbar Elizabeth from that succession because of her 'heretical opinion and illegitimacy, and characteristics in which she resembled her mother'. Mary would have preferred her heir to be Margaret Douglas, to whom she had already shown great favour. Mary, the Imperial ambassador noted, still resented the injuries inflicted on her mother 'by the machinations of Anne Boleyn'.

Mary had won the throne by a chivalric venture; albeit one which cast her as the knight/contender rather than the lady/prize. That makes it the more striking that her reign, her rhetoric, did *not* see – was not justified by – use of the courtly love tropes her sister Elizabeth would manipulate so successfully. But in so far as a young Mary had registered the phenomenon of courtly love, she must have perceived it as a disreputable game – an illicit weapon, a potentially lethal piece of folly. And, of course, the weapon of Anne, the enemy.

What Mary sought was a socially sanctioned as well as personally fulfilling love. A partnership of equals, happily confined within the bounds of matrimony. Would it be Mary's attitude that spurred her sister into an opposing view, so that courtly love became so vital a part of Elizabeth's armoury – of her identity? We can never know whether in their father's lifetime, in all those long days when they shared a household, they ever talked about books, poetry, ideas; but it is surely a possibility.

* * *

At the end of July, at Winchester Cathedral, Mary I married Philip of Spain. The ceremony was resplendent, the bride and groom both dressed in white and gold (though Mary chose a plain gold band for her wedding ring because, she said, so maidens were married in the olden days). But there had been awkward negotiation behind the scenes.

Long before Philip's arrival Mary had told the Imperial ambassador that in her private capacity she would love and obey her husband, 'but if he wished to encroach in the government of the kingdom she would be unable to permit it'. Mary's ambassador had been instructed by her council to stress that 'if the marriage took place the government of the realm should always remain in her Majesty and not in the prince'. Bishop Gardiner preached that Philip 'should be rather a subject than otherwise; and that the Queen should rule all things as she doth now'. The marriage treaty – published in January to reassure the public – had painstakingly laid out all the provisos that should indeed keep Philip within bounds. But against that was set the huge weight of social assumption, and personal feeling too.

As Henri II of France put it, once Philip was married to Mary, 'a husband may do much with his wife'. It would, he said, be hard for a woman 'to refuse her husband anything that he shall earnestly require of her', adding that he knew marital authority to be 'very strong with ladies'. The old Catholic marriage service had Mary promising 'to be compliant and obedient . . . as much in mind as in body'; though, once again, the messages were ambiguous.

At the feast which followed the ceremony, Mary Tudor was served on gold plate, and Philip of Spain merely on silver. Philip moved into the rooms once known as the queen's apartments, Mary taking the king's. Two days after his marriage, Philip assured Mary's council that he was available to advise, but that on any question 'they must consult the Queen, and he would do his best to assist'. But Mary for her part insisted that Philip should always be informed of the council's discussions; that all council papers were to be signed by him as well as herself. Habsburg negotiators insisted that his name should precede hers on official documents – 'Philip and Mary by the grace of God King and Queen of England'. They claimed that 'no law human or divine, nor his highness's prestige and good name' would allow otherwise. But the English Parliament would refuse to grant Philip a matrimonial crown.

And, on a personal level, the alliance Mary achieved was never likely to offer the combination she sought: of romantic love and happy domesticity. When the question of marriage had first been broached, Mary's reaction – the Imperial ambassador reported – had been excited nervous laughter. She demanded to see a portrait before she could make up her mind. She sent word to Charles V that: 'If Philip were disposed to be amorous, such was not her desire, for she was the age your Majesty knew of and had never harboured thoughts of love.' But her comportment suggests a different story.

Philip, for his part, was never going to be personally eager for a marriage with his father's cousin, eleven years older than he. In contradiction to the posthumous picture of an older Philip as a dour religious fanatic, the man who came to England loved music and jousting: he was something of a party prince. Though Mary would cling to the belief that, as she told the Venetian ambassador, her husband 'was free from the love of any other woman', Philip was in fact if anything a womaniser; happy to play the gallant all over Europe. At a feast in Milan he let the loveliest ladies drink from his own glass, enjoying their praise for his prowess in the tourney; in Binche, at an elaborately staged chivalric feast, he was one of the knights who had to win past obstacles in their way to rescue prisoners from a Dark Tower. In Brussels, he gave a banquet to celebrate the death and rebirth of the god of love. Finding themselves in Winchester for the wedding, one of the first things the Spanish nobles did was to seek out the Round Table of King Arthur.

Philip personally impressed many in England. A servant of the Lennoxes noted that his face was 'well favoured, with a broad forehead and grey eyes, straight-nosed and manly countenance', his body so well proportioned 'as nature cannot work a more perfect pattern'. Of 'stout [strong] stomach, pregnant wit, and of most gentle nature', reported another observer. He was, moreover, prepared to follow established practice in putting a chivalric gloss on a pragmatic business and play the role of loving and attentive spouse.

One Spaniard was able to describe Philip and Mary as 'the happiest couple in the world, and more in love than words can say. His Majesty never leaves her, and when they are on the road he is ever by her side, helping her to mount and dismount.' Rather less enthusiastically, however, he added that the queen was 'not at all beautiful: small, and rather flabby than fat ... She is a perfect saint and dresses badly.' Philip's confidant Ruy Gomez wrote home that his master 'is trying to be as gracious as possible to [Mary] so as not to fall short in any way of his duty'. Philip 'understands that this marriage was effected not for the flesh but for the restoration of the realm'.

And it did look as though the marriage would fulfil its primary purpose of producing a Catholic heir. In the autumn Mary was convinced she was pregnant. In the second half of April 1555 Elizabeth was summoned from Woodstock to Hampton Court. The assumption was that she would witness her sister's triumph. What she saw, in hideously drawn-out slow motion, would be Mary's tragedy.

There were rumours at the end of the month that the queen had been delivered of a son, and the nation's bells rang out, joyfully. But it was a mistake – or perhaps, a miscarriage? Still in pain, still with a swollen belly, Mary – pitifully, embarrassingly – was still also in hope. She waited in her birthing chamber through May . . . through June . . . through July. Slowly, it became evident even to her that this was a phantom pregnancy. Or perhaps, as the French ambassador heard early in May, the whole thing, swollen belly and all, had been the result of 'some woeful malady'. In August Mary quietly left her chamber.

She found that more bad news awaited her. Duty called her husband back to the Continent, where his father Charles V was planning to abdicate, leaving Spain and all its vast foreign territories to Philip. (The role of Holy Roman Emperor would go to Charles's brother Ferdinand.) Perhaps Philip was not too reluctant to answer the call. Mary was now nearing forty, and it seemed all too likely her obstetric history would echo that of her mother. Mary saw him go with a brave public face and a private flood of tears; grieving as much, the Venetian ambassador was told, 'as may be imagined with regard to a person extraordinarily in love'. As Mary's old tutor Vives had warned young women (more prey, he said, to their emotions than men): 'it is in your power to let love in, but once you have let it in, you no longer belong to yourself, but to it. You cannot drive it out at your pleasure, but it will be able and will take pleasure in ousting you from your own house . . .'

Mary had brought to her convenient marriage an inconvenient and indeed crippling weight of emotional baggage. She, like her father, had made the mistake of seeking romance in what should have been a matter of political expediency. Perhaps Mary's humiliation and anger, her 'tears, regrets', appeared to Elizabeth in the guise of another lesson. In October she received permission to leave court; and not for Woodstock, but for her own estate at Hatfield, there to begin what, for the next three years, would essentially be a waiting game.

The split between the two sisters – and the two faiths – was becoming clearer. In February 1555 the burnings of heretics began that gave 'Bloody' Mary her posthumous sobriquet. Almost three hundred would die in agony: probably an unwelcome surprise to Mary herself, who envisaged the savage penalty as a short, sharp cautionary measure.

The description later given by the martyrologist John Foxe – how one victim, when the fire 'had taken hold upon both his legs and shoulders he, as one feeling no smart, washed his hands in the flame as though it had been in cold water' – cannot begin to mask the horrifying reality. Cranmer was one of the most pitiful victims: imprisoned on Mary's accession, recanting his Protestant faith in terror, only to withdraw his recantation on the very day he faced the fire. And the figurehead for the new faith was still the queen's half-sister.

Elizabeth was also a factor with which the absent Philip had to contend – a pawn to be played in the cause of Habsburg policy. Was she anything more? There were suggestions that Philip had been personally drawn to the slim, vibrant, red-headed Elizabeth. Certainly as Philip's absence wore on, Mary's grief – in what the Venetian called her 'extreme need' of him – was turning to anger. There were stories of her haranguing his portrait; of a mirror thrown across the room in fury. Mary could easily, she wrote to Philip in one letter about his plans for Elizabeth, 'become jealous and uneasy about you'.

But politics gave Philip more than sufficient reason to protect Elizabeth for the rest of Mary's reign. The popular Catholic successor, should Queen Mary die childless, was not Margaret Douglas but the fourteen-year-old Mary, Queen of Scots, being raised at the French court as future bride to the dauphin. And Spain had no wish to see the throne of England pass to an heir so wholly committed to the French cause. In November 1556 Elizabeth was invited back to court for Christmas in the hopes she could be converted to Spain's interest by marriage to a Catholic cousin of Philip of Spain: the titular Duke of Savoy. But the brevity of Elizabeth's visit – the fact that in the first week of December she was on her way back to Hatfield – suggested the force with which she had refused the suggestion she should wed him.

In the spring of 1557 Philip himself returned to England. France and Spain had resumed active hostilities, and he hoped both to secure England's involvement on Spain's side and to put pressure on Elizabeth. The French ambassador warned Elizabeth that there was a plot to carry her abroad by force. Other marriage proposals included Don Carlos, Philip's mad pre-teenage son by his first marriage; and later the crown prince (soon to be king) of Sweden. To the first, Elizabeth 'said plainly that she would not marry' – 'no, though I were offered the greatest prince in all Europe'. To the second, she said she liked her single status too well to change it: so well 'as I persuade myself' there was no other comparable. Perhaps the very fact of having endlessly to reiterate her position, in the face of repeated coercion, was itself reinforcing her conviction. But by now, surely, she saw dangling temptingly before her eyes the real possibility of herself on the throne of England. And it was a place she had no desire to share.

Philip's main purpose in returning to England was precisely what everyone had feared when he married Mary: to draw England into a foreign war. Parliament and people were more than reluctant. The French ambassador declared that the queen, caught between their desire and Philip's, was on the verge 'of bankrupting either her own mind or her kingdom'. But Mary expounded to her council 'the obedience which she owed her husband and the power which he had over her as much by divine as by human law'. In June a herald was sent to the French court, to throw down the gauntlet – literally. Henri II dismissively declared that 'as the herald came in the name of a woman it was unnecessary for him to listen to anything further . . . Consider how I stand when a woman sends to defy me to war.'

Philip left Dover in July, with a six thousand-strong English army. Mary would never see him again. In January 1558 the French took

Calais, England's last remaining continental outpost: a massive humiliation for both queen and country. A few years later Sir Thomas Smith would recall that: 'I never saw England weaker in strength, money, men and riches . . . Here was nothing but fining, headinging [beheading], hanging, quartering and burning, taxing, levying and beggaring, and losing our strongholds abroad.'

At least, that month Mary felt able to inform Philip his visit of the summer had left her pregnant. But few shared her conviction. By April Mary herself knew she was wrong. Over the course of the summer it became clear she was gravely ill: perhaps with a tumour of the stomach. And by the terms of her father's will, Elizabeth was still Mary's heir.

The Venetian ambassador had written the year before that 'all eyes and hearts' were turned towards Elizabeth, as Mary's successor. And Elizabeth had not been idle, during the three years she had spent based at Hatfield. She had been forming a network of friends and supporters; among them William Cecil, the Cambridge-trained bureaucrat and committed Protestant who would emerge as the leading statesman of the decades ahead. Among them also was Robert Dudley. Elizabeth would later say that he sold lands to raise money for her.

In early October Queen Mary's condition worsened. On 28 October she added a codicil to her will. Acknowledging that she had as yet no 'fruit nor heir of my body', she conceded that in the absence of such she would be followed by 'my next heir and successor by the laws of this realm'. Ten days later she was brought to acknowledge more specifically that this meant Elizabeth. In the early morning of 17 November, quietly, Mary died. Margaret Douglas was the chief mourner at her funeral.

The historian William Camden, writing early in the next century, said that though young to rule at twenty-five, Elizabeth was 'rarely qualified by resolution and adversity'; adversity described in a prayer of Elizabeth's own, published in the first years of her reign:

When I was surrounded and thrown about by various snares of enemies, Thou has preserved me with Thy constant protection from prison and the most extreme danger; and though I was freed only at the very last moment, Thou has entrusted me on earth with royal sovereignty and majesty.

God had, as Elizabeth put it, 'willed me not to be some wretched girl from the meanest rank of the common people, who would pass her life miserably in poverty and squalor, but to a kingdom Thou has destined me'. Now it remained only to fulfil that destiny.

To do so, Elizabeth would use every technique in her repertoire. Her half-sister had ruled as England's first queen regnant; but Mary had done so under the ultimate spiritual authority of her father in God, the Pope, to say nothing of the possible authority of her earthly husband. Elizabeth would do something yet more subversive – with the aid of a doctrine that had itself suborned men's rules. Britain's last medieval monarch would invoke – adopt, adapt – the patterns of a past age to mask the fact that she was doing something revolutionary. And if courtly love had seemed to be coming to the end of its long history, now, on the contrary, it would be reborn.

PART V

1558–1584

Amor de lonh: love from afar

I grieve, yet dare not show my discontent;
I love, and yet am forced to seem to hate,
I dote, but dare not what I meant;
I seem stark mute, yet inwardly do prate.
I am, and am not, freeze, and yet I burn,
Since from myself my other self I turn.

Elizabeth I, 'On Monsieur's Departure'

18

'the King that is to be'

1558–1563

I<small>T WAS</small> E<small>LIZABETH</small>'s day of triumph. Less than five years before, she had left the Tower as a prisoner on parole, still in fear of her life. On 14 January 1559 she rode out (after the brief stay new monarchs traditionally made there) on the way to Westminster, and her coronation the next day. She herself was quick to note the gulf that separated past from present. After all, it bolstered the sense of the queen as God's chosen that He had delivered her, she declared, as He delivered Daniel from the lions' den.

A dazzling figure, in twenty-three yards of cloth of gold and silver, trimmed with ermine, she was carried through the City, propped up on huge satin cushions, in a litter drawn by two mules. Thirty-nine ladies dressed in crimson, with cloth-of-gold sleeves, followed behind her – and behind the commanding red-and-gilt form of Robert Dudley, who rode immediately after the queen's litter, in his new capacity as Master of Horse.

Pageants greeted her along the way. On Gracechurch Street she met the first of them – the 'Pageant of the Roses'. On a three-tiered platform, reflecting the Tudor dynasty, stood, first, Henry VII and Elizabeth of York, suitably marked by red and white roses. Above them, behind a Tudor rose, stood Henry VIII and Anne Boleyn, reunited at last. (Perhaps this was Anne's day of triumph, too.) On the top level stood the image of Elizabeth herself. She, of course, stood alone . . . So far.

*   *   *

It is only hindsight that identifies Elizabeth so closely with the virgin state. When she came to the throne in 1558, that was far from obvious to contemporaries.

There was, Elizabeth herself would later observe wryly, 'a strong idea in the world that a woman cannot live unless she is married'. The Holy Roman Emperor's envoy was quick to assure his master that she should ('as is woman's way') be eager 'to marry and be provided for. For that she should wish to remain a maid and never marry is inconceivable'. This was one barrier her sister had not broken for her.

Mary Tudor's Catholicism, and Catholic marriage, had made England once again kissing cousins with the bulk of Europe. Elizabeth's Protestantism returned her country to the isolation triggered by their father. (It would perhaps be that political and to a degree cultural isolation that allowed the spirit of courtly love – elsewhere fading – still to haunt England's shores.) But the pressing need was to find some safety for an England that one of Elizabeth's own agents described as 'a bone between two dogs' – France and Spain. To most of her contemporaries the obvious route lay in the alliance of a shrewd foreign marriage: in the words of William Cecil, queen and realm's 'only known and likely surety'.

Elizabeth would prove to be breaking two moulds, as female queen and as unmarried woman. And from her first, vulnerable, days on the throne, she would need to exercise more than usual virtuosity in the presentation of her female monarchy.

She would do so (with typically thrifty practicality) by adopting existing codes – not just of courtly love, when the time came, but of biblical heroines, of Diana and, crucially, of the Virgin Mary. But Elizabeth's right to rule derived from the rejection of papal authority. To Catholics who held her parents' marriage invalid, she was no queen at all. In France, King Henri was proclaiming his daughter-in-law Mary Stuart as England's rightful sovereign. And the Protestant attitude towards a woman's authority was itself still in negotiation.

John Knox was only one of the Protestant writers who had inveighed against the Catholic female rulers Mary Tudor and Marie de Guise. In his *First Blast of the Trumpet Against the Monstrous Regiment of*

Women, published only that summer, Knox had declared, all too vividly, that to put a crown on a woman's head was as unreasonable 'as to put a saddle upon the back of an unruly cow'. It was 'the subversion of good order, of all equity and justice' – 'a thing most repugnant to nature, that women rule and govern over men'. Knox was only one who had now hastily to rethink his position, writing to the Swiss theologian John Calvin to discuss the problem. Calvin's own view had likewise always been that life under a female sovereign should 'be ranked no less than slavery'.

A kind of resolution was achieved by presenting Elizabeth as an exceptional woman. The courtly lady was raised above the rest of her sex; so too, in a different way, were the biblical heroines such as Judith and Esther, and Deborah who figured in the coronation pageantry. But it remained an uneasy compromise.

Within four days of Queen Mary's death, on 21 November the Spanish ambassador had written to Philip II that 'everything depends upon the husband this woman [Elizabeth] may take'. He urged that the husband should be Philip himself; but the Spanish would have to move quickly, since both Elizabeth and her ministers 'will listen to any ambassadors who may come to treat of marriage'. Three weeks later, on 14 December, he wrote again: 'Everybody thinks that she will not marry a foreigner, and they cannot make out whom she favours, so that every day some new cry is raised about a husband.' But Philip's reluctant offer, he wrote, was made only 'to serve God' and forestall the new queen's making any changes in England's religion. Elizabeth, complaining of Philip's lack of enthusiasm, did not take it.

Over the following months many other candidates would indeed emerge. Among the suitors closer to home, the 47-year-old Earl of Arundel and the diplomat Sir William Pickering were perhaps never likely candidates; but the Earl of Arran – Protestant heir to the Scottish throne and thus a natural focus for Scotland's disaffected nobility – could give England a useful counterweight to the ascendancy France had long held just north of England's border. Eric of Sweden returned to the assault he had begun in Mary's day, and the Holy Roman Emperor (Charles V's brother Ferdinand) suggested one of his younger sons.

The Imperial proposal foundered on Elizabeth's declared reluctance to marry a man she had never seen. Elizabeth swore – perhaps remembering her father's experience with Anne of Cleves – that she would never put her trust in portraits and told her Swedish suitor that 'we shall never choose any absent husband'. Mischievously, she suggested that the archduke should come to England for inspection.

The emperor himself would later complain that among kings and queens this determination was 'entirely novel and unprecedented, and we cannot approve of it'. But Elizabeth's firmness on this point was part of a broader attitude equally puzzling to her contemporaries. In the words of one ambassadorial despatch: 'nothing would suffice to make her think of marrying, or even treating of marriage; but the person she was to marry pleasing her so much as to cause her to desire what at present she has no wish for.' In one particular sense, sixteenth-century opinion would be behind her, since it was believed female orgasm was necessary for conception, and an agreeable husband was thus the surest route to an heir. Nonetheless, the Spanish ambassador would voice the general opinion when he declared that Elizabeth 'says the most extraordinary things'.

Less than three months after her accession, Elizabeth's own House of Commons drafted a petition, urging her to marry quickly in order to ensure the succession. If she should remain 'unmarried and, as it were, a vestal virgin', it would be 'contrary to public respects'. They were, of course, figuring exactly the course and image she would choose . . . But at the time her reluctance might be taken as a mere parade of maidenly aloofness – no more than a move in the courtly game. In the first months and years of her reign, the real obstacle to a foreign marriage for Elizabeth seemed to take a more physical form – the notably tall, dark and handsome form of Robert Dudley.

Robert Dudley's new role as Master of Horse gave him a uniquely privileged access to her company. Of course, some of the other men who would be central to her monarchy already clustered around Elizabeth: chief among them William Cecil, who would be the great statesman of her regime. But Cecil's forte would be as a bureaucrat – the archetypal (and, in the courtly story, slightly contemptible) clerk always opposed to the knight.

It was Robert who rode with Elizabeth, danced with her, oversaw her safety; who appealed to the now-released flamboyant side of her personality. Robert who wrote, half in terror and half admiration, of her boldness in the saddle – how she had made him order her 'good gallopers' from Ireland, and 'spareth not to try as fast as they can go'. Robert, the expert jouster who starred in tournaments like those that marked Elizabeth's accession. Robert who adopted the cinquefoil, the five-petalled form of the May blossom as another of his symbols. Robert who represented pleasure and sensuality.

Their romantic relationship developed swiftly. In her first spring as queen the Spanish ambassador was writing that: 'Lord Robert has come so much into favour that he does whatever he likes with affairs. It is even said that Her Majesty visits him in his chamber day and night . . .' Nine months later the ambassador's successor in the post would be writing of 'my Lord Robert, in whom it is easy to recognise the King that is to be'.

Though Robert Dudley was a married man, his wife Amy played no part in her husband's court life. Theirs appears to have been a youthful marriage that had long outworn its appeal. And the Spanish ambassador had written that 'they say' Robert's wife 'has a malady in one of her breasts'. An envoy in Europe likewise reported that Amy 'has been ailing some time', and that if she were to die, various persons believed 'the Queen might easily take [Dudley] for her husband'.

The Imperial ambassador wrote that: 'It is generally stated that it is his fault that the Queen does not marry.' That Dudley and the queen had 'a secret understanding' that they would marry after Amy's death. But England, he said, would not sit quiet under such a match: 'if she marry the said Mylord Robert, she will incur so much enmity that she may one evening lay herself down as Queen of England and rise up the next morning as plain Mistress Elizabeth . . .'

Elizabeth's old governess Kat Ashley went down on her knees to beseech her erstwhile charge to marry elsewhere and put an end to the rumours, 'telling Her Majesty that her behaviour towards the Master of Horse occasioned much evil speaking'. She might have added that Elizabeth was facing one of the very situations against which Christine de Pizan had warned: risking her own reputation by advancing a man. But Elizabeth's answer (to the gossipmongers of Europe, as much as to

Kat) was that she needed Robert because 'in this world she had so much sorrow and tribulation and so little joy'. How, she asked, could she be suspected of anything improper, when she was always surrounded by her women? 'I do not live in a corner,' she told a Spanish envoy once. 'A thousand eyes see all I do.' But in fact Elizabeth did often consult alone with her ministers and senior courtiers, of whom Robert was one.

There seems to have been a fairly universal assumption that the unfortunate Amy Dudley could be disregarded – would somehow quietly disappear from the picture. But when Amy Dudley *did* quit the stage, it was in an explosion of scandal that still resonates to this day. On 8 September 1560 Amy Dudley was found dead at the bottom of a staircase in the Oxfordshire house where she had been staying, with her neck broken.

There were and are four possible explanations for Amy's death: suicide; natural causes, whether accident or illness; murder at the hands of someone hoping to incriminate Robert Dudley; or murder on the orders of Robert Dudley (who was himself far away with the court that day). There is some circumstantial evidence in support of each theory. For suicide: Amy's maid spoke of her mistress's despair, of how Amy had been down on her knees praying to God to deliver her. And Amy had, most unusually for a Tudor aristocrat, chosen to dismiss all her attendants and be alone that day. For natural causes: those tales of her ill health (and any illness could mean medication which was itself more destructive than the malady). But it is the murder theories that grip the imagination now, and did in 1560.

Was the obvious theory the correct one? Mary Stuart in France certainly thought so, sneering that the Queen of England was about to marry her horsemaster, who had murdered his wife to make way for her. In England, a coroner's jury swiftly brought in a verdict of misadventure. But as the news spread through Europe, Sir Nicholas Throckmorton at the French court was only one ambassador writing home to Cecil about 'dishonourable and naughty reports ... which every hair of my head stareth at and my ears glow to hear'.

But, against that, surely Dudley was sufficiently experienced a politician to know what would happen: that far from facilitating his marriage to the queen, the scandal surrounding Amy's death would itself (in the short term, at least) make it impossible for he and Elizabeth to marry. It was, in the event, someone else who profited from Amy's tragedy. Robert Dudley and William Cecil had been tussling for influence over Elizabeth, and Dudley had been winning the battle. Cecil had been out of favour just before Amy's death. Just after it, he was back in control. Against that, of course, would Cecil really have risked not merely Dudley's but Elizabeth's reputation by ordering the killing? His desk would be littered with ambassadors' letters, lamenting those 'dishonourable and naughty reports'.

There can, now, be no certainty about Amy's fate. What we need to consider is Elizabeth's reaction – and she reacted as queen, not as the lovesick young woman some might have thought her. She sent Dudley away from court, pending further inquiry. She certainly accepted the self-evident truth: that marrying him (for the moment) was impossible.

Many through the centuries have seen this as Elizabeth's tragedy. But it could be viewed very differently. Elizabeth told her Parliament of 1559 that from her first 'years of understanding' she 'haply chose this kind of life in which I yet live, which I assure you for mine own part hath hitherto best contented myself and I trust hath been most acceptable to God'. Robert Dudley himself backed that up, saying later that he had known Elizabeth since she was eight years old – and that from that time, she had sworn never to marry.

If ambition for a grand alliance, obedience to the ruler's will or the fear of danger, Elizabeth told the Parliament of 1559, 'could have drawn or dissuaded me from this kind of life, I had not now remained in this estate wherein you see me'. But she had always 'continued in this determination'. In the end, she said 'this shall be for me sufficient: that a marble stone shall declare that a queen, having reigned such a time, lived and died a virgin'. It would, however, be almost twenty years before her councillors were forced to accept the fact.

A few years down the line, with the scandal of Amy Dudley's death perhaps fading into memory, another Parliament in January 1563 would again urge Elizabeth to marry: explicitly, to marry *anybody*. 'Whomsoever it be that your Majesty shall choose, we protest and promise with all humility and reverence to honor, love, and serve as to our most bounden duty shall appertain.' Politicians and people, both desperate for the security of an assured succession, would accept even Dudley as sire to an heir of Elizabeth's body. It was a mandate to choose him if she would, but Elizabeth did not take it. Indeed, her comportment in the time immediately after Amy's death was not that of a woman who'd had all her hopes destroyed. It was that of a woman who had triumphed in some emotional way.

The pressure for Elizabeth to marry and produce heirs did not let up; the more so since there were others at court greedily eyeing her crown. Margaret Douglas, Lady Lennox, held a pair of trump cards in the shape of her sons – two of them now – with rights in the succession to both the English and (through their father) the Scottish crowns. In 1561 events had brought the most famous Catholic claimant to the fore when the death of François II, France's new king, left Mary, Queen of Scots a widow. Margaret instantly began to plot a marriage between Mary and her own eldest son Lord Darnley, though the idea would not bear fruit for some time.

Margaret's Catholicism was at once a strength and a weak point; appealing to those who rejected a Protestant queen, but giving Cecil an excuse to watch her so closely that, Margaret complained, she felt a virtual prisoner. Indeed, early in 1562, on information from one of Cecil's spies, Margaret and her husband would for some months find themselves literally prisoners. Not only was Lady Lennox accused of potentially treasonous communication with foreign envoys, but she had been in contact with 'witches and soothsayers'. But the descendants of Margaret Tudor were not the only spectres rearing up before Elizabeth's frightened eyes.

A possible Protestant rival was Jane Grey's sister Katherine. In 1561 Elizabeth learnt with fury that Katherine, the previous autumn, had made a secret marriage with Edward Seymour, Earl of Hertford, son and heir to Protector Somerset. There is no doubt this was a love match, as evidenced both by their letters and by the number of passionate assignations they proved to have held. But Elizabeth was convinced the marriage (made just at the time of the Amy Dudley crisis) was meant also to position Katherine to steal her throne; a fear only increased when, in the Tower of London where she and Hertford had both been imprisoned, Katherine gave birth to a son.

Fear of Katherine would for a time make Elizabeth almost enthusi-astic about the Stuart claim of Mary, Queen of Scots; and even of the Lennoxes. Eighteen months later, the Hertfords' offence would be compounded by the birth of another child (Hertford having bribed two Tower guards to unlock their doors). They were moved to sepa-rate, and distant, country houses. Katherine – another Tudor romantic – wrote frantically to Hertford of her 'boundless love for my sweet bedfellow, that I once lay beside with joyful heart and shall again'. Her hopeful prophecy was wrong. She died five years later, still in captivity, never having seen her husband again.

But by that time, Katherine's sister Mary, youngest of the three Grey siblings, had likewise made a secret marriage, though with a very differ-ent partner. Her husband Thomas Keyes was the queen's Serjeant Porter, of much lower rank than Mary. (He was also, Cecil wrote, the tallest in the court while Mary was the smallest; the Spanish ambassador described her as being little, ugly and crook-backed.) It is possible that, like Katherine de Valois more than a century before – and like her own mother Frances Brandon, whose second marriage had been to her Master of Horse – Mary thought safety lay in alliance to a man never made to be a royal consort. If so, she was wrong. Mary spent seven years under house arrest, released only after the death of Thomas, whose health had not survived his harsher imprisonment in the Fleet. Truly, Elizabeth was both getting and giving further lessons in the dangers of love.

And for all her statesmen sought the queen's marriage, there were political dangers in any path other than celibacy. The position of a husband in relation to a reigning queen was a vexed one.[*] To marry a foreign prince was to risk her country's autonomy: her brother had cut his still-unmarried sisters from his will, fearing 'the utter subversion of the commonwealth of this our realm, which God forbid'. Their father Henry had written of his fear that if a woman shall chance to rule, 'she cannot continue long without a husband, which by God's law must then be her governor and head, and so finally shall direct the realm'.

---

[*] Even in the age of constitutional monarchy, some of the concerns evident around the marriages of the sixteenth-century queens were voiced again when Victoria married Albert – and when the future Elizabeth II married Prince Philip of Greece.

And all those gloomy prophecies seemed to have come true when Mary Tudor's Spanish marriage had seen England dragged into a war not of her making.

Marriage to a subject brought the risk of faction in the country, as Mary Stuart across the border would soon find. Moreover, it left unanswered the fundamental question: in an age where the husband expected to rule the wife, how could a queen both reign and wed? When, in 1565, the Queen of Scots did marry Lord Darnley, his assumption would be that this gave him the consort's crown – and the supremacy. 'Suppose I be of the baser degree, yet am I your husband and your head,' Darnley told Mary.

It was an assumption prevalent enough to trouble contemporaries. John Aylmer, writing in answer to John Knox's *First Blast*, had tried unconvincingly to rationalise the position of the married female ruler. 'Say you, God hath appointed her to be the subject to her husband . . . therefore she may not be the head. I grant that, so far as pertaining to the bands of marriage, and the offices of a wife, she must be a subject: but as a Magistrate she may be her husband's head.' She could be his inferior in 'matters of wedlock', and yet his leader in 'the guiding of the commonwealth', he claimed. But it was a claim fraught with difficulty.

There were other, personal, reasons why Elizabeth might not want to marry. Everything in her early experience taught her to see sex and marriage as danger; from the fate of her mother (and, after Anne, her kinswoman Katheryn Howard) to the devastating consequences of Thomas Seymour's advances. As a girl at Hatfield she had been surrounded by ladies each suffering a disastrous marital history; as a queen she saw her premier noble, the Duke of Norfolk, lose three wives in childbed. Small wonder that, as she once told the French ambassador, when she tried to make up her mind to marriage, it was 'as if my heart were torn out of my body'.

Many years later Elizabeth would tell the Earl of Sussex that she hated the idea of marriage more each day, 'for reasons which she would not divulge to a twin soul, if she had one, much less to a living creature'. At the end of Elizabeth's life her godson Sir John Harington wrote of her that: 'In mind, she hath ever had an aversion and (as many think) in body some indisposition to the act of marriage.' There was speculation, from the Spanish ambassador who reported soon after her accession that 'for a certain reason which [my spies] have recently given me, I believe she will not bear children', to the playwright Ben Jonson who after her death claimed that 'she had a membrane on her, which made her incapable of man' ('though for her delight she tried many', he added). Conjecture at the time, however, dwelt not on Elizabeth's posthumous reputation as the 'Virgin Queen' but on whether she was a virgin at all. And at this stage, there was no doubt as to the name of her possible lover.

Years later, when Elizabeth was an old woman, Henri IV of France would joke that one of the great conundrums of Europe was whether Queen Elizabeth was a maid or no. (His mother-in-law Catherine de Medici had warned Elizabeth that the best way a powerful woman could be attacked was through 'dishonourable tales' which saw her 'slandered wrongfully'.) Various of Elizabeth's subjects would indeed report scurrilous stories: even that she never went on summer progress but to be delivered of a secret child.

But at this point in her reign, when the question was a pressing one, not merely a subject for malicious gossip, the Imperial envoy, assessing whether Elizabeth could be considered a suitable bride, concluded that though 'Her Majesty shows her liking for Lord Robert more markedly than is consistent with her reputation and dignity', Elizabeth's ladies 'all swear by all that is holy that Her Majesty has most certainly never been forgetful of her honour'. On the whole, other ambassadors agreed.

In the autumn of 1562 Elizabeth fell dangerously ill of smallpox. As she put it later: 'Death possessed every joint of me.' Believing herself to be about to face the judgement of her Maker, she took this moment to declare that, 'although she loved and had always loved Lord Robert dearly, as God was her witness, nothing improper had ever passed between them'.

That said (as Elizabeth's parents had found), the rules of courtly love might offer a particular definition of propriety.[*] Elizabeth also asked, unrealistically, that in the event of her death Robert Dudley should be

---

[*] The same definition that, centuries later, would allow a devout Horatio Nelson to swear in a church ceremony that the love he shared with Emma Hamilton had always been pure: this though she had, while married to another man, borne Nelson's child.

protector of the country – and, she asked that his personal servant should be given a large sum of money, in what might seem a bid for the man's continued discretion.

The rumours would persist, as witness the appearance, in the 1580s, at the Spanish court of the interestingly named 'Arthur Dudley', who claimed to be Robert and Elizabeth's son. But even the Spanish could not manage to believe 'Arthur Dudley's' story; and in fact, whatever love play she and Robert enjoyed behind closed doors, it is hard to believe the wary Elizabeth would have gone so far as to put herself at risk of an extramarital pregnancy.

It is not quite true to say that in the years following Amy Dudley's death Elizabeth's relationship with Robert Dudley settled down. Through the 1560s and well into the 1570s speculation about a possible marriage – or, conversely, reports of dreadful quarrels – would ebb and flow. Rumours circulated in the early 1560s that Elizabeth had actually married Robert secretly. She teasingly told the Spanish ambassador her ladies had been asking whether to kiss Dudley's hand. But weeks later, the Swedish diplomat Robert Keyle was reporting the queen as telling him 'in the Chamber of Presence (all the nobility being there) that she would never marry him, nor none so mean [i.e. lowly] as he'.

It placed Dudley in an impossible position. For Elizabeth, their relationship was a tool to use in her diplomatic courtship with a long series of foreign princes. Dismissing him as her long-suffering servitor when she needed to present herself as available, she would then tell ambassadors, when any foreign suitor came too close to victory, that Robert was the only man she could ever love. His very visible pursuit gave point to her much-vaunted chastity: as Anne de Beaujeu had written, where lay the virtue in defending the castle if no one were besieging it?

She set him up as her stalking horse – remember Dante setting up another lady to distract observers from his love for Beatrice? – and perhaps her whipping boy. The carrot and the stick: she was still refusing to grant him a peerage; but she gave him rooms next to her own in all the palaces; gave him pensions and properties. It suited Elizabeth very well to keep her 'Sweet Robin' always by her side, enacting the role of quasi-consort without the Crown Matrimonial, or even the matrimony, which might have given him the mastery.

'I cannot do without my Lord Robert, for he is like my little dog, and whenever he comes into a room, everyone at once assumes that I myself am near,' she said once, humiliatingly. Under these circumstances perhaps Robert, and Elizabeth's other courtiers, needed urgently to find a form in which to couch their enduring subservience to a sometimes aloof and unrewarding queen. Over the long years ahead, Robert Dudley would essentially – despite occasional schemings behind her back he would no doubt have seen as necessary – remain almost heroically loyal both to Elizabeth and to her throne. But there would be an ever-growing need to discover a language for that loyalty.

19

'satiety and fullness'

1563–1575

I F THE FIRST years of her reign had been all about conventional marriages (or love stories), there would, as those years wore on, loom the challenge of finding a public coding for Elizabeth's unmarried female monarchy; and perhaps for the emotional dynamics she used to sustain it. Courtly love – with Elizabeth's own twists – would provide one. At almost every point the rules of courtly love match the relationship between Elizabeth and her courtiers – explain its nature as nothing else has done.

The courtly lady was meant to be capricious, demanding, testing her lover's utter fidelity. Caprice and demand were Elizabeth's specialities. The literal language of courtly love, the role reversal that seemed to cede the woman power, is echoed in the complex position of a reigning queen. As sovereign, she was presumed to have 'two bodies' – two identities: as a flesh and blood woman; and as a genderless, presumed masculine, epitome of monarchy. Elizabeth habitually referred to herself as a 'prince'. And as her reign wore on critics would rail against women's usurpation of masculine dress, doublets and jerkins, trends initiated by the queen herself. (Women literally wearing the trousers? Eleanor of Aquitaine had likewise been criticised for donning men's clothing to ride astride.)

True, the original heroines of the courtly love story married – but then, Elizabeth (like Mary before her) would figure herself as married to her country and would display the ring that symbolised the union. And if the courtly lady was supposed to be of higher rank, and thus able to dispense patronage, no one had more patronage at her disposal than a reigning queen. Even more significantly, the courtly lady was supposed to provide a superior moral example which, if her adorer learnt from it, would improve his knightly status. You could not get much higher, morally, than a woman who was married by the ritual of the coronation to God, and by rhetoric and affection to her country. Castiglione's *Book of the Courtier* was translated by Sir Thomas Hoby three years into Elizabeth's reign, urging that the courtly lady should be loved by the perfect courtier 'and that she should love him in turn, so that both may attain absolute perfection'.

Though Protestant clerics like John Knox might reject the idea that women, sinful daughters of Eve, might wield any moral authority, the Church Elizabeth had inherited from her father saw sacred and profane love jointly directed towards the secular ruler who was also God's representative on earth. The role of a spiritual lodestar that Beatrice and Laura performed for Dante and Petrarch was ideal for an anointed queen giving spiritual example to a nation. It would, as her reign developed, allow for all of England to act as Elizabeth's courtly lover.

Courtly love made the practical necessity of homage paid by Elizabeth's courtiers seem also spiritual, admirable. It gave an acceptable gloss, too, to Elizabeth's own behaviour – behaviour which was a matter both of tactics and of temperament. Historians down the centuries have seen it as the product of an unhappily frustrated sexuality. (The Freudian age shifted the focus, without changing the fundamental assumption to any real degree.) In terms of courtly love, however, what she did looks more like artistry.

But how long could the game continue with the same actors? One summer of the 1560s Elizabeth wrote a verse on the flyleaf of her French psalter:

No crooked leg, no bleared eye,
No part deformed out of kind,
Nor yet so ugly half can be
As the inward, suspicious mind

A note from William Cecil suggests it was sparked by annoyance with Robert Dudley. Though jealousy (if Andreas Capellanus is to be believed) was an integral part of the courtly love story, Elizabeth now felt the need to show Robert he was not the only candidate available . . . and perhaps that she could do without him, if necessary.

Back in 1561 Elizabeth herself had first felt the presence of a political rival when the widowed Mary, Queen of Scots returned to her native shores from France. 'Two queens in one isle . . .' The question of who Mary would next marry had urgent implications for English policy. A Scottish alliance with either France or Spain would bring a powerful foreign presence to England's northern border.

As Elizabeth's nearest royal relative, the Queen of Scots sought above all to be named as Elizabeth's heir. Elizabeth was determined to avoid ceding Mary such dangerous prominence in English affairs, while using the tantalising possibility as bait. She sought to control the choice of Mary's husband, insisting it should be someone from Elizabeth's own country. But the relationship between the two queens was complex in personal as well as political terms.

A relationship which often saw Mary, nine years the younger, cast as Elizabeth's daughter was also often figured as a love story, with Mary kissing the ring Elizabeth had sent her and swearing it would never leave her finger, any more than the one given by her husband François. Indeed, a joke ran between the two courts – if only one of them could be turned into a man, so that Elizabeth and Mary themselves might marry!

Instead, in 1563 Elizabeth proposed Robert Dudley as Mary's husband. She gave him a peerage at last – the earldom of Leicester – to make him slightly more suitable as a bridegroom, but this remained a close-to-insulting suggestion with which the Scots queen was never likely to agree. And Elizabeth was seen publicly to tickle Robert at the investiture: 'putting her hand in his neck to kittle him smilingly'.

Perhaps Elizabeth's demeaning suggestion played its part in pushing Mary into that marriage with Lord Darnley which his mother Margaret Douglas had long sought. Margaret found herself back in the Tower for her part in arranging it. But the marriage would quickly prove disastrous – within months of the ceremony in spring 1565, observers were shocked to report that Mary had grown to hate her husband, while Darnley's attempts to insist on what he saw as his rights as king consort highlighted the problems posed by the marriage of any queen regnant.

One of the great conundrums is why the famously beautiful – and supposedly amorous – Mary does not feature more largely in the courtly love story. She had been to some degree caught in its trap early in her Scottish rule, accepting, in pure courtly tradition, the sighing adoration of the poet Pierre de Chastelard. But Chastelard seems to have taken this for encouragement. He was twice found hiding under the queen's bed; and, the second time it happened, hauled off to execution, still protesting his adoration for a mistress 'so beautiful and so cruel'.

If Mary needed a lesson, she would have learnt it here – the more so since Chastelard had been armed. It seemed possible he was hiding in her room to kill her – whether from misguided passion or from political motives hiding under a courtly cloak. (Or, that he was there to discredit her with seeming evidence of sexual immorality.) But is it fanciful to suspect that – for all the romantic weight later centuries have laden on her figure – Mary herself, reared in France, already took a more practical approach to these matters? She had grown up in the sphere of the famously beautiful Diane de Poitiers, who had been revered mistress to not one, but two French kings; she had seen her father-in-law Henri II die of the injuries received in a tournament. Her youth had been dominated by two women – her mother Marie de Guise ruling as her regent in Scotland, and her mother-in-law Catherine de Medici – who exercised real power. But the result seems to have been that she saw the game of courtly love for what it was: a play.

In England, meanwhile, Elizabeth's extraordinary action in offering Robert Dudley to Mary had another effect closer to home. Perhaps it began to convince the new Earl of Leicester that Elizabeth would never marry him, since, in the summer of 1565, he was flirting with another red-headed beauty. Lettice Knollys was the queen's second cousin (her mother being Mary Boleyn's daughter). She was also at the time married, and any talk of Leicester seemed to have passed off quietly. But perhaps that is why in 1565 a 'much offended' Elizabeth herself could be seen flirting with Thomas Heneage, a young man with a family history of service to the Tudors who had entered her own service some five years before.

But Heneage was not the major new figure on the scene. That role belonged to another man: one whom Heneage would later back in the great game of court politics, and who would prove to take rank among the special favourites of Elizabeth's reign.

Third son of an undistinguished Northamptonshire gentleman, Christopher Hatton had been born in 1540, and succeeded to the family estate in his minority, on the deaths of his father and elder brothers. After a spell at Oxford his guardians had sent him to the Inns of Court, where he was 'Master of the Game' in the 1561 Christmas revels at the Inner Temple. He may thus have caught the queen's eye still in his early twenties, before he ever had occasion to practise the law he had studied; but he entered history around the time he turned thirty.

The first date of his coming to court is not recorded, but Sir Robert Naunton in the early seventeenth century wrote that he came there 'by the galliard', since it was his dancing – and his 'tall and proportionable' person – that first brought him to the queen's attention. As William Camden puts it, 'being young and of a comely tallness of body and countenance, he got into such favour with the Queen that she took him into her band of fifty Gentleman-pensioners'. From there he rose to be a Gentleman of the Privy Chamber, and the recipient of a steady stream of grants and offices: a lease of properties in 1568; more lands and offices (albeit still minor ones) almost every year thereafter. He became a Member of Parliament in 1571 and, the following year, a courtier sufficiently prominent and wealthy to offer the queen a beautiful jewel as a New Year's gift.

The gifts he received in return were certainly enough to arouse the jealousy of Leicester, who is said to have offered to bring in a dancing master who could cavort even better than Hatton. He was suggesting that this was the young man's only claim to fame. But in fact one of Hatton's most winning attributes seems to have been what Camden called 'the modest sweetness of his manners'. Though every great Elizabethan courtier might expect to be besieged by letters appealing for his intercession with the queen, the volume of letters to and from Christopher Hatton, edited by the antiquary Nicholas Harris Nicolas in 1847, displays a warming confidence that all those who appealed to him might find a sympathetic ear. As the Duke of Norfolk would later write to his ten-year-old son on the eve of his execution, Mr Hatton was 'a marvellous constant friend'.

He was certainly an agreeably ardent letter writer where Elizabeth was concerned. 'No death, no, nor hell, shall ever win of me my consent so far to wrong myself again as to be absent from you one day,' he wrote to her when sickness had forced him to leave court.

> God grant my return. I will perform this vow. I lack that I live by. The more I find this lack, the further I go from you . . . Would God I were with you but for one hour. My wits are overwrought with thoughts. I find myself amazed. Bear with me, my most dear sweet Lady. Passion overcometh me. I can write no more. Love me, for I love you.

In another letter he urged her: 'Live for ever, most excellent creature; and love some man, to shew yourself thankful for God's high labour in you.' The adoration couched in such extravagant language was perhaps hardly meant to be believed – but in Hatton, as in Leicester himself, time would prove that the hyperbole ran alongside a seemingly genuine affection.

Thomas Elyot's influential 1531 *Book Named the Governor* described the ruler's watchful friends and advisers as his 'eyes and ears and hands and feet'. Elizabeth called Leicester her 'eyes', reflected often by a scrawled symbol in their letters, and Hatton was now her 'Lids'. Perhaps it is true that Elizabeth's incessant use of nicknames (often animalising nicknames, and usually the more domesticated or less threatening animals) may have been one way to trivialise the men around her and keep them in their place. But here her use of 'eyes' and 'lids' may reflect the way she wanted these two to work together. In the years ahead the most notable among this first generation of men around Elizabeth – Leicester, Cecil, Hatton – would, against the odds, achieve a measure of collaboration.

Leicester was now known around Europe as 'the great Lord': great in the wealth Elizabeth had given him, and in his ability to distribute goods and patronage further down the food chain of the endless hungry mouths at court. He was now established as a political entity, with his own preoccupations and his preferred policies, his contacts abroad, his network of paid informers. He had been made a Privy Councillor in 1562, after Elizabeth's smallpox, and had become one of the tiny handful on whom most of the business of England relied.

Yet there remained the central anomaly for him as for other favourites: that his power, his wealth, his executive ability ultimately relied on one thing only – his influence over the queen. His greatest utility to the other ministers, even, lay in his ability both to support and to handle her: a vision of his role that potentially presented a challenge to his masculinity.* No wonder that, while Elizabeth's first great favourites rushed to give a more palatable chivalric gloss to their humiliating position, they could be found clustering together as often as they could, quarrelling . . . For comfort, maybe.

There was yet another new figure on the scene; and one who, unlike Hatton, everyone hated. The young Earl of Oxford was a compelling but erratic figure. In 1571, at twenty-one, he came to court; and his rank, since he had succeeded to his father's title at twelve, meant it hardly needed his skill at dancing to catch the queen's attention.

A former ward of the queen herself and of William Cecil (or, as he should now be known, Lord Burghley), Oxford was well educated, trained in music and the classics, in modern languages and cosmography. He was particularly gifted at the joust, where again he intruded himself on the queen's notice. He was, moreover, a poet of some note, and a patron of plays – hence the theory that he was in fact the author of Shakespeare's work. Oxford also patronised the translation of a whole series of continental 'romances of chivalry' and would himself be the leader of one group of the early Elizabethan court poets.

It was noted that the queen 'delighteth more in his personage and his dancing and valiantness than any other . . . If it were not for his fickle head he would pass any of them shortly.' But Oxford's head was

---

* Just as, centuries later, Prince Philip's principal role would be his personal support for Elizabeth II: a traditionally feminine role with which he struggled, reportedly. While Leicester would be particularly significant in shaping Elizabeth I's public image, Philip in the early years of his wife's reign likewise remoulded the image of her monarchy.

indeed a fickle one. Still in his teens, he had killed one of Burghley's servants, though the scandal was hushed up. Hatton spoke no more than the truth when he warned Elizabeth to beware of the 'Boar' – for so she named Oxford – whose tusks might raze and tear. Better the Sheep (in Elizabeth's litany of nicknames, Hatton was often her sheep or her 'Mutton'), 'he hath no tooth to bite'.

Indeed, only a couple of years later Oxford fled England for the Continent; perhaps just to escape his creditors. But the reason may have been his Catholic sympathies – or even a more specifically treasonable involvement in the inept plotting of his kinsman the Duke of Norfolk.

The second half of the 1560s had seen the rapid unravelling of Mary Stuart's Scottish rule. Early in 1566 Mary's suspicious and unstable husband Lord Darnley had been complicit in the murder of her secretary, David Rizzio. Just a year later Mary herself would be suspected of complicity in Darnley's murder, and compound the offence by an indecently speedy marriage to the Earl of Bothwell, widely believed to have been the prime mover in the affair.

The letter Elizabeth wrote to Mary then reflects her awareness of the downside of the sisterhood of queens: that failure or moral turpitude on the part of one reflected dangerously on the other. But when in 1568 Mary, deposed from her throne, fled south over the border to seek refuge in England, the problem for Elizabeth only worsened.

A commission at York, headed by the Duke of Norfolk, was scandalised by the so-called Casket Letters (in fact almost certainly faked or doctored), which seemed to prove Mary to have been Bothwell's long-time lover and accomplice. The proceedings reflect an austerely moralistic view of adultery which has nothing to do with the courtly fantasy. But over the almost twenty years of her English captivity that followed, young English Catholics would, in the words of Lisa Hilton, offer 'their lives as love tokens' to the famously beautiful Scots queen.

Trouble first came to a head with the Revolt of the Northern Earls, a dangerous armed uprising in 1569 by the old, Catholic-leaning, aristocracy, already dissatisfied with the new men Elizabeth had around her. They failed to place Mary on Elizabeth's throne, but their revolt had become entangled with another plan – that Mary should marry the Duke of Norfolk himself, Elizabeth's own kinsman and premier noble. The Scots queen had given her ardent support, writing to Norfolk as to her husband, and embroidering for him the cruelly telling design of a knife pruning a barren vine (a reference to the childless Elizabeth). Norfolk's complicity was known to the authorities, and he himself placed in the Tower, before the northern earls rode southwards. But it threw a harsh light on the danger posed by Norfolk and Norfolk's kin – and also by Mary.

The revolt was put down, savagely. The leading rebels fled abroad, while Norfolk was released into house arrest the following summer. But events did not end there. In the early spring of 1570 the Pope issued a Bull, *Regnans in excelsis*, depriving the heretic Elizabeth of 'her pretended right to her realm'. This placed English Catholics in an impossible situation – and Elizabeth in grave and lasting danger.

In the spring of 1571 Mary wrote to Norfolk with details of the Ridolfi plot (named for the Italian agent who was its chief machinator) and by the autumn Norfolk was back in the Tower. Brought to trial in January 1572 before a jury of his peers, the sentence was never in doubt, though it would be June before Elizabeth could bring herself to allow the execution to go ahead: the first beheading of her reign.

Norfolk's execution paled beside what came later in that summer of 1572, but both in their different ways were products of the religious divisions sweeping ominously across Europe. In August, in France, those divisions came to a terrible head. Admiral Coligny, leader of the Huguenots, the French Protestants, was assassinated by French Catholic forces that included both the Guise family (the Queen of Scots' relatives) and the queen mother, Catherine de Medici.

What became known as the Massacre of St Bartholomew's Day was a bloodbath in which perhaps ten thousand Protestants were killed. The violence raged through France for weeks and even months – and changed the mental map of Europe. Elizabeth put her court into mourning when she heard the news, and her favourites and ministers, staunch Protestants all, stood firm behind her.

One caught up in the trouble was Philip Sidney, the son of Leicester's sister Mary. The earl, still with no heir of his own body, had always taken the warmest interest in 'my boy'. Now a young Sidney, down from Oxford, had found himself in Paris about to be convulsed by violence, and having to take refuge in Francis Walsingham's house. The experience permanently coloured his – like Walsingham's – attitudes.

Something else happened in the autumn of 1572; hardly pressing on the world stage, but significant in our context. The courtier and poet Edward Dyer (today best remembered for 'My mind to me a kingdom is') wrote to his friend Christopher Hatton warning him about his behaviour towards the queen: 'who though she do descend very much in her sex as a woman, yet may we not forget her place, and the nature of it as our Sovereign'.

Anyone who seemed to be challenging that hierarchy, Dyer told Hatton, should be very careful, for fear lest the queen thought he was trying 'to imprison her fancy'. There were other and better ways to manage her, Dyer advised: 'acknowledge your duty' to her and (a subtle touch) 'never seem deeply to condemn her frailties, but rather joyfully to commend such things as should be in her, as though they were in her indeed'.

Royal favourites, like racehorses, had often a team of backers and trainers behind them. Dyer warns Hatton against too much importunity, against criticism and jealousy. But the most striking phrase in Dyer's letter lies here: 'though in the beginning when her Majesty sought you (after her good manner), she did bear with rugged dealing of yours, until she had what she fancied, yet now, after satiety and fullness, it will rather hurt than help you'.

Satiety and fullness? Elizabeth having 'what she fancied'? Small wonder, perhaps, that even at the time, there were suggestions that Hatton had (as one Mather, a conspirator against Elizabeth, phrased it) 'more recourse to Her Majesty in her Privy Chamber than reason would suffer if she were so virtuous and well-inclined as some [noiseth] her'. Hatton himself might be said to have contributed to the fantasy. Sending her a ring said to ward off the plague, he wrote that it was meant to be worn 'between the sweet dugs [breasts]'.

But looked at more closely, Hatton's letters leave little doubt that this sexual innuendo was only a pleasurable fantasy. His most impassioned declarations of love come allied to what are effectively pleas that Elizabeth should marry him . . . hardly likely. If marriage with the titled Leicester would have been disadvantageous for Elizabeth, then marriage with Christopher Hatton – not even 'Sir' Christopher until she knighted him in 1577 – would have been an insult to her sovereignty. Indeed, it was probably the knowledge that Hatton could never aspire so high that allowed Elizabeth to enjoy his verbal love play.

Neither Elizabeth's other courtiers nor the foreign ambassadors reacted to Hatton with the alarmed attention they would have paid had they really believed he had gained sexual ascendancy over her. The eroticised language was in general currency: Francis Bacon would write of Elizabeth's 'wonderful art of keeping servants in satisfaction, and yet in appetite'.

Dyer urges Hatton to follow the path he lays down, promising that then 'your place shall keep you in worship, your presence in favour, your followers will stand to you, at the least you shall have no bold enemies, and you shall dwell in the ways to take all advantages wisely, and honestly to serve your turn at times'. That 'honestly serve your turn' is key. Clearly, Dyer is thinking in terms of more than Hatton's own individual advancement. Though Hatton is not remembered first in political terms, that is unfair. His apprenticeship was served in the personal arena, but Elizabeth would then begin to make use of him professionally – just as had happened with Leicester.

Hatton would prove himself over the years as a significant Parliamentary orator and Elizabeth's voice in the Commons – mediator, even, between Elizabeth and her House. In the 1576 session he was appointed to commissions on everything from ports and coinage to the queen's marriage. In 1577 he became Vice Chamberlain of the Royal Household, a knight and a Privy Councillor. (He also became a notable backer of voyages of exploration such as Martin Frobisher's attempt to find the North-West Passage, which was backed also by other leading statesmen including Leicester and Oxford. It is striking how strongly all Elizabeth's favourites would interest themselves in adventure abroad, perhaps to get out from under her controlling wing!)

Perhaps it is time to look from a fresh angle at the nature of Elizabeth's relations with her favourites – at the balance between sex appeal and statesmanship. All of Elizabeth's personal favourites would be also among her most useful governmental servants, but this elision of roles was – during some of the censorious centuries between Elizabeth's day and ours – seen as exemplifying her feminine weakness: how even she could be in thrall to unworthy men.

The misogynistic assumption was long that Elizabeth – even Elizabeth! – here let her heart (or some other part of her anatomy) rule her head. The fear was that men first noted for their personal appeal might then win undue political influence. The question of a ruler's favourite, and the influence they might wield, was always a vexed one – but never more so than when the ruler was a woman, and the socially accepted dominance of the male over the female had to be added into the mix. A king might have his favourite ministers for business and his mistresses for pleasure; and if the bounds were broken, as with Edward II, there was a price to pay. But now, with a female ruler, who even knew where the boundaries lay?

The amount of power Elizabeth actually ceded to her favourites is a matter of dispute. 'I conclude that she [Elizabeth] was absolute and sovereign mistress of her grace and that those to whom she distributed her favors were never more than tenants at will and stood on no better ground than her princely pleasure and their own good behaviour,' Robert Naunton wrote. Elizabeth's statesman Fulke Greville likewise (contrasting the queen with her susceptible successor James, who did indeed seem under the sway of a series of handsome young men) wrote that: 'in the latitudes which some modern princes allow to their favourites, it seems this queen reservedly kept entrenched within her native strengths and sceptre'.

What is more, a favourite, in terms of court life, could be a useful animal: conduit through which the ruler could distribute patronage; mouthpiece and manager; scapegoat when necessary. As John Clapham, one of Burghley's adherents, put it, 'she seldom or never denied any suit that was moved unto her . . . but the suitor received the answer of denial by some other; a thankless office, and commonly performed by persons of greatest place, who ofttimes bear the blame of many things wherein themselves are not guilty, while no imputation must be laid upon the prince.' (The function of scapegoat was one Anne Boleyn had to some degree performed for Henry.)

Perhaps, instead of seeing her favourites as her weak spot, we should ask whether Elizabeth was drawn only to individuals exceptional in mind as well as body. She was able, at the least, to bring out men's abilities. The trends of history have varied between giving Elizabeth herself credit for the successes of her reign, and seeing her as the frontwoman for her ministers. But to assemble such a team around her – to command their enduring service, to wield them all into one fighting unit – was not the least of her talents.

Certainly (just as he had come to form a working relationship with Burghley) Leicester's hostility towards Hatton came to melt in the face of Hatton's noted amiability. The tone of Leicester's letters to the queen had by now become almost domestic. Perhaps the very extravagance of the courtly game allowed the men to distance themselves from it to some degree. Or perhaps, after all these years of devoted service, Leicester's attention, at least, was beginning to turn another way.

The loves of an older generation were beginning to pass out of sight. Margaret Douglas had been greatly saddened, in 1571, by the assassination of her husband the Earl of Lennox. He had been living in Scotland as regent for his and Margaret's infant grandson James VI; but the Lennox Jewel, in the Royal Collection, is tribute to their enduring love. The heart-shaped locket opens to reveal two hearts pierced by arrows, and the initials MSL – Margaret and Matthew Stuart Lennox – with the avowal that only 'Death will dissolve' this marriage. King James was only five years old when his grandfather was shot in the back and brought back to Stirling Castle to die, in his last hours sending his love to his 'Meg'.

Margaret's grief was 'poignant and perpetual'. She had now lost her 'choicest comforts': both her son and her 'mate'. But for Elizabeth, Margaret had yet one sting in the tail. At the end of 1574 she conspired with that other great Tudor matriarch Bess of Hardwick to arrange a marriage between her younger son Charles Stuart and one of Bess's daughters. Given Charles's royal blood, this was a matter of state. Queen and Council were profoundly unconvinced by the plea that this was merely a case of two young people and their 'own liking' – that Charles was 'so far in love that belike he is sick without her'. Margaret found herself once more committed to house arrest. 'Thrice have I been cast into prison, not for matters of treason but for love matters,' she complained.

She was soon released, dying some three years later at her own house in Hackney. Her son had predeceased her; but Charles's marriage had produced a daughter, Arbella Stuart, who in turn would come to occupy the dizzying, dangerous position of Queen Elizabeth's possible heir. And who, in her cousin James's reign, would in her turn find herself in the Tower for an unsanctioned marriage . . . Perhaps – though this is another story – through Margaret some strain of the Tudor romanticism would find its way into the Stuart dynasty.

'against my nature'

1575–1584

W HEN, IN THE summer of 1575, Queen Elizabeth rode up to Kenilworth, the grand Warwickshire seat she had given the Earl of Leicester, she was greeted by a piece of Arthurian pageantry. The Lady of the Lake, aboard a 'moveable island, bright blazing with torches', was borne towards her across the great lake, to assure Elizabeth that though she had kept the castle since Arthur's day, it was now the queen's. Elizabeth was heard to mutter that she rather thought she owned it already.

The published chronicle of this fortnight's visit suggests the 'Princely Pleasures' at Kenilworth might almost have borne comparison with the Field of Cloth of Gold. Hunting, feasting, rustic sports; the fireworks the best an Italian pyrotechnic expert could provide. When Elizabeth admired the new garden Leicester had built, but regretted, capriciously, that it could not be seen from her apartments (themselves decked out in silver fabric of peach and purple), he had a duplicate created under her window overnight . . . Well, in the account written by one of his gentlemen, anyway.

But during her visit Elizabeth's eyes and ears were battered also by a parade of entertainments orchestrated to urge her towards matrimony. Even the clock dials were stopped at two o'clock to suggest 'two, pairs, and couples'.

Did Leicester truly believe the great entertainment might yet persuade her to marry him? That year, after all, the painter Zuccaro was commissioned to make twin portraits of the queen and the earl, as if they were an established partnership. But he had surely given up all real hopes. Sometime before the Kenilworth visit Leicester had made a contract – or, as she would later claim, a secret marriage – with another lady, Douglass Sheffield; and that alliance had resulted in a son.

The entertainments Leicester commissioned at Kenilworth tended to promote not only marriage, but also military action: they tended to show women in jeopardy, in need of being rescued by a protective masculinity. One of the queen's greatest skills was to find a currency – distinct from the male camaraderie, the accolades of the tourney – with which to negotiate the royal transactions of favour and reward that worked for her female monarchy. But the men around her were equally capable of dressing a political agenda in a cloak of chivalry. In 1575 Leicester cherished burning hopes of leading an army to the Netherlands, where the Dutch Protestants were under ever-greater pressure from their Spanish Catholic overlords.

On this occasion, at least, Elizabeth was having none of it – as she made clear by spurring away at the end of her Kenilworth visit, leaving panting behind the tame poet from whom Leicester had commissioned verses favouring marriage over virginity. Her resistance was not only to a costly foreign war, but to the passive coding imposed on her by this version of chivalry. As queen regnant she was a figure at once masculine and feminine. She needed to be both hero and heroine of the story.

A letter from the Earl of Leicester to Sir Nicholas Throckmorton during these irritable years shows the bitterness he – even he! – could feel after some unintentional offence. 'Foul faults have been pardoned in some; my hope was that only one might be forgiven – yea, forgotten – me. If many days' service and not a few years' proof have [not] made trial of unremovable fidelity enough, what shall I think of all that past favour, [when] my first oversight [brings about] as it were an utter casting off of all that was before.'

There had always been marked downturns in his relationship with the queen, but their tone with each other was becoming more consistently fractious; perhaps as any real hope Leicester had of her hand began to die away. Or, as he came to understand the skill – and the ruthlessness – with which the queen made use of him: invoking his role as her acknowledged adorer whenever the pressure to marry a foreign suitor grew too great, but never coming close to fulfilling the apparent promise.

Three years later, in the summer of 1578, Elizabeth made a visit to another of Robert Dudley's homes – to Wanstead, just east of London. In the entertainment devised for her there two suitors competed for the hand of the Lady of the May. The handsome forester and a weedy shepherd suggested, all too obviously, Leicester and Burghley, but the song sung by the foresters recalled what Wyatt had written about Elizabeth's mother.

> Two thousand wildest deer in the wild woods I have,
> Them can I take, but you I cannot hold.

When, at the end of the entertainment, Elizabeth was given a necklace of agates shaped, daringly, like Catholic rosary beads, she was told that when Leicester said his 'Our Father' every day he added the words 'and Elizabeth'. Leicester was now figuring himself as 'good man Robert', Elizabeth's bedesman, 'with all his *aves*, in his solitary walk'. But that is doubly ironic.

On the one hand Leicester, always a more ardent Protestant than his queen, was drawing ever closer to the Puritan cause. On the other, any echoes of ritual courtship belie the actuality of his changing relationship with Elizabeth. Just weeks before, Leicester had secretly married Lettice Knollys, the lady with whom he had flirted years before, but who had since become a widow. And this was definitely a marriage, regularised by a further ceremony in the autumn, but already in a different league entirely from the putative 'marriage' with Douglass Sheffield, which Douglass was pressured to disown.

Is it just coincidence that in June Christopher Hatton was writing to Leicester of the queen's 'great melancholy', of her dreams of 'a marriage that might seem injurious to her'? Elizabeth's ability *not* to know what she needed to – firmly to take fantasy for fact – was key to the success of her courtly strategy.

But the quasi-rosary gift made to Elizabeth at Wanstead was perhaps significant in yet another way. The mid-1570s saw the real start of the cultural and political construct which figured Elizabeth as an alternative to the Virgin Mary. When the fleet of the Catholic Holy League defeated that of the Ottoman Empire in 1571, it was declared that the real victor was the Virgin Mary. The Catholic Counter-Reformation sponsored a renewed cult of the Mother of God.

Many of the symbols used to represent Elizabeth – rose, pearl, moon, star, phoenix and ermine – had been used also for Mary. The cult of Mary had been particularly popular in England during the late Middle Ages and into the Tudor years; the invocation of her image had been a regular trope of queenship, used even by Anne Boleyn.

After Elizabeth's death she would be hailed as a second Virgin, who had given birth to Christ's true gospel just as the Virgin Mary had given birth to Christ himself. Elizabeth, as sovereign, had assumed certain religious functions from the start of her reign, but as the 1570s turned to the 1580s the promotion of her as essentially a saint or a goddess took on a different tone. It was now that the term 'Virgin Queen' came into currency. In her mid-forties, the queen was passing out of the reproductive years and it was as if once one female stereo-type, the fertile mother, could no longer be applied to her, there was a pressing need for another.

Even the celebrations for Elizabeth's Accession Day every year were coming to be known as 'the queen's holy day', with the religious accompaniments of sermons and bell-ringing. No wonder Burghley could write of her visit to him at Theobalds as 'consecrating' his house. Men wore the queen's portrait as once they might have worn a holy image. As one courtier would later put it, 'We worshipped no saints, but we prayed to ladies in the Queen's time.'

George Gower's 'Sieve Portrait' of Elizabeth dates to 1579, and the sieve prominently displayed in the queen's hand is a reference to a slandered Vestal Virgin, whose feat of carrying a sieve-full of water through the Roman streets without spilling a drop was considered to prove her chastity. The mystical power of virginity had the imprimatur of history: St Jerome linked Mary's virginity with the gift of life she brought. From the female saints to the pure knights of Camelot (and these years saw a fresh peak of interest in the queen's ancestor King Arthur; the link between them carefully illustrated in a genealogical table in the Cecils' house) the world was full of images of the power of sexual virtue. The very word 'virgin' came from the Latin *virtus*, strength – and Elizabeth herself would invoke her virginity to convey strength, rather than maidenly frailty.

It is hard to know exactly who was behind this image-making. But we do know that legend – story – was a part of Elizabeth's own mental world. It is there when she told the French ambassador that she had tried to be a good mother (i.e. mother figure, mentor) to the Queen of Scots but that Mary's plots meant she deserved 'nothing other than a wicked stepmother' – clear reference to the villain-figure of fairy story. It is hard *not* to see Elizabeth's dialogue with the Scottish ambassador Sir James Melville – her demands as to whether she or Mary were the fairer, the taller, the better musician – as a kind of 'Mirror, mirror on the wall'.

All in all, it was a heady emotional and cultural, as well as political, mix that paved the way for the last great crisis in the history of Elizabeth's courtships: the question of a French marriage for the queen.

The idea had been mooted back in 1570 that Elizabeth might marry Henri, Duc d'Anjou, brother to the young French King Charles IX. Henri was twenty years younger than Elizabeth, promiscuously bisexual, and fervently Catholic: nonetheless, even Leicester seemed prepared to concede that 'our estate requireth a match'. The balance of power in Europe, so long a precarious balance between France and Spain, was tipping the latter's way and France, like England, needed allies.

Both of the principal parties, however, were notably reluctant; and in December 1571 the French had suggested that Elizabeth might instead marry Anjou's (even) younger brother François, Duc d'Alençon. Alençon was less religiously strict than his brother, more interested in women, 'less like a mule', as the English ambassador put it. But all talk of marriages foundered – for a time – on the events of 1572: the Massacre of St Bartholomew's Day. It was no time to be talking of marriage to a French Catholic prince.

A few years on, however, the climate had cooled sufficiently for a marriage between Elizabeth and Alençon to be once more in ques-tion.* England's need for allies had been made the more evident by the

---

* Alençon had, when Charles died in 1574 and Henri inherited the French throne, himself inherited Henri's former title as Duc d'Anjou. For clarity's sake, however, I shall continue to refer to him as Alençon.

increasing infiltration of Elizabeth's country by Catholic priests – and by the situation in the Netherlands, where the ongoing Protestant rebellion had resulted in a vengeful Spanish army camped just across the waters. The French marriage was an issue that would divide her ministers like no other – but those divisions were nothing to the ones within Elizabeth's own head.

This should, by all the rules of sixteenth-century royalty, have been a pragmatic rather than a personal story. But Elizabeth (displaying the same anachronistic concerns her forebears had done) protested that for her own 'satisfaction' she would need to see Alençon in the flesh. She was not prepared to cast this alliance wholly in political terms, and after one wounded explosion on her part, Leicester was forced to warn Walsingham to 'avoid the suspicion of her Majesty that you doubt Monsieur's love to her too much'.

January 1579 saw the arrival of Jean de Simier, Alençon's personal envoy and close friend: 'a most choice courtier, exquisitely skilled in love toys, pleasant conceits and court dalliances', as William Camden described him.* Soon Simier – *singe* – was Elizabeth's 'monkey'. His master Alençon's letters, meanwhile, were couched in terms of such literary romance Elizabeth told him they should be carved in marble, rather than just written on parchment.

The ongoing negotiations were practical ones. The French were demanding Alençon should be crowned king; 'a matter that greatly toucheth our regality'. But on Elizabeth's side at least there continued to be also a strong personal element to the story. The French, she insisted, had made it clear by letters and 'most earnest speeches and protestations . . . that not our fortune but our person was the only thing that was sought'.

Perhaps her determination to see herself, at forty-five, as desirable and desired was a chance to put the now-married Leicester in his place. For this may have been Simier's masterstroke: one story suggests that in July 1579 it was he who broke to Elizabeth the news of Leicester's secret marriage with Lettice Knollys. Whether or not she had already

---

* Simier's polished exterior concealed a violent past. He had recently murdered his brother, for having an affair with his wife – much like the sinful lovers in Dante's *Inferno*!

any suspicion, Elizabeth was furious at this publicly acknowledged fact: the more so for the fact that the Knollys family 'appertaineth to us in blood', as she wrote. Wiser counsels dissuaded Elizabeth from her first impulse, which was to put Leicester in the Tower. But now the way was paved for the arrival, the following month, of the suitor, Alençon, himself.

From the very start, the visit took on the tones of courtly fantasy. Arriving at Greenwich early in the morning after travelling through the night, Alençon had (Simier said) to be dissuaded from going instantly to Elizabeth to kiss her hand. When forced instead to go to bed he declared: 'Would to God it was by your side.' When they met, later that day, Elizabeth declared that she had 'never in my life seen a creature more agreeable to me'; yes, Alençon might be, as she had been warned, both small and pockmarked but, in a very public parade of affection, he was able to make himself so agreeable as to be soon Elizabeth's 'Frog'. Ten days after his arrival, however – to the massive relief of Leicester and Hatton – the death of a friend summoned Alençon back to France.

Elizabeth would write to Alençon with what sounds like real intimacy (and perhaps it is significant that she would write to him in French). 'My dearest, I give you now a fair mirror to see there very clearly the foolishness of my understanding . . . See where the love that I bear you carries me – to act against my nature.' Though, as with her own courtiers, her letters turn in the end to a note of reproach. 'It seems to me that in commemorating the history of the dealings between us, it pleases you to tell me at length of the hazards, losses, and machinations that you have endured for my sake . . . I think that the king will repute me for such a one as goes a-wooing, which will always be a fine reputation for a woman!' she would write in 1582.

Not to be outdone, Alençon claimed to say his prayers before her portrait; wrote letters, so the French envoy claimed proudly, 'ardent enough to set fire to water'. Burghley, who strongly favoured the match, kept up the pressure on Elizabeth, subtly reminding her this might be her last chance of love; that even Leicester had left her; that without a replacement she would be 'alone, though a hundred are about'.

But other voices spoke against the match, and more publicly. Alençon was barely back across the Channel when the Puritan John Stubbs wrote a pamphlet entitled *A Gaping Gulphe wherein England is like to be swallowed*. Stating the fundamental problem – that the English equated a foreign marriage with subjection, and a Catholic prince with tyranny – he added, unpalatably, the suggestion that the queen was too old to face childbirth for the first time, that Alençon could have only a mercenary motive in seeking to marry a woman so much older than he. Elizabeth, he wrote, was being 'led blindfold as a poor lamb to the slaughter' . . . It was instead Stubbs who was led to Westminster Palace Green, there to have his right hand hacked off, to the evident disapprobation of a silent crowd.

Stubbs was far from the only critic. Another – strongly supported by his uncle – was Leicester's nephew Philip Sidney. Sidney's open *Letter to Queen Elizabeth touching her marriage with Monsieur* suggested that Alençon blew hot and cold in his affections towards her; failed properly to appreciate 'the perfections of your body and mind'. It was never likely Leicester's nephew, his work circulated only in a private and aristocratic circle, would suffer the same hideous penalty as Stubbs. But a friend advised him to consider where he should go if forced into exile; and indeed Sidney would withdraw to Wilton, home to his sister Mary, the Countess of Pembroke.

When in October the queen asked the Privy Council for advice, Leicester and Hatton mustered a majority of councillors against the match, while Burghley led the smaller party in favour. When, after thirteen hours of solid debate, they returned a hung verdict, Elizabeth was distraught. She had anticipated, she said, in tears, 'a universal request made for her to proceed in this marriage'. On 10 November she told her councillors 'she had determined to marry'. On 24 November she agreed that she and Simier (as Alençon's proxy) should sign the marriage articles – which, however (as she wrote to Alençon, 'my dearest'), gave her two months to convince her people to 'rejoice and approve'.

But as the two months came and went, it began to look as though Elizabeth was trying to keep the French on a string, dangling Alençon as she had so long dandled Leicester (who for years had been 'more than a bondsman', as he now complained bitterly). Burghley, horrified, warned her of the dangers of such a course: 'those that would trick princes, trick themselves'. But then again – while Elizabeth wore the frog jewel from Alençon, publicly kissed the gloves that he had given her, wrote a stream of letters praising his 'constancy' – Alençon himself showed no burning desire to press his suit. It was the European political situation that in August 1580 pushed Elizabeth into inviting French commissioners to come and discuss terms of a marriage treaty. But when they did not at once appear, the Venetian ambassador in Paris heard that Alençon (who, despite his own Catholicism, was now fighting at the head of the Dutch Protestants in the Netherlands) was also remembering Elizabeth's 'advanced age and repulsive physical nature'.

In September 1580 Hatton wrote to the queen: 'Against love and ambition your Highness hath holden a long war; they are violent affections that encumber the hearts of men: but now, my most dear Sovereign, it is more than time to yield, or else this love will leave you in war and disquietness of yourself and estate'. His letter had begun by figuring himself:

> on my knees with such reverence as becometh your most obliged bondman; and with like humility, in my most dutiful and grateful manner, I do offer in God's presence myself, my life, and all that I am or is me, to be disposed to the end, and my death to do your service, in inviolable faith and sincerity.

The rhetoric could hardly have gone further had Elizabeth been indeed a divinity. But what is also notable is that in terms of both politics and personal ambition, Hatton's and Leicester's attitudes were becoming less consistently hostile to the French match than might have been expected. And emotionally, perhaps even an element of relief crept into play.

In January 1581, at last, came news that the French commissioners were on their way. In March they arrived, to be greeted by a positive storm of festivities. May saw an allegorical 'Triumph' in the tiltyard as knights attempted to assail the Fortress of Perfect Beauty. As musicians played from inside the fortress mound, the Sons of Desire pelted its walls with flowers and 'fancies' while cannons fired scented powder. Unlike the Siege of the Château Vert, almost sixty years before, Lady Beauty successfully resisted the attack. A horde of her knights stormed into the tiltyard to the defence of the fortress, and a knight in snakeskin, accompanied by a doctor whose shield bore a woman's face, was defeated by the queen's champion, Sir Henry Lee. Just so, the message made clear: Elizabeth should have none of Alençon, the snake in the grass . . . Well, the entertainment had been written by Philip Sidney.

And Elizabeth seemed to have taken on board the message. Some of her concerns were those old near-insoluble political problems: the question of Alençon's religion; the fear of England's being sucked into war against Spain. Others were more personal: her worry about the difference of age. One moment she seemed to decide she wanted a marriage-free treaty, a simple league of alliance; the next she told the commissioners to draw up terms for a marriage, but stipulated that Alençon would have to come himself to ratify them.

Her own messages to Alençon were equally contradictory. In one letter she warned him that 'her body was hers' – though her soul was 'wholly dedicated to him'. It suggests Elizabeth still sought to be, as Naunton described her, 'absolute and sovereign mistress of her grace'. But her letters could also sound a very different note: 'Monsieur, my dearest, grant pardon to the poor old woman who honours you as much (I dare say) as any young wench whom you ever will find . . . she who governs desires to have the grace to be able to serve you in some manner.' It sounds a little as though the courtly rules were being reversed. Elizabeth compared herself to a beaten dog he could not turn away. Alençon was the first serious suitor she had met in the flesh with whom she stood on terms of royal near-equality.

'When Her Majesty is pressed to marry she seemeth to affect a league, and when a league is proposed then she liketh better a marriage,' Walsingham wrote to Burghley when Elizabeth sent him to persuade the French of her sincerity. Exasperated beyond endurance, Walsingham added that he would count it 'a great favour' if she would send him to the Tower instead.

In the autumn Alençon arrived back in England, and the ritual exchange of gifts resumed. He brought Elizabeth a diamond ring; she responded (with a slightly more elaborate symbolism) by giving him a key that fitted every room of the palace, as well as a jewel-encrusted arquebus. Rumour said she took him a cup of broth in bed each morning and, so the Spanish ambassador heard, when they were alone Elizabeth would pledge herself to Alençon 'as much as any woman could to a man'. But only when they were alone.

The French ambassador managed to force the issue, catching her walking with Alençon in the gallery of Whitehall palace. The French king, he said, wanted to know the queen's intention from her own lips. 'She replied, "You may write this to the King: that the Duke of Anjou [Alençon] shall be my husband." She turned to the Duc and kissed him on the mouth, drawing a ring from her own hand and giving it to him as a pledge.' Calling her courtiers around her she publicly repeated her vow. It was said both Leicester and Hatton were among the number who burst into tears.

But the night brought different – wiser? – counsels. Or was it that Elizabeth's visceral reluctance to marry once again overwhelmed her in the end? The next morning, she sent for Alençon and told him that two more such sleepless nights would see her in her grave and that she could not marry him after all.

Not that that was the end of the story. As Elizabeth dithered – as Alençon loitered in England, muttering about 'the lightness of women' – it became apparent both parties could get what they most wanted without the strain of trying to turn this fantasy of love into a reality.

England's rapprochement with France had already frightened Spain into less bellicose behaviour, while Alençon, as the price of his departure, won substantial English funds to help his Netherlands campaign. The Spanish ambassador heard that in her own bedchamber, when the deal was struck, Elizabeth danced for joy. Alençon's journey to the coast in the spring of 1582 took on the nature of a party – for all that Elizabeth was soon to be heard sighing that she wished her frog were once more swimming in the Thames.

Her poem 'On Monsieur's Departure' was probably written now; and though it is in some sense a display of literary virtuosity, the editors of her collected *Works* point out that Elizabeth's rare poems were kept in jealous privacy, unlike the letters and speeches written with an audience in mind. It is hard not to suspect those skilful Petrarchan contraries also reflect her own real conflict.

I grieve, yet dare not show my discontent;
I love, and yet am forced to seem to hate,
I dote, but dare not what I meant;
I seem stark mute, yet inwardly do prate.
I am, and am not, freeze, and yet I burn,
Since from myself my other self I turn.

Love-melancholy was regarded as a vehicle of extreme heat and cold, and love, in its courtly sense, was said to make men the opposite of themselves. As Andreas Capellanus put it: 'Beauty, which we call Venus, cannot subsist without contrariety.' Chaucer, translating Petrarch and describing for the English 'this wondrous malady', had written: 'For heat of cold, for cold of heat, I die', and Wyatt had echoed to the contrasting extremities. Elizabeth was writing in a long-established literary tradition. But she had just come up against reality.

It was Leicester who escorted Alençon back to the Netherlands, and when he stayed away too long, Hatton had to write in a panic, summoning him home to soothe a tetchy queen. The game was back in the hands of the regular players. But was it one they still felt able to play?

Perhaps Leicester was now reluctant to keep up the parade of being Elizabeth's suitor. The position to which – when they were on good terms – he could aspire (and which the French, if she married Alençon, had offered to maintain) was akin to that of Elizabeth's brother. She was a woman short of blood relations, and for all the difference in their rank, Leicester had become family. But in the summer of 1581, when Lettice gave birth to a son, Lord Denbigh, Leicester seemed to have achieved the goal of every nobleman: a family, a dynasty, of his own. Small wonder he became increasingly unwilling to collaborate in the queen's wilful determination to ignore his marriage.

A letter he wrote to her – probably in 1583, after the defeat of yet another plot against her life – sounds an ecstatically religious note. The goodness of God had saved her against so many devils – 'You may see what it is to cleave unto Him; He rewardeth beyond all deserts, and so is it daily seen how He payeth those that be dissemblers with Him.'

The casual error of history long painted Leicester and Elizabeth's other favourites as personally ambitious and thus amoral popinjays. In fact, Leicester had a long connection with the Puritan cause: he was a patriot, and a believer in his queen, but it is doubtful he would have recognised the Platonic concept familiar to Dante of a human love leading to a sacred. Perhaps, even, his increased religiosity changed his attitude to the other roles he was called upon to play.

Nor were Elizabeth's other old favourites much source of satisfaction to her. On his return to England Oxford had become associated with a group of aristocratic Catholics, and his star once more fell dramatically when, in the spring of 1581, his mistress Anne Vavasour, one of Elizabeth's maids of honour, had given birth to his illegitimate son, in the queen's own palace. Both were placed in the Tower and, though Oxford was soon released and forcibly reconciled with his wife, Burghley's daughter, the gilt was off the gingerbread; the more so since an armed brawl with one of Anne's relatives was only the first skirmish in a feud worthy of Montague and Capulet.

Oxford's old rival Sidney, too, was to some degree estranged from the court. It was likely around 1580 and at Wilton that Sidney began to write his *Arcadia*, the pastoral romance, Virginia Woolf would say, in which 'all the seeds of English fiction lie latent'. It contains a number of possible reflections on Elizabeth; and not flattering ones: ageing women curled and painted, queens handicapped by their own vanity and desire.

Elizabeth for her part, though she used him on certain diplomatic missions, never altogether warmed to Sidney; perhaps aware of the criticism implicit under a courtly surface or recognising that his own romantic appeal made him dangerous. Sidney's legend would live on as long as his queen's, due in large part to the idea of his love for Penelope Devereux, daughter of Leicester's wife Lettice.

Penelope had been dangled as a prospective bride for Sidney but instead, soon after she came to court in 1581, had been married to Lord Rich – 'the rich Lord Rich'. At some point subsequently – once, in best courtly tradition, she was safely married to another man? – Sidney began to write to her the great sonnet sequence *Astrophil and Stella*. Its powerful analysis of the pain of passion led to the long assumption she was in truth his lost love or married mistress. But Katherine Duncan-Jones raised the question of whether he was really deeply in love with her or whether 'the whole Astrophil-Stella love affair was a kind of literary charade, in which both real-life participants knew exactly what was going on'. Elizabeth had played the courtly game more skilfully than any, but as her reign wore on there came a question. Was it the men around her, or was it she, most in danger of taking it seriously?

Another woman was doing her bit to burst the bubble in which Elizabeth sought to live. In the early 1580s the imprisoned and increasingly embittered Mary, Queen of Scots penned an (undated) 'scandal letter', later found among Burghley's papers.

Mary was writing, theoretically, to clear herself of the scandalous charge that she had been having an affair with her gaoler, the Earl of Shrewsbury, estranged husband to the famous Bess of Hardwick. But she was eager to pass the ball of scandal into Elizabeth's court, and get the Countess of Shrewsbury into trouble, too.

Bess (wrote Mary) had said that one to whom Elizabeth had made a promise of marriage 'had made love to you an infinite number of times with all the license and intimacy which can be used between man and wife. But that undoubtedly you were not like other women . . . and you would never lose your liberty to make love and always have your pleasure with new lovers.'

Mary accused Elizabeth of 'various indecent liberties' with Simier, of trying to lure Alençon into bed; of pursuing Hatton until he was forced to leave court in a vain attempt to protect his modesty. Elizabeth, like her mother before her – and like some versions of Guinevere – was being cast as the sexual aggressor; the seeker rather than the sought. Mary added that Elizabeth's courtiers had often to turn away to hide their laughter as they paid their extravagant compliments. If the queen read the letter, it could only have dealt a wounding blow to her vision of herself as the sought-after, the infinitely desirable, the courtly lady. Conventional wisdom suggests – since Elizabeth gave no sign of having received such a wound – she did *not* see the letter; that Burghley kept it from her. But one of the queen's talents was at once to know and not to know. Several of her predecessors had found that this ranked as one of the most useful gifts of any medieval monarch, and in this too Elizabeth was a true descendant of her forebears.

In fact, by the 1580s Mary's allegation about Elizabeth and Leicester was seriously out of date. Nothing could end their relationship while both parties were alive. But something had changed significantly.

The old dream of courtly love had given a *language* to Leicester's long relationship with his queen – had indeed made possible its durability. But by its nature the relationship of these two had consisted at first of real hopes and desires pressing urgently to be satisfied, and later of a familial, almost a quasi-marital, domesticity. When Leicester sought also an actual, a legally sanctioned, marriage of the kind that could give him heirs (and maybe the position of superiority a man expected in the sixteenth century), Elizabeth was forced to acknowledge the difference between the dream and the reality. Perhaps that was at the root of her violent anger.

Leicester had never been naturally cast as a courtly lover – had performed the role only with difficulty. Hatton's letters show that he took the language, the fantasy of love further; but in the end what stands out about Hatton, too, is his real and lasting affection for Elizabeth. Naunton reports Hatton once saying that the queen did fish for men's souls, and had so sweet a bait that no one could escape her net. And though the image sounds menacing, no one can doubt that Hatton had given his soul gladly.

In the years ahead, however, a new generation would push this fantasy of courtly worship to its greatest height; an escalation in which Elizabeth herself, perhaps, would never quite believe. In doing so, they would expose the hollowness of the reality – the unpalatable brew of compulsion and ambition that lay behind the fantasy.

PART VI

1584–1603

Congé: a poem of farewell, particularly common among the *trouvères*

When I was fair and young, and favor graced me,
Of many was I sought their mistress for to be.
But I did scorn them all, and answered them therefore,
    'Go, go, go seek some otherwhere,
        Importune me no more.'
How many weeping eyes I made to pine with woe;
How many sighing hearts I have no skill to show.
Yet I the prouder grew, and answered them therefore,
    'Go, go, go seek some otherwhere,
        Importune me no more.'
Then spake fair Venus' son, that proud victorious boy,
And said: 'Fine dame, since that you be so coy,
I will pluck your plumes that you shall say no more
    "Go, go, go seek some otherwhere,
        Importune me no more."'
When he had spake these words, such change grew in my breast
That neither night nor day since that, I could take any rest.
Then lo, I did repent that I had said before,
    'Go, go, go seek some otherwhere,
        Importune me no more.'
Finis
Elizabetha Regina.

Elizabeth I, c.1580s

21

'this old song'

1584–1587

E LIZABETH HAD SAILED into the 1580s on a high note, despite the departure of Alençon. Even her fiftieth birthday, in September 1583, had not seriously dented her confidence. There was precedent for it: one Arthurian tale had described Guinevere as past fifty, but still the most beautiful woman in the world . . . Perhaps the ending of her years of fertility, the years in which she could reasonably be pressured to marry, brought a kind of freedom; a chance – an imperative – to redefine her identity. For the men around her, on the other hand, time was moving differently. Leicester, Hatton and the rest were growing less able endlessly to play the same games: to launch the ritual assaults and rivalries.

In the summer of 1584, in the space of just a few short weeks, three events – three deaths – brought everyone's positions into sharper focus. On 10 June, in the Netherlands, the Duc d'Alençon died. Though her feelings about his courtship may have been mixed, Elizabeth was not entirely insincere as she wrote to Catherine de Medici that his mother's grief 'cannot be greater than my own . . . I find no consolation except death, which I hope will soon reunite us. Madame, if you were able to see the image of my heart, you would see the portrait of a body without a soul.'

Alençon's death left the Netherlands Protestants bereft, lacking the figurehead who had brought with him the hope of foreign aid. Just a month later came a new blow – the assassination of the Protestant leader William of Orange by a Catholic fanatic presumed to be in

Spain's pay. In England, Leicester was very far from giving up his eminence in England's affairs – or his ambitions to lead an army to the relief of his co-religionists in the Netherlands. Now the cause seemed more urgent than ever.

But just days later, before July was out, he received a third and more personal blow – the death of his infant heir Lord Denbigh. Leicester was with the court at Nonsuch when the news of Denbigh's illness came. Neglecting to take formal leave of the queen, he rushed straight to Wanstead and Lettice's side. His parents had doted on their 'noble Imp'.

Hatton wrote to him consolingly: 'Of men's hearts you enjoy more than millions, which, on my soul, do love you no less than children or brethren. Leave sorrow, therefore, my good Lord, and be glad with us, which much rejoice in you.' 'Your good friendship never wanteth,' Leicester wrote back gratefully. But with Lettice now in her forties, and he himself in poor health, Leicester knew he had probably lost his chance of a dynasty. It gave all the more importance to the young men of his extended family: his nephew Philip Sidney; and his stepson, of whom we shall hear shortly.

In the years ahead, images of Elizabeth would increasingly cease to reflect her real face as it aged – would become an elaborately allegorical illusion; as devoid of real identity as the object of any courtly lover's poetry. But the men around her had access neither to her ability to command collective make-believe, nor to her maquillage. Hatton like Leicester was beginning to age before his time. 'Charming white-haired old gentlemen' was how a foreign visitor described the first generation of the queen's favourites, unable now to match her energy or convincingly to offer the flattery she demanded.

There were new men arrived at court who could do that more easily.

The single most famous story of Walter Ralegh – not yet 'Sir Walter' – was recorded only by one Thomas Fuller, born some quarter of a century later.[*] 'This Captain Raleigh coming out of Ireland to the

---

[*] He himself spelt his name both as Ralegh and Raleigh; contemporaries used some dozen variants including Rawlie, which last offered the word-conscious Elizabethans the chance for puns on his sometimes abrasive style. 'I have heard but rawly of you,' James I joked on meeting him.

English Court in good habit (his clothes being then a considerable part of his estate) found the Queen walking, till, meeting with a plashy place, she seemed to scruple going thereon. Presently Raleigh cast and spread his new plush cloak on the ground; whereupon the Queen trod gently.' The staggering cost of court clothes gives added point to the story – but the fact it could be believed says something about Ralegh's flamboyant reputation.

It is hard to be certain when Walter Ralegh was born, though his biographer Anna Beer thinks 1554 likely. He was not of the elite class whose early years were recorded. He was the fifth son of a mere Devonshire gentleman; and one with two previous families already to provide for, while his mother likewise had other sons from a previous marriage.

But we do know that, with his way wholly to make, Ralegh went to the French wars at what even contemporaries recognised as a very young age, probably in the troop of his cousin Henry Champernowne. In October 1569 he was writing from near Poitiers where the Protestant forces, of which he was a small part, were in retreat from those of the Catholic government. Ralegh throughout his life would prove at least as competent with the pen as with the sword. But notable, too, is the degree to which adventures beyond English shores would figure in Ralegh's career, and of others in Elizabeth's later years. It was as if a door were being shouldered open, breaking the enforced isolation of Protestant England from the bulk of Catholic Europe and bringing with it, in the long run, an end to some outworn cultural mores.

The peace of 1570 meant a return from the French wars – and for Ralegh, some years in obscurity. But in 1579 trouble once again brought opportunity. Rebellion broke out in Ireland – that perennial trouble spot – and as forces were assembled the following summer, 'Captain Ralegh' can be found leading his hundred men across the water.

Soon after he arrived, troops under Ralegh's command were chiefly responsible for the massacre of defeated troops at Smerwick. He was unabashed by the harsh realities of war, or the even harsher treatment meted out by the English to the Irish they regarded as little better than savages. It was Ralegh's half-brother Humphrey Gilbert who had an entire village decapitated and the heads stuck up to decorate the path to his tent, the better to intimidate the local chiefs. But Ralegh's reports home showed a lively awareness of all sides to the Irish situation; and he was sending them to the queen's chief gatherer of information, Francis Walsingham. Straightforward reportage was blended with political advice. All the less surprising, then, that when in December 1581 Walter Ralegh was sent back to England with despatches, he wound up at court. No less a person than the queen herself decreed that there he should stay.

He did not arrive as a complete outsider. That huge extended family had its advantages, since some were now people of influence. Ralegh's mother, moreover, had been born a Champernowne, the same family that had produced Elizabeth's beloved governess Kat Ashley. But just as it is hard fully to account for Ralegh's prominence in legend – unless, like Churchill, history would look favourably on him because he wrote it – it is hard to find the mechanisms for Ralegh's evident influence. He would never in his life become a Privy Councillor, usually the high-water mark of having made it politically, in Elizabethan terms.

His appeal to Elizabeth, however, was obvious. A miniature by Nicholas Hilliard from 1585 shows Ralegh with a vast ruff and flowers in his hair. Sir Robert Naunton remembered him as having 'a good presence, in a handsome and well compacted person, a strong natural wit, and a better judgement, with a bold and plausible tongue' – adding that he took care 'by diligence' to enforce 'some natural learning' to a great perfection. Dark, six feet tall, he was blessed with a naturally curling – positively priapic! – beard that reflected his irrepressible chutzpah. We are back to the loaded question of whether Elizabeth valued most his masculine appeal, or his political utility.

Naunton would remember how Ralegh 'had gotten the Queen's ear in a trice, and she began to be taken with his elocution, and loved to hear his reasons to her demands. And the truth is, she took him for a kind of oracle, which nettled them all.' An absent Leicester took alarm at the news that Ralegh, at court, was speaking against him (for all that Ralegh had once been a humble client to Leicester himself). Even the queen's godson Sir John Harington wrote edgily of the newcomer:

He doth extol her speech, admire her feature,
He calls himself her vassal, and her creature.

Thus while he daubs his speech with flattery's plaster,
And calls himself her slave, he grows our master.
Still getting what he lists without control,
By singing this old song, *re mi fa sol.*

By March 1583 Ralegh was in a position to write to Humphrey Gilbert, sending him a jewel from the queen. In May he was writing to Lord Burghley about the Earl of Oxford's ongoing troubles after Burghley, himself Elizabeth's chief minister, had felt it worthwhile to solicit Ralegh's aid. When Oxford was allowed back to court, Ralegh was described as being 'a great mean herein'. Truly the fifth son who still spoke with a West Country burr had come a long way.

A foreign visitor in 1584 recorded that the queen 'was said to love [Ralegh] now beyond all the others; and this may be true, because two years ago he could scarcely keep one servant, and now with her bounty he can keep five hundred'. Elizabeth had given him Durham House on the Strand, a veritable palace (Edward VI had lived there, and Jane Grey been wed there) which Ralegh furnished lavishly with plunderings from around the world, with porcelains and 'pied silks'; and where he began collecting around him an extraordinary circle of thinkers – the mathematician and astronomer Thomas Harriott, the Hakluyts, the astrologer John Dee. One of Elizabeth's early gifts to Ralegh was a patent for exploration of the New World, where he hoped to establish 'Virginia' in the queen's honour. With the support of keen imperialists like Dee and Richard Hackluyt he established the ill-fated colony of Roanoke, in what is now North Carolina. Huge estates in Ireland, where again he hoped to establish an English colony; a patent for the sale of wine; a licence to export broadcloth ... Perhaps it is hardly surprising that Ralegh would never have many friends at an envious court.

As far back as the end of 1582, Christopher Hatton was being warned by Heneage that 'water' ('Walter' Ralegh) had been 'more welcome than were fit for so cold a season'. Hatton himself had sent the queen allusive gifts of a book, a bodkin and a tiny bucket ... She sent back a dove: the bird from the Ark that showed Noah there was no more need to fear the rising water. Elizabeth's 'mutton' was further reassured by the queen's message that water and the creatures who belong to it were not so appealing to her as some thought, 'her food having been ever more of flesh than of fish'. But a few years later, on progress, Hatton was hurt to find Ralegh occupying the room that had once been his.

Hatton sent the queen a true lover's knot and (Heneage reassured him) Elizabeth swore she 'would rather see [Ralegh] hanged than equal him with you'. But in fact, Hatton's own letters to Elizabeth – like those of Leicester before him – were becoming less lover-like than they had been; more practical, more prone to quarrel and apology.

A letter he wrote to Elizabeth in 1584, apologising for having offended her 'by lack of attendance on your princely presence', affirms 'in the presence of God, that I have followed and loved the footsteps of your most princely person with all faith and sincerity' – but nonetheless puts it to her straightly that he had cause for his 'too high presumptions'. Hatton was becoming ever more fully the politician: one speech of 'above two hours', on the danger from Spain, made a particular impression on Parliament. Clearly, in terms of fun and flattery, the way to Elizabeth was open for newcomers. In 1585 Elizabeth knighted 'Sir' Walter Ralegh. And his path was the clearer for the fact that Leicester – like Hatton – now had other concerns.

In 1585 Leicester realised his long-held dream of leading an army to help the beleaguered Protestants in the Spanish Netherlands. Alas, the Netherlands campaign was little short of disastrous. The queen had dithered a dozen times about letting him go, saying she could not do without him, until Leicester wrote to Walsingham that he was 'weary of life and all'.

'Her Majesty I see will make trial of me how I love her and what will discourage me from her service,' he complained, in words that would be echoed almost exactly by his stepson Essex a decade later, 'but resolved I am that no worldly respect shall draw me back from my faithful discharge of my duty towards her, though she shall show to hate me, as goeth very near, for I find no love or favour at all.' Bad went to worse when – greeted as a quasi-king in the Netherlands, hailed in entertainments as 'a second Arthur' – he allowed the flattery to go to his head, and accepted the title of governor-general.

Elizabeth's reaction was furious. 'How contemptuously we conceive ourselves to be used by you . . . We could never have imagined (had we not seen it fall out in experience) that a man raised up by ourself and extraordinarily favored by us, above any other subject of this land, would have in so contemptible a sort broken our commandment in a cause that so greatly toucheth us in honour.' Leicester was wounded to the quick. 'At the least I think she would never have so condemned any other man before she heard him . . . For my faithful, true and loving heart to her and my country, I have undone myself.'

The hostility did not last, of course. At the end of March Ralegh (to whom Leicester had written asking for the services of some specialised troops) was reassuring the earl that 'the queen is in very good terms with you, and, thanks be to God, well pacified, and you are again her "sweet Robin"'. By April the queen's next letter to Leicester was haughty, but conciliatory. 'Right trusty and well-beloved cousin and councillor, we greet you well. It is always thought in the opinion of the world a hard bargain when both parties are leasoned [slandered], and so doth fall out the case between us two . . .'

On the political front things were less emollient. The troops Leicester had managed to raise were ill-conditioned and worse equipped, while he himself had no significant military experience to match that of the Spanish commander, the great Duke of Parma. Still, for most of 1586 his men managed to hold back the Spanish tide. And at least Elizabeth was writing in her old familiar mood: 'Rob, I am afraid you will suppose by my wandering writings that a midsummer moon hath taken large possession of my brains this month . . .' She signed off: 'Now will I end, that do I imagine I talk still with you, and therefore loathly say farewell, [eyes symbol], though ever I pray God bless you from all harm, and save you from all foes with my million and legion of thanks for all your pains and care. As you know, ever the same, E.R.'

But in September 1586 the Battle of Zutphen saw the tragic death of Leicester's nephew Philip Sidney, slowly succumbing to gangrene from the wounds he received. Stories that Sidney had given his own water to a dying soldier only added to the legend of the country's hero. One of the early voices clamouring for England's involvement in the international Protestant cause, Sidney had in 1585 been appointed Governor of Flushing in the Netherlands. Now his body was taken there to lie in state before being brought home for burial in St Paul's. Hundreds of

Londoners lined the streets to watch the funeral procession; his horse was ridden by a page trailing a broken lance.

Another, however, would also take prominent part in that spectacular funeral procession, taking upon himself Sidney's mantle as chivalric, and as Protestant, hero. It was after the Battle of Zutphen that the Earl of Leicester saw fit to knight his stepson the Earl of Essex in the field.

Robert Devereux, 2nd Earl of Essex, was born on 10 November 1565 – or, just possibly, on the same date in 1566 or 1567. A Devereux had come over with the Conqueror; a later one fought for Richard III at Bosworth, but the family had then committed to the Tudor line, and the loyalty of Robert's father Walter saw him created 1st Earl of Essex in 1572, though the title came with no commensurate fortune. By this time the young Robert was being carefully educated at the family seat of Chartley in Staffordshire: in Latin and dancing; writing and swordsmanship.

In 1573 Robert's father volunteered for the task of crushing rebellion in Ireland. The crusade to impose a Protestant and, it seemed, civilising influence upon the wild Catholic Irish was one beloved of the bulk of Elizabeth's leading counsellors; the more so since the turbulent country could easily provide a back door to England's Catholic enemies. But when Essex died at Dublin Castle, the rumour mill was busy.

The symptoms suggest dysentery but Essex himself suspected 'some evil received in my drink', and his doctors dosed him with unicorn's horn (in reality the tusk of a narwhal), that well-known specific against poison. Not only was it suspected that Lady Essex, the beautiful Lettice Knollys, had long been having an affair with Leicester, but gossip suggested Leicester rather than Essex was really the father of young Robert. Lettice was a particularly forceful woman whose son would become the focus of her life, as he was for his sisters Dorothy and Penelope – that same Penelope famous as Philip Sidney's 'Stella'. But a post-mortem into the death of Lettice's husband found natural causes; and her ten-year-old son passed into the custody of his new guardian, Lord Burghley, and was duly enrolled at Trinity College, Cambridge.

But his mother's marriage to the Earl of Leicester soon brought another vital influence into the young earl's life. When in 1581 Essex left Cambridge as Master of Arts he went to live at Lamphey in Pembrokeshire, and he said later that he could easily 'have bent his mind to a retired course'. But his new stepfather Leicester saw a different use for him, and took him to court. The young Essex arrived in time to break fifty-seven lances fighting fifteen challengers in the Accession Day tilts of 1584. This visit, however, did not last long. When Leicester sailed for the Netherlands in 1585 he took Essex with him. But after the Battle of Zutphen, after Philip Sidney's death, they both sailed home again, to confront a new threat.

Catholic enemies in England as well as abroad had never ceased to be a pressing danger. Central to the trouble now, as ever, was Mary, Queen of Scots. The second half of 1586 – those months when Leicester's campaign in the Netherlands took a decisive downturn – had seen also the revelation of the Babington conspiracy: the attempt, by a group of aristocratic young English hotheads, to place Mary on Elizabeth's throne with the help of a foreign army.

Francis Walsingham's agents had long known of the plan – even fostered it, with the aim of giving the Scots queen enough rope to knot the noose around her own neck. Their scheme worked: by the time, in the autumn, Babington and his fellow conspirators met the horrible traitor's death, there was evidence to move against Mary, too.

Leicester was summoned hastily back from the Netherlands, to hold the queen's hand at this crisis of her reign. But all Elizabeth's first favourites – Leicester, Hatton, Oxford – took leading parts in the process that, on 8 February 1587 at Fotheringhay, brought Mary to the block. No chivalric end by the sword for her, as there had been for Anne Boleyn. The death of the most romantic queen in Christendom was a piece of common butchery, given a blackly comic turn at the end. As the executioner picked up Mary's severed head, declaring that thus died all Queen Elizabeth's enemies, the head itself, topped with grey bristles, rolled away across the floor, leaving him holding aloft a red wig.

Mary *had* managed to work her magic; to forge a historical statement from the horror. When her ladies stripped off her outer robe, she stood up in a petticoat of crimson: the colour of Catholic martyrdom.

But this was the iconography she had chosen that would carry her legend into the centuries ahead. The religious, not the romantic or the courtly, story.

Perhaps Elizabeth's grief at the death of her sister queen was not entirely feigned; but, after a suitable period in the cold for the ministers who had, she said, executed the death warrant without her volition, the waters of court antagonisms and allegiances closed over Mary's severed head. Abroad, however, it was a different story: if Mary could be refigured as Catholic martyr, in whose name Philip of Spain could prepare his mighty Armada, Elizabeth was increasingly cast as champion of Protestant Europe.

In France, Henri of Navarre, the Huguenot contender for the French throne, launched an impassioned plea for Elizabeth's aid, but did so in the language of courtly love. This warrior queen had yet to be wooed as a woman. Elizabeth's withholding of her outright support was like the inch-by-inch granting of favours of the courtly lady; the Protestants' despair like that of the lover.

And if the young Earl of Essex saw himself as new chivalric champion of the Protestant cause, there was no doubt of the mistress he should serve: Elizabeth, the Queen's Majesty.

22

'Cold love'

1587–1590

I F LEICESTER HAD brought his stepson Essex to court to combat Ralegh's attraction, the plan seemed to be working. In May 1587 it was reported that: 'When [the Queen] is abroad, nobody near her but my lord of Essex . . . at night my Lord is at cards, or one game or another with her, that he cometh not to his own lodging till birds sing in the morning.' With auburn hair like his mother's and eyes dark like Elizabeth's own, Essex was ardent and athletic; his egotism and ambition not yet apparent under the veil of his brilliance and his youthful charm. Tall and gangling, his very clumsiness in dance and carelessness in dress appealed to the jaded palate of a queen who dubbed him her 'wild horse'.

Despite the dramatic difference in their ages, Essex was prepared to offer Elizabeth the same lavish flattery his elders had done. Whatever the underlying reality, this (as with the Alençon courtship) was never to be cast as a matter of business between an attractive young man and an older woman who could advance him. When Leicester sailed back to the Netherlands, he left behind an Essex now staying in Leicester's own apartments near the queen's.

It was not all plain sailing, however. As early as July, Essex dared to protest that Ralegh had too much influence over the queen. Elizabeth had, Essex wrote in temper, refused to meet his sister Dorothy, who had provoked royal anger by an unsanctioned marriage, and Essex had been dissatisfied with the royal 'excuses'. Interesting word, when used of the queen . . . her 'wild horse' was clearly feeling his oats.

Essex told Elizabeth, hotly, that she had snubbed Dorothy 'only to please that knave Ralegh'. It seemed, he protested, that the queen 'could not well endure anything to be spoken against him . . . I did let her know whether I had cause to disdain his competition of love, or whether I could have comfort to give myself over to the service of a mistress that was in awe of such a man.'

While the younger generation of favourites bickered, the older were moving on. Hatton's evolution into skilled political manipulator was now complete. In 1587 Elizabeth made him lord chancellor, and though Camden reported that the legal establishment 'took it very offensively . . . Yet bare he the place with the greatest state of all that, and what was lacking in him in knowledge of the law, he laboured to supply by equity and justice.' Ironically, Ralegh too would become a Parliamentary stalwart.

A poetic exchange between Ralegh and the queen, provisionally dated to around this time, expresses the balance of power between the pair. Ralegh begins:

> Fortune hath taken away my love,
> My life's joy and my soul's heaven above.
> Fortune hath taken thee away, my princess,
> My world's joy and my true fantasy's mistress.

Elizabeth's answer began on a demeaning nickname:

> Ah, silly Pug, wert thou so sore afraid?
> Mourn not, my Wat, nor be thou so dismayed.
> It passeth fickle Fortune's power and skill
> To force my heart to think thee any ill.

Whereas Elizabeth herself, here, is more powerful even than Fortune, she ends by condescendingly adjuring Ralegh to get his courage up:

> Revive again and live without all dread,
> The less afraid, the better thou shalt speed.

It is a little like their famous exchange when Ralegh first came to court. 'Fain would I climb, yet fear I to fall,' Ralegh reputedly scratched on a window pane. To which the queen retorted: 'If thy heart fails thee, climb not at all.' In 1587 Elizabeth promised Ralegh the prime position of Captain of her Guard (though events – not least Hatton's determination to cling on to the role – meant he would not take up the position for another few years). But she also allowed Essex to inherit Leicester's position as Master of Horse. Both were roles that gave particularly close access to the sovereign.

With the approach of the Spanish Armada in 1588, Leicester and Essex rode on either side of the queen as she went to deliver her famous speech at Tilbury. Elizabeth had wanted to make her stand on the south coast, closer to the action, but Leicester urged against it with the warmth of long affection as well as courtly flattery.

'Now for your person, being the most sacred and dainty thing we have in this world to care for, a man must tremble when he thinks of it; specially finding your Majesty to have that princely courage, to transport yourself to the utmost confines of the realm to meet your enemies and defend your people. I cannot, most dear Queen, consent to that,' he had written. So it is the name Tilbury, and Elizabeth's speech from there, that has gone down in history.

Elizabeth took up and ran with Leicester's protective fantasy.

My loving people, I have been persuaded by some that are careful of my safety to take heed how I committed myself to armed multitudes, for fear of treachery. But I tell you that I would not desire to live to distrust my faithful and loving people . . . Wherefore I am come among you at this time but for my recreation and pleasure, being resolved in the midst and heat of the battle to live and die amongst you all, to lay down for my God and for my kingdom and for my people mine honor and my blood even in the dust.

I know I have the body but of a weak and feeble woman, but I have the heart and stomach of a king and of a king of England too – and take foul scorn that Parma or any prince of Europe should dare to invade the borders of my realm

She herself would be the troops' 'general, judge, and rewarder', she said. Or did she? There was no direct eyewitness account of the speech recorded. But an alternative version noted by Lisa Hilton – a text underneath a contemporary painting in a Norfolk church – tackles the gender issue even more aggressively: 'The enemy may challenge my sex for that I am a woman, so may I likewise charge their mould, for they are but men.'

An official version of the queen's speech was, however, written down by Leonel Sharp, a chaplain in the Earl of Leicester's service, then printed up and sent skimming through Europe within a week. Sharp described Elizabeth riding through her squadrons like 'an armed Pallas'. She had made a point of leaving her ladies behind, and rode through the troops with the sword of state carried before her – or, as Camden put it two decades later, walking up and down 'sometimes like a Woman, and anon, with the countenance and pace of a Soldier'.

It is only later chroniclers who describe her as having worn helmet and breastplate, the image that has come down to posterity, but the idea was in currency. Many years earlier, one ambassador reported that Elizabeth had been practising riding a warhorse, to lead a charge against Spain; like a latter-day Boudicca (or, see below, a Britomart – or indeed a Catherine of Aragon or Marguerite of Anjou).

In fact, the troops stirred by Elizabeth's words would never be needed. The Spanish fleet had been dispersed by the time she spoke at Tilbury, more by 'God's wind' than by any English efforts. But no one knew that at the time. Rumours spoke all the other way – of the embarkation of a Spanish invasion army. It would be weeks before England could be sure of Spain's catastrophe.

But pageantry apart, the queen's 'weak and feeble' woman's body had always forbade her displaying the warlike masculine aspect of monarchy. For almost thirty years Leicester had supported her, stood in for her, whenever she was required to do so; now it seemed he was sharing the role. It was Essex who led the victory celebrations. Leicester, with the queen, watched from a window. But weeks later Leicester was dead of a sudden illness, leaving Elizabeth both bereft and distraught.

For 'some days' in the report from the Spanish agent, she shut herself in her own chamber, refusing (wrote Walsingham) to 'suffer anybody to have access to her', or to tackle affairs. She wrote to Shrewsbury of her loss as 'a thing whereof we can admit no comfort, otherwise [than] by submitting our will to God's inevitable appointment'. Leicester left a 'Rope of fair white Pearls, to number six hundred' to his 'most dear, and most gracious Sovereign, whose creature under God I have been, and who hath been a most beautiful, and a most princely Mistress unto me'. (One of the executors of his will was Christopher Hatton, 'mine old dear friend'.)

Elizabeth, Leicester wrote, had exalted him:

> as well in advancing me to many Honours, as in maintaining me many Ways by her Goodness and Liberality. And as my best Recompense to her most excellent Majesty can be from so mean a Man, chiefly in Prayer to God, for whilst there was any Breath in this Body, I never failed it, even as for mine own Soul. And as it was my greatest Joy, in my Life Time, to serve her to her Contentation, so it is not unwelcome to me, being the Will of God to die, and end this Life for her Service.

It is instructive to set this will, couched in the most elevated terms, against the brief homely letter Leicester sent to Elizabeth just before his death – before he had any sense he was about to die. The queen's 'poor old servant', on his way to the medicinal baths at Buxton, sent to know 'how my gracious lady doth, and what ease of her late pain she finds, being the chiefest thing in the world I do pray for'. There might almost be a gentle mockery of the courtly tradition when he signs off by promising: 'I humbly kiss your foot'. Elizabeth kept it by her bed, labelled 'his last letter', in her own hand. But both sides of the relationship ring true.

Leicester had – in the somewhat desultory fashion of a practical man, rather than a dreamer – figured himself as her courtly lover. But he had been in truth her ally and admirer, gallant and confidant. And if Leicester had brought his stepson to court as his surrogate ('Your son,' Essex had signed himself, 'most ready to do you service'), both Essex and the grieving Elizabeth would try to keep up the pretence.

Life at court as the 1580s drew towards their close was shaping up as a battle: a battle for Elizabeth's heart and mind. And Robert Devereux, Essex, had the great trump card of Elizabeth's love for dead Robert

Dudley. It would be speculated in Essex's early heyday that he was 'like enough, if he had a few more years, to carry Leicester's credit and sway'. Others at court, moreover, were ready temporarily to ally with Essex simply to strike back at the ubiquitous Ralegh: the council (Burghley and his rising son Robert Cecil included) would cover up the scandal when Essex challenged Ralegh to a duel.

By Christmas 1588 Elizabeth was sufficiently recovered from Leicester's death to resume her card games with Essex (though still ready to answer him furiously if he complained of Ralegh's influence). In January 1589 the queen granted him the lucrative farm of (the right to levy tax on) sweet wines Leicester had enjoyed. When in 1589 Ralegh found himself back in Ireland ('not the commonwealth but the common woe', he had described it to Leicester) many put it down to Essex's influence.

But Essex's rise was not a foregone conclusion. He was visibly 'full of humours'. And his ambition was to be Leicester's heir not just in court favour but in international affairs – to be the Protestant hero against Philip of Spain. In April 1589 Francis Drake set sail towards the Azores, with the twin aims of intercepting Spanish ships on the way home from the New World, and helping a pretender to the Portuguese throne seize back control of that country from Spain. Essex galloped to the coast without permission and set sail with the fleet, missing the furious letter Elizabeth sent after him. 'Your sudden and undutiful departure from our presence and your place of attendance, you may easily conceive how offensive it is, and ought to be, unto us. Our great favours bestowed on you without deserts hath drawn you thus to neglect and forget your duty.' She had, she declared, no intention of tolerating 'this your disordered part'.

To the fleet commanders she wrote that 'these be no childish actions'. Yet in a sense she treated them as a child's naughtiness. Maybe it was the best thing she could do, faced with the female ruler's perennial problem of dealing with the intransigence of the military men in the field. In action Essex had been the first to land, wading through water shoulder high. This was 'but a sally of youth', the queen declared when he was back at Nonsuch in July.

It seems likely that it was Essex who at this time commissioned a miniature painting from Nicholas Hilliard. 'Young Man Among Roses' shows a swooningly elegant youth, dressed in Elizabeth's colours of black and white (white – the colour of purity), leaning pensively, hand to heart, against a tree trunk twined with eglantine. Eglantine, the wild rose, was the Queen's favourite flower; the tree trunk probably symbolises constancy.

But interpretations have included the idea that the trunk's soaring (masculine?) strength represents the concept of the queen's dual nature, at once female and male. Or, alternatively, was Essex, however presumptuously, inviting her to twine herself around his masculine solidity? A portrait of Ralegh shows him, too, wearing black and white, decked with pearls, his cloak stitched with moonbeams, under a rainbow – the motto 'Amor et Virtute', Love and Virtue.

Essex had already developed something of a reputation as a womaniser around court. The spring of 1590 saw his courtship of and secret wedding to Frances Walsingham, Philip Sidney's widow. The appeal may have been that connection with Sidney, whom Essex idolised, Frances's elegant sexuality . . . or the spy network set up by her father Sir Francis, and now ripe for the picking. Walsingham's own death that April left a power vacuum, into which Essex determined to step.

The secret of his marriage was out by October, by which time Frances was likely six months pregnant. The queen's chance discovery aroused her 'passion', both because the match had been made without her consent, and because she considered Essex had married beneath his rank. One John Stanhope, however, noted interestingly that Elizabeth had reacted 'more temperately than was looked for'. Was she already privately aware that, by now, her courtiers' devotion was hollow at the core? She was placated by Essex's suggestion that his wife should live retired from court – and perhaps by the fact that, though their son was born the following January, Essex showed no sign of feeling constrained by his marriage vows.

He was reaching out. The great question of this latter part of the Virgin Queen's reign was that of the succession. (History knows Elizabeth lived until 1603, but that would have come as a surprise to contemporaries. As early as 1589 Essex wrote that she could not live long.) The best, though far from only, candidate was James VI of Scotland, to whom Essex now wrote coded letters: a contact that could count as treason by the rules of the sixteenth century.

He described himself in the letters as a 'Weary knight' whose present state of life was 'Thrall': the code cast Elizabeth as Venus and James as Victor. Barely less controversially, he was also in correspondence with the Huguenot King Henri IV of France who – at war with the Catholic League dominating his country, and desperate for the English aid Elizabeth herself was reluctant to give – flatteringly addressed Essex as '*mon cousin*'. He may even have been making flattering overtures of his own to the queen's impressionable young kinswoman Arbella Stuart, who many expected to succeed her.

Elizabeth, however, was by no means willing to give up the ghost. These years saw the acceleration of the Gloriana cult. In 1590 the annual celebration of the queen's Accession Day was marked by a tilt organised by Sir Henry Lee, whose retirement ceremony celebrated Elizabeth as a virgin mother 'whom neither time nor age can wither'. Essex appeared in gleaming black armour, covered in a surcoat heavily embroidered with pearls. Coal-black horses pulled the carriage in which Essex sat with his back to the driver, who was dressed as 'Gloomy Time'.

In the standard allegory, drawn from Petrarch, carnal love was overcome by chastity; death by time, fame and eternity. Elizabeth, angered by what she saw as Essex's warmongering urge to aid the French Protestants, ignored his pageantry. But in a sense was Essex volunteering to defend the ageing queen against Time itself?

Was Elizabeth's feeling for Essex the laughable passion of an ageing woman for a pretty gigolo – did he exploit it cynically? It has been suggested that many of 'Essex's' letters were actually the work of his secretaries. Or was his appeal for Elizabeth that of a surrogate son; was it from frustrated maternity that she forgave him so frequently? There may be an element of truth in this – but if so, there was an element of the incestuous in the story.

For underneath the courtly love game, in Essex's letters it is hard not to see some reality of emotion; if not necessarily the emotion protested in the lavish hyperbole of praise. There was the sense that as he and Elizabeth wrote to each other they were both exploring their place in the world. Their identity. And though Essex may or may not have wanted Elizabeth, he wanted *something*, badly. And in the grabby war for access to power, a courtier would use any weapon that came to hand: even . . . poetry?

When in 1589 Walter Ralegh returned to court from Ireland, he was accompanied by one Edmund Spenser – a clothmaker's son from London who had worked his way through Cambridge to administrative service in Ireland. He had found fame among his fellow poets as author of the influential *The Shepheardes' Calender*, but another work, *Mother Hubberd's Tale*, had satirised too many people at court . . . Now Spenser had one more chance to win favour. The first three volumes of his epic *The Faerie Queene*, published in 1590, had as their central conceit the marriage of the queen with 'Prince Arthur'. At this late date in the Tudor century, Elizabeth I's reputation could still be boosted by Arthurian fantasy.

> She is the mighty Queene of Faerie,
> Whose faire retrait I on my shield do beare;
> She is the flowre of grace and chastitie,
> Throughout the world renowned far and neare

And faerie had mileage on it, in terms of chivalric romance: the early Guinevere had been a one-time *fée*, often abducted by an otherworldly lover, and the early Romance stories blended sword with sorcery. But if this were the last great literary tribute paid to the courtly love story, it was far from a simple or a whole-hearted one.

The Faerie Queene was, Spenser wrote, 'a continued Allegory aimed, or a dark conceit'. He planned twelve books to illustrate the twelve moral virtues laid down by Aristotle. The massive poem, moreover, was left unfinished by Spenser's death, which also left questions about his final intent. But the six completed 'books', which centred on the virtues of holiness, temperance, chastity, friendship, justice and courtesy, each have some six thousand lines – and each of the twelve cantos in each book may well contain enough action for a novella – while the stanza form Spenser invented is purposely as slow and exploratory as the quest of an Arthurian knight.

The poem comes loaded with a weight of symbolism critics still strive to unpick. But on one level of allegory, it is possible to make a simplistic identification of various characters with Elizabeth and her courtiers. Of course Elizabeth is the Faerie Queen who sends Prince Arthur on missions of chivalry, but she has other identities. The maiden Una, whose virtues tame a lion, represents truth; but thus she also symbolises the Protestant Church and *perhaps* Elizabeth herself in her young days as a Protestant princess. By this reading, the famous tournament of Spenser's book figures Elizabeth's Church as a battleground to be won. Prince Arthur may stand not only for King Arthur of Camelot but for virtue itself, as embodied at Elizabeth's court by the leaders of the Protestant aristocracy such as Leicester and Essex.

Arthur's squire Timias is usually identified with Walter Ralegh. In Book IV (published a few years later in 1596 at a time when Ralegh was out of favour for an illicit marriage), Timias is rejected by his adored Belphoebe when she sees him with another lady. The unlucky Timias is also bitten by the figure representing slander – the wonderfully named Blatant Beast.

Belphoebe stands for chastity but she is also, like Una, another incarnation of Elizabeth. Spenser called various figures 'mirrors' of the queen, but often the 'mirrors' seem to be the cruelly distorting mirrors of a fairground. Yes, Elizabeth figures as the ageing Cynthia, subject to change or 'Mutabilitie'; as Diana; and as Mercilla, the peace-loving queen who presides over the trial of Duessa, the deceitful enchantress usually seen as Mary, Queen of Scots. But there *might* be aspects of Elizabeth even in Radigund, the man-hating Queen of the Amazons who takes prisoner the knight Artegall and has him dressed in woman's clothes. He is eventually rescued by his lover Britomart, a female knight representative of chastity and thus herself also of Elizabeth. It seems that Spenser the ardent Protestant could both laud Britomart/Elizabeth's military aid to the Netherlands (Mercilla sees Arthur off to the rescue of Queen 'Belge'), and deplore the debilitating effect that some of his heroines seem to have on the men around them.

C.S. Lewis, and other critics since, see courtly love here exposed as virtue's enemy. The foes of Britomart, in her character of chastity, are Malecasta and Busirane, who Lewis identifies with courtly love. The beautiful but unchaste Malecasta presides over the Castle Joyous where Cupid holds sway, and the attendant knights who dote on her 'might have stepped out of the *Roman de la Rose*. The enchanter Busirane presides over the dreadful but alluring castle where the Masque of Cupid is performed, and the Masque embodies, says Lewis, 'all the sorrows of Isoud among the lepers, and Launcelot mad in the woods, of Guinevere at the stake or Guinevere made nun and penitent'. The much-lauded chastity here 'turns out to mean not virginity but virtuous love' – ultimately, married love: 'the triumphant union of romantic passion with Christian monogamy'. Spenser, to Lewis, sees courtly love as the enemy of chastity – is writing 'the final struggle between the romance of marriage and the romance of adultery'.

Is that why though Spenser was presented to Elizabeth – read to her, received a pension – he never received a court post? But then, though he had little choice but to make use of it, Spenser had no love for court: a world of luxury in a time of economic hardship; a world of young men led by an ageing woman. In *Colin Clouts Come Home Again* – its title drawing on a poem of Skelton's – he made his feelings about the place clear. He soon returned to Ireland; only, eight years later, to find himself driven from his castle home by Irish forces.

Perhaps it is telling that Spenser – the man who so hated the court; the man who wrote the elegy to courtly love – had connections to all Elizabeth's leading courtiers. The poet's debts to Leicester and Ralegh apart, Christopher Hatton was one of the dedicatees of *The Faerie Queene*. And when in 1599, in London, Spenser died of plague, Essex would pay for his burial in Westminster Abbey, where his fellow poets threw their pens into his grave.

Spenser's feelings on the court were shared by many of his contemporaries in this increasingly disillusioned time. Young men felt caged and frustrated as they tried to barter their hold on a powerful woman's querulous affections into power in the world outside, the world of arms. In the 1590s this anger would express itself viciously in literature. Perhaps there had always been a toxic current of sexual frustration in courtly love, with all the venom that implies: a resentment of the courtly mistress whose influence could either empower or emasculate. Now it was coming to the fore.

Walter Ralegh was himself a poet: one of the 'crew of courtly makers' who flourished in Elizabeth's latter years.

Of womankind such indeed is the love,
Or the word 'love' abused,
Under which many childish desires
And conceits are excused.
But Love is a durable fire
In the mind ever burning,
Never sick, never old, never dead.
From itself never turning.

He wrote hymns to Elizabeth, hailing her as his 'life's soul and my soul's heaven above / My only light and my true fancy's mistress'. But Germaine Greer has noted how poignantly the hyperbole of some of Ralegh's poetry contrasts with the words of his real affection, such as the letter he wrote to his wife Bess on the eve of what he thought was his execution: 'bear my destruction gently, and with a heart like thyself . . .'. As Ralegh wrote in another poem, passions were like floods and streams – 'The shallow murmur, but the deep are dumb'.

The court poets were turning against courtship. In a poetic riposte to Thomas Heneage's praise of love, Ralegh would bid farewell to 'false love, thou oracle of lies . . . fever of the mind'. The Earl of Essex likewise took pride in *not* singing 'of wanton love-sick lays / Of trickling toys to feed fantastic ears'. In this at least, Essex and Ralegh were as one. For even Essex turned to verse, to express not only courtly sentiments, but their very reverse. One (undated) song attributed to him and set to music by John Dowland is a denial of the courtly love ethic, with its sense of exquisite pain.

Can she excuse my wrongs with Virtue's cloak?
Shall I call her good when she proves unkind?
Are those clear fires which vanish into smoke?
Must I praise the leaves where no fruit I find?
No, no, where shadows do for bodies stand
Thou may'st be abused if thy sight be dimned
Cold love is like to words written on sand
Or to bubbles which on the water swim
Will thou be thus abused still
Seeing that she will right thee never?

If thou cans't not o'ercome her will
Thy love will thus be fruitless ever
Better a thousand times to die
Than for to live thus still tormented
Dear, but remember it was I
Who for thy sake did die contented.

And now the sea was coming in to wash those words on the sand away.

23

'confusion and contrariety'

1590–1599

THE 1580s HAD proved at once the apogee and the tipping point of Elizabeth's reign. But, increasingly, its drama had been acted out by a new band of players. The most significant emotional relationship in Elizabeth I's adult life had surely been that with Robert Dudley, Earl of Leicester. And yet for all of Leicester's importance, he could almost disappear into the chronicle of the first decades of Elizabeth's reign. His influence, like that of many female consorts, extended largely behind the scenes: figuratively if not literally 'pillow talk'. Those years were all 'about' the queen; and Leicester (like Hatton, and of course Burghley) was ultimately content it should be so.

With the later favourites it was very different. Essex can seem to dominate the scene, as indeed he was determined to do. Ralegh was as striking a figure, in a different way. These later favourites were, you might say, more aggressively protective of their masculinity: less ready to adopt the postures of courtly love in anything other than a literary way.

The death of Christopher Hatton in November 1591, aged just fifty-one, confirmed the end of an era. His last months were spent on important political business, which showed just how far he had come from the dancing devotee of earlier years. His prosecution of a group of Puritan leaders reflected the way he had time and again (like a knight, if in prosaic armour) taken a leading part in the investigation and prosecution of those who threatened the queen.

The court was witnessing a changing of the guard. The space of little more than three years had also seen the deaths not only of Leicester and his brother the Earl of Warwick but of their fellow props of government Francis Walsingham and Walter Mildmay, long-time chancellor of the exchequer. Elizabeth was losing a councillor a year. Even Oxford, while he would outlive his royal mistress, was from the end of the 1580s removed from the life of the court and its 'reptilia', preferring his 'Country Muses', and the activities of his company of players. Only William Cecil, Lord Burghley, remained.

But as Essex and Ralegh competed for the queen's attention, and political authority, they were both aware of another threat. William Cecil's son Robert – small, hunchbacked, as clever as his father – would never be a competitor in the romantic stakes; nor would his relationship with either Essex or Ralegh be consistently hostile. Essex had in part grown up in William Cecil's care; while conversely, in the crucial endgame at the turn of the century, Ralegh would ally with Robert Cecil for the destruction of Essex. The telescoping perspective of history can all too easily suggest fixed positions, but on the ground, court politics saw a constant shifting of alliances mutable as sand when the waves come in.

But the Cecils – 'pen gents', bureaucrats; the clerks presented as counterpoise to the knights in the courtly story – did consistently represent an alternative, less militaristic, vision for England's future. And in May 1591 the queen's visit to Burghley's resplendent pleasure palace of Theobalds made clear it was one she took very seriously. She knighted young Robert Cecil, suggesting she would soon give him a place on the Privy Council.

In June, however, Elizabeth agreed that Essex should be allowed to lead the military campaign to help the Protestant Henri confirm his claim to the French throne. Elizabeth wrote about Essex to Henri: 'If, which I most fear, the rashness of his youth does not make him too precipitate, you will never have cause to doubt his boldness in your service . . . I must appear a very foolish creature, only I repeat to you that he will rather require the bridle than the spur.'

She was always admonishing Essex himself not to venture his person in combat. Compare and contrast Tilbury, only three years before, where it had been Leicester admonishing her not to adventure *her* person – 'the most sacred and dainty thing we have in this world to care for' – against the Spanish soldiery. Now it was as though the courtly roles had been reversed, although Essex, at this stage, still wrote by courtly rules. 'I am jealous of all the world, and have cause, since all other men that have either open eyes or sensible hearts are my competitors.'

Essex's French campaign was a disaster. He set out, with a train of pages decked out in orange velvet, to greet his force of more than three thousand men near Dieppe. His orders were to recapture Rouen from the Catholic forces, from whence Henri could secure the Channel ports, thus lifting the threat of invasion for England. Henri's sights, however, were set on seizing Paris; and, not for the last time, Essex felt more sympathy for the goals of a fellow man of action than for those of a cautious woman. Essex and Henri bonded over four days of feasting and leaping contests, but the ensuing fighting cost the life of Essex's younger brother, 'the half-arch of my house', without giving England significant gains.

To Robert Cecil, Essex complained that, having read the queen's letter of reproach, 'I thought I should never see end of my affliction. I want words to express my just grief . . . judge uprightly between the Queen and me, whether she be not an unkind lady, and I an unfortunate servant.' To Elizabeth herself he had written some days earlier that: 'no unkindness from you, though it break my heart, can diminish my affection; but I will end my life complaining of your injustice, and approving mine own constancy'.

Recalled, Essex (like Henry V before him) concluded his abortive venture by issuing an anachronistic challenge to personal combat to the Governor of Rouen. 'I will maintain that the cause of King Henri is more just than that of your League, and that my mistress is more beautiful than yours.' It showed him a believer in the chivalric creed, rather than one who used it wholly cynically. It did not, however, show him as an appropriate military commander.

Elizabeth for her part was threatening to make Essex 'an example to the entire world' if he failed to obey her order to return. He had evidently, she said, 'small desire to see her'. But he wrote to his 'most fair, most dear, and most excellent Sovereign' that: 'The two windows of your Privy Chamber shall be the poles of my sphere . . . While Your Majesty gives me leave to say I love you, my fortune is as my affection, unmatchable. If ever you deny me that liberty, you may end my life, but never shake my constancy, for were the sweetness of your nature turned into the greatest bitterness that could be, it is not in your power, as great a Queen as you are, to make me love you less.' With hindsight, his avowal strikes a bitterly ironic note.

Yet in January 1592 he was back at court, and envisaging a turning point in his career. From the start of 1592 Essex really began building his network of friends and supporters. Socially, his closest ally was that new young star the Earl of Southampton, who would be Shakespeare's patron; politically, he took on the Bacon brothers, Francis and Anthony, as his advisers. The Bacons urged Essex, instead of merely warmongering abroad, to seek a 'domestical greatness'. And he was increasingly convinced that statesman was another role he could play. Hatton's death had confirmed the sense of a new generation of leaders at court, while Essex's closest competitor Ralegh was in disgrace.

That spring the queen discovered that, the year before, Ralegh had made a secret marriage with one of her Gentlewomen of the Privy Chamber, Bess Throckmorton – an affront on two levels, since not only did Elizabeth always resent the attention of her favourites turning elsewhere, but she was *in loco parentis* to her young maids, and had been thwarted in her duty of care – betrayed, moreover, by some of those closest to her. At the end of March 1592 Bess secretly gave birth to a boy (one of his godfathers, surprisingly, the Earl of Essex); at the end of April Ralegh set off on what promised to be one of his most ambitious naval ventures – to Panama, to attack the Spanish treasure fleet – only to be summoned back to answer a formal inquiry, placed under house arrest and, to his dismay, refused access to the queen.

The imprisoned Ralegh described himself as 'a fish cast on dry land, gasping for breath': and indeed, the queen's attention was the oxygen by which he lived. He wrote to Robert Cecil a letter of lament for his estrangement clearly intended for Elizabeth herself:

My heart was never broken till this day that I hear the Queen goes away so far off, whom I have followed so many years with so great

love and desire ... I that was wont to behold her riding like
Alexander, hunting like Diana, walking like Venus – the gentle
wind blowing her fair hair about her pure cheeks like a nymph,
sometimes sitting in that shade like a goddess, sometimes singing
like an angel, sometimes playing like Orpheus.

In vain. August saw both Ralegh and his wife in the Tower of London.

It was probably now that Ralegh began to write his most significant
poem, *The Ocean to Scinthia* (Cynthia). Long, infinitely complex, its
central thrust is nonetheless clear. Walter Ralegh (Wat – Water), ocean,
laments the failure of his relationship with Cynthia, the virgin moon.
A relationship on which, until his 'fancy erred' – in falling in love with
another woman? – all his fortune depended.

> Whom Love defends, what fortune overthrows?
> When she did well, what did there else amiss?
> When she did ill what empires could have pleased?
> No other power affecting woe or bliss
> She gave, she took, she wounded, she appeased.

Cynthia was all-powerful; and the position of a courtier in relation to
his capricious queen could hardly be better described. But perhaps
Ralegh's poem makes clear, too, his dissatisfaction with this state of
affairs? He was, he protested, unable to alter his love, even if the beloved
had become 'a Lion then, no more a milk white Dove'. But then he
changes: had it all been a sham, on his side? 'My love was false, my
labours were deceit'. His long blazon of Cynthia's perfections ends by
dismissing them:

> These be the Tyrants that in fetters tie
> Their wounded vassals, yet not kill or cure
> But glory in their lasting misery.

Anna Beer discusses how the poem represents a journey to the dark
side of love: how Cynthia's 'seeming beauties' hide bitter cruelty – how
to take this all-too-human woman for a goddess had been 'outworn
conceit'. How 'that fair resemblance [appearance] weareth out of

date' . . . and how, in Elizabeth's female court, the 'hardest steel' was giving way, 'eaten with softest rust'.

But in the event, Ralegh's stay in the Tower was brief. His September release was facilitated by news that the ships sent out on that expedition to Panama he had planned had captured a rich prize: the Portuguese galleon *Madre de Dios* laden with treasure, but which, in Ralegh's absence, was being looted as the ships reached port.

As 1592 turned to 1593 and the queen contemplated, in September, the milestone of her sixtieth birthday, the times were harsh. A series of disastrous harvests compounded economic hardship, while the victims of repeated plague epidemics were hardly worse off than many of the veterans of Elizabeth's wars, left to beg on the streets once their service was over. In July 1593, in France, Henri IV converted to Catholicism, famously declaring that Paris was worth a Mass.

Henri would continue to play the courtly game with Elizabeth; the following year he intercepted a portrait of herself she had sent to his sister, claiming it was infused with divine spirit, that he could not bear to part with such beauty . . . Henri by now had his patter down pat. Elizabeth's diplomat Sir Henry Unton had a year or two earlier shown him her miniature, declaring that he served 'a far more excellent Mistress' than any of Henri's. Henri kissed it several times with great reverence, Sir Henry keeping a jealously firm hold, and afterwards claiming it had done more good than all his ambassadorial eloquence. But underneath the courtly language, Henri's action had left England isolated, and Elizabeth feeling she had been played for a fool.

The queen suffered repeated bouts of melancholy in these years, for consolation translating the work of the early Christian philosopher Boethius, with its picture of God testing His beloved children. (A volume of Boethius had been inscribed by her grandmother, Elizabeth of York.) A courtly lady tested her lover in much the same way – though in their relationship it was Essex who repeatedly tested Elizabeth's affection. Her position as ruler did not allow her to be wholly passive and adored.

In February 1593 the queen made Essex a Privy Councillor, and the admittedly partisan Anthony Bagot reported that: 'his Lordship is become a new man – clean forsaking all his former youthful tricks, carrying himself with honourable gravity, and singularly liked of both in Parliament and at Council-table, for his speeches and judgement'. But against that, Essex's inveterate habit of taking any political defeat as personal was making it ever harder for him to share a council table with the Cecils.

Soon afterwards, Essex's determination to win the post of attorney general for Francis Bacon showed the strength of the forces ranged against him. Angrily, he told Robert Cecil that: 'the Attorneyship for Francis is that I must have; and in that will I spend all my power, might, authority and amity'. Instead, the queen gave the post to a more experienced (and more supportive) Cecil candidate, Sir Edward Coke. But by that time, Essex and the Cecils were locked into another contest; one reflecting little credit on either party.

Through Anthony Bacon's contacts the earl had been building up a formidable network of informers. It was one of these who first described, as Essex excitedly wrote, 'a most dangerous and desperate treason'. A plot to assassinate the queen, no less, and perhaps by a traitor alarmingly close at hand.

Elizabeth was incredulous when Essex first burst in, accusing her trusted physician Dr Lopez, a Portuguese Jew, of conspiring against her. A 'rash and temerious youth', she called him – but Essex was not to be denied: the more so, it was said, because Lopez had treated the earl for a less-than-respectable disease, and had spoken of it less than discreetly. Essex waged a campaign of attrition against the old man, who probably did indeed have a second, subsidiary, career as a spy – but in the Cecils' employ.

But when in the spring of 1594 Essex succeeded in having Lopez brought to trial, the competition between him and the Cecils was over who could gain most credit for his conviction. In June Dr Lopez (almost certainly innocent of evil intent) suffered the full horror of a traitor's death. As the court increasingly divided into hostile groups, the earl considered himself to be riding high.

He seemed still to have the personal pull. On Twelfth Night 1594 Elizabeth was seated on a high throne, richly dressed and looking, said one observer, Mr Standen, 'as beautiful as ever I saw her'. Next to her was Essex, 'with whom she often devised in sweet and favourable manner'. Walter Bourchier Devereux, editing his ancestors' papers in the 1850s, places around this time the undated, single most intriguing letter from Essex to his mistress:

> The delights of this place cannot make me unmindful of one in whose sweet company I have joyed as much as the happiest man doth in the highest contentment; and if my horse could run as fast as my thoughts do fly, I would as often make mine eyes rich in beholding the treasure of my love as my desires do triumph when I seem to myself in a strong imagination to conquer your resisting will.

As with Hatton before him, the phraseology suggests (surely deliberately) sexual conquest: as with Hatton, suggestion was surely all it was. Gregorio Leti's 1682 *La Vita della Regina Elisabetta* describes a series of ambassadors pacing the anteroom to Elizabeth's chamber and debating sardonically what she and Essex (like Leicester before him) were doing behind the closed door. But as before stated, Leti is an unreliable source.

Accession Day 1595 saw the performance of a play: a hermit, a soldier and a statesman trying in vain to persuade a knight to abandon his love, forsake the mistress 'whose virtues made all his thoughts divine', and turn instead to prayers, to politics or to war. Needless to say, the knight 'would never forsake his mistress's love – his mistress, whose virtue made all his thoughts divine'. The entertainment was drawn up by Bacon. But 1595 brought trouble for Essex: much of his own making.

He was belatedly exposed as the father of an illegitimate child born, several years before, to one of the queen's maids of honour, Elizabeth Southwell. More seriously, he seemed ever more to be meddling in the dangerous matter of the succession – to raise which, said the queen hysterically, was to set her own winding sheet before her eyes. King James of Scotland, after a disagreement with Elizabeth, had appealed to his 'Right trusty and well-beloved cousin' Essex to urge her against evil counsellors, and Anthony Bacon's contacts in Scotland opened the way to further indirect communication.

In the autumn a damning book arrived in England, written by the pseudonymous Doleman (almost certainly the Jesuit Robert Persons):

A Conference About the Next Succession to the Crown. The book assessed the claims of each possible contender, deciding, as a Catholic was likely to do, in favour of the Spanish Infanta (daughter to Philip of Spain: himself, like his English enemy, a descendant of John of Gaunt). But it also called upon Essex to play the kingmaker – or queenmaker – after Elizabeth's death. No other 'could have a greater part or sway in the deciding of this great affair'. Essex himself read so provocative a claim with horror. He may indeed have been right to believe the intent was to discredit him; and Elizabeth was shrewd enough to take it at its true worth. All the same, a seed had been sown.

Immediately after the book's appearance Essex retired to his house in the Strand, and fell prey to one of the psychosomatic illnesses to which he was prone. But soon he was back, and arguing as vehemently as ever for an attack on Spain, in support of the French king Henri. It seemed Philip was preparing another Armada; and faced with that threat, even the Cecils – like Ralegh, like the queen's kinsman Lord Admiral Howard – agreed it was time for England to take up the sword.[*]

With Essex and Howard in joint command, the fleet set sail on 1 June 1596. The queen's instructions were for the destruction of Spanish ships, and the capture of Spanish treasure to swell England's empty coffers. The establishment of an English base on Spanish soil was, she said, on no account to be attempted . . . An instruction that went out of Essex's head as soon as he set eyes on Cádiz. The English did succeed in smashing the Spanish fleet, lying in harbour, but allowed thirty-four rich Spanish merchant vessels – a fabulous prize, if only they had managed to seize them – to be set afire by their own commander, while Essex instead led a land force to seize control of the city. A report described him scaling the walls singlehanded. The city's women were not only let pass by the conquerors but 'suffered to take with them all their apparel'. Maybe chivalry had something to it, after all.

Essex sent to the council at home an impassioned letter begging them to give him the right to hold the city as a military bridgehead on

---

[*] Ralegh, indeed, had long been conducting his own privateering – and profitable – campaign against Spanish shipping. Even his venture up the Orinoco in 1595 had been a deliberate counter-move to Philip II's expansion in South America.

the Continent, in the teeth of what he clearly saw as Elizabeth's weak feminine folly. (As he wrote once to his secretary Reynolds, 'I know I shall never do her service but against her will.') The Cecils, of course, showed his letter to the queen.

Orders came back: Cádiz was to be burnt, razed to the ground, and then abandoned. Essex greeted the news with 'bitterly passionate' speech. He viewed it as a personal betrayal – the more so for the fact the queen had retaliated for his disobedience by announcing Robert Cecil's appointment as principal secretary.

Once again Essex had managed to snatch defeat from the jaws of victory. He returned to England without the much-needed treasure, but with a popular reputation as a military hero which, however, did him the reverse of service in the queen's eyes. She had always mistrusted military men, who led where she as a woman could not – and Essex seemed increasingly to embody that toxic masculinity.

Contemporaries were aware of that toxic quality. On 4 October 1596 Francis Bacon penned (whether or not it was ever sent) a letter of advice to his patron: worth comparing with Dyer's letter to Christopher Hatton, a quarter of a century before. Essex seemed to the queen, Bacon wrote, 'a man of a nature not to be ruled; that hath the advantage of [her] affection and knoweth it; of an estate not grounded to his greatness; of a popular reputation; of a military dependence . . . I doubt whether there can be a more dangerous image than this represented to any monarch living, much more to a lady of Her Majesty's apprehension.' Essex was the first royal favourite to have such a popular presence – the people had never loved Leicester or Hatton (let alone Gaveston or Mortimer). It was a sign of the changing times that while it had recently been a badge of honour to carry Elizabeth's image, in 1600 the Privy Council was having to forbid the sale of images of Essex and other noblemen – rivals to Elizabeth's role as her people's princess, if not actually to her throne.

It was the queen's unkind dealing, Bacon had written earlier, which might at last persuade Essex 'to self-love'. In his own interests he should play down his military ambitions; enter more into court games; his compliments should be warmer – less formal – and his courtship less perfunctory than it had become. Good advice, but Essex was the last man to take it. Essex, as his new adviser Henry Cuffe said, 'can conceal nothing; he carries his love and his hatred on his forehead'. And that face reflected back to Elizabeth an image she did not wish to see.

Approaching her mid-sixties, the queen was visibly ageing. From a distance the illusion held – a tourist dazzled by her robes and jewels said she seemed no more than twenty. But other foreign visitors described her face as 'very aged. It is long and thin, and her teeth are very yellow and unequal . . . Many of them are missing so that one cannot understand her easily when she speaks quickly'. There is a story that through the last decade of her reign the queen eschewed mirrors; but she was too shrewd not to find them in men's eyes – or in those of the lively young girls who waited upon her, and knew every secret behind the 'Mask of Youth'. When one of her maids, Lady Mary Howard, appeared in a particularly elaborate velvet dress, Elizabeth reacted with sarcastic hostility. But Mary Howard was said at the time to have been involved with Essex. Her real offence may have been not the gold-trimmed dress itself, but the man for whom she wore it. Essex's name was also linked, Elizabeth Southwell apart, with a Mrs Russell and Elizabeth Brydges, and the queen's goddaughter Elizabeth Stanley.

Sir Robert Naunton wrote later of the problems in the relationship of Elizabeth and Essex: 'The first was a violent indulgency of the Queen which is incident to old age where it encounters with a pleasing and suitable object . . . The second was a fault in the object of her grace, my Lord himself, who drew in too fast like a child sucking on an overuberous nurse'. Had there been 'a more decent decorum' in either of them things might have proceeded differently. Without it, they were 'like an instrument ill tuned and lapsing to discord'.

Yet still they seemed tied one to the other – by practical needs, yes, but also by some kind of visceral link.[*] There is a vehemence in the earl's letters as well as in the queen's which suggests real emotion of *some* sort. One of his letters declares that: 'Since I was first so happy as to know what love meant, I was never one day, nor one hour, free from

---

[*] So visceral as to have led to a theory – without foundation, but significant nonetheless – that Essex was not merely a surrogate son for Elizabeth, a reminder of Leicester, but an illegitimate child of the pair.

hope and jealousy, and as long as you do me right, they are the inseparable companions of my life.'

But for all that, Essex (like his rival Ralegh?) failed really to understand or appreciate Elizabeth as Leicester (and Hatton, and the Cecils)
had done. It is notable that he dared write to her, as his predecessors
never did, on terms almost of equality. He saw as pure weakness the
qualities of vacillation and dissimulation which, carefully deployed,
had been one of the best weapons in Elizabeth's wars. He had built up
the bonfire of courtly love to the point where it became a pyre. But, like
the queen's ever-sparser locks, perhaps the parade of courtly love itself
was wearing a little thin.

Compared to the cynicism of the 1590s, there seemed to have been
almost a mood of innocence about the court of Elizabeth's earlier
years. Sir John Harington recalled a 'kind of weariness' of that time:
'*mundus senescit*: that the world waxed old'. Trouble came not only
with the increasing hostility between Essex and the Cecils, but with
the young men's open dissatisfaction with an old woman's government. There was a climate of sexual licence which suggested the queen
had lost her grip on her hive – and, worse, lost the moral authority
which should both have sanctified her status within the game of courtly
love, and defied those who doubted a woman's right to rule. The dete-
rioration in the relationship of Elizabeth and Essex was just the symbol
of a more fundamental decline.

Essex could write a long chain of letters from Elizabeth's 'humblest
and most affectionate vassal' – or 'humblest and devoutest vassal' – or
'the most your own of all your Maj. creatures'. He could protest his
'dearest, faithful, and infinite affection' (or his 'infinite, pure, and
humble affection': Essex's invention was clearly running out). He could
ask Cecil to let his sovereign know 'I do spiritually kiss her fair royal
hands, and think of them as a man should think of so fair flesh'. But he
confided to Anthony Bacon that: 'I am as much distasted with the
glorious greatness of a favourite, as I was before with the supposed
happiness of a courtier.'

When, early in 1597, the strange pair quarrelled and Essex retired to
his bed, Elizabeth cried out in fury: 'I shall break him of his will and
pull down his great heart.' Ralegh was – no coincidence – once more
back at court after his long spell in the wilderness; and back in favour.

On 2 June Rowland Whyte was reporting to Robert Sidney that Robert Cecil had conducted Ralegh to the queen, 'who used him very graciously . . . In the evening he rid abroad with the Queen and had private conference with her; and now he comes boldly to the Privy Chamber as he was wont.' Essex in his paranoia saw enemies everywhere; yet even with the Cecils, even with Ralegh, he could unite to promote another naval venture against the common enemy: Spain.

But the so-called Islands Voyage was an unmitigated disaster. Again, Essex's instructions were to sail to the Azores and capture the summer treasure fleet, pausing on the way to wreak as much havoc as possible on the Spanish port where Philip was said to be preparing yet another Armada. From the very start, before they had even left English waters, the fleet was beset by a series of terrible storms. Essex, the queen's 'dismounted' servant, wrote to his mistress in confusion, and to Cecil of his and his fellow commanders' urgent need to hear of the queen's 'bearing, with her wonted magnanimity, these hard and cross beginnings'.

It was two months later when a depleted fleet could finally leave harbour, only to find no trace of the Spanish treasure ships when finally they reached the Azores. The chain of genuinely appalling luck – for the bad weather followed them southwards – was compounded by a chain of bad judgements as Ralegh and Essex squabbled. This may have been in Essex's mind when he wrote to the queen that absent men were at the mercy of 'many reports, interpretations and taxations [i.e. accusations]'. But Elizabeth was a just mistress, he wrote hopefully, and would understand Essex's 'true zeal to your service, perfect obedience to your commandments, and matchless affection to your dearest person'. So far so courtly – not so the sign-off. 'And if you believe not this, you are not just, nor do not right.'

The fleet finally returned home in October empty-handed to find that, in their absence, another Armada had indeed approached England and been defeated only by the stormy weather. Essex returned home, moreover, to find Robert Cecil being appointed to the lucrative position of chancellor of the duchy of Lancaster and another rival, Lord Admiral Howard, created earl of Nottingham and lord steward, in which capacity he outranked Essex. Retiring to his own house at

Wanstead and declaring himself ill, refusing to see visitors, Essex indulged in a sustained sulk. He was, he wrote to Elizabeth, 'overcome with unkindness, as before I was conquered by beauty'. Friends urged in vain that he should return to court, warning that absence of even the most favourite subject gave way to forgetfulness, forgetfulness gave way to wrath – 'and the wrath of a prince is as the roaring of a lion'. The queen snapped that 'a prince was not to be contested withal by a subject', but was finally persuaded in December to create Essex Earl Marshal of England, giving him once again the precedence. But the seeming victory came at serious cost to his credibility.

On 1 June 1598, at a meeting of the Privy Council, Elizabeth disregarded Essex's opinion in the matter of choosing a new governor for Ireland. Losing his temper, he shot her a scornful look, then, in defiance of all etiquette, deliberately turned his back. Losing her temper in turn, she dealt him a great box around the ears and told him to go and be hanged. Instinctively, he reached for his sword – which, fortunately, stayed in its scabbard as Nottingham seized him. As the guards wrestled him out of the chamber, he shouted that he would not have taken such an insult even from Elizabeth's father. The inference – that he rated her, as a mere woman, much lower – was clear. It was soon after this that he made his infamous comment: that the queen's conditions 'were as crooked as her carcass'. Without that comment, Ralegh would claim later, Essex might have met a very different fate.

That August, William Cecil, old Lord Burghley, died at last; in his illness fed nourishing broth by the queen's own hand. The next month, Philip of Spain also died after long agony: a man who over the years had perhaps occupied almost as large a place in Elizabeth's imagination. Besides leaving her ever more isolated, this fresh changing of the guard only intensified awareness that the long Anglo-Spanish war was becoming a luxury neither side could afford. Robert Cecil led the delegation to France, England's ally in the war, to discuss the possibility of peace. Essex of course was outraged – but the indulging of Essex had begun to look like another expensive luxury. 'He hath played long enough upon her, and she means to play awhile upon him,' one observer on 30 August reported Elizabeth as saying, 'and so stand as much upon her greatness as he hath done upon his stomach.'

Petulantly, outrageously, Essex now wrote to her: 'your Majesty hath, by the intolerable wrong you have done both me and yourself, not only broken all laws of affection, but done against the honour of your sex'. Scoldingly, he added: 'I cannot think your mind so dishonourable but that you punish yourself for it, how little soever you care for me.' He was denying that moral superiority the sovereign and the courtly mistress were alike supposed to possess.[*]

In another letter he declared: 'I do confess that, as a man, I have been more subject to your natural beauty, than as a subject to the power of a king; for your own justice doth conclude this [the former] within law, but the other my affection made to be infinite.' But now this subjection, he implies, was at an end. Elizabeth had sent Essex a message, saying she valued herself at as great a price as he valued himself. The extraordinary thing was that she should feel the need to.

Sir Henry Lee, advising him to make amends, urged Essex: 'She is your sovereign . . . consider my Lord how great she is with whom you deal.' His was but one voice sounding the same note. But Essex had, as he wrote to Lord Keeper Thomas Egerton, 'been content to do her Majesty the service of a clerk, but can never serve her as a villain or a slave'.

'What, cannot princes err? Cannot subjects receive wrong? Is an earthly power or authority infinite? Pardon me, pardon me, my good Lord, I can never subscribe to these principles.' One observer noted that Essex's greatness 'was now judged to depend as much on her Majesty's fear of him as her love to him'. But something was about to break, and that something was the situation in Ireland.

The situation in Ireland was a perennial thorn in England's side. Particular danger lay in the fact that Ireland's staunch Catholicism might open a back door for Spain. But the long revolt against English rule had been given a new boost by the dynamic leadership of the Earl of Tyrone. Now sudden Irish advances made the sending of a punitive

---

[*] Perhaps, even, a parallel could be drawn between the decline of courtly love and a decline in the level of reverence for the monarchy inculcated by Elizabeth's father. If so, it would have formidable repercussions in the next century: the century in which Essex's son would serve as a Parliamentary general in the Civil War.

force imperative, and Essex was the obvious choice to command it. On 25 March 1599 his commission was signed. Essex knew the task was a poisoned chalice but he was, as he put it, 'bound my own reputation to use no tergiversation'. Two days later he set out with a large force at his command and a lord lieutenant's authority.

The next six months were (as so often in the story of Essex's military adventures) a very sorry saga. Initial success in Ireland was undercut at every stage by dissent between the commander and the council; by delay in despatch of the further men and horses he demanded; by Essex's own extraordinary delay (with which Elizabeth did not hesitate to reproach him) in actually coming to grips with Tyrone. His letters to the council lamented that it was impossible 'at once to please and serve her Majesty'.

To the queen herself he wrote 'from a mind delighting in sorrow; from spirits wasted with travail, care, and grief; from a heart torn in pieces with passion'; he spoke of ransoming his soul 'out of the hateful prison of my body'. He addressed himself 'to a goddess not at leisure to hear my prayers', but the homage was distinctly perfunctory. Others of Elizabeth's favourites had also written in pained terms, but no one ever accused Essex of a lack of self-pity.

Elizabeth's letters to him in Ireland reflect a kind of bafflement: 'we are doubtful what to prescribe you at any time, or what to build upon your writing to us,' she wrote in one epistle whose very length betrays her uncertainty as to whether her commands will be obeyed. By the end of July almost three quarters of the English forces had fallen sick, slipped home or even joined the rebels . . . as, it almost seemed, Essex himself was prepared to do.

For when Essex finally faced Tyrone, it was not with sword in hand, but to agree a truce for which he by no means had the queen's sanction. Indeed, the reports heard with horror in London raised an unthinkable possibility: that Essex could return to impose his will on England with the support of Tyrone's Irish army.

'It appeareth by your journal that you and the traitor [Tyrone] spoke half an hour together without any body's hearing,' wrote Elizabeth in understandable fury, 'wherein, though we that trust you with our kingdom are far from mistrusting you with a traitor, yet both for comeliness, example, and your own discharge, we marvel you would carry it no better . . .' These were the fears, the conditions and the threats that brought Essex back from Ireland in September, quitting his post without permission. Galloping from the coast with a small band of supporters, with angry fear to spur him every step of the way, he arrived at Nonsuch early in the morning; 'so full of dirt and mire that his very face was full of it', as a shocked Rowland Whyte wrote to his employer Robert Sidney.

His small band of followers were left in the courtyard, to thwart pursuit, as he pressed on alone, through chamber after chamber meant to protect the queen's privacy. It would, after all, be a brave guard who presented his halberd and barred the way to the commander of England's army.

It was a woman's world into which he pressed; one native only to the queen's ladies. It was they who, at this late date in Elizabeth's reign, did the spadework behind the scenes to create the mask of majesty. Trussed the queen into her corsets and settled the hard pointed stomacher; pinned the wig of red curls on her head. Tied on the hoops that would hold out the skirts; laced the sleeves onto the bodice and hauled into place the stiff heavy overdress, glittering with jewels and groaning with embroidery. Though the queen, as a woman, could never wear armour on the field of battle, she stood up in her own protective carapace.

Ruff and jewels for a top dressing; the thick layer of white paint, powdered carmine for the thin lips hiding blackened teeth. Finally the illusion of Gloriana was complete. Enough of an illusion that men could pretend to believe in it, anyway.

But none of this had been done when Essex burst into the queen's chamber so early that she – by her own confession 'no morning woman' – was barely out of bed. He saw her with her own sparse grey hair around her wrinkled face: a sight no man was supposed to see. Essex had played out the courtly fantasy: pretended hers was a timeless beauty. Now that pretence lay naked and exposed, hollow for all to behold.

It must have taken every ounce of the queen's undoubted courage to stay unflinching in her seat, to greet him calmly and kindly, extend her hand for his kiss. But Elizabeth Tudor had always been at her best in an emergency.

*   *   *

When Essex burst into the queen's bedchamber, no one knew what kind of crisis was brewing. Even if this were not a *coup d'état*, to return against orders – to break into her presence – was a shocking insult to the queen's authority. Elizabeth had tried to believe Essex was another Leicester; but when she criticised Leicester's conduct in the Netherlands, he had reacted very differently. Years ago, Elizabeth had been appalled when she heard violent men had dared burst into the chamber of the Scots queen Mary, 'as if she were a public woman [a prostitute]', murdering her servant Rizzio. Now Elizabeth herself was in almost the same boat.

Time and again she had yielded to Essex's pleas, and given him leadership of her armies. Each time, she had to fan into flame the hope that this time – this time! – he would lead them with prudence and with loyalty. Now that flame flickered and died, sputtering into darkness amid the rushes on the floor.

Essex emerged from Elizabeth's bedchamber declaring that after such 'trouble and storm' in Ireland he had found 'a sweet calm' at home. He was deceiving himself. His unsanctioned intrusion was followed by another, midday, meeting, where he declared her still 'very gracious', but a third meeting the same day found her 'much changed'. Essex was ordered to keep to his room and, the next afternoon, to face the Privy Council and justify himself as best he could for 'His disobedience to Her Majesty's instructions . . . his contemptuous disregard of duty in returning without leave. And, last, his overbold going to Her Majesty's presence in her bedchamber.' He was ordered from Nonsuch that night. He and Elizabeth would never see each other again.

Essex was ordered into house arrest – forbidden even to write to his wife, newly delivered of a daughter. Meanwhile, Elizabeth's anger mounted. Her godson John Harington reported her as saying: 'By God's Son, I am no Queen; that man is above me.' Meanwhile, Essex himself was writing the 'unfeigned submission of the saddest soul on earth'.

As the strain made him ill, 'of the stone, stranguillon, and grinding of the kidneys', said one letter, she relented to a degree, and observers noted that she 'had water in her eyes' when she spoke of him. The general opinion in December was that 'he cannot live many days', since 'he begins to swell'. Elizabeth's reaction was again to send soup . . . Up with the rocket, down with the stick: Ralegh, hearing she was relenting towards his rival, 'is fallen sick upon it'.

But Essex as always seemed set on increasing his offence. At this of all moments he had circulated an engraving of himself in armour, against a background of his military successes, describing him as the paradigm of virtue, wisdom, honour – and, even, as God's elected. Small wonder if the queen thought she was the one suffering the 'intolerable wrong'.

This is but one of the many letters which, since I saw your Majesty, I wrote, but never sent unto you; for, to write freely to a Lady that lies in wait for all things I do or say, were too much hazard . . . your Majesty seeth the state of my mind, full of confusion and contrariety. I sometimes think of running, and then remember what it will be to come in armour triumphing into that presence, out of which both by your own voice I was commanded, and by your hands thrust out. But God knows this is no sudden accident. You may tell those that thirst and gape after my ruin, that you have now an advantage, that, being in passion, I spake rashly. It is well you have that you looked for, and so have I.

Letter, undated, from the Earl of Essex to Queen Elizabeth

24

'Affection's false'

1599–1603

EVEN IF THE play called courtly love were almost over, the
protagonists would not so easily leave the stage. It was said of
Essex that he had only one enemy – himself – and only one
friend – the queen. Now that friend seemed to have turned her face
away. Nonetheless, in February 1600 Elizabeth cancelled the scheduled trial of Essex, the very night before it was due to take place.

Perhaps she was moved by an oleaginous letter he had sent her,
declaring that he was 'humbly and unfeignedly' willingly to admit his
offence, that her 'princely and angel-like nature' would be best
displayed by having 'your mercy blazed by the tongue of Your Majesty's
once happy, but now most sorrowful orator'. By the end of the month
word was that 'we should see him a cockhorse again'. (The same writer
noted that 'My Lord of Essex hath been somewhat crazy this week.')
Elizabeth was still unwilling utterly to ruin him. He was allowed to
return to Essex House in the Strand, albeit in the custody of a warder
who kept all the keys and forbade all visitors.

Essex – 'pining, languishing, despairing' – kept up the pressure. A
stream of lachrymose letters swore that he was 'a servant whose humble
and infinite affection cannot be matched'; wrote of the queen's 'gracious,
princely, and divine nature' – 'a lady, a nymph or an angel, who, when
all the world frowns upon me, cannot look with other than gracious
eyes'.

He would write with an almost worrying regularity of Elizabeth's
'fair correcting hand' – of wishing to kiss the rod it held. (There was

perhaps something of the *dompteuse*, the trainer, if not actually the dominatrix in Elizabeth.*)

Essex, however, was too late: Elizabeth saw through the pretence of passion (passion, as he claimed unconvincingly a few months later, 'tyrannous to me, but reverent to your Maj'). And Essex's cause was far from helped by an attempt to publish the defence of his own actions he had begun writing on his way home from Cádiz. On 5 June he was brought back along the Strand to Egerton's York House to face a day's interrogation by the queen's councillors; 'from eight of the clock in the morning until almost nine at night, without either meat or drink. He kneeled two hours by the clock,' one of his supporters wrote indignantly. The upshot was that Elizabeth, while granting him his freedom, stripped him of all his offices and banished him from court forever.

But the real crux was yet to come. Through the summer he wrote again, frantically, to his 'most dear and most admired Sovereign', begging her 'to let me once prostrate myself at your feet'. It was autumn when Elizabeth finally – and, for Essex, disastrously – decided not to renew his lease on the farm of sweet wines: 'my chiefest maintenance', he pleaded, panic-stricken, and his only means of compounding with his creditors. (Unless, he said, his creditors would 'take for payment many ounces of my blood'.) On 17 November he was trying desperately to sound the old note: 'no soul had ever such an impression of your perfections, no alteration shewed such an effect of your power, nor so heart ever felt such a joy of your triumph' – but in vain. Was Elizabeth's anger fuelled by realisation that his protestations were directed so nakedly to a financial end?

'An unruly horse must be abated of its provender', William Camden reported the queen to have said. Perhaps she still hoped to tame Essex; in fact, she made him desperate. That, too, is something Cecil might have foreseen. The techniques of entrapment, of creating a conspiracy

---

* I cherish on my own bookshelves a 1960s volume which describes how the courtly lover 'assumes a childlike or feminine attitude, with voyeuristic tendencies, complicated by memories of spankings in boyhood'. But, ready mockery apart, it is worth remembering that Andreas Capellanus was at one with Havelock Ellis in allying love and suffering, pleasure and pain ... and viewing the courtly mistress as the ultimate exemplar of maternal tough love.

– of giving rebels just enough rope with which to hang themselves – were those the elder Cecil had used against Mary, Queen of Scots, that other glamorous threat to Elizabeth's throne.

Essex had long been making dangerous connections – dangerous in more senses than one. He had in 1598 again taken up the correspondence with James VI in Scotland, and spoke now of 'sending emissaries' into Ireland, where his sister Penelope's lover Charles Blount, Lord Mountjoy, had taken over command of the campaign. Emissaries to do what, exactly? Were the troops under Mountjoy's lead to pressure Elizabeth into returning Essex to favour and promising James the succession after her death? Or were they to place James – or even, conceivably, Essex himself – on the still-living Elizabeth's throne? That autumn (though pamphlets in the streets and sermons from the pulpits proclaimed Essex's rights) it became clear that neither Mountjoy nor James was foolish enough to hazard so much for what Mountjoy scathingly described as Essex's 'private ambition'.

'Ambition thwarted in its career doth speedily lead on to madness', as Sir John Harington wrote of the earl. Harington recorded in his journal how Essex 'shifteth from sorrow and repentance to rage and rebellion so suddenly as well proveth him devoid of good reason or right mind'. And when before Christmas Essex melodramatically wrote to James that he was 'summoned of all sides' to save his country, to rid the queen of her evil councillors, he was tying a noose for his own neck.

It started with a play – and a play written by the protégé of Essex's associate the Earl of Southampton. It took some persuasion to make the actors of the Globe perform Shakespeare's old story of Richard II on the afternoon of Saturday 7 February 1601. Though Essex's supporters attended the performance, he himself did not. But the play's theme – of a failing Richard, betrayed by his own sense of a king's divine right, and replaced by a vigorous Henry IV – would lie behind the most serious charges levelled against Essex in the weeks ahead.

Was Essex even then planning actual rebellion? The number of malcontents massing in the courtyard of Essex House, the report of muskets being oiled, might seem to say yes; the fact Essex spent part of that Saturday playing tennis and the evening hosting a supper party seems to say no. But that performance shook Cecil and the Privy Council into sending for him, and a genuine fear may have sparked the events of the next day. Essex believed that Ralegh had a band of men ready to assassinate him: and perhaps Ralegh was playing an invidious role.

It is just possible, again, that the scare was put about deliberately, to panic Essex into over-hasty action. Early on Sunday morning Ralegh took a small boat on the Thames, downriver towards Essex House, and on it had a private meeting with Ferdinando Gorges, Essex's hench-man but Ralegh's distant kin. We have only Gorges's word for what was said – but Gorges would in the end testify against his former patron.

Certainly, too, a panic-stricken speed provides the only excuse for the sheer incompetence of the Essex rebellion. It is hard to read the events of 8 February without a sense of farce; from the moment Essex locked into his bookroom the officials sent to reason with him, to the one where the rebels made a three-hour break for refreshment, and a change of Essex's sweaty clothes.

He, Southampton and some 150 supporters, striding through the streets of London, calling out for the citizens to rise in his defence, had been dismayed by the lack of response. One Sheriff Smyth had prom-ised to raise the City; when the promise proved vain, Essex lost his nerve. While he ate and drank, his supporters slipped away. The City's barriers were raised, preventing his return down Fleet Street, while the council demanded Essex surrender to the authorities. The queen, meanwhile, likewise made a good midday meal, declaring the God who had placed her on her throne would certainly preserve her on it. Later, she told the French ambassador that if Essex had reached Whitehall, she herself would have gone out to confront him 'in order to know which of them ruled'.

The rebels made their way back to Essex House by boat at dusk, to find the officials held as hostages had escaped, and the house was almost surrounded by government forces. The barricades of books and furniture hastily thrown up would not stand against the cannon being dragged from the Tower. Essex spent a two-hour truce burning his most private papers, notably his letters from King James, but around 10 p.m. he surrendered; to be taken, with Southampton, to the Tower. The rebellion was over twelve hours after it had begun – thanks, as one observer put it, 'to the providence and celerity of the Secretary': Cecil. The trial that followed would prove a confrontation between the two.

Elizabeth had often infuriated her councillors by dilatoriness in despatching those who threatened her. But now, all was done in haste. The Earl of Essex was brought to trial on 19 February, with all the government's heavy guns wheeled out. Francis Bacon, his one-time adviser, was his chief accuser.

Sir Edward Coke claimed that Essex had schemed to make himself 'Robert, king of England'. Essex hotly denied it: 'God, which knoweth the secrets of all hearts, knoweth that I never sought the crown of England . . . only seeking to secure access to the presence of the queen, that I might speedily have unfolded my griefs unto her Majesty against my private enemies.'

The most important of those 'enemies', setting Ralegh aside, was Cecil, who, Essex said, had been reported to him as saying that the Infanta of Spain had the best claim to the throne of England. From behind a screen Cecil himself stepped forward to refute the accusation, dramatically.

'I stand for loyalty, which I never lost,' said Cecil. 'You stand for treachery, wherewith your heart is possessed. I have said the King of Scots is a competitor, and I have said the King of Spain is a competitor, and you, I have said, are a competitor. You would depose the queen. You would be King of England . . .'

For the first three decades of Elizabeth's long reign not only she, like her predecessor, but all those who hoped either to inherit or to seize her throne had been women. It seems telling that now, at the last, all the most serious of these 'competitors' were men. Telling, too, that the indictment against Essex was couched in almost sexualised terms that repeatedly saw him pressing through 'resistance' to 'seize', 'possess', 'master' the queen, who had in fact shown herself singularly stalwart, but who was now presented as a frightened female in distress. It was as though Essex stood charged with having broken the chivalric rules, as much as the laws of the land.

The outcome of the trial was never in doubt. Essex was sentenced to the traitor's death – hanging, drawing and quartering – though it would be commuted to a simple beheading, as usual for the aristocracy. Essex's last days in the Tower do him little credit. In an explosion of hysterical guilt he denounced not only himself but also his supporters; notably his sister Penelope, who had served his interests 'more like a slave than a sister', as she responded bitterly.

Almost twenty years later, a story would emerge of a ring Essex tried to send Elizabeth on the eve of his death. It was a jewel the queen had once given him in proof of her love; now he sought to return it in a bid for pity, only to have it intercepted by an enemy. The tale is, alas, a pretty fabrication, without evidence – but the question is why we have clung to it down the years, to the degree that the ring is still on display, near Elizabeth's funeral effigy, in Westminster Abbey.

Essex's execution was to be private, inside the Tower. Elizabeth had always feared his popularity and, though it had not risen to join the earl's rebellion, London now seethed with sympathy. Two headsmen ('so that if one faint, the other may perform it') and their 'bloody tool', the axe, were all smuggled secretly into the Tower. Ralegh had given evidence at Essex's trial, and would be expected to attend the execution in his capacity as Captain of the Guard. In fact, he withdrew to the armoury at the crucial moment to avoid accusations of triumphing over his fallen rival – but, carefully nurtured by Essex's followers, the charge would continue to dog him anyway.

Histrionically, on the scaffold, Essex blamed himself for his rebellion: 'this great, this bloody, this crying, this infectious sin'. Seconds later the third blow of the axe severed his head from his body. As with the other deaths she had ordered – of Mary Stuart, of the Duke of Norfolk before her – Elizabeth had wavered, in the days before his death. But – by her own standards – only briefly.

It can be curiously hard to see the figure of the ageing Elizabeth behind the flamboyant stories of the men around her. While Essex was in his last disgrace, the queen attended a court wedding, at which she was invited to dance by the character representing Affection. ' "Affection!" said the Queen; "Affection's false"; yet Her Majesty rose and danced.' It is salutary to remember – even earlier in the reign, when it was all 'about' Elizabeth – how much of the talk had indeed been about her 'affection'. Who she would or would not marry; the licence she gave or did not give to her sexuality. Did even a queen regnant, even this queen regnant, become less visible once that possibility was past?

Eight months after Essex's death, in October 1601, Elizabeth made her 'Golden Speech'. 'Though God hath raised me high,' she told her people, 'yet this I count the glory of my crown, that I have reigned with your loves.' But her speech was made to placate the Parliament that had forced her to back down over proposed monopolies, and the very fact she had to make it reflected a change. The courtly love of Elizabeth and Essex was not the only relationship which had faltered. So too, in these last years of her reign, had that between Elizabeth and her people.

The French ambassador de Beaumont described the queen speaking of Essex almost with tears; recalling how she had seen the trouble inherent in his nature; had warned him not to touch her sceptre. A conversation recorded by the antiquary William Lambarde might suggest that Elizabeth had come to see her affection for Essex, and indeed Essex himself, as having been manipulated by others around them with 'the wit of the fox'. The fox had been a popular name for the elder Cecil, Lord Burghley; Essex himself had used the term of Ralegh.

Hard on the heels of Essex's downfall, Cecil seized the chance to start his own correspondence with James. His relationship with Essex, he assured the Scots king, had originally been founded on 'so many reciprocal benefits interchanged in our growing fortunes'. In his secret correspondence with James, Cecil promised after Elizabeth's death swiftly to translate James of Scotland to the English throne.

In the two years that remained to her after the loss of Essex, Elizabeth could still show flashes of energy and of brilliance, dancing two galliards with the Duc de Nevers, striding energetically through her garden at Oatlands. But she felt 'creeping Time' at her gate – and Cecil was far from the only one to turn his eyes, just as Elizabeth had always feared, towards the rising sun.

It was reported in November 1602 that the queen had 'a new inclination, supposed to be for the Earl of Clanrickarde, a handsome, brave Irishman, who is said to resemble Essex' – and who, indeed, had married Essex's widow Frances. But Clanrickarde, de Beaumont says, 'is cold, and hath not sufficient understanding to lift himself'. Or, he found the courtly game of love one he had no wish to play.

Elizabeth's godson John Harington described her, Hamlet-like, thrusting a rusty sword into the arras of the private chamber where, after the Essex rebellion, she spent more and more time. She told a kinsman that 'I am tied with a chain of iron about my neck, and the case is altered with me.' In the early months of 1603 it was clear the end was nigh. On 25 February, the second anniversary of Essex's death, the queen disappeared into her chambers, appearing in public only days later, and in such melancholy that observers guessed that she too would shortly die. Her death came on 24 March, and James's accession passed 'without so many ripples as might shake a cockle boat', Cecil recorded proudly.

There was a coda to the story of courtly love and the Tudor dynasty. The life of Arbella Stuart – granddaughter of Margaret Douglas and Bess of Hardwick – had been dominated by her tantalising proximity to the English throne. In the 1580s, with Arbella in her teens, Queen Elizabeth had, cynically, fostered the idea that the girl might be her heir, telling the wife of the French ambassador that 'she will one day be even as I am and a lady mistress. But I will have gone before.' Throughout the 1590s, however, Arbella was carefully kept away from court, and from political prominence, isolated in Hardwick Hall, which she described as 'my prison', strictly watched by her grandmother and still unmarried as her twenties ticked away. But in the first weeks of 1603, as Elizabeth lay dying, the horrified authorities discovered Arbella making what must surely be seen as a bid for the throne – an attempt to contract a marriage with another possible royal claimant: the grandson of Katherine Grey.

A government hardman was sent north to investigate, and under the strain Arbella's stability – even her sanity – gave way. But the rambling letters of self-exculpation she sent to the Privy Council reiterate one very interesting fantasy. Anything she had done, she claimed, was at the instigation of an unnamed 'dearest and best-beloved' at court – someone 'great with her Majesty' who had urged her to 'try' – to test – the queen's love.

This improbable lover was, Arbella claimed, one who 'can take nothing ill at my hand ... [though] I have dealt unkindly, shrewdly, proudly with him'; whose love she might compare 'to gold which hath been so often purified that I cannot find one fault, jealousy only excepted'; one of whose chief virtues was 'secrecy' – that discretion, like that ardent jealousy, so often urged on the courtly lover. Indeed, the relationship she recounted was in many ways a perfect rendition of the courtly dream; a dream of which the bookish and deeply cultured Arbella must often have read.

As the weeks of interrogation – and Arbella's letters – went on, this was far from the last appearance of her putative lover ('my little, little love') whose identity she would never reveal. (Pressed beyond endurance, she declared, absurdly, that it was her cousin the King of Scots: a married man she had so far never met.) In fact he was surely a fantasy figure, though one coloured by the memory of someone real: the dead Earl of Essex. The longest and most confused of her letters (seven thousand words long) was written on Ash Wednesday: the anniversary of his execution.

If Arbella had been bidding for the throne, then, of course, she failed. But, summoned to the court of the new King James, she did win liberty from Hardwick and her grandmother's custody. And there was after all one allegiance they shared. Within weeks, the new king – who hastened to release the Earl of Southampton from the Tower where he still languished, who showered favour on Essex's family – would be referring to Essex as 'my martyr'. Robert Cecil was rightly received into King James's confidence as the architect of his accession. But well before his own death in 1612, Cecil came to think with regret of his former mistress.

Walter Ralegh would, within months of James's arrival, be on trial for a treasonous plot to replace him on the throne with Arbella Stuart. Escaping execution, he was nonetheless imprisoned in the Tower for almost fifteen years – until 1617, when he was released in order to conduct another expedition to South America in search of El Dorado. Failing to find the land of gold – but provoking Spanish hostility – he was executed on his return in October 1618: the last flamboyant figure of the Elizabethan age.

The cult of courtly love had made possible Elizabeth's unmarried female monarchy. But in doing so, ironically, it had ensured the end of the Tudor dynasty. That contradiction is entirely in tune with the essentially anomalous courtly love story. Elizabeth, childless, was succeeded by a man reared in a very different tradition – in the harsh Protestantism that allowed not even the homage offered, in the Catholic Church, to the female saints or the Virgin Mary. It was in a sense Essex's way, the masculine way, that would be the path immediately ahead.

James VI and I would himself not be above using old legend; would describe himself as the new 'Arthur . . . Come by good right to claim my seat and throne.' But James disliked music and dancing; fell asleep during plays and masques; was reported as 'very rude and uncivil'. His court became a byword for sexual licence; but he was unsympathetic to any delicate games of love.* And James would help to ensure that romantic ideals – or rather, any ideal that seemed to allow power to a woman – had little currency in the coming century.

Lytton Strachey in 1928 saw in the Earl of Essex the last of the Middle Ages; the flame 'of antique knighthood'. The 'spectral agony of an abolished world is discernible through the tragic lineaments of a personal disaster,' he wrote in his groundbreaking *Elizabeth and Essex* biography.

Lisa Hilton suggests that 'Perhaps Essex can be seen, like Anne Boleyn before him, as yet another victim of the game of love': a reversal of the usual idea that he exploited Elizabeth's ageing vulnerability. In direct contradiction to most historical male/female relationships, Essex was not the whole of Elizabeth's life, but she did ultimately control the whole of his. But it can be hard, looking back, to decide where the balance of power in this relationship really lay.

I began writing this book with the idea that courtly love was a tool ready to the hand of the ambitious, most notably Anne Boleyn and Essex. That it was the Tudors themselves who were fools for love, taking in deadly earnest what should have been a game. I wound up believing almost the reverse: that the royal Tudors were the ones skilfully manipulating its tropes. It was, after all, Anne and Essex, and indeed poor Katheryn Howard, for whom the consequences had been quite literally deadly.

---

* James's personal obsessions were hunting – and the pursuit of supposed (and usually female) witches: the persecution of whom would characterise Catholic and Protestant alike.

Postscript

HE STORY CHRONICLED in this book began with a figure – Eleanor of Aquitaine – outside the scope of its pages. The Tudor saga should end with another, even more famous. William Shakespeare, the great poet of Elizabeth's reign as well as James's, plays with, against, over and above the conventions of courtly love.* Indeed, it would be the work of a whole other book to list the places in which Shakespeare's words – whether written seriously, or in affectionate mockery – echo those either of the courtly love theorists, or of Tudor worthies.

Romeo and Juliet, that eternal number one in the romantic charts, is full of the tropes of courtly love: love at first sight, secrecy, love ending in tragedy. Yet Shakespeare's mockery of the fantasies of love is omnipresent: 'My mistress' eyes are nothing like the sun ... If snow be white, why then her breasts are dun.' In *Love's Labour's Lost*, his ladies prick the balloon of the lords' courtly charade, exposing it for a hollow thing.† And yet again ... even in that play, out of the ruins of ritual romance grows some hope of real affection.

* Wrote the great John Dover Wilson in 1935: 'I believe, as many others have believed, that this conception [of Hamlet] first came to Shakespeare from the career and personality of his patron's hero, the brilliant, melancholy and ill-fated Earl of Essex.'
† During the Christmas revels of 1594, around the time Shakespeare probably wrote *Love's Labour's Lost*, the law students of Gray's Inn, under the auspices of Francis Bacon, held a mock court in which members forswore the company of women, exactly as the lords do in the play.

Time and again Shakespeare's plays – *Twelfth Night, As You Like It* – begin with the fantasy, the fancy, of love. They end, if we are lucky, by at least opening up the possibility of something more durable. Germaine Greer in *The Female Eunuch* saw Shakespeare even as providing the mythology for a 'new ideology of marriage'. Was this, in the end, 'What The Tudors Did For Us', to adapt the title of a popular television series? To give us a version of courtly love we would be able to use, despite all its anomalies?

Of course the story of courtly love would not come to an abrupt end with Shakespeare's death in 1616, any more than with Elizabeth's in 1603. But to trace its influence through the next four hundred years of literature (even just English literature!) would be the work of another book – or three. Germaine Greer, continuing the remarks quoted in the Introduction, followed the story from Petrarch to Luther, and from the Renaissance to the novels of Samuel Richardson in the eighteenth century.

Courtly love would indeed help to shape the novel: that new form that came in with the Romantic age, and sought to ally the ideal of romantic love with that of matrimony. But the novel would exemplify the way in which the oddities and anomalies of courtly love itself would continue to pop up, like perennial weeds in a flowerbed.

Over the next two centuries, true, the novel was frequently, even predominantly, concerned with romance, and with romance which did pave the way for marriage – was not, as Greer described courtly love, 'quite inimical' to it. But from the worlds of literature beloved of every bookish girl to the traditional Mills & Boon, the romance tends to end with some version of Jane Eyre's immortal words: 'Reader, I married him.'

Great exceptions from *Anna Karenina* to *Madame Bovary* and *Middlemarch* may explore the challenge of married love. Few attempt to offer an answer to it; perhaps on the principle that a happy family has no story (or at least, as Tolstoy suggested, no individuality). No more than their earliest courtly predecessors do the bulk of traditional stories, from film to fairy tale, attempt to lay down a route map for the continued life of romance within marriage. Greer concluded her chapter with the myth of happy-ever-after, which 'isn't true and it never was, and now for sure it never will be'. Well, let's hope it may be . . . But let's not rely on courtly love to show us the way.

We need to give this great fantasy its due weight. To remember the words of two great writers not only of, but on, the novel; since the novel would be the form in which, for vital generations of change, the dreams and aspirations of women were enshrined. Virginia Woolf in *A Room of One's Own* regretted that *this* novel was deemed important, because it dealt with war; *that* was dismissed, because it dealt with the feelings of women in a drawing room – or a tower. Jane Austen lamented in *Northanger Abbey* that novels themselves were dismissed as an unworthy – and, implicitly, a female-oriented – form.

We need to accept the part the long dream of courtly love has played in all our psyches. And then, perhaps, after almost a thousand years, we need finally to exorcise the ghost. To put it away.

Appendix

The Many Faces of Guinevere

GUINEVERE HAD BEEN encountered many times before Chrétien de Troyes brought her centre stage: a position she would continue to occupy. It is from an early world – a world, even, where writers do not feel the need to apportion Christian blame – that she first enters the Arthurian story.

The older stories carry with them the misty whiff of legend off the Welsh hills. Often this early Guinevere would be a sorceress – a wonder woman. The very name Gwenhwyvar means 'the white ghost', while the goddess manifest in three forms, as in the list of Arthur's queens from the Welsh Triads, is an idea from Celtic mythology.

In the real world of Celtic queenship, Guinevere could have been her husband's equal, able to lead armies like Boudicca or take lovers like Cartimandua. Even when, in 1190, Layamon, a parish priest living on the upper reaches of the River Severn, came to write his *Brut* – the narrative poem that has been called the first real Middle English literature – his 'Wenhaver' is queen in a world (Anglo-Saxon in feeling) where women don't merely inspire knights, but instead themselves do deeds of valour and of cruelty.

Guinevere's women scour the battlefield to slaughter the army of her abductor: in her husband's dream she stretches out her hand and draws down the roof of his hall, a figure of anger and potency whom Arthur hacks to pieces in revenge. In the *Rise of Gawain*, in years ahead, Gwendolena is not only Arthur's wife but also a powerful prophetess.

In one of the earliest stories of the *Mabinogion* she is included in a catalogue of Arthur's possessions: his ship, his mantle, his sword Caletvwlch and wife Gwenhwyvar – one of the 'gentle gold-torqued women of the island'. But even this passive Guinevere plays a role that is an archetype of mythology. For centuries Guinevere would feature repeatedly as the victim of abduction – often with an element of superstition about it.

In the saint's life of St Gildas written by Caradoc of Llancarfan probably between 1130 and 1150, Gildas comes to 'the summer country' (Somerset?), whose ruler King Meluas violates and carries off Guennuuar, wife of 'the tyrant Arthur', and hides her behind the reeds and rivers of Glastonbury, which here has some of the features of a Celtic otherworldly kingdom.* It takes Arthur and his Cornish armies a year to find her, while the great annual cycle of the seasons rolls by; a pattern celebrated in pre-Christian mythology.

In the early Welsh poem *Ymddiddan rhwng Arthur a Gwenhwyfar*, Melwas comes disguised to Arthur's court because he has heard of Guinevere's beauty, 'Gwenhwyfar of the deer's glance'. Sometimes she is carried off by a fairy lover, an otherworldly figure, who had loved her when she was herself a *fée*. A willing Persephone, or Deidre.

Quite soon, in story after story – French and German, as well as British – the more earthly figure of Mordred (Medraut), often the king's nephew or illegitimate son and supplanter, would be actually abducting Guinevere, with or without her consent.

One triad on 'Three unrestrained ravagings of the island of Britain' has Mordred coming to Arthur's court where he 'dragged Gwenhwyvar from her royal chair and then struck a blow upon her'. Another suggests that it was a quarrel between Gwenhwyvar and her sister Gwennhwyfach that led to the Battle of Camlan where Arthur fell. ('That is why these Battles were called Futile, because they were brought about by such a barren cause as this.') Guinevere was already a fateful queen who brings trouble – but not necessarily burdened with the weight of sexual guilt later centuries would load on her.

---

* Caradoc described how Glastonbury was 'an impregnable refuge', thanks in part to its 'boggy ground' – a phenomenon all too familiar to revellers at the modern Glastonbury Festival!

In the 1130s the Welsh cleric Geoffrey of Monmouth – translating into Latin, he said, a 'very ancient book' in the British language – described deeds 'handed down joyfully in oral tradition . . . by many peoples'. His *History of the Kings of Britain* was largely fictionalised – but it was taken, nonetheless, as giving the first authoritative version of the Arthurian story.

Geoffrey's Arthur marries Guanhuvara, or Gwanhumara, of Roman descent, brought up in the household of Duke Cador – the most beautiful woman in the whole island. He gives little of her character but, instead, a lengthy description of her coronation, four queens walking before her, carrying white doves. The ceremony perhaps implies that Guinevere had some rights in the crown herself – which may explain why, when Arthur is away, his nephew Mordred not only takes the crown but lives adulterously and incestuously with Guinevere. This may refer to an old custom whereby rights in the crown and the land descended in the female line, and a successful war leader could claim them by marriage. When Guinevere, in so many early versions of the story, is appropriated by her husband's supplanter, we need to be aware that the pre-Conquest kings Ethelbald and Cnut would marry their predecessor's wives as another way of colonising their territory.

But it also reflects the times in which Geoffrey himself lived. This was the time of the Anarchy – the civil war over whether the throne of England should be inherited by Henry I's daughter Matilda, or by his nephew Stephen. Geoffrey's insistence on Arthur's journeying into France may even have been a propaganda weapon aimed at encouraging Matilda's French adherents. His descriptions of Arthur's court of Caerleon are full of twelfth-century detail, and of the new innovations – tournament and heraldry – introduced into England in part by Matilda's Plantagenet husband.

One of the sources Geoffrey used was the *Historia Brittonum*, usually credited (though some modern scholarship disputes this) to the Welsh monk Nennius, writing in the early ninth century. The figures of Nennius's own day may themselves have helped colour his picture of the Arthurian story.

Nennius wrote on the border of Wales and Mercia – Mercia being widely known as the territory of Offa (he of the eponymous dyke), who ruled it through the second half of the eighth century. We know a good deal about Offa – about his great hall at Tamworth, 'its high roof gilded, its mead-benches decked in gold'; about the sword given him by Charlemagne; about how his influence extended even to continental Europe, and to the papacy. But most unusually we know about his queen, the noted beauty Cynethryth or Cwenethryth.

The Frankish scholar Alcuin charged Offa's son and heir to learn 'authority' from his father and 'compassion' from his mother. But Roger of Wendover wrote that she, rather than her husband, was responsible for the treacherous murder of their son-in-law, the King of East Anglia; and that because of her dangerous reputation the title of queen was subsequently forbidden to the wives of the Mercian kings. We know that letters were written to them jointly; that Offa broke with tradition in having coins struck with the image of his wife, as well as himself, thus giving a formal recognition to the role of consort, of the kind we would recognise today. That Cwenethryth survived her husband to enter a convent and became its abbess . . . As did Guinevere, in all the later stories.

This is not to suggest that Offa and Cwenethryth 'were' Arthur and Guinevere. But a queen so famous in Nennius's day may – for anyone looking back over Britain's history – have added her own legend to his bald narrative. After all, this is a trope we have seen here time and again: the cross-fertilisation of history with the soaring fantasy of sheer, inimitable story.

Interest in Guinevere has never gone away. In *Camelot* the 1960 musical, Julie Andrews, somewhat improbably, took the role on Broadway before Vanessa Redgrave starred in the movie. Recent screen incarnations have seen her as Keira Knightley's weapon-wielding Pictish princess in the 2004 film *King Arthur* or the black servant Gwen of TV's *Merlin*; the 2021 film *The Green Knight*, adapted from the tale of Sir Gawain, gives Guinevere a secondary role. Looking a little further back, we have, more conventionally, Cherie Lunghi in the 1981 John Boorman film *Excalibur* and Julia Ormond in the 1995 *First Knight*. That is to ignore a number of modern novels by, notably, Marion Zimmer Bradley, beginning in the early 1980s. Her Guinevere is, however, something of a weak sister:

other novels would reimagine Guinevere from a feminist perspective, investing her with greater agency than she had known since the very earliest incarnations. The New Age interests of recent years have even given her back her supernatural ties.

Camelot was adapted from T.H. White's 1958 *The Once and Future King*; White drew on Malory. But two centuries of comparative neglect had followed the Tudor era, and the dominance of Malory's *Morte*. The Age of Enlightenment had no use for legend, other than as a historical curiosity. It was inevitably in the Romantic era, the antiquarian late eighteenth century, that a new interest in the Arthurian myth, and with it the tropes of courtly love, really got under way. During the Victorian period – like the twelfth and sixteenth centuries, an era of great social change – the rediscovered ideal of chivalry came to permeate every aspect of culture. That, surely, is how it survived so vigorously through to the present day.

The turreted architecture with which we are all familiar was only one face of the Gothic Revival. The historical novels of Sir Walter Scott reflected the new interest – but the Romantic era also ushered in an age of factual research and rediscovery, with scholars across Europe searching for the epics of their national past, and texts like *Beowulf* and *The Song of Roland* coming back into the light. In the 1820s Malory's *Morte* was republished three times; between 1838 and 1849 Lady Charlotte Guest published her translation, from the Welsh, of the *Mabinogion* – oral tales from before the Conquest, written down in the late fourteenth century and featuring King Arthur as (in Lady Charlotte's view) 'the noblest creature that ever lived in fiction'. In the nineteenth century, as in earlier times, this echoing, evocative Celtic voice from a little-known land took Europe by storm. In 1839 the Eglinton Tournament – organised at his Scottish castle by the 13th Earl of Eglinton – saw knights compete in carefully authentic armour, while costumed ladies cheered them on. In 1865, in *Sesame and Lilies*, John Ruskin urged women to be 'queens to your lovers; queens to your husbands and your sons; queens of a higher mystery to the world beyond'. (He specifically rejected the idea that this relationship worked only for 'the lover and mistress, not the husband and wife', urging instead that marriage should be 'the seal which marks the bowed transition of temporary into untiring service'.) More than forty years on,

Baden-Powell's *Scouting for Boys* urged his juvenile knights to rescue women in distress – and credited the nine rules of his 'Knight's Code' to no less a person than King Arthur: a piece of historical fantasy of which Andreas Capellanus or Geoffrey of Monmouth might well have been proud.

But the Victorian rediscovery of the Arthurian tales – under another queen regnant, as in Elizabeth's day; and signalling another age of reassessment of women's position – showed two very different faces. Tennyson the Poet Laureate was leader of the camp which figured Prince Albert, the Prince Consort, as a second Arthur – but the tale of Guinevere was so different from the home life of Tennyson's own dear queen! His *Idylls of the King* has a repentant Guinevere literally prostrate at Arthur's feet, as he thunders at her from the moral heights, eventually to forgive her 'as Eternal God forgives'.

Considering Guinevere's complaint that her husband was:

. . . cold,
High, self-contain'd, and passionless, not like him,
Not like my Lancelot

our sympathies are likely to lie with the lady. But help was at hand, and coming as much from the realm of visual art as from poetry.

In 1858 – just as he, Rossetti, Burne-Jones and others were decorating the walls of the Oxford Union library with Arthurian frescoes – William Morris published *The Defence of Guenevere*, a poetic account of the queen's life told largely in the first person, and portraying her as a proud woman who 'never shrunk / But spoke on bravely'. Suddenly, her story was everywhere, not least because the Pre-Raphaelites saw here a reflection of their own tangled love affairs.

Within the complexities of the Morris/Rossetti triangle, Jane Morris (William's model and wife, Rossetti's muse and platonic lover) was identified as the modern Guinevere. The Pre-Raphaelites talked much about the 'passion of the soul'; a passion which might or might not involve physical sex. Courtly love was reborn; an alternative version of the fashionable chivalry to the one offered by Tennyson's virtuous knights. As such, it was adopted by Benjamin Disraeli, who took to describing Queen Victoria as 'the Faery', in reference to *The Faerie Queene*.

Aubrey Beardsley was another devotee, who near the end of the nineteenth century produced Art Nouveau illustrations of Guinevere. By that time the idea of the new courtly love – of a 'pure', if technically sometimes adulterous, romance which had nothing to do with marriage – was already in currency among a clever upper-class coterie. Known as the Souls, their members included the Tennant sisters, Lord Curzon, Lord Balfour and a number of leading hostesses. When the great seducer (traveller, poet, anti-imperialist) Wilfrid Scawen Blunt went to Wales to stay with a fellow member, Lady Windsor, they walked round a medieval castle, both dressed in white, talking about Lancelot and Guinevere.

As Scawen Blunt wrote of the Arthurian legends:

Tales touching still, and still thro' time renowned
Though less, methinks, for their high deeds who wear
Their crests so proudly, than for the lost sound
Of Lancelot's steps at the Queen's chamber door.

Those steps beat through the Tudor palaces – outside them, too, in the horse's hooves on the tournament ground. In the steps of the dance, where Henry and his great love took hands: in Anne Boleyn's frantic steps, the whirl of her skirts, as she held their daughter in Henry's face, trying to win his mercy. In the patter of Katheryn Howard's tiny feet as she tried to run away from a destiny no teenager should have to face. In the walks Elizabeth paced talking with the men who were her ministers; and the measures she trod with her favourites: often the same men, at the end of the day. In the insistent hasty thud of Essex's muddy boots as he raced back from Ireland . . .

That might seem to have brought the steps to a halt. And yet, somehow, we still hear them today.

Acknowledgements

T HE PERSON I need first to thank, now and always, is Alison
Weir, who generously found time to read this book in draft
stage, and make many helpful suggestions. The very idea was
born on a swaying Alison Weir Tours bus, when I delivered a talk on
'The Tudors in Love'; and both she and Nicola Tallis encouraged me to
take it further. Indeed, I should like also to thank the many AWT
guests who have now become friends.

This is a pandemic production. True, it was conceived and
commissioned in the halcyon days when it was possible to hold
discussions over a convivial lunch. (As I write this, I can only hope it
will be published into the same climate.) But much of the real work
was done under lockdown conditions; which means special thanks
are due to the staff of the London Library, whose service in posting
out even the most recherché of volumes was over and above the call
of duty. One side effect of the pandemic was to make even more
precious the few people one was allowed to see: firstly, of course, my
husband Derek Malcolm, who accepted with unexpectedly good
grace that he was sharing lockdown with a cast of characters from
the twelfth century. But also our dear friends and neighbours Paul
Louis and Sheba Phombeah, to whose active support and constant
encouragement I owe so much. Thanks too to Jane Williams for her
part in keeping me up to the mark. Anyone who fails to understand
the concept of Petrarchan contraries has clearly never taken one of
her Pilates classes!

From the professional sphere, I should like to thank firstly my editor Sam Carter for his enduring commitment to the project and – like Rida Vaquas, also of Oneworld – for sharing his own knowledge of the medieval period. Work under lockdown conditions imposed extra burdens on everybody: to Tamsin Shelton it gave the task of dealing with my technological ineptitude, as well as the regular demands of a copy-edit. All thanks are due also to my ever-supportive agent, Donald Winchester. On this as every book I have ever written, I owe an immense debt of gratitude to my old friend and colleague Margaret Gaskin, for her invaluable role in shaping, trimming, correcting and generally birthing my early text.

A book with as broad a historical sweep as this one can only leave the author standing on the shoulders of others – giants all – to a degree even beyond the norm. If I have failed correctly to interpret their work I can only apologise: any errors here, of course, are mine alone. Every person who aided my other books on the Tudor period, moreover, has essentially played a part here. One thing, however, has sadly changed this time around. During the course of the virus, separated by lockdown, I lost my beloved stepfather, Professor R.G. West, whose example always inspired me to try to do better. Richard – always in my memories.

Notes and Further Reading

To attempt a complete bibliography or source notes for this book would result in an impossibly lengthy appendix, as the waist-high piles of battered volumes littering the floor of my study could attest. I have written four previous books on the Tudor or pre-Tudor period, and everything I read, every document I studied for each of those, has played some part here.

In *Blood Sisters: The Women Behind the Wars of the Roses* (HarperPress, 2012) I covered the period 1445–1509; in *Game of Queens: The Women Who Made Sixteenth-Century Europe* (Oneworld, 2016) I discussed women who played a significant part in rule, from the accession of Isabella of Castile in 1474 to, roughly, the execution of Mary, Queen of Scots in 1587. *Elizabeth & Leicester* (Bantam, 2007) covered the life of Elizabeth I until 1588; and *Arbella: England's Lost Queen* (Bantam, 2004) explored the politics of the latter part of her reign through the story of the girl who might have succeeded her. I therefore refer the reader to the notes and bibliographies of each of those books: only works with the most direct relevance can be mentioned here. The very limited notes are likewise given only where I feel a particular need to acknowledge a debt or address a confusion.

Or, quite simply, when I can't resist.

Introduction

'C.S. Lewis . . . described it as a centuries-long force': C.S. Lewis, *The Allegory of Love: A Study in Medieval Tradition* (Oxford University Press, 1977), p. 4.

'D.W. Robertson complained': See *The Meaning of Courtly Love*, ed. F.X. Newman (State University of New York Press, 1968), p. 17.

'Greer . . . points out': Germaine Greer, *The Female Eunuch* (Harper Perennial, 2006), p. 222.

'A friend of the young Diana Spencer reported': Tina Brown, *The Diana Chronicles* (Arrow, 2017), p. 66.

Part I: Origins

The terms and definitions at the top of each Part are drawn from *The Courtly Love Tradition* by Bernard O'Donoghue (Manchester University Press, 1982).

Chapter 1: Chrétien, the Countess and the Chaplain (12th century)

Amid a vast body of literature, two books were particularly important to my understanding of the whole concept of courtly love. The first, chronologically, was *The Allegory of Love* by C.S. Lewis, which I encountered as a schoolgirl (first published in 1936, though any page references are from the 1977 reprint). As vital in a different way was *The Origin and Meaning of Courtly Love: A Critical Study of European Scholarship* by Roger Boase (Manchester University Press, 1977). Among the five conference papers which make up *The Meaning of Courtly Love* is the important 'The Concept of Courtly Love as an Impediment to the Understanding of Medieval Texts' by D.W. Robertson, Jr. (It is worth pointing out that the mid-/late twentieth-century dismissal of courtly love by Robertson and others bred its own rebuttal: see *The Origin and Meaning of Courtly Love*, p. 122, where Boase notes 'a mood of scepticism concerning the use of the term Courtly Love which it has been the intention of this book to dispel'.)

Of the central texts, for Chrétien de Troyes, see *Arthurian Romances*, translated with an introduction and notes by William W. Kibler

(Penguin, 1991). See also *A Companion to Chrétien de Troyes*, ed. Norris J. Lacy and Joan Tasker Grimbert (D.S. Brewer, 2005). See also *Andreas Capellanus On Love*, ed. and trans. P.G. Walsh (Duckworth, 1982).

'the name "courtly love" came into widespread use': Gaston Paris is usually credited with having coined the term in his 1883 article 'Lancelot du Lac: le Conte de la Charrette'; this late invention was taken by detractors as evidence that the concept had no medieval actuality. The credit is, however, not entirely deserved: the medievalist Jean Frappier noted use of '*cortez'amors*' in the twelfth century and '*Amor cortes*' in the thirteenth. The English term 'courtly love' can be found, twice, in the late Elizabethan poem *Orchestra: or a Poeme of Dauncing* by Sir John Davies.

'the story of Lancelot and Queen Guinevere has been told': This should be made clear throughout this book and its Appendix. Yet in the wide field of Arthurian study, assessment of the treatment of Guinevere herself long remained a curiously patchy business, to be pieced together from work on other, male-oriented, myths, whether of Sir Gawain or of the Grail. See, however, *Women and Arthurian Literature: Seizing the Sword* by Marion Wynne-Davies (Macmillan, 1996); also (though Lancelot is not the other man of this story) *An Arthurian Triangle: A Study of the Development and Characterization of Arthur, Guinevere and Mordred* (E.J. Brill, 1984) by Peter Korell. *The Book of Guinevere* by Andrea Hopkins (Saraband, 1996) is brief and picture-led but nonetheless fascinating. As this book was going into production, I discovered *The Once & Future Queen: Guinevere in Arthurian Legend* by Nicole Evelina (Lawson Gartner, 2017). Had I done so earlier I might have saved myself a lot of work, but I have at least the pleasure of recommending it here; not least for the lead it gives into a whole world of feminist Arthurian scholarship.

'analogy . . . between the chess game and the cult of love': See Marilyn Yalom, *Birth of the Chess Queen* (Pandora Press, 2004).

'C.S. Lewis pointed out': Lewis, *The Allegory of Love*, p. 2.

'a new "self-fashioning"': As in Stephen Greenblatt's groundbreaking *Renaissance Self-Fashioning: From More to Shakespeare* (University of Chicago Press, 1980).

'a religion of profane love': Boase, *The Origin and Meaning of Courtly Love*, p. 85.

'harbingers of the Reformation'; 'grew out of the Cathar or Albigensian heresy': See Boase, *The Origin and Meaning of Courtly Love*, pp. 77–81.

'the pathological nature of love': See Boase, *The Origin and Meaning of Courtly Love*, pp. 62–75 for this theory.

'Reay Tannahill': See Reay Tannahill, *Sex in History* (Abacus, 1981), p. 253.

'William Marshal . . . had risen through his valour': See Thomas Asbridge, *The Greatest Knight: The Remarkable Life of William Marshal, the Power Behind Five English Thrones* (Simon & Schuster, 2015). More than eight centuries on, his character would inform that of William Thatcher, played by Heath Ledger in *A Knight's Tale*.

'too hot to handle': Any connection with Chrétien would depend on his Lancelot having been written slightly later than is thought (i.e. between 1177 and 1181), and indeed on gossip having spread. But there is, of course, the possibility of revision or excision.

'tropes of troubadour song': See Matilda Tomaryn Bruckner, 'Le Chevalier de la Charrette', in *A Companion to Chrétien de Troyes*, p. 145: 'loss of self, humbling service to the lady that paradoxically raises the lover to her superior level, the split of heart and body, dying for love, antitheses of wisdom and folly, measure and "desmezura", pain and joy, etc.'

'Andreas based the first two parts of his book': Ovid takes three books to give advice on winning and keeping the opposite sex. Andreas likewise offers three books: but while the first two are on how to keep and how to win love (his rules vouchsafed to one of Arthur's knights), the third is used to condemn it. Ovid did something not dissimilar in a subsequent work, *Remedia Amoris* (The Cure for Love).

Chapter 2: Realpolitik and the *Roman* (13th century)

On the extraordinary life of Eleanor of Aquitaine, see *Eleanor of Aquitaine, by the Wrath of God, Queen of England* by Alison Weir (Jonathan Cape, 1999); and the same author's broader-ranging and more recent *Queens of the Crusades: Eleanor of Aquitaine and Her Successors* (Jonathan Cape, 2020). The other book I found particularly helpful, as exploring the relationship between fact and fiction in the context of Eleanor's story, was *Eleanor of Aquitaine: Queen and Legend* by D.D.R. Owen (Blackwell, 1993). On Isabella of France, see *Isabella: She-Wolf of France, Queen of England* by Alison Weir (Jonathan Cape, 2005). I owe also a very particular debt to Lisa Hilton's *Queens Consort: England's Medieval Queens* (Weidenfeld & Nicolson, 2008).

For the *Roman de la Rose*, see *The Romance of the Rose*: a new translation by Frances Horgan (Oxford University Press, 1994).

'Jersey-born Norman poet Wace': Wace took the first steps in adapting Geoffrey's chronicle-based tale for a more courtly Anglo-Norman audience. Fewer battles; an Arthur who Wace describes as 'one of Love's lovers'; ladies who figure both as inspirers and rewarders; and that procession of dismal demoiselles whose woes trigger most quests . . . Wace gives, too, a description of Guinevere as Arthur claps eyes on her: 'marvellous dainty was the maiden in person and vesture; right queenly of bearing; passing sweet and ready of tongue'.

'[Eleanor] is often credited . . . with having helped inspire': Of course, we are now in dodgy territory. It is a dangerous, a disreputable, game to try to pin a real-life tag, like a donkey's tail, onto the back of any literary construct, whether Guinevere, or Shakespeare's Dark Lady. It suggests precisely the kind of romantic (sloppy?)

thinking that has seen the whole idea of courtly love dismissed as unfit for any serious student of history. This, however, is to throw out the baby with the bathwater. As Owen writes, truth 'was infinitely malleable in the Middle Ages . . . Whilst on the one hand . . . the medieval mind was apt to envisage real events in terms of favorite fictions, people also felt the urge on occasion to make life imitate art by acting in the manner of the heroes and heroines of legend' (Owen, *Eleanor of Aquitaine*, p. 2). Owen also suggests that, conversely, writers may have used Eleanor 'to give the ring of truth to their favourite characters' (ibid.); and that Eleanor was aware of 'her present status as a latter-day Guenevere' (ibid., p. 40). 'The medieval narrative poets and, increasingly from the thirteenth century, writers of prose were apt to smuggle into their works disguised references to real characters and events' (ibid., p. 161).

'progressive degrading of Guenevere's character': See Owen, *Eleanor of Aquitaine*, pp. 184–5.

'Vulgate Cycle': Aka the 'Pseudo-Map Cycle' or 'Lancelot-Grail', the Vulgate Cycle consists of three main stories: on Merlin, on the Grail Quest, and on Lancelot, which last romance is, however, itself often broken into three. The Vulgate Cycle was swiftly rewritten into what is now known as the Post-Vulgate Cycle, which would de-emphasise the romance of Lancelot and Guinevere in favour of the quest for the Holy Grail.

'he had played King Arthur': Conversely, a poem known as the 'Lament of Edward II' and thought by some to have been written by the imprisoned king himself might be said to cast Edward as the betrayed Arthur, leaving Mortimer an unusually dastardly Lancelot.

'into one mystery': See Derek Brewer, *A New Introduction to Chaucer* (Longman, 1984), p. 60. Brewer sees this as the start of the literary tradition referenced more than three centuries later by Thomas Middleton when he wrote in *The Changeling* that Love 'has an intellect that runs through all . . . brings all home'.

'an increasingly rigid climate': 'The decline in the positive symbolism of women . . . is but one facet of a pervasive intellectual constraint.' See Joan M. Ferrante, *Women as Image in Medieval Literature* (Columbia University Press, 1975), p. 11.

Chapter 3: The *Commedia*, Chaucer and Christine (14th century)

Among many editions, Dante's *The Divine Comedy* was notably translated and edited by John D. Sinclair (Oxford University Press, between 1939 and 1946); for his life, see James Burge, *Dante's Invention* (The History Press, 2010).

For Chaucer's complete works, see *The Riverside Chaucer*, ed. Larry D. Benson (Oxford University Press, 1988), also *The Complete Works of Geoffrey Chaucer*, ed. F.N. Robinson (Houghton Mifflin, 1957); and for a critical overview, Brewer, *A New Introduction to Chaucer*. For

Chaucer and courtly love, see Larry D. Benson, 'Courtly Love and Chivalry in the Later Middle Ages' (http://sites.fas.harvard.edu/~chaucer/special/lifemann/love/ben-love.htm).

For Christine de Pizan, see *A Medieval Woman's Mirror of Honor: The Treasury of the City of Ladies*, trans. Charity Cannon Willard, ed. Madeleine Pelner Cosman (Bard Hall Press and Persea Books, 1989), with a valuable introduction; also, Jacqueline Broad and Karen Green, *A History of Women's Political Thought in Europe 1400–1700* (Cambridge University Press, 2009).

For general background, see also Henrietta Leyser, *Medieval Women: A Social History of Women in England 450–1500* (Weidenfeld & Nicolson, 1995); and Marty Newman Williams and Anne Echols, *Between Pit and Pedestal: Women in the Middle Ages* (Markus Wiener, 1994).

'Neoplatonic currents of thought': Boase, *The Origin and Meaning of Courtly Love*, p. 83: 'Neoplatonism, which was, after all, a "religion of eros", might explain how a love which for Christians was sinful could have been exalted as pure and ennobling.'

'John of Gaunt': See Alison Weir, *Katherine Swynford: The Story of John of Gaunt and his Scandalous Duchess* (Jonathan Cape, 2007); Norman F. Cantor, *The Last Knight: The Twilight of the Middle Ages and the Birth of the Modern Era* (Free Press, 2004). A new biography – *The Red Prince* by Helen Carr (Oneworld, 2021) – was published as I write.

'the Lollards . . . foreshadowed Protestantism': This was, after all, the time of the 'Papal Schism' in the Catholic Church, which saw the election of multiple rival popes, based in both Rome and Avignon. It was also the time of the anonymous piece of Christian mysticism, *The Cloud of Unknowing*, which couched Christian yearning in courtly terms: 'Beat constantly against the cloud of unknowing between you and your God with a piercing dart of longing love . . . For if this loving impulse is properly rooted in the soul, it contains all the virtues.'

'a cast of heroines': There has been considerable critical debate in recent years as to whether Chaucer takes rank as a writer supportive of women or the reverse: one who, for example, follows the worst of courtly love tradition and 'whitens' his Duchess Blanche out of any real existence. Here, surely, is the answer. For more on feminist criticism of Chaucer see Brewer, *A New Introduction to Chaucer*, p. 106. See also p. 255 on 'the centrality of marriage to Chaucer's general conception of love'.

'the Stanzaic Morte Arthur': Guinevere, in this version, acts as a moral corrective even on her husband, warning him about the corruption of his court. This Guinevere is an emotional creature who takes to her sickbed when Lancelot seems to leave her for the Maid of Astolat (or Ascolat). He visits her and, with tears running down her cheeks, she sets him free. After Mordred seeks to abduct her, she flees to the nunnery of

Amesbury where she and Lancelot have a final interview. She once again sends Lancelot away because her eyes are turned to God, refusing his request for a last kiss. He too becomes a hermit and their last benison is this: they die simultaneously.

Chapter 4: Lancaster (1400–1461)

I wrote about the latter part of this period in *Blood Sisters*, and for the players in the so-called Wars of the Roses, a more extensive bibliography can be found there. Two particularly useful books, however, were J.L. Laynesmith, *The Last Medieval Queens: English Queenship, 1445–1503* (Oxford University Press, 2004) and Helen Castor, *She-Wolves: The Women Who Ruled England Before Elizabeth* (Faber and Faber, 2010). For Marguerite of Anjou see also Helen E. Maurer, *Margaret of Anjou: Queenship and Power in Late Medieval England* (The Boydell Press, 2003).

On Margaret Beaufort, two works are of paramount importance: Nicola Tallis, *Uncrowned Queen: The Fateful Life of Margaret Beaufort, Tudor Matriarch* (Michael O'Mara, 2019); and Michael K. Jones and Malcolm G. Underwood, *The King's Mother: Lady Margaret Beaufort, Countess of Richmond and Derby* (Cambridge University Press, 1992).

The start of the Tudor dynasty, with Owen Tudor, signals also the start of my debt to Leanda de Lisle's *Tudor: A Family Story* (Chatto & Windus, 2013), which debt continues up to the end of the Tudor era. I should like to pay a similarly broad tribute to *The Private Lives of the Tudors: Uncovering the Secrets of Britain's Greatest Dynasty* by Tracy Borman (Hodder & Stoughton, 2016).

'Duke . . . of Gloucester': Gloucester – a deeply cultured man whose name is borne even today by Oxford's Duke Humfrey's Library – himself made a secret marriage which was the cause of widespread controversy. The story of this 1423 marriage to the flamboyant heiress Jacqueline of Hainault – coupled with his subsequent marriage to his mistress Eleanor Cobham, and her 1441 trial and imprisonment for witchcraft – makes a fascinating narrative, albeit one for which there is no space in this book.
'extraordinary revival in the cult of chivalry': Or rather, as Helen Cooper puts it, introducing Thomas Malory's *Le Morte Darthur*, below, p. xi, 'its practitioners seem to have thought of it as a revival, but it is hard to find actual precedents'.

Chapter 5: York (1461–1485)

On Elizabeth Woodville (and her daughter) see Laynesmith, *The Last Medieval Queens*, but also Arlene Okerlund, *Elizabeth Wydeville: The Slandered Queen* (Tempus, 2005); David Baldwin, *Elizabeth Woodville: Mother of the Princes in the Tower* (Sutton, 2002); Anne Crawford, *Yorkists: The History of a Dynasty* (Hambledon Continuum, 2006); and Philippa Gregory, David Baldwin and Michael Jones, *The Women of the Cousins' War: The Duchess, the Queen and the King's Mother* (Simon & Schuster, 2011).

On Thomas Malory see Christina Hardyment, *Malory: The Life and Times of King Arthur's Chronicler* (Harper Perennial, 2006); for Malory's *Morte* see *Le Morte Darthur: The Winchester Manuscript*, ed. Helen Cooper (Oxford University Press, 1998); also *Malory: Works*, ed. Eugène Vinaver (Oxford University Press, 1954). NB the possibility mooted that Malory's work was intended as different tales, edited together by Caxton into the form we now know – and that had Malory lived, he may himself have revised it.

'Toulouse had celebrated': From 1323, the *Consistori dels Sept Trobadors* (or *Consistori del Gay Saber*) commissioned a number of works to 'rejuvenate' the courtly tradition.

'romantic popular version of this first meeting': For more details on the historiography of Edward IV's encounter with Elizabeth Woodville, see *Blood Sisters*, pp. 83–8. Essentially, however, the details of the popular tale crumble at a touch. Hall had Edward hunting in the forest of Wychwood near Grafton and coming to the Woodville home for refreshment; but other traditions say Whittlebury Forest. It was suggested that Edward rode south in 1461, after his victory at the Battle of Towton; yet it is well into 1463 before Elizabeth Woodville next appears in the records, in a dispute over her dowry from her first husband. Indeed, in mid-April 1464 Elizabeth Woodville was still negotiating for her dower lands, seemingly unaware she would soon be acknowledged as queen.

'Mancini . . . More': See *Blood Sisters*, pp. 354, 357 for a discussion as to the sources for this period; particularly those describing the lives of the women involved. Notable among them is the *History of King Richard the Third* written some years later by Sir Thomas More. Revered and indeed canonised for the stance he took under Henry VIII, More – irresistibly for the modern historian – gives long and vivid accounts of conversations at which, however, he could not possibly have been present. His book is useful in that his – like so many other literary works discussed in this book – was essentially a work of fiction sufficiently in tune with its day to be accepted by contemporaries. But the *History* has nonetheless to be read in view of More's avowed purpose: to provide a warning against tyranny, rather than an objective narrative of events.

'Elizabeth . . . eager to fall in with her uncle's plans': In 1619 the antiquary George Buck reported finding a letter written in February 1465 by Elizabeth to the Duke of Norfolk, in which the writer 'prayed him as before to be a mediator for her in the cause of the marriage to the king, who, as she writes, was her only joy and maker in this world, and that she was his in heart and in thoughts, in body, and in all. And then she intimated that the better half of February was past, and that she feared the queen would never die.' But modern scholarship has revealed major alterations to the badly damaged manuscript original. A subsequent editor inserted the most scandalous words. It is entirely possible that (even assuming such a letter, now lost, did indeed exist; even assuming Elizabeth wrote it) that she refers to another, uncontroversial, foreign marriage under discussion at that time. See Alison Hanham, 'Sir George Buck and Princess Elizabeth's Letter: A Problem in Detection', *Ricardian*, 7, 1987; and Arthur Kincaid, 'Buck and the Elizabeth of York Letter', *Ricardian*, 8, 1988.

Part II

Chapter 6: 'nothing uxorious' (1485–1502)

The dour reputation of Henry VII was revitalised by Thomas Penn's *Winter King: The Dawn of Tudor England* (Allen Lane, 2011), following on from S.B. Chrimes's *Henry VII* (Eyre Methuen, 1972). The somewhat passive image of Henry's wife benefited greatly from Alison Weir's *Elizabeth of York: The First Tudor Queen* (Jonathan Cape, 2013). Notable among earlier work is Arlene Naylor Okerlund's *Elizabeth of York* (Palgrave Macmillan, 2009).

'companionable and respective, and without jealousy': A stable and adult emotion, in other words – whereas courtly love, by contrast, has been linked in psychoanalytic evaluations with rejection anxieties, voyeurism, infantilism, and described, in the words of the psychologist and historian Richard A. Koenigsberg, as 'an institutionalised response to the Oedipus complex'. Koenigsberg compared Capellanus's observations on jealousy to Freud's opinion in 'First contribution to the psychology of love' that the woman acquires her full value for the man only when there is some occasion for jealousy; when the love object is overvalued, and the subject of a rescue fantasy. (Freud – perhaps predictably! – saw this as deriving from a mother fixation of infantile origin.) See Melvin W. Askew, 'Courtly Love as Neurosis' (https://www.pep-web.org/document.php?id=paq.035.0469b).

Chapter 7: 'to marry whom he choose' (1502–1509)

For Margaret Tudor (and her successors in Scotland) see Linda Porter's compelling *Crown of Thistles: The Fatal Inheritance of Mary Queen of Scots* (Macmillan, 2013), while Margaret and her sister Mary are the subjects of Maria Perry's *Sisters to the King* (André Deutsch, 1998).

On Catherine, Garrett Mattingly's *Catherine of Aragon* (Jonathan Cape, 1942) still retains its appeal; more recently see Giles Tremlett's *Catherine of Aragon: Henry's Spanish Queen* (Faber and Faber, 2011); and Patrick Williams's *Katharine of Aragon* (Amberley, 2013). See also Julia Fox, *Sister Queens: Katherine of Aragon & Juana Queen of Castile* (Weidenfeld & Nicolson, 2011).

It is perhaps here that one should introduce the three eponymous classics on Henry's wives, being, in chronological order, Alison Weir's *The Six Wives of Henry VIII* (Bodley Head, 1991); Antonia Fraser's *The Six Wives of Henry VIII* (Weidenfeld & Nicolson, 1992); and David Starkey's *Six Wives: The Queens of Henry VIII* (Chatto & Windus, 2003). To these I must add the wonderfully detailed *The Six Wives & Many Mistresses of Henry VIII: The Women's Stories* by Amy License (Amberley, 2014).

David Starkey's *Henry: Virtuous Prince* (HarperPress, 2008) is particularly valuable on Henry's education and formative influences. See also Robert Hutchinson, *Young Henry: The Rise of Henry VIII* (Weidenfeld & Nicolson, 2011).

'At Windsor': One of Philip's retinue noted that the 'excessive' opulence of Windsor, the parade of gold, of treasures, of liveries was like something that might have been found in a royal palace a century before. It was yet another example of the way in which Henry VII used the past to smooth the present path.

'Dunbar . . . explored both old and new traditions': In *The Tua Mariit Wemen and the Wedo* (The Two Married Women and the Widow) Dunbar evinced his readiness to mock courtly love – to make clear just how far apart were the idealised lover and the real woman.

Chapter 8: 'Sir Loyal Heart' (1509–1515)

For Henry's interest in the Arthurian stories, see David Starkey, 'King Henry and King Arthur', *Arthurian Literature*, 16, 1998, pp. 171–96.

See also Dai Morgan Evans, ' "King Arthur" and Cadbury Castle, Somerset', *The Antiquaries Journal*, 86, 2006, pp. 227–53. For Henry's court culture see *Henry VIII: A European Court in England*, ed. David Starkey (Collins & Brown, 1991).

For Mary Tudor see Erin A. Sadlack, *The French Queen's Letters: Mary Tudor Brandon and the Politics of Marriage in Sixteenth-Century Europe* (Palgrave Macmillan, 2011); and Sarah Bryson, *La Reine Blanche: Mary Tudor, A Life in Letters* (Amberley, 2018); also Perry, *Sisters to the King*. For Brandon, see S.J. Gunn, *Charles Brandon, Duke of Suffolk c.1484–1545* (Blackwell, 1988).

For more on Margaret of Austria, see *Game of Queens*: the most authoritative single biography available in English remains Jane de Iongh, *Margaret of Austria: Regent of the Netherlands*, trans. M.D. Herter Norton (Jonathan Cape, 1954).

'the new learning . . . and a fresh appreciation of the old': See John E. Stevens, *Music and Poetry in the Early Tudor Court* (Methuen, 1961).

'La Belle Dame Sans Merci': See Dana M. Symons's introduction and notes to the text: https://d.lib.rochester.edu/teams/text/symons-chaucerian-dream-visions-and-complaints-la-belle-dame-sans-mercy-introduction; also Richard Firth Green, 'The Familia Regis and the Familia Cupidinis', in *English Court Culture in the Later Middle Ages*, ed. V.J. Scattergood and J.W. Sherborne (Duckworth, 1983). Note that a title is really all that Chartier's work can be said to share with that of Keats!

'frantic, self-exculpatory letter': Margaret of Austria is believed to be the author of two long letters, signed 'M', in the British Library's Cotton MS (Titus B. i. f. 142). They are in the handwriting of Sir Richard Wingfield, Henry VIII's ambassador, and it was presumably he who translated them into English from the original French. The British Library will admit only that 'M' can 'probably' be identified as Margaret, but the internal evidence would strongly suggest it.

'Anne de Beaujeu': Her manual, *Anne of France: Lessons for my Daughter*, has been translated and edited by Sharon L. Jansen (D.S. Brewer, 2004).

Chapter 9: 'mine own heart and mind' (1515–1525)

For Mary Boleyn, see Alison Weir, *Mary Boleyn: 'The Great and Infamous Whore'* (Jonathan Cape, 2011).

'recent scholarship has considered': For interesting discussion of Mary's authorial voice (and of the malleable line between history and fiction) see Sadlack, *The French Queen's Letters*, especially p. 10: 'Mary would adhere to the code set by romances she knew, such as Froissart's *Meliador* and Malory's *Morte d'Arthur*, and attempt to shape events the way their heroines would ... throughout her life Mary enhanced her authority to act, to persuade nobles and even kings to do her bidding, by inhabiting the role of a lady in a romance.'

'wandered onstage into the wrong play': Gunn describes a seventeenth-century tale which figured Henry and Brandon as first meeting in a forest, where they combined forces to save a lady (Gunn, *Charles Brandon*, p. 1). One report says that the English people at first resented Brandon's appropriation of Mary Tudor, but were reconciled by reports of his knightly prowess: the codes of chivalry still permitted young men to rise.

'6th Earl of Angus': Angus's maternal grandfather old Lord Drummond, who broke all protocol by boxing the ears of the official sent to tell Margaret she would no longer rule, was father to one Margaret Drummond who had been mistress to James IV – and who, romantic legend said, had been poisoned to make way for his marriage to Margaret Tudor!

'Mary Boleyn': Though Mary was the second of only two certain mistresses in Henry's career, the start of that relationship is confused. A Catholic source, Cardinal Pole, in 1538 would write that Henry had 'violated' Mary, i.e. raped her. The term 'rape' itself, however, could mean an act of ravishment – removal of property – against a married woman's husband, rather than against herself. Both Thomas Malory and Geoffrey Chaucer had, probably in these terms, been accused of rape. Then again, in 1537, a man called William Webbe would declare that Henry had summarily seized his own 'pretty wench' away from him. But this may reflect the disregard always held by the chivalric code for women from the lower orders of society.

Part III

Wyatt's poems are taken from *Sir Thomas Wyatt: The Complete Poems*, ed. R.A. Rebholz (Penguin, 1978); in which, however – correctly – none are titled.

Chapter 10: 'My Mistress and friend' (1525–1527)

Anne Boleyn has generated an immense volume of literature: the single most comprehensive and enduring whole-life biography, however, remains Eric Ives, *The Life and Death of Anne Boleyn* (Blackwell, 2004). More controversial views can be found in G.W. Bernard, *Anne Boleyn: Fatal Attractions* (Yale, 2010), chief exponent of the theory that Anne was to some degree guilty of adultery; and in Retha M. Warnicke, *The Rise and Fall of Anne Boleyn: Family Politics at the Court of Henry VIII* (Cambridge University Press, 1989). Warnicke also wrote of Anne in *Wicked Women of Tudor England: Queens, Aristocrats, Commoners* (Palgrave Macmillan, 2012), and in an essay described below. Literature dealing specifically with Anne's fall from grace will be referenced in another chapter.

Henry's letters to Anne Boleyn have been digitised by the Vatican Library: https://digi.vatlib.it/view/MSS_Vat.lat.3731.pt.A. They are available in printed (and translated) form, with many other invaluable texts concerning Anne, in Elizabeth Norton, *Anne Boleyn: In Her Own Words & the Words of Those Who Knew Her* (Amberley, 2011).

For Wyatt see, particularly, Nicola Shulman, *Graven With Diamonds: The Many Lives of Thomas Wyatt: Courtier, Poet, Assassin, Spy* (Short Books, 2011); and Susan Bridgen, *Thomas Wyatt: The Heart's Forest* (Faber and Faber, 2012); also Ingeborg Heine-Harabasz, 'Courtly Love as Camouflage in the Poems of Sir Thomas Wyatt' (http://ifa.amu.edu. pl/sap/files/14/20_Heine-Harabasz.pdf).

The dispatches of Eustace Chapuys can be found in CSP Spanish (4, part 2, and subsequent) – or, to give it its correct title, the *Calendar of Letters and State Papers relating to English Affairs, preserved principally in the Archives of Simancas*, ed. M.A.S. Hume et al., (1892–9). The same *Calendar* also contains the despatches of subsequent Spanish ambassadors, of particular significance during the early reign of Elizabeth I.

'memoirs or manuals of instruction': See *Game of Queens*, for which they were an important source. Some form of autobiographical writing survives for five of the French royal women of the sixteenth century: Anne de Beaujeu, Louise of Savoy, Marguerite of Navarre, Jeanne d'Albret and Marguerite de Valois.

'Anne stayed on at the French court': The Catholic, and hostile, William Rastell would describe Anne Boleyn as known at the French court to be 'the Hackney of England', a hackney signifying a horse anyone can ride, i.e. a prostitute; but this probably represents a confusion with her sister Mary. The Elizabethan Catholic propagandist Nicholas Sander likewise described, inaccurately, a fifteen-year-old Anne as sexually incontinent 'with her father's butler, and then with his chaplain', sent in disgrace to France, where she gained a scandalous reputation as 'the English mare'.

'a man called Bonnivet': See Patricia F. and Rouben C. Cholakian, *Marguerite of Navarre* (Columbia University Press, 2006), pp. 21–38 for their development of the idea that passages in the *Heptameron* are autobiographical.

'not so much heartbroken as gazumped': Shulman, *Graven With Diamonds*, p. 156.

'a huge risk crossing King Henry': One theory, however, suggests Wyatt did take the risk, but for a particular cause. At the start of 1528, Wyatt would dedicate *The Quiet of Mind*, a translation of Plutarch, to the increasingly isolated Queen Catherine. In *Thomas Wyatt: The Heart's Forest* pp. 136–153 Susan Bridgen suggests he may actually have been Catherine's man deliberately, dangerously, trying to discredit Anne.

'Seventeen letters from Henry VIII to Anne Boleyn': My suggested chronology largely, though not entirely, conforms with that suggested by Eric Ives, who, however, did not attempt to place all the letters.

'exercises in the rhetoric of courtly love': Retha M. Warnicke explores the whole question of the courtly ethic in this relationship in 'The Conventions of Courtly Love and Anne Boleyn', in *State, Sovereigns & Society in Early Modern England*, ed. Charles Carlton (Sutton, 1998), pp. 103–18. Her concern, broadly speaking, is to deny the idea that the one was behind the fate of the other – to point out, indeed, that 'historians began to depend upon this romantic model [courtly love] for gender analysis just as literary critics were confining it to the world of fiction and denying that it had ever been an actual, social phenomenon'. She does so, however, from a curiously restrictive standpoint, taking the ideal and influence of courtly love to be exhibited only in C.S. Lewis's 'straight-jacketed model': a model she sees as being adopted by Eric Ives and others. I would suggest that this vision of the transmission of so pervasive an ideal is itself a limited one.

Warnicke states that 'no didactic texts circulating in Tudor England approved [this] model of courtly love'. True. To make a modern analogy, however, the violent ethos of the video game is likewise not taught in schools – but we worry about its effect on children, anyway. And having admitted that 'some literary conventions had begun, however, to shape and alter social institutions', Warnicke goes on to confirm that 'the eloquence of courtly love had filtered into the wooing and wedding market'.

'*Noli me tangere*': For discussion of this poem, see Shulman, *Graven With Diamonds*, pp. 107–10.

Chapter 11: 'our desired end' (1527–1533)

For Thomas Cromwell, see recent biographies: Tracy Borman, *Thomas Cromwell: The Untold Story of Henry VIII's Most Faithful Servant* (Hodder & Stoughton, 2014) and Diarmaid MacCulloch, *Thomas Cromwell: A Life* (Allen Lane, 2018).

Chapter 12: 'the most happy' (1533–early spring 1536)

Suzannah Lipscomb's *1536: The Year that Changed Henry VIII* (Lion, 2009) examines the year of Anne's fall.

'Black Book of the Garter': Roland Hui, 'Anne Boleyn as "The Lady of the Garter": A Rediscovered Image of Henry VIII's Second Queen' (https://tudorfaces.blogspot. com/2017/04/anne-boleyn-as-lady-of-garter.html).

'major change in his reign and his personality': Others, however, deny such a change; or see it happening in 1525–7, consequent on an earlier jousting injury; or in 1533, or later. See Lipscomb, *1536*, pp. 24–6 for discussion.

Chapter 13: 'the spotted queen' (April/May 1536)

Alison Weir's *The Lady in the Tower: The Fall of Anne Boleyn* (Jonathan Cape, 2009) is a riveting forensic analysis of the circumstances leading up to Anne's execution.

'Jane Rochford, George Boleyn's wife': This sister-in-law has had as contested an afterlife as Anne herself: her culpability or otherwise hotly debated. See Julia Fox, *Jane Boleyn: The Infamous Lady Rochford* (Weidenfeld & Nicolson, 2007).

'to test – to "prove" – her': The 'Patient Griselda' trope; but, also, a repeated trope of courtly love. When lovers 'love each other with an equal ardour . . . they will turn against one another without any valid reason . . . All these devices are aimed at testing and proving what each is seeking in the other,' wrote Ibn Hazm in *The Ring of the Dove* in the eleventh century.

'Sir William Kingston described': See Weir, *The Lady in the Tower*, pp. 337–44 for discussion of all our sources of information as to Anne's final weeks.

'Most historians see no reason': The honourable exception being G.W. Bernard, see above.

'Anne had protested her innocence': For transcript and discussion of the dubiously authentic letter to Henry in which Anne is said also to have protested that innocence, see Weir, *The Lady in the Tower*, pp. 171–5.

Part IV

Chapter 14: 'My faithful, true and loving heart' (1536–1540)

For Margaret Douglas, see Alison Weir, *The Lost Tudor Princess: A Life of Margaret Douglas, Countess of Lennox* (Jonathan Cape, 2015). The Devonshire Manuscript has been digitised by the British Library: http://www.bl.uk/manuscripts/FullDisplay.aspx?ref=Add_MS_17492.

A Social Edition of the Devonshire MS (BL Add. MS 17492) (http:// en.wikibooks.org) offers also a formidable body of textual, palaeographic and literary analysis; attributions; and biographical material on contributors. Academic essays I found particularly helpful include Elizabeth Heale, 'Women and the Courtly Love Lyric: The Devonshire MS (BL Additional.17492)', *The Modern Language Review*, 90, 1995, pp. 296–313. See also Seth Lerer, *Courtly Letters in the Age of Henry VIII* (Cambridge University Press, 1997) and Catherine Bates, 'Wyatt, Surrey, and the Henrician Court', in *Early Modern English Poetry: A Critical Companion*, ed. Patrick Cheney, Andrew Hadfield, and Garrett Sullivan, Jr. (Oxford University Press, 2007).

On Henry VIII's last four wives, see the group biographies mentioned above; Elizabeth Norton has written biographies of Jane Seymour and Anne of Cleves.

'Nicola Shulman memorably described': See Shulman, *Graven With Diamonds*, p. 142.

Chapter 15: 'it makes my heart die' (1540–1547)

Of Henry's wives, only Katheryn Howard has as interesting (albeit far shorter) a historiography as her kinswoman Anne Boleyn. The interest lies not only in the horror of her early death, but the challenge posed by the blatant sexuality (deserved or undeserved?) of her reputation. Traditionally, writers *have* tended to see her as sexually motivated and the less admirable for it; in 2004 David Starkey was unusual in seeing her as not necessarily guilty of adultery with Culpeper, but was none-theless happy to categorise her as an archetypal bad girl. Even those writers who seek to defend her find it necessary to use this as their battleground.

Joanna Denny's *Katherine Howard: A Tudor Conspiracy* (Little, Brown, 2007) suggested alternatively (as has been suggested also in the case of Anne Boleyn) that she needed another man to father the child Henry was now unable to give her. But Retha M. Warnicke sees her, in her earlier relationships, as a victim of sexual abuse: one of the women who despite the appearance of resistance 'were thought to have possessed "interior consent"' (Warnicke, *Wicked Women of Tudor England*, p. 51). This view is shared by Josephine Wilkinson in *Katherine Howard: The Tragic Story of Henry VIII's Fifth Queen* (John Murray, 2016).

Warnicke also suggests that Katheryn's letter to Culpeper – an 'odd specimen of the romance genre' (Warnicke, *Wicked Women of Tudor England*, p. 69) – may show instead that he was essentially attempting to blackmail her. The idea is developed by Conor Byrne – *Katherine Howard: Henry VIII's Slandered Queen* (The History Press, 2019) – who sees Katheryn, like her predecessors, as a victim of 'fertility politics' (p. 18), since there was contemporary discussion of the fact Katheryn was yet another wife to fail to give Henry an heir; and interestingly discusses her relationship with Culpeper in terms of the courtly love tradition.

Gareth Russell's *Young & Damned & Fair: The Life and Tragedy of Catherine Howard at the Court of Henry VIII* (William Collins, 2017) in some ways returns to the traditional view of Katheryn, but is careful to contextualise it; exploring her world as much as it does her own 'horribly compelling' story.

See – by contrast – biographies of the very different queen who 'survived': Linda Porter, *Katherine the Queen: The Remarkable Life of Katherine Parr* (Macmillan, 2010) and Elizabeth Norton, *Catherine Parr* (Amberley, 2011).

Chapter 16: 'shameful slanders' (1547–1553)

For Elizabeth's youth and education, see David Starkey, *Elizabeth: Apprenticeship* (Chatto & Windus, 2000).

For Jane Grey, see Nicola Tallis, *Crown of Blood: the Deadly Inheritance of Lady Jane Grey* (Michael O'Mara, 2016), which helpfully discusses the sources of information about her life. For Jane's siblings, see Leanda de Lisle, *The Sisters Who Would Be Queen: Mary, Katherine and Lady Jane Grey: A Tudor Tragedy* (HarperPress, 2009).

'Diarmaid MacCulloch': MacCulloch's great *Reformation: Europe's House Divided 1490–1700* (Allen Lane, 2003) is an essential background to the era. The conveniently succinct remarks quoted, however, come from the same author's television series *Sex and the Church* (BBC2, April 2015).

'as England's first queen regnant': The twelfth century had seen Henry I's attempt to secure the succession for his daughter Matilda: the result was the Anarchy, as she and Henry's nephew Stephen of Blois contended for control of the country. Interestingly in this context, Henry attempted to make Matilda more palatable to the nobles by decreeing that England would not be subject to the rule of her husband. See *Game of Queens* for the debate about female monarchy in the sixteenth century; and Charles Beem, *The Lioness Roared: The Problems of Female Rule in English History* (Palgrave Macmillan, 2008).

Chapter 17: 'a husband may do much' (1553–1558)

The once-dubious reputation of 'Bloody' Mary has greatly benefited from Anna Whitelock's *Mary Tudor: England's First Queen* (Bloomsbury, 2009), following Linda Porter's *Mary Tudor: The First Queen* (Portrait, 2007) and Judith Mary Richards's *Mary Tudor* (Routledge, 2008). See also Sarah Duncan, *Mary I: Gender, Power, and Ceremony in the Reign of England's First Queen* (Palgrave Macmillan, 2012) and *Tudor Queenship: the Reigns of Mary and Elizabeth*, ed. Alice Hunt and Anna Whitelock (Palgrave Macmillan, 2010). For Mary's husband, see Henry Kamen, *Philip of Spain* (Yale University Press, 1997).

Part V

Chapter 18: 'the King that is to be' (1558–1563)

For Queen Elizabeth's own letters, speeches and poems, see *Elizabeth I: Collected Works*, ed. Leah S. Marcus, Janel Mueller and Mary Beth Rose (University of Chicago Press, 2000). This invaluable volume also includes not only discussion of attribution where necessary, but relevant supplementary documents, e.g. Parliament's pleas to Elizabeth to marry.

The sheer volume of biographies of Elizabeth make it necessary to skip directly to modern days, when to Alison Weir's *Elizabeth the Queen* (Jonathan Cape, 1998) and Anne Somerset's *Elizabeth I* (Weidenfeld & Nicolson, 1991) has now been added Lisa Hilton's *Elizabeth: Renaissance Prince* (Weidenfeld & Nicolson, 2014). Anyone writing specifically on Elizabeth's personal relationships, however, has first to pay tribute to Martin Hume's classic *The Courtships of Queen Elizabeth* (Eveleigh Nash, 1904). Important older work also includes that of Frederick Chamberlin in *The Private Character of Queen*

Elizabeth (John Lane, 1920) and Milton Waldman in *Elizabeth and Leicester* (Collins, 1944); while both Waldman and Elizabeth Jenkins in *Elizabeth and Leicester* (Gollancz, 1958) also wrote of this, perhaps the most important of Elizabeth's relationships. Notable on the inter-relation between Elizabeth's personal and political lives are Carole Levin's *The Heart and Stomach of a King; Elizabeth I and the Politics of Sex and Power* (University of Pennsylvania Press, 1994) and Susan Doran's *Monarchy and Matrimony* (Routledge, 1996).

Other academic work I found helpful on, particularly, Elizabeth's self-creation includes Susan Frye's *Elizabeth I: The Competition for Representation* (Oxford University Press, 1993); Ilona Bell, *Elizabeth I: The Voice of a Monarch* (Palgrave Macmillan, 2010); *Elizabeth I in Writing: Language, Power and Representation in Early Modern England*, ed. Donatella Montini and Iolanda Plescia (Palgrave Macmillan, 2018); and Rayne Allinson, *A Monarchy of Letters: Royal Correspondence and English Diplomacy in the Reign of Elizabeth* (Palgrave Macmillan, 2012); see also *Dissing Elizabeth: Negative Representations of Gloriana*, ed. Julia M. Walker (Duke University Press, 1998). On Elizabeth's portraits, the expert remains Roy Strong, *Gloriana: The Portraits of Queen Elizabeth I* (Pimlico, 2003).

Notable among biographies of Robert Dudley is Derek Wilson's *Sweet Robin; A Biography of Robert Dudley Earl of Leicester 1553–1558* (Allison & Busby, 1988), with *The Uncrowned Kings of England: The Black Legend of the Dudleys* (Constable, 2005) by the same author. See also Simon Adams, *Leicester and the Court: Essays on Elizabethan Politics* (Manchester University Press, 2002).

See *Elizabeth & Leicester*, pp. 371–87 for a more detailed list of sources both primary and secondary.

'the virgin state': Though it has been noted that even a portrait of Elizabeth in her coronation robes (in the National Portrait Gallery: painted c.1600 but believed to be a copy of an earlier lost original) strongly resembles that of Richard II, another monarch famous for his chastity.

'Amy Dudley's death': See *Elizabeth & Leicester*, pp. 99–123, also pp. 379–81, for a longer discussion of the evidence and possible conclusions. Some years after the publication of that book, Chris Skidmore's *Death and the Virgin: Elizabeth, Dudley and the Mysterious Fate of Amy Robsart* (Weidenfeld & Nicolson, 2010) drew on the coroner's report into Amy's death: lost for centuries but newly rediscovered. This, while it does not radically alter the situation, makes an act of violence more likely. Without giving away all Skidmore's conclusions, the vital point here is that he does not see either Dudley or Elizabeth as murderers – and indeed, introduces a new suspect into the equation.

'a membrane on her': Michael Bloch (known as biographer and associate of the Duke and Duchess of Windsor) suggested that Elizabeth (possibly like Wallis Simpson) suffered from Androgen Insensitivity Syndrome: that she was born with male chromosomes but, failing to produce also male hormones, developed outwardly as a woman. An interesting idea in light of the androgynous, the gender role reversal, aspect of the courtly love theory. Hilton, *Elizabeth*, p. 317 cites Christopher Haig describing Elizabeth 'perfectly, as a "political hermaphrodite"'. See also William Monter, *The Rise of Female Kings in Europe 1300–1800* (Yale University Press, 2011), pp. 43–4 on the identification of queens regnant as male.

'Arthur Dudley': See *Elizabeth & Leicester*, Appendix II, pp. 351–63.

Chapter 19: 'satiety and fullness' (1563–1575)

On Christopher Hatton, the first resource is Sir Nicholas Harris Nicolas, *Memoirs of the Life and Times of Sir Christopher Hatton, K.G.* (1847), which includes Hatton's letters to Elizabeth, and Dyer's letter of advice to Hatton. See also Alice Gilmore Vines, *Neither Fire Nor Steel: Sir Christopher Hatton* (Nelson-Hall, 1978).

On the Earl of Oxford, see B.M. Ward, *The Seventeenth Earl of Oxford 1550–1604 from Contemporary Documents* (John Murray, 1928); and Alan H. Nelson, *Monstrous Adversary: The Life of Edward de Vere, 17th Earl of Oxford* (Liverpool University Press, 2003).

On the issue of favourites in general, see Simon Adams, 'Favourites and Factions', in *The Tudor Monarchy*, ed. John Guy (Arnold, 1997); *The World of the Favourite, c.1550–1675*, ed. J.H. Elliott and Laurence Brockliss (Yale University Press, 1999); and *Princes, Patronage and the Nobility: The Court at the Beginning of the Modern Age c.1450–1600*, ed. Ronald G. Asch and Adolf M. Birke (Oxford University Press, 1991). A more accessible volume – on which many of us grew up! – is Neville Williams's *All the Queen's Men* (Weidenfeld & Nicolson, 1972).

On Mary, Queen of Scots, see John Guy, *'My Heart is My Own': The Life of Mary Queen of Scots* (Harper Perennial, 2004); also Kate Williams, *Rival Queens: The Betrayal of Mary, Queen of Scots* (Hutchinson, 2018).

'their lives as love tokens': Hilton, *Elizabeth*, p. 251.

'balance between sex appeal and statesmanship': Martin Hume's classic *Courtships of Queen Elizabeth*, in the first years of the twentieth century, described her political courtships rather than what he memorably described as her 'non-political philanderings'. But as I wrote in *Elizabeth & Leicester*, Elizabeth's statecraft and her sexuality were inextricably intertwined . . . 'The personal is political' was a slogan of modern feminism. But it was just as applicable in the court of England, in the late sixteenth century. To quote Walter Ralegh's biographers Nicholls and Williams in *Sir Walter Raleigh in Life and Legend*, cited below, pp.26–8: 'favour often follows a process of very careful political calculation . . . Access led to familiarity, familiarity led to an objective assessment of ability, and this assessment weighed the man's capacity to undertake particular political or ceremonial tasks.'

Chapter 20: 'against my nature' (1575–1584)

On Philip Sidney, see Katherine Duncan-Jones, *Sir Philip Sidney: Courtier Poet* (Yale University Press, 1991).

'Sieve Portrait': A subsequent version of the Sieve Portrait, one with which Roy Strong believes Hatton to be particularly associated, along with the magus John Dee, makes use of Petrarchan imagery. Dee was fiercely concerned with the promotion of Elizabeth's imperial claims and, by way of justification, her descent from King Arthur (see Strong, *Gloriana*, p. 93). Dee's biographer Peter J. French noted 'a spectacular recrudescence of interest in Arthur' in precisely these years.

'villain-figure of fairy story': Jo Eldridge Carney, *Fairy Tale Queens* (Palgrave Macmillan, 2012), p. 7.

'to write his *Arcadia*': The book was published only after Sidney's death, by which time Sidney himself had revised, almost to the point of rewriting, his original *Old Arcadia*; his sister then published a version on which she too had worked, hence the well-known title *The Countess of Pembroke's Arcadia*. For Sidney's attitude to relations between the sexes, see Duncan-Jones, *Sir Philip Sidney*, particularly pp. 2, 180, 206, 211, 314–5.

'a kind of literary charade': Duncan-Jones, *Sir Philip Sidney*, pp. 240–1 raises the possibility that – with all the provisos as to the unwisdom of applying modern labels to such a different culture – Sidney was what we would see as homosexual. His closest friends Fulke Greville and Dyer never married and Sidney in poetry 'gives this triple friendship the pre-eminence normally accorded to heterosexual unions'. I would myself tentatively raise the same speculation about Christopher Hatton. See also Stanley Wells, *Shakespeare, Sex and Love* (Oxford University Press, 2012); also Alan Bray, *Homosexuality in Renaissance England* (Columbia University Press, 1996).

'expose the hollowness of the reality': Lytton Strachey, in *Elizabeth and Essex: A Tragic History* (Chatto & Windus, 1928), pp. 25–6: 'as her charms grew less, her insistence on their presence grew greater. She had been content with the devoted homage of her contemporaries; but from the young men who surrounded her in old age she required – and received – the expressions of devoted passion. The affairs of State went on in a fandango of sighs, ecstasies, and protestations.'

Part VI

'When I was fair and young': The poem quoted appears on pp. 303–5 of *Elizabeth I: Collected Works* with a discussion of its attribution to Elizabeth.

Chapter 21: 'this old song' (1584–1587)

In *Elizabeth: The Forgotten Years* (Viking, 2016) John Guy explored the period 1584 to 1603; following the academic discussion of Elizabeth's 'second reign' he earlier edited *The Reign of Elizabeth I: Court and Culture in the Last Decade* (Cambridge University Press, 1995). As he points out, this latter part of the Elizabethan era had previously been treated with cursory speed by earlier biographers and even historians.

Walter Ralegh has recently been the subject of strong studies: see Anna Beer, *Patriot or Traitor: The Life and Death of Sir Walter Ralegh* (Oneworld, 2018); Mark Nicholls and Penry Williams, *Sir Walter Raleigh in Life and Legend* (Bloomsbury, 2011). Among older work, Norman Lloyd Williams's *Sir Walter Raleigh* (Cassell, 1962) includes transcripts of contemporary documents and much of Ralegh's poetry.

'his appeal to Elizabeth': As with Hatton (above) – and with Leicester and Essex – so with Ralegh. Nicholls and Williams, *Sir Walter Raleigh in Life and Legend*, pp. 26–8: 'Courtly gestures and political lovemaking should never obscure the political realities on which favour was grounded . . . How far the personal then drew these decisions further is anybody's guess.' In *Patriot or Traitor*, Beer likewise sees the link between queen and courtier as 'an eroticised political relationship, not a political sexual relationship, and Elizabeth was on top' (p. 75).

'Lettice was a particularly forceful woman': Her demanding affection is evinced by letters to her adult son begging that he 'bestow some time a few idle lines on your mother who otherwise may grow jealous that you love her not so well as she deserves'. It sounds a little like Queen Elizabeth's own unseasonable demands for reassurance and flattery. See Nicola Tallis, *Elizabeth's Rival: The Tumultuous Tale of Lettice Knollys, Countess of Leicester* (Michael O'Mara, 2017).

'the Protestants' despair like that of the lover': In *Elizabeth*, Lisa Hilton notes that Elizabeth, in the performance of her court ceremonial, 'can be seen positioning herself intellectually as both stylised mistress and Protestant martyr' (p. 212). (Paulus Melissus, the German Protestant poet and one of Sidney's circle, addressed her in a poetic cocktail of the chivalric – erotic, even – and the religious.) But the just comparison perhaps became less apt with the passing of the years. Courtly love and the harsher Calvinist Protestantism of the later century were never going to agree.

Chapter 22: 'Cold love' (1587–1590)

Essex's correspondence is drawn from Walter Bourchier Devereux, *Lives and Letters of the Devereux, Earls of Essex, in the reigns of Elizabeth, James I, and Charles I: 1540–1646* (John Murray, 1853). See also G.B. Harrison, *The Life and Death of Robert Devereux, Earl of Essex* (Cassell & Co, 1937) and Robert Lacey, *Robert, Earl of Essex, an Elizabethan Icarus* (Weidenfeld and Nicolson, 1971). Among valuable academic work, see Paul Hammer, *The Polarisation of Elizabethan Politics: The Political Career of Robert Devereux, 2nd Earl of Essex* (Cambridge University Press, revised edition 2008). The personal relationship of Elizabeth and Essex, however, has been surprisingly little covered – perhaps because it does not show either protagonist in a flattering light? The post-Freudian vision of Lytton Strachey, in his groundbreaking psychobiography *Elizabeth and Essex*, has never yet been successfully superseded: albeit that he saw an Elizabeth suffering 'a deep-seated repugnance to the crucial act of intercourse' but nonetheless 'filled with delicious agitation by the glorious figures of men'.

On Spenser and *The Faerie Queene*: *The Faerie Queene* ed. A.C. Hamilton et al. (Longman, 2001); see Donald Stump, *Spenser's Heavenly Elizabeth: Providential History in The Faerie Queene* (Palgrave Macmillan, 2019).

'wild horse': Inept at the usually important pastime of dancing, where Essex was described as 'no graceful goer', Sir Henry Wotton would describe Essex's beautiful hands, his silence at meals which he ate greedily but with his attention elsewhere, and his love of baths.

'famous speech at Tilbury': See *Elizabeth I: Collected Works*, pp. 325–6 for notes on the sources of and variations on this speech, the precise words of which are disputed, though the gist is never in doubt. See also *Elizabeth & Leicester*, p. 286; and Hilton, *Elizabeth*, pp. 275–6 for yet a further, little known, version.

'the Faerie Queen who sends Prince Arthur on missions of chivalry': C.S. Lewis (pp. 336, 353) suggests with conviction that the books Spenser never wrote would have come to their crescendo in the Faerie Queen's relationship with Prince Arthur. That she too would in effect marry . . . Lewis (p. 298) concludes his book on the history of *fin'amor* by seeing Spenser as writing 'the final defeat of courtly love by the romantic conception of marriage'.

'Una . . . represents Truth': Stump sees Una rather as the church forming around Anne Boleyn; her knight's defeat of the dragon Errour as Anne's winning over Henry to the true faith; and the untrue charge of infidelity against Una as the charges levelled against Anne. See Stump, *Spenser's Heavenly Elizabeth*, p. 24.

'the triumphant union of romantic passion with Christian monogamy': This Lewis (pp. 359–60) definitely sees as a good: to read Spenser – he says, in a phrase more reminiscent of our era than of his – 'is to grow in mental health'. Lewis's view was that the centuries would reveal Spenser as 'the great mediator between the Middle Ages and the modern poets . . . In the history of sentiment he is the greatest among the founders of that romantic conception of marriage which is the basis of all our love literature from Shakespeare to Meredith.'

'Germaine Greer has noted': See Germaine Greer, *Shakespeare's Wife* (Bloomsbury, 2007), p. 257.

Chapter 23: 'confusion and contrariety' (1590–1599)

'the Earl of Southampton . . . Shakespeare's patron': And, like the Earl of Oxford before him, suggested by anti-Stratfordians as a candidate for the authorship of Shakespeare's plays. It has been suggested without plausibility that Southampton was Oxford's and Elizabeth's son.

Chapter 24: 'Affection's false' (1599–1603)

'Charles Blount': Charles Blount, long-term lover and then husband to Essex's sister Penelope, transformed from a youthful rival of, to a significant ally for, Essex himself. He is not, however, to be confused with Christopher Blount, who would become the third husband of Essex's mother Lettice, and an even closer friend of Essex's; though the two Blounts were distant relations.

'replace him on the throne with Arbella Stuart': Arbella survived the use of her name in this plot. Seven years later, however, she succeeded in making a secret marriage with another of Katherine Grey's grandsons: a marriage in which affection does seem to have been involved, but which struck alarm into the hearts of the authorities. Through imprisonment, dramatic escape, and death in the Tower, Arbella's thoughts stayed with the husband from whom she had been reft, writing to him that she thought herself 'a pattern of misfortune in enjoying so great a blessing as you so little a while'.

'James's personal obsessions . . . witches': See MacCulloch, *Reformation*, pp. 561–70 for the role the fear of witchcraft played in the sixteenth century: and perhaps in the decline of women's power. It has been said that the 'Age of Queens' also birthed the great age of the witch hunt. Between 1400 and 1800 from forty to fifty thousand people died in Europe and colonial North America on charges of witchcraft, the number mounting from 1560, when, in England, the burnings of heretics as such slowed. Witchcraft was seen as natural successor to heresy, with the difference that it was particularly (though far from exclusively) associated with women.

'of antique knighthood': Strachey, *Elizabeth and Essex*, p. 2.
'victim of the game of love': Hilton, *Elizabeth*, p. 314.

Postscript

'Germaine Greer in *The Female Eunuch*': See Greer, *The Female Eunuch*, p. 235.
'John Dover Wilson': See John Dover Wilson, *What Happens in Hamlet* (Cambridge University Press, 1974), p. 228.

Appendix

For the Victorian revival of the Arthurian legends, and the ideals of chivalry and courtly love, see *The Return to Camelot: Chivalry and the English Gentleman* by Mark Girouard (Yale University Press, 1981), pp. 197–218 and 255.

Index